# Almost Chosen People

## A CENTENNIAL BOOK

One hundred books
published between 1990 and 1995
bear this special imprint of
the University of California Press.
We have chosen each Centennial Book
as an example of the Press's finest
publishing and bookmaking traditions
as we celebrate the beginning of
our second century.

## UNIVERSITY OF CALIFORNIA PRESS

*Founded in 1893*

# Almost Chosen People

## Oblique Biographies in the American Grain

Michael Zuckerman

UNIVERSITY OF CALIFORNIA PRESS

*Berkeley / Los Angeles / Oxford*

University of California Press
Berkeley and Los Angeles, California

University of California Press, Ltd.
Oxford, England

Library of Congress Cataloging-in-Publication Data
Zuckerman, Michael, 1939-
    Almost chosen people : oblique biographies in the American grain /
Michael Zuckerman.
        p.      cm.
    "A Centennial book"—P.
    Includes bibliographical references and index.
    ISBN 0–520–06651–0 (alk. paper)
    1. National characteristics, American.   2. United States—
Civilization.   3. United States—Biography.   I. Title.
E169.1.Z883 1993
973'.099—dc20                                              92–5779

Printed in the United States of America
9 8 7 6 5 4 3 2 1

9168741

*To Sharon Ann Holt
my chosen person*

# Contents

# Introduction

Maybe it was bound to turn out as it did. Maybe I only fasten on Frances as an emblem. Maybe I still see the world more than I would wish through my mother's eyes.

Certainly my mother did her gentle best to shield me from Frances. The woman affronted every aspiration by which my mother lived and wished the rest of her brood to live—every aspiration but one. My mother cherished family as much as she treasured respectability and refinement. And Frances was as much my father's sister as Aunt Elsie and Aunt Fritzi were.

My mother was a paragon of propriety. She framed my fate. She shaped my sense of goodness, truth, and beauty in ways I will never shake. But she could not keep me from my fascination with Frances.

When I was five years old, Frances—whom I could never comfortably call Aunt Frances—frightened me. Small children dwell unduly on the external aspects of things. My other uncles and aunts were attractive men and women. Uncle Murry was to me more dashing than the stars of the Saturday matinees. Aunt Sheila was even more ethereally, angelically beautiful than my mother.

But even when I was ten, and twelve, and fourteen, Frances still made me feel deeply uneasy. Try as I would, I could not get around it. She seemed to me truly a hag. In the memories that still tease at me, she is toothless. I know that she was not. Reason rebukes recollection, assuring me that she was merely missing some teeth. But reason does not dispel my feeling that there was something craggy and fierce about her, as there was about the old crones in the Arthur Szyk illustrations of Andersen's fairy tales that haunted my dreams at the time. She spoke with a gap-toothed lisp, and she keened more than she spoke. She smelled sour.

I trembled to ask my parents about her, and I did not understand much of the little I did learn. I do not know to this day whether she was a prostitute or just an unmarried woman who lived with a succession of men who hardly ever came with her to family affairs. I do know that she must have made my mother queasy, and my father too, though he was the most accepting man I have ever known. She was the only one of all my aunts and uncles and cousins who was not routinely invited to our birthday parties and holiday celebrations.

Maybe a lot of historians of my generation had a Frances in the family. Maybe a lot of them felt as deeply uneasy as I did.

I grew up in the 1940s and 1950s, the last decades when American life offered even the slightest semblance of coherence. I grew up under the sway of my mother, because she was the strongest of a clan of strong, willful men and women. Her father came to America to make his fortune and actually did as others dreamed; he died a millionaire steel manufacturer. My father's father crossed the Atlantic with the same fond fantasy and wound up the proprietor of a prospering delicatessen; by all accounts, he was a difficult man who dealt imperiously with people. My father abjured such ambitions and disdained such domination; he was, nonetheless, a brilliant and adored attorney. My mother prevailed over them all.

Her triumph did not depend on what my father ruefully called her whim of iron. It did not depend on her way with people, either, or her eloquence, or even her wisdom. It rested rather on one of those recurrent coincidences of personal predilection and cultural history. As my other elders did not, my mother meant to assimilate, to be more American than the Americans, and to help her family to do the same. She assented ardently to the ways of the Protestant establishment, at a historical moment when those ways could actually entice assent.

My grandfathers were so preoccupied with their own businesses that they never troubled to ponder much the business of being Americans. My father did trouble, did not see much in it, and kept his distance. But my mother studied the professed ideals of the affluent assiduously. She identified with all that the establishment esteemed and devoted herself earnestly to instructing the rest of us—her sisters and brothers, her cousins, my sisters and me—in the ethos and arcana of elite culture. She found apt pupils, for we were as keen to shed the encumbrances of old country identities as she was. At a time that the American dream was still a credibly coherent one, she incarnated that coherence for us.

Frances gave me my earliest intimation that the crystalline cosmos my mother conjured might be cracked.

Later, there would be more than mere intimations. As I grew older, I would be privy to indiscreet adult conversations. I would get increasingly frank answers to increasingly impertinent questions. And I would learn how little was as it looked on its stylish suburban surface: how many apparently exemplary businessmen could scarcely separate their financial affairs from their extramarital affairs, how many seemingly cordial couples could scarcely abide each other's company.

More than that, I would learn that the men mired in their corporate peccadilloes and the couples immured in their marital miseries were not just figures on a far ground, among my father's clients and my mother's friends. They were also close at hand, among my own blood relations.

We certainly seemed a shining family. My grandparents lived well, even luxuriously, and sent their sons to elite colleges. My father was a flourishing lawyer. A couple of my uncles were soaringly successful salesmen who made far more money than my father did. Another uncle just missed the Yale Younger Poets Prize and became a world-traveled public relations agent and advertising copywriter. Another stood to inherit his father's furniture factory. One aunt was an insurance agent, another a very independent businesswoman. In my own generation there would be several college professors, a couple of entrepreneurs, a rich corporate executive, a multinational consultant, a celebrated interpreter, a financier, a couple of doctors.

But such sheen was deceptive. My millionaire grandfather married, very late in life, a glamorous younger woman whose enchantments gained her the lion's share of his fortune. The rancor that their brief liaison stirred in my mother and her sisters and brothers suffused our family gatherings for years. My maiden aunt was not quite a maiden at all. She married, very young, a brutal older man whose carnal demands devastated her. The trauma inflicted on her by their transient union left her sexually anesthetized the rest of her days.

Revelations tumbled after revelations. One uncle ran away from home when he was twelve; for the first six months he was on the road he refused his parents the comfort of a card assuring them that he was alive, and he never did return to them. Another uncle did his last day's work before he was forty; he realized that he was handsome enough to be kept handsomely by a succession of male lovers. An aunt and uncle built a wall within their modest row house; they figured that that would cost less than a divorce and that they would only have to speak to each other to maintain a facade on family occasions.

And all of those disclosures and discoveries paled in the early hours of that shattering morning when the police called and asked us to come to the airport motel. My youngest sister was still in Mexico. My younger sister was sleeping. My mother stayed home to be with her. I went, in fear and trembling. My father was far too late returning from a business trip.

I revered my father. I showed it in an odd way, sharing with him a hundred raging, ranging arguments—a single, interminable, adolescence-long argument, actually—about politics and poetry and psychoanalysis and anything else that was dear to him. He delighted, I learned later, to see me try my intellectual wings. I tried them, I realize now, because I trusted that he did not doubt my reverence for him.

I also shared with him an odd, powerful affection for Edwin Arlington Robinson and especially his odd, powerful poem "Richard Cory." The poem preys upon me even as I write, for my father too, that "calm summer night," went out and "put a bullet through his head." I still don't entirely understand why.

Years later, I tried to tote it all up. In my mother's and father's generation, there were my runaway uncle, my gay uncle, my lesbian aunt, my asexual aunt, a battered wife, an incurable philanderer, a militant vegetarian, an embezzler, a compulsive gambler, a suicide. In my own generation, among my cousins, there were a satanist, a mystic, a severe stutterer, another sexual anesthetic, another suicide.

But even as a boy, even before I knew enough to attempt such an accounting, I knew that there was Frances. Even before I was overtaken by the untoward imaginings and unruly impulses of adolescence, even before I was rocked by my father's self-annihilation, I knew that there were more things in heaven and earth than were authorized in my mother's philosophy. I knew that there were mysteries in life.

It is almost impossible to imagine now—three decades have made such a difference—but young men and women of my generation wanted to be novelists. I did.

I wrote a novella when I was twenty. Summer love and modern consciousness. I reread it when I was thirty, to some embarrassment and a certain embarrassed pride. I have not looked at it since, and I would be hard-pressed to put my hands on it today.

But I was in earnest then, even before my father blew his brains out. I sent my novella off to a publisher. I kept notebooks full of fine phrases, snatches of dialogue, sketches of characters, and the choreographies of a couple of novels.

I also went to graduate school to do a doctorate in American civilization.

I was in earnest about the doctorate, too. It would be silly to say I was not. Academic life seemed a lot more appealing than a career in the law, once I noticed that other lawyers were not like my father.

By the time I registered for the LSATs and applied to law schools, I had made it my business to talk to a fair number of lawyers. My father struck me as the only one of them who was not dispirited by what he did for a living. And by the time my father died, I had already fallen under the spell of my second great teacher, Murray Murphey.

Murray beckoned to me as he beckoned to others, without even seeming to try. He had a gift great teachers have, of simultaneously intimating the imminence of marvelous revelations and projecting his own inability to attain such revelations unaided. There was nothing of self-pity in him. Still, he seemed Sisyphean. Some of us tried to comfort him in other ways. Some of us took up his monumental intellectual project. We would help him accomplish the end he put so palpably before us, of unriddling the mysteries of the American character.

I went off to graduate school to do a doctorate in his field, American Civilization, and I went as one of his blessed band. I had been granted an illumination. Others might see American Civilization, or American Studies as it was more commonly called, in terms of great texts, great ideas, the great conversation that constituted American history and literature as they were taught in the early sixties. Murray's students knew civilization as another name for culture. We meant to study Americans as anthropologists studied Trobrianders or Kwakiutls. So the twitting of friends who alleged surprise that anyone would claim that America had a civilization was nothing to us. We were not trying to prove American literature worthy of keeping company with French or Russian or to prove American history worthy of study alongside Italian or British. We were forging an interdiscipline that did not exist. We would be anthropologists of a nation-state, historical psychologists of a complex culture. We would discover the deep springs of American life.

Soon enough, that mission would truly hold me. Soon enough, that vision would consume me. But as I began my graduate study, that mission and that vision were not the main motives that drove me. It would be silly to say they were. More than I sought scholarly success, I wanted the free time I fancied that scholars had.

So far as I could see, professors taught two or three courses a term, six or nine hours a week. People like Murray tried to tell me that teaching was a full-time job like any other. They described the daily drudgeries of preparing classes, keeping office hours, and grading papers. They conjured committee meetings and administrative obligations. They gave me my first glimpses of the academic routines that still fill my days, for better and for worse.

I thought I took their advice into account, supposing myself fortunately forewarned and sublimely sophisticated. I allowed another half-dozen, even another dozen hours a week outside the classroom. I still came up with the better part of the week for real writing.

It was the same inane calculation so many of my generation made. It was sufficient to finish most of us as novelists and make most of the rest academic novelists. It would certainly have been sufficient to finish me if I had persisted in my ambitions. I was unduly attracted to the novel of ideas to begin with.

The only reason I did not persist was that I sat on the wrong side of a professor one foul gray day one foul gray Cambridge winter. It was the beginning of spring term, the first meeting, or more likely the second, of Bernard Bailyn's seminar in early American history. There were ten of us in the class, mostly first-year students like myself. Bailyn had given us a list of ten topics for research papers, each of them as inscrutable as he was. Each of us was to choose one of them.

I happened to be sitting a few seats to his right, or perhaps his left. He happened to go around the room starting to his left, or perhaps his right. By the time he got to me, the only topics that had intrigued me at all were long gone. The three that were left appeared arid beyond any plausible pedagogic purpose. In frustration and not a little fury, I chose the one that seemed the most drearily pedantic of the three: voting procedures in eighteenth-century Massachusetts.

Bailyn gave each of us a couple of leads with which to begin. The ones he gave me led nowhere. I was at a loss. Precious weeks passed. I tried one long shot after another, my efforts as desultory as they were desperate. And then, reaching for anything, I made the right move.

I had been looking for direct descriptions of voting procedures. There were none. If I had been a better anthropologist, I would have saved myself the trouble. People do not describe in detail the quotidian conventions of their existence. They describe in detail the behaviors that violate those conventions. It finally occurred to me that I might find explications of the ordinary buried in accounts of the extraordinary. I might find appeals to proper procedures implicit in complaints of impropriety.

There was an abundance of such complaints in the petitions of the towns of the colony to the central government that sat in Boston. I dug into them like a man possessed. I did not fathom my fervor then. I barely fathom it now. I did have weeks of false starts to make up, but there was no need to make them all up at once; graduate students were allowed Incompletes, and most took them, without stigma. I did have to keep my grades up to assure my financial aid, but there was no real pressure at that point; fellowships were based on performance in the fall, and I knew, long before the spring term was over, that I was secure for the following year. It was something else.

Scientists have written of their experience in certain collaborative enterprises—the Manhattan Project, for example—as utopian. I had, in the sudden intensity of my research, my own solitary utopian community. I tore through the massive volumes in the Massachusetts State Archives. I devoured their thousands of petitions, their hundreds of stories, so many of them separately impenetrable, the assemblage of them collectively importunate. My growing grasp of voting procedures was merely the most trifling aspect of my excitement. I was getting a glimmering of the values that governed local life in eighteenth-century Massachusetts, the values whose infringement occasioned the petitions, and they were nothing like the values of town-meeting democracy that the civics texts celebrated.

I was becoming an anthropologist after all. I sensed myself at the threshold of another world. I took to reading all the petitions, not just the ones that referred to elections. I began evolving in my mind a model of the generative matrix from which community action flowed. I began hypothesizing actions and attitudes I had not even encountered in the archives and designing tests of my hypotheses. I ransacked the town histories and the town records. I had to see if the norms I thought I saw implicit in the exceptional circumstances that led people to complain of their condition were also explicit, or at least legible, in everyday affairs.

A culture was coming to life before my astonished eyes. Or, rather, a myriad of little local cultures were emerging, each aloof from the vast abstractions of "Puritanism," "New England," and "the New England

Mind" that controlled scholarship at the time. I felt a creative frenzy more compelling than any I had known in writing my novella. I was discovering that I could seize—and be seized by—history as utterly as I could take hold of fiction and that I could say in history most of what I wanted to say in fiction. Indeed, I was discovering that writing history was more challenging, and more fun, than writing novels. The material was not so totally at my authorial disposal. The evidence was recalcitrant. It sometimes took me where I had no notion of going. It occasionally even took me where I was disinclined to go. In my novella, I drew on all I had learned of the world. In this historical study, I had to learn more. I had to listen to voices and values that were not my own yet possessed an integrity and passion that required recognition if my research and writing were to be satisfying.

Such imperatives suited me splendidly. In the spring of 1962, America was, for all practical purposes, still in the Eisenhower era. The brief years of John Kennedy's presidency changed almost nothing of our music, our dress, our sexual proprieties, or our platitudinous politics. Except for blacks, the sixties did not begin until after the assassination. I was still searching for ways to affirm that life admitted of more possibilities than the WASP establishment of imperial America could countenance, more variation than the insipid middle-class morality of the suburb would acknowledge. A history that could catch the lives Americans had led before the culture congealed seemed to offer one such way.

Looking back, I am not disturbed by my reasoning, but I am a little disconcerted by my rage. It still seems to me impossible to exaggerate the smarminess of that era or the smug certainty of Americans that all people everywhere aspired to achieve our own puny and constricted existence. But why was I so adamant to deliver my diatribe against such chauvinism? Why was I so bitter, when my own prospect could hardly have been more promising? Why did my bitterness intensify as my adolescent sexual frustration ebbed?

Perhaps it was my very bookishness: so many modern novels, such precocious wallowing in literary experiment and perversity, so much anthropology and philosophy (and so little history, oddly, and that little so ethnocentric and positivistic that it contributed nearly nothing to my emerging ideas of culture). Perhaps it was my very privilege: such loving parents, such trepidatious trust to allow me to spend my summers hitchhiking wherever the rides ran across the United States and Canada and Mexico and Europe, such good fortune in friends and in early loves and losses with young women. Who knows?

Somehow I had arrived at ideas of a kind of social justice in which all might be as blessed as I was and none need be cramped and deformed as the official culture of the era demanded. Somehow I had come to a commitment. I meant to minister to America. I would surely have been a rabbi in some other time, some other place, if only I believed, if only audiences believed.

I lie, of course. I would have been a prophet, not a rabbi. Modesty is only an outward affectation of mine.

As I pursued my doctoral studies over the ensuing years, and as I learned more of the vast variety of the American past, it began to dawn on me that I did not have to cry in the wilderness nor call on my countrymen to be what they had never been before. I had only to show them what they had been and seduce their allowance of the legitimacy of it all. America had been stolen from Americans by the Protestant elite and its assorted academic, journalistic, and religious errandboys. There had always been other lives, other impulses, other dreams.

There is an emergent historiographical orthodoxy that attributes the "new social history" of the seventies to European influences such as the *Annales* school in France. That historiography is hogwash. Even in the hermetic terms of the filiation of academic ideas, the new history owed much more to Karl Marx and a disparate array of native sources than it ever did to tony French figures. Even insofar as we took our cues from others, the writings that mattered to me and to the new social historians I knew were works of blunt empirical audacity such as the Kinsey reports and pieces of pyrotechnic journalism such as the early *Esquire* essays of Tom Wolfe. The mentors who mattered to us were men and women like Murray Murphey, who drew on the rich populist and progressive traditions of American pragmatism and social science to try to touch the experience of an entire people rather than to privilege its elite.

But if it is fatuous to ascribe the new social history to the example of the *sixième section* or the Cambridge Group for the History of Population and Social Structure, it is only marginally more accurate to credit the transformation to the inspiration of American scholars and scholarly institutions. The new social history simply did not derive from a disembodied academic process. It arose in response to the sit-ins in the South, and the March on Washington, and the dismal deathwatch over Schwerner, Goodman, and Chaney in the fateful Freedom Summer of 1964. It arose in resentment of the pointless and proliferating repressions of American society. It arose in revulsion from the sodden pieties and bombastic pomposities of the establishment. As surely as any of the other movements of the sixties did, it arose in rage for a larger life.

None of this was so transparent at the time. But from the first I had intuitions of unwritten histories that needed to be known. From the first those intuitions must have been fired by my mounting fascination with my family and my increasing experience of my country.

I had taken to hitchhiking. When school was done, I would put a few changes of clothes in my backpack, strap my sleeping bag on top, and set out for the summer, criss-crossing America, riding on my thumb and my nerve and the rough kindnesses of my countrymen. I rode with truckers and state troopers, with plumbers and fruit pickers, with more salesmen than I could count. Too many of them made me homosexual propositions. Far too many of them had a bottle or a flask and drank from it as they drove. Almost all of them had a gun or a knife that they brandished meaningfully before me. And all of them had tales to tell.

I listened in innocent astonishment to stories of precocious sexuality, mindless marital promiscuity, and orgy. I began for the first time to sense the fury of the battle of the sexes in America. I felt as I never had before the seething hatred of Southerners for Northerners, of whites for blacks, of Protestants for Catholics, of working people for their bosses. Sometimes the very continent seemed swathed in lust and animosity.

I listened in equally wide-eyed wonder to stories of hardihood beyond any I ever encountered at home. The people who gave me rides were people prepared to take chances, not only for themselves but also for others. Again and again they told me tales of trust, of sacrifice, and of a readiness to run risks for the sake of family, friends, and strangers. They did not ask my admiration or expect my applause. They took their fellow-feeling for granted, as an elemental decency if not an obligation. They were, to be sure, lonely people. As often as not, they picked me up to have someone to talk to, to keep from falling asleep at the wheel, to share the ache of their isolation. But they were also good people. As often as not, they picked me up simply to lend a wayfarer a helping hand: to take me where I was going, to treat me to dinner, to offer me the hospitality of their homes for the night and breakfast next morning besides. Sometimes the country seemed suffused with a human grandeur to match the immensity and loveliness of the land.

The festering enmities and the Christian *caritas* alike gave the lie to the truisms of liberal individualism that were then taken by historians to be the essential if not the only American outlook on life. On every hand, scholars in the early sixties asserted the sway of legitimate self-interest in American culture. At Harvard, Louis Hartz and his insistence on the absolute ideological hegemony of the liberal tradition mesmer-ized graduate students in four or five different departments. At other schools, other teachers and other product-differentiated formulations doubtless did the same. But none of them caught the variety of voices I heard on the road. Americans were much more interesting than the aca-demics and their theories supposed. None of those splendid schemata explained or even acknowledged the meanness or the mutual regard, the resentment or the idealism, that were the coin of the realm. It was, as Marianne Moore once said, "an honor to witness such confusion."

I have no idea how I held so long to my presumptions of prim, middle-class propriety, when my every summer exposed an array of other ambitions and axioms. I cannot imagine how I shared so easily in the sheltered discourse of my Harvard days, when almost my every ride revealed a vaster range of vile, violent, yearning, daring, and indeed noble dreams than could be encompassed in those tight little islands of Ivy League arrogance.

Years later, I would come across a luminous anecdote of the early months of the Kennedy administration. As David Halberstam told it, in *The Best and the Brightest,* David Riesman was having lunch with a couple of his cocksure colleagues who were commuting between Cam-bridge and the capital. Talk turned to the conflict in Vietnam. The New Frontiersmen spoke righteously and exhilaratedly of the administra-tion's emerging initiatives in counterinsurgency warfare. Riesman lis-tened, increasingly dismayed by their hubris,

until finally he stopped them and asked if they had ever been to Utah. *Utah!* No, they said, not Utah, but why Utah, had Riesman ever been there? No, Riesman answered, but he had read a good deal about the Church of the Latter-Day Saints, and it occurred to him that his friends did not know much about America, about how deep the evangelical streak was. "You all think you can manage limited wars and that you're dealing with an elite society which is just waiting for your leadership. It's not that way at all," he said. "It's not an Eastern elite society run for Harvard and the Council on Foreign Relations."

But even before I left Harvard, I was beginning to realize that my principal advantage over my classmates and competitors was that I had been to Utah. I had climbed its painted mountains and explored its in-tricate Indian ruins. I had been stranded in its deserts and slept in its railroad sandhouses to get out of its sudden lashing rains. I had been proselytized by half a dozen Mormon missionaries. I had been taken into a dozen homes, as a scruffy stranger, and I had left, more than once, as a veritable member of the family. I knew something of Utah's hypocrisies and quite a bit about its majesties.

I had been to Louisiana, too, and Alabama and the Carolinas and Mississippi. I had had a hundred rides, heard a thousand stories, and shivered in terror more times than I could count. I had eaten the grits and the red-eye gravy, the catfish and the chess pie. I had been to the churches and the tent meetings. I had flirted with the women.

I had been to the prairies and the mountains and the rain forests, to Nebraska and Colorado and the Pacific Northwest. I had set my sights on big cities and ended up spending more time in small towns. I had plotted my routes by the great highways and wound up riding my miles on the back roads. I had aimed to spend nights in state parks and found myself spending them in cemeteries and city jails. If I did not truly know America, I did know that there was more to it than the prissy individualism of my self-congratulatory cosmopolitan colleagues.

I was as alienated from cosmopolitanism as I was incorrigibly attached to it. I meant to dismantle its myths, demystify its presumptions and platitudes, and restore the American people to their past. It was an outlandish and immature ambition. I cling to it still.

In my earliest work, including one of the essays here, I disputed some shibboleths of town-meeting democracy. In a number of subsequent studies, including some here, I considered other items of received wisdom. Again and again it seemed to me that things were not as they seemed, or not, at any rate, as they seemed in the conventional accounts. Life was larger than official legend allowed. It was larger, indeed, than I myself saw when I wrote.

In my dissertation, I let loose a diatribe against the Harvard I hated and the New England I hated and the elite American orthodoxy I did not adore unduly either. Or at least I thought I did at the time. As I look back, I realize that I wrought more than I knew and that I could hardly have done otherwise. Sustained research cannot be conducted, month after month, year after year, without a modicum of ambivalence and a consequent curiosity. So as I grow older I come to be intrigued by the coercive ethical community I damned in the dissertation. I come to appreciate elements of interest and even of mystery in the pattern of self-suppression that I assailed in the book.

I have learned to relish this inner colloquy. I have learned to learn from the belated self-interrogation that writing permits and to be a little chary of my ready righteousness. The animus of these essays often seems clear enough, against all those like the persecuting Puritans or the negrophobic Jefferson who would contract the possibilities of our common life. But the energy of these pieces is often more complex. I can only assume that I was drawn to the Puritans because their very narrowness enabled them to dig deeper, to Jefferson because his aversion to blacks stood in such striking contrast to his avidity for everything else, to Horatio Alger because his obsession with success extended its definition and made social space for gentler impulses, to Doctor Spock because his capitulation to the corporate economy opened new spheres of feeling.

Occasionally, these interior conversations work their way outward into print. My piece on identity in early America, for example, maintains the emphasis of my initial thinking on the communal constraint of individualism while also attempting to reconcile it with my subsequent sense of the exaggeration of individualism in the New World.

More often, I reach no reconciliation. So far from seeking synthesis or coming to a calm resolution, I push postures to tenable extremities. In this regard I would write as D. H. Lawrence did, extending experiments to the point where their empirical, ethical, and esthetic consequences can be judged. Sometimes one of my essays takes tacit issue with another, as sometimes a later Lawrence character or novel implicitly rebukes the endeavor of an earlier one.

Careful readers have caught me more than once on the inner contradictions of these disparate pieces. I see no reason to expose all of them, but at least one blatant one might best be addressed. The essays on relatively recent America hold up an older society of authentic individuality as a standard by which to assess the erosion of autonomy in contemporary life. Yet the essays on that older society acknowledge no such sway of genuine individuality. On the contrary, they insist upon the primacy of communal pressures that extorted conformity or otherwise impelled people to flee from freedom. They allow, at most, a liberty to manipulate masks and to manage impressions. Their very iconoclasm ineluctably subverts the iconoclasm of the essays on the contemporary scene and saps the urgency of those essays besides.

I am not sure how to respond to such criticism. I struggle to square my condemnation of the bad old days, in my writings about the remote past, with my commendation of the good old days, in my writings about the recent past. I strain to connect my castigation of collective controls over individuals in the colonial era with my lamentation for the decay of independence in our own time.

Perhaps I should put it all down to dyspepsia. Perhaps I should seek refuge in Emersonian claptrap about consistency and the hobgoblin of little minds. Perhaps I should simply concede a failure of rigorous integrity and confess my cynical presumption when I wrote the essays that a collection such as this would never come along to embarrass me.

Or perhaps I should not. Perhaps the contradictions can be redeemed. Perhaps the essays themselves can be understood as elements of a more intricate conversation that is itself tempered by history. For it seems to me impossible to doubt that the directions of American development have changed profoundly since the end of the Second World War.

Over the past half-century, our primary public institutions have grown distended and dissolute in the pursuit of an unprecedented imperial project. Over that same span, we citizens have very nearly given up all opposition to the demands that our curdled corporate establishment makes upon us.

Two centuries ago, at the conclusion of the constitutional convention in Philadelphia, Benjamin Franklin remarked that the delegates had given us a republic, if we could keep it. Generation after generation, through all the temptations of westward expansion, all the traumas of civil war, all the turmoil of urban industrial growth, we kept it. Only in our own era have we given it over, to uphold as we suppose the imperial garrison.

In the name of national security, we have essentially abandoned politics and the tension between the claims of self and society that our politics expressed. Voting returns show that, for the first time in our history, most of us do not even bother to cast a ballot. Surveys show that most of us no longer even define citizenship in such minimal terms. We now see the good citizen simply as the man or woman who does not break the law. We reelect virtually any incumbent who runs. We submit to almost every exaction of executive privilege. We admit unabashedly to the public opinion polltakers who ask that we would lie and commit crimes if told to do so by our superiors.

To be sure, our apathy, docility, and doglike amiability are continuous in some considerable degree with cultural patterns that have been evident since the seventeenth century. We have never been preoccupied with politics, nor averse to surveillance, nor disdainful of the demands of others. Nonetheless, we have never had so criminally expansive an executive or so criminally complaisant a Congress, either. We have never routinized so ruthlessly our prying into people's lives or surrendered so supinely our privacy. And these matters of degree do matter. History and its subtle modulations condition the apparent continuities of our national course.

If some contradictions among these papers can thus be relieved by the ways in which things may be different even when they seem the same, others can be resolved by the ways in which other things remain the same even when they scarcely seem at all. The explicit analysis of a number of these studies emphasizes social pressures upon individuals. The implicit tension of these studies takes its rise from the unruly indisposition of those individuals to suffer those pressures and from the incipient anarchy of American life.

By their very emigration from their various old countries, Americans revealed themselves. They were the men and women of those ancestral villages and towns who were least entangled in tradition, least tied to kinfolk and friends, least encumbered by obligations to others, and least warmed by reciprocities with others.

On just that account, as Tocqueville saw, they were the men and women most caught up in conformity, most susceptible to the appeals of abstract affiliation. In their very loneliness, as Mencken maintained, they sacrificed themselves "in order to belong to something larger and safer" than they could find in isolation.

But always the fond fantasy of self-sufficiency remained, and often the real residue besides. Official culture—the subject of so many of these essays—advanced in deadly antagonism to the muffled American dream of anarchy and is unintelligible without it. The Puritans relied upon the apparatus of the town meeting to blunt the wayward indiscipline and insouciant antiauthoritarianism that they took to be typified in Thomas Morton and his promiscuous revelers at Merry Mount. Our own imperial presidents rely upon the armamentarium of the warfare state to offset the permissiveness and flaccidity that they take to be typified in Doctor Spock.

Americans have always wished to be free. The country has always smoldered with yearnings for a primal liberation and leveling that the culture has set itself to tame. And sometimes the inchoate egalitarianism that pulses in the popular ethic has crystallized in comradeship rather than resentment. Sometimes it has found its voice in poetry rather than politics, arousing irresistible popular responses. I think of Tom Paine's

*Common Sense* and of the masses who took to heart its defiance of denunciations from the "better sort." I think of Thomas Jefferson imagining endless revolution and renewal, of Andrew Jackson inviting his
muddybooted adherents to consecrate the White House with him at his
inaugural, of Harriet Beecher Stowe electrifying the conscience of the
North with her unabashed appeal to outlaw values.

I do not deceive myself that these crystallizations and the responses
they evoked ever constituted the prevalent pattern of our lives. I do believe that they were our occasions of cultural communion, in the sense
in which the great German sociologist Schmalenbach specified the
term. Though they could never be sustained, they caught our consciousness of our deepest and dearest selves. Though they resisted rou-
tinization, they remained more tantalizingly within reach in America
than anywhere else in the Western world. Indeed, just because they did,
they had to be counteracted more strenuously than anywhere else in the
Western world, by elites who have always been more preoccupied with
suppressing or co-opting them than elites anywhere else in the Western
world.

Our very nationality springs from a document that declared all men
created equal. Our national pantheon enshrines an array of founders
and politicians, artists and religious leaders—William Penn and Abra-
ham Lincoln, Walt Whitman and Roger Williams and Martin Luther
King—who were willing to dare the radical doctrine of the inner light
and the spiritual parity it implied. If American norms have generally
been conformist and collective, they have generally rested uneasily upon
Americans. So when I appeal as I occasionally do to a freer past than I
ordinarily describe, I appeal to those liminal moments and subversive
traditions that voiced some of the inmost aspirations and expressed
something of the experience of the mass of Americans.

We have always been an antinomian nation, for better and for worse.
We are being brought to order now, for better and for worse. And even
our domestication—our submission to the requisitions of the military-
industrial regime and our compensatory resort to an ethic of radical
private validation in our emotional lives—reflects our resilient lawless-
ness, for better and for worse.

None of these essays are actually biographical. Not a one of them begins at its subject's birth and traces his career. Not a one of them attempts a "life" of Byrd or Barnum or anyone else.

A couple of them appear only because they bear indirectly on the rest, which themselves have but an oblique biographical aspect. "The Fabrication of Identity in Early America" aims to establish conditions of character formation in the colonies and, by extension, in the new nation. "The Social Context of Democracy in Massachusetts" seeks to set a communal counterpoint to the other accounts, which focus more manifestly on individuals.

Yet even these other accounts concern themselves less, in the end, with the individuals on whom they center than with the social issues and cultural themes that those individuals intimate. My endeavor in all these obliquely biographical essays is to capture a moment of emergence that is refracted through particular persons but resonates through far larger cultural configurations.

Each of these essays is implicitly if not overtly embattled, because history seems to me nothing if not a story of conflict and contingency. I write about Jefferson and St. Domingue because I think he helped cast there a negrophobic die that could have been cast otherwise. I write about Alger and Spock because I believe they reveal shifting American definitions of success and self and the changing content of American conceptions of masculinity and femininity. I write about Franklin and Barnum because I am convinced that they illuminate vicissitudes of self-advancement and impression-management in times of turbulence.

Each of these essays is also embattled because each is a confrontation with American mythology, an effort to engage sacred cows in their own pastures. Explicitly in some cases, tacitly in others, I assume that if we understand our icons better, we will understand ourselves more deeply. I offer my unconventional readings of my very conventional subjects not because I would be willfully perverse but because the conventional readings seem to me willfully obtuse and inattentive. They simply do not accord their subjects serious scrutiny. The very people they put forth as paragons of orthodoxy are far more subtle and even subversive than they allow, and far more human for it.

Yet I do not in these essays accord my subjects a full measure of humanity either, at least not in the sense in which conventional biographers do. Because my concern is ultimately with collective values more than with individual character, and with cultural moments more than with personal careers, I do not delve much into my subjects' motives. I do not attempt earnestly to answer the questions that are bound to arise even in oblique biographies. What made these men tick? *Why* was Jefferson so fixated on blackness? *Why* did Franklin disdain integrity, or Barnum believe a sucker born every minute?

Once I thought that the essential business of the historian was with just such matters of motivation and explanation. Once, I dismissed all else as mere description.

Once I believed that the only adequate explanations were those predicated on learned behavior and the accumulation of experience. Once I disdained all recourse to heredity and innateness as obscurantism and worse. Now, after five children and another thirty years of living, I am not so sure.

I do still take experiential factors to be more influential than any others. That is why I am still a historian, and still fascinated by conundrums of national character. But that is not to assert very much. Even so stalwart a sociobiologist as E. O. Wilson acknowledges that eighty percent of animal social behavior is to be attributed to environmental elements rather than to genetic ones.

I just do not take that preponderant part to be the most perplexing or intriguing part any more. I take almost for granted that there are profound similarities among my children. I marvel that there are also deep differences, and I muse endlessly upon them. I cannot account for them by birth order, gender, or any other explanatory principle that presumes the primacy of experience. Indeed, I cannot account for them at all. Some of them were evident from the instant each child came from the womb, in the lustiness or tentativity with which he cried, the quickness with which she gained her composure, and more.

Just as I cannot explain the variation in my children's temperaments, so I cannot explain Jefferson's racism or Franklin's romantic relativism. I can place such men in their class situation and set them in their social circumstances, but I do not thereby grasp the distinctive ideas and attitudes that drew me to those men and made me care to comprehend them in the first place. I do not thereby make any significant sense of why Thomas Morton could abide the Puritans so much more amiably than they could endure him or why William Byrd was driven to keep a diary when so few of his fellow planters did.

As with my children, and as with my Aunt Frances before them, so with these oblique biographies. I come finally to opacity and obstinacy, to contingency and quandary. I come to mystery.

It does not disturb me. I am more patient with the recalcitrance of things than I once was, and I know better now than I once did that there are many modes of explication. Some questions are simply more accessible than others.

Isaac Newton fathered a new physics by abjuring a question that had informed an older physics for centuries—why did bodies fall as they did?—for a far more fruitful inquiry—what followed from positing as an axiom that bodies fell as they did? His contemporary critics maintained that he had missed the point of their enterprise, mistaking the proper physicist's concern with causes for a far more superficial focus on consequences. But the science of succeeding centuries, which advanced under the Newtonian paradigm, proved that there was still sufficient causal and explanatory work to go around.

On a far less lofty frequency, I would entice my fellow historians and my readers to move toward a similar paradigm change. I would defer explanation of character and seek instead its specification, writing of individuals primarily as a means to understand aggregates. I study Thomas Morton less to get at him and his appealing ways than to try to fathom the Puritans and their more appalling practices. I look into the lives of Franklin and Barnum less to learn about those extraordinary promoters than to come to some comprehension of the nascent mass audiences that embraced their promotions.

Occasionally I catch something explanatory, and even predictive. My analysis of the interior logic of Horatio Alger's stories, and of their author's patent unease with the masculine role as his era defined it, prefigured by several years the archival discovery that Alger was himself homosexual. My treatment of the essential impulsion of Doctor Spock's baby care books anticipated the celebrated revisions of the fourth edition, in which he was able to eliminate the sexism of the first three editions but did not even try to reconsider the corporate careerism that was always more central to his advice.

But I do not take such spasms of predictive power to be the test of my interpretations. I do not aim to unravel the origins of things, linearly. The social world does not seem to me the determinate sort of place that is susceptible to such conventional causal explanations.

I do aim to trace the relations of things, circularly. I aim to do it in contexts of contingency, and I only wish that I did it more compellingly than I do.

I do aim, too, to search out the social in the personal and to tease intimations of collective culture out of individual action and ideation. If none of these essays is actually biographical, that is because I do not ultimately put much stock in biography. Especially in these years of the yuppies, when amok ideologues on every hand insist on the sufficiency of the individual and asperse every effort to recall men and women to concern for the common weal, it seems imperative to say that the great issue in America is not, and has never been, how individuals live. It is, and has always been, how they live together.

ONE

# The Fabrication of Identity in Early America

In the study of the American character there have been two primary positions. One has emphasized the ascendancy of individualism, with its values of self-interest and self-reliance. The other has stressed the sway of the community, with its corollaries of sociability, conformism, and endemic insecurity of self. Exponents of each have been indisposed to take seriously the claims of the other, and advocates of the only significant alternative have taken them both too seriously by setting those static characterizations in historical sequence.

Consider, for instance, the recent historiography of the New England town. Almost every examination of the subject that has not affirmed an abiding communalism or an irrepressible individualism has described an evolution, or devolution, of close communal modes into more modern individuality. And on just that account such studies constitute, collectively, an advancing embarrassment. The ones among them that predicate either a constant corporate or a constant liberal inclination among the townspeople simply talk past one another, while, taken together, the ones that posit a passage from a self-subordinating to a self-seeking orientation place that passage in every generation from the founding of the colonies to the middle of the twentieth century.

Darrett Rutman affirms a transformation of communal ideals and the emergence of a profusion of private purposes and practices in the very first decade of settlement. William Haller presumes the persistence of

From *William and Mary Quarterly*, 3d ser., 34 (1977), 183–214.

more medieval ways through the first generation and argues their abandonment only after 1660. Kenneth Lockridge insists that the ancient
frame of values remained intact through the second generation but not
the third. Richard Bushman postulates a pristine traditionalism clear
through the seventeenth century and asserts its erosion in the Great
Awakening. John J. Waters alleges a placid homogeneity through the
revivals and portrays its irrevocable impairment in the period of the
Revolution. Benjamin Labaree maintains that customs of corporate solidarity survived the Revolution but not the depression of the early nineteenth century and the War of 1812. And others extend the same paradigm through the nineteenth century, into the twentieth, and indeed
into our own age.[1]

Amid differences so protracted and inconclusive, it might be wise to
suppose that every side brings out at least an aspect of the truth. On
such a supposition it would be less urgent to ascertain and account for
the priority of communalism or individualism than to plot the pattern
within which both could burgeon at once. It would then be immensely
suggestive that, exactly in the years through which America was first
colonized by Englishmen, both the self-awareness and self-assertion
that inform the modern psyche and the coercive mutuality that marks
the modern community achieved something of their subsequent scope.
Even as the settlers of the seventeenth century craved self-suppressive
communalism, they also sought larger liberties for themselves and drew
distinctions between social role and a sense of inner identity. Like many
in the mother country, they established elaborate geographies of con-

1. Darrett B. Rutman, *Winthrop's Boston: Portrait of a Puritan Town, 1630–1649*
(Chapel Hill, N.C., 1965); William Haller, Jr., *The Puritan Frontier: Town-Planting in
New England Colonial Development, 1630–1660* (New York, 1951); Kenneth A. Lock-
ridge, *A New England Town, The First Hundred Years: Dedham, Massachusetts, 1636–1736*
(New York, 1970); Richard L. Bushman, *From Puritan to Yankee: Character and the Social
Order in Connecticut, 1690–1765* (Cambridge, Mass., 1967); John J. Waters, Jr., *The Otis
Family in Provincial and Revolutionary Massachusetts* (Chapel Hill, N.C., 1968); Benjamin
W. Labaree, *Patriots and Partisans: The Merchants of Newburyport, 1764–1815* (Cambridge,
Mass., 1962). For successive generations in the nineteenth and twentieth centuries see,
for example, Michael B. Katz, *The Irony of Early School Reform: Educational Innovation in
Mid-Nineteenth Century Massachusetts* (Cambridge, Mass., 1968); Leonard L. Richards,
*"Gentlemen of Property and Standing": Anti-Abolition Mobs in Jacksonian America* (New
York, 1970); Michael H. Frisch, *Town into City: Springfield, Massachusetts, and the Meaning
of Community, 1840–1880* (Cambridge, Mass., 1972); Stephan Thernstrom, *Poverty and
Progress: Social Mobility in a Nineteenth Century City* (Cambridge, Mass., 1964); W. Lloyd
Warner and J. O. Low, *The Social System of the Modern Factory. The Strike: A Social Analysis*,
Yankee City Series, no. 4 (New Haven, Conn., 1947); William M. Dobriner, "The Natu-
ral History of a Reluctant Suburb," *Yale Review*, n.s., 49 (1960): 399–412.

sciousness on the basis of a "separation between the behaving and the scrutinizing self."[2]

The early colonists were at once more free and more controlled, more concerned about themselves and more attentive to the opinions of their neighbors, than their European forebears had been; and Americans since have carried these fissions further. Like the men and women who planted the first colonies, they have continued to have two revolutions in train, in opposite directions, at the same time. They have grown more individuated *and* more regimented, more tolerant *and* more repressive. They have come increasingly to move, as Philip Rieff has said, in a milieu "of orgy and routine which constitutes modernization."[3]

Modernization may, indeed, afford a context in which it is possible to comprehend both the communal and the individualistic elements of American life. For in such a context these tendencies do not appear as antithetic as they have ordinarily done. On the contrary, they seem more nearly to have been inseparable expressions of a single dislocation, each destined to grow with the other.

It would be rash to hold that the individual's relation to society has ever been anything but problematic in the career of western Christendom, but it would be myopic not to notice that that relation became markedly more tortured in the late sixteenth and seventeenth centuries. Something seems then to have come unhinged in the ways people were wont to live with one another and in their aspirations for, and anxieties about, group life. Something seems to have driven them simultaneously to seek a new purity of personal identity and covenanted community alike.

Interpretation of the early modern character must accordingly comprehend the sources of such centrifugality, for Western people had not always been impelled to those extremities. In the Middle Ages they had admitted oppositions, but "the distinctive feature of medieval thought" was that it absorbed "contrasts which later were to be presented as irrec-

2. David Riesman, Nathan Glazer, and Reuel Denney, *The Lonely Crowd: A Study of the Changing American Character* (New Haven, Conn., 1950), 44. For a discussion of the antithesis between the "inner man" and the "outer man" see Norman S. Fiering, "Will and Intellect in the New England Mind," *William and Mary Quarterly*, 3d ser., 29 (1972): 515–58. For a similar distinction as indigenous to English Protestantism, and indeed to Christianity itself, see Charles H. George and Katherine George, *The Protestant Mind of the English Reformation, 1570–1640* (Princeton, N.J., 1961), 295–97, and Robert N. Bellah, "Religious Evolution," *American Sociological Review* 29 (1964): 358–74.

3. Philip Rieff, *Fellow Teachers* (New York, 1973), 113.

oncilable antitheses." The medieval church was "more ecumenical, more genially encompassing, more permissive doctrinally, than either the sixteenth-century Protestant churches or the post-Trentine Catholic Church." It allowed degrees of dissident freedom, in mysticism and in the religious orders, which Protestant congregations of the early modern era, organized as they were in antagonism to such catholicity, contracted to counterposed options of conformity or secession.[4]

The pluralism of medieval proclivities was sharply at odds with the dichotomous ordering of experience that emerged after the Reformation. Men and women of the Middle Ages did not distinguish as strenuously as their descendants would between work and leisure, madness and sanity, or youth and maturity. They did not set apart as scrupulously the spheres of religion, science, and magic, or "rationalize" as relentlessly the realms of the economy, the polity, and the society. They did not isolate conscience from temporal affairs, as Luther would, and they did not segregate science from morality or natural law from revelation, as Bacon would. Indeed, they did not sunder nature and grace, and they did not even separate any too carefully the domains of the sacred and the secular. Pilgrimages were pretexts for lovers' trysts; prostitutes pursued their trade in the churches; the earthiest of erotic relations were depicted in the most elevated of religious terms. And in discounting all these differentiations, people tended, as Huizinga said, to "reduce all things to a general type," so that "the power to discern and describe individual traits was never attained."[5]

4. R. H. Tawney, *Religion and the Rise of Capitalism: A Historical Study* (New York, 1926), 20; Eugene F. Rice, Jr., *The Foundations of Early Modern Europe, 1460–1559,* in The Norton History of Modern Europe, ed. Felix Gilbert (New York, 1971), 147.

5. J. Huizinga, *The Waning of the Middle Ages: A Study of the Forms of Life, Thought and Art in France and the Netherlands in the XIVth and XVth Centuries* (London, 1924), 196. This paragraph follows Huizinga more generally; see, for example, ibid., 44, 111, 137, 140–41, 142, 144–45, 195, 196, 207–8, 236–37, and also Keith Thomas, *Religion and the Decline of Magic* (New York, 1971); Philippe Ariès, *Centuries of Childhood: A Social History of Family Life* (New York, 1962); and Michel Foucault, *Madness and Civilization: A History of Insanity in the Age of Reason,* trans. Richard Howard (New York, 1965). On the significance of the recognition of the sacred for individuation see Benjamin Nelson in "Perspectives on the Therapeutic in the Context of Contemporary Sociology: A Dialogue between Benjamin Nelson and Dennis Wrong," *Salmagundi* 20 (1972): 186. On the centrality of casuistry as an institutional expression of the connectedness of nature and grace, and of the temporal and spiritual realms in the Middle Ages, and on the attenuation of the practice of casuistry among the early Protestants, see ibid., 169–70, and Benjamin Nelson, "Self-Images and Systems of Spiritual Direction in the History of European Civilization," in *The Quest for Self-Control: Classical Philosophies and Scientific Research,* ed. Samuel Z. Klausner (New York, 1965), 61–72.

Such diffusion suggests patterns of muffled individuality to which we also have testimony from present-day tribal societies around the globe. Among the Samoans of the South Pacific, for instance, Margaret Mead reported a similar disinclination to acknowledge individual differences or admit any consequential "consciousness of personality." Among the Balinese of Indonesia Clifford Geertz discovered a comparable "anonymization of persons." Among peoples as far-flung and diverse as the Dinka of the Sudan, the Wintu of northern California, and the Amahuaca of the upper Amazon, anthropologists have found evidence of individuation underdeveloped by modern Western standards—a lesser presence, in language and often in life, of an idea of each human being as a center of personal agency, of a valuation of each as unique, and, in truth, of the very "concept of an established separate self."[6]

In such settings, in which the individual finds his social environment

6. Margaret Mead, *Coming of Age in Samoa: A Psychological Study of Primitive Youth for Western Civilization* (New York, 1928), 224, 215, and chap. 13, *passim.* Clifford Geertz, *Person, Time, and Conduct in Bali: An Essay in Cultural Analysis,* Yale University Southeast Asian Studies Cultural Report Series, no. 14 (New Haven, Conn., 1966), 54; Dorothy Lee, "The Conception of Self among the Wintu Indians," *Journal of Abnormal and Social Psychology* 45 (1950): 539. On the Dinka see Mary Douglas, *Purity and Danger: An Analysis of Concepts of Pollution and Taboo* (New York, 1966), 84; on the Wintu see Lee, "Conception of Self," 538–43, and D. Demetracopoulou Lee, "Linguistic Reflection of Wintu Thought," *International Journal of American Linguistics* 10 (1944): 181–87; on the Amahuaca see Manuel Córdova-Rios and F. Bruce Lamb, *Wizard of the Upper Amazon* (New York, 1971), and Andrew Weil, *The Natural Mind: A New Way of Looking at Drugs and the Higher Consciousness* (Boston, 1972), 184. See also, for example, Douglas, *Purity and Danger,* 88; Nelson in "Perspectives on the Therapeutic," 186; Bellah, "Religious Evolution"; Colin M. Turnbull, "Human Nature and Primal Man," *Social Research* 40 (1973): 528–30; Francis L. K. Hsu, "Kinship and Ways of Life: An Exploration," in *Psychological Anthropology,* ed. Francis L. K. Hsu (Homewood, Ill., 1961), esp. 418; Helen Merrell Lynd, *On Shame and the Search for Identity* (New York, 1950), 157–59; Richard N. Henderson, *The King in Every Man: Evolutionary Trends in Onitsha Ibo Society and Culture* (New Haven, Conn., 1972), 13, 124, 503–4; Donald N. Levine, *Wax and Gold: Tradition and Innovation in Ethiopian Culture* (Chicago, 1965), 238–86; and a host of older if somewhat disreputable assertions of similar points by Edward Tylor, James Frazer, Émile Durkheim, Lucien Lévy-Bruhl, and Marcel Mauss.

The issue of the premodern personality is vastly vexed, since some degrees and types of self-awareness seem to be present in, and essential to, even the most primitive societies. For suggestive efforts to explicate differences of quality and quantity despite such minima see Levine, *Wax and Gold,* 239–41; Turnbull, "Human Nature," 528–30; Geertz, *Person, Time, and Conduct,* 43, 53–55, 58–59, 69–70; and Edward Shorter, "Comment," *History of Childhood Quarterly* 1 (1973–74): 593–94. On the basis of these analyses it seems plausible to suppose that other cultures, including most Western cultures before the early modern era, may have afforded no very notable scope for the express cultivation of the individuality they did contain. In that light it is striking that the word "self" was not compounded as a prefix in English before the late sixteenth and early seventeenth centuries. See Logan Pearsall Smith, *The English Language* (London, 1912), 236–37.

"emotionally continuous with himself," the self is, as Benjamin Nelson has said, "an intermittent emergent."[7] And if the early modern epoch was the time of the self's decisive emergence in the West, the origins of that development are probably to be traced to the ways in which men and women of that era were wrenched loose from customary contexts of community and domesticity. For as Philippe Ariès, Michel Foucault, and Marshall McLuhan, among others, have shown, the rage for categorization and compartmentalization that shaped the new bourgeois culture of the seventeenth century made distinctions central that had scarcely been salient for medieval folk, embedded as they were in a more intricate and multifarious web of human relations.

The society of the Middle Ages was at once intensely immediate and immensely complex. The mass of men and women lived in an intimate world in which kinfolk, neighbors, and unnumbered ancient customs mediated the impingement of more distant authorities. Central government was hardly able even to curb local magnates, let alone control townspeople and villagers in the disparate jurisdictions of the realm. Peasants shielded themselves from the exactions of lords by recourse to prerogatives of ancestral usage and by enrollment under multiple masters, as well as by reliance upon their legitimate rights as members of a village and a family. For every sphere of medieval existence conferred its distinctive entitlements and exemptions, and "according to the different departments of their activity, men passed from one to the other of these zones of law." Family law, agrarian law, the customary law of the manor, the regulations of the community, and contractual obligations all cut across one another; and this multiplicity of legal codes was paralleled by a proliferation of courts to administer them. Even in the England of the Plantagenets, where royal courts and a kind of national law were relatively effective, a profusion of local tribunals persisted. Manorial, bor-

---

7. Dorothy Lee, "Are Basic Needs Ultimate?" *Journal of Abnormal and Social Psychology* 43 (1948): 393; Nelson in "Perspectives on the Therapeutic," 184. On emergent individuation among the ancient Greeks see, for example, E. R. Dodds, *The Greeks and the Irrational* (Berkeley and Los Angeles, 1951), and Bruno Snell, *The Discovery of the Mind: The Greek Origins of European Thought* (Cambridge, Mass., 1953); among the early Christians see Bellah, "Religious Evolution," and Gustav Mensching, "Folk and Universal Religion," in *Religion, Culture and Society: A Reader on the Sociology of Religion,* ed. Louis Schneider (New York, 1964), 254–61; and on the "twelfth-century renaissance" see M. D. Chenu, *Nature, Man and Society in the Twelfth Century: Essays on New Theological Perspectives in the Latin West,* trans. and ed. Jerome Taylor and Lester K. Little (Chicago, 1968); Colin Morris, *The Discovery of the Individual, 1050–1200* (London, 1972); and the introduction to John F. Benton, ed., *Self and Society in Medieval France: The Memoirs of Abbot Guibert of Nogent (1064?–c. 1125),* rev. ed. (New York, 1970), 7–33.

ough, county, and ecclesiastical courts preserved "a flourishing life of their own." And the administration of the law was but one aspect of the life of a myriad of counties, hundreds, villages, manors, towns, boroughs, guilds, bishoprics, abbeys, parishes, monasteries, and chapters, all of which maintained a substantial measure of self-determination. Each regulated its own life in accordance with its venerable customs and entitlements and its current exigencies. Each possessed and protected its own privileges and immunities, in a medieval universe both personal and pluralistic.[8]

Modernization represented, in many respects, an abandonment of the richness and complexity of this medieval round of life. Like the nativistic revivals sometimes seen among tribal populations, it simplified a "gigantic game" grown "over-complicated" and altogether "too much for people." Men and women of the early modern age meant to tame what E. M. W. Tillyard called the "bursting and pullulating world" of their ancestors. They aimed to "hack their way through" what Perry Miller called "the scholastic undergrowth" of "the fifteenth-century morass." And in their readiness to renounce the multiplicity of the medieval habit, they gave up as if gladly that panoply of intermediate agencies of authority and objects of affection that had hedged their parents' lives.[9]

In crucial measure, the movement toward modernity was encompassed in this stripping down of the old plenitude of powers and in the attendant transition from ways of plurality to ways of polarity. In politics, kings began to level the realm, imposing new norms of uniformity of rights and obligations on what had been an extravagantly irregular system of baronial prerogatives and local privileges. In religion, Protestants set out to level the cosmos itself, denying the efficacy of the Virgin,

8. Marc Bloch, *Feudal Society*, trans. L. A. Manyon (Chicago, 1961), 112; Michael R. Powicke, *The Community of the Realm, 1154–1485* (New York, 1973), 45. See, more generally, Joseph Strayer, "The Development of Feudal Institutions," in *Twelfth-Century Europe and the Foundations of Modern Society*, ed. Marshall Claggett, Gaines Post, and Robert Reynolds (Madison, Wis., 1961), and Bloch, *Feudal Society*, 63–64, 65, 66, 75, 82–83, 111, 116, 125–30, 185, 211, 212, 242, 264, 359, 360, 361–62, 363, 364, 367, 370–71, 382, 409. A convenient summary is Powicke, *Community of the Realm*, chaps. 3 and 4.

9. E. M. W. Tillyard, *The Elizabethan World Picture* (London, 1943), 4, 92–93; Perry Miller, *The New England Mind: The Seventeenth Century* (New York, 1939), 157; Michael Walzer, *The Revolution of the Saints: A Study of the Origins of Radical Politics* (Cambridge, Mass., 1965), 151–52; and cf. Michel Foucault, *The Order of Things: An Archaeology of the Human Sciences* (New York, 1970). On the notion of nativistic revivals see James Mooney, *The Ghost-Dance Religion*, in Smithsonian Institution, Bureau of Ethnology, *Fourteenth Annual Report* (Washington, D.C., 1896); Ralph Linton, "Nativistic Movements," *American Anthropologist*, n.s., 45 (1943): 230–40; and Anthony F. C. Wallace, "Revitalization Movements," *American Anthropologist* 58 (1956): 264–80.

the angels, the saints, the pope, and a vast variety of magical forces to intervene between God and human beings. A new-fledged passion for books and words initiated an unprecedented contraction of the very modalities of the senses. The medieval church had assumed, in its ritual and its elaborate trappings, that all its worshipers' senses were to be served. The dissenting offshoots of the early modern age declared, in their insistence on plainness, that the sensory range of their congregations' response was to be stringently restricted. Catholic exegesis had proliferated meanings. Protestant explication of texts afforded as far as possible only single meanings, so as to provide unequivocal instruction. The Christianity of the Middle Ages affirmed that its mystery was the richer for its ambiguity. The religion of the Reformers favored didactic sermons and allegories over such ambiguity, appending marginal notes even to its allegories lest those limited meanings be missed.[10]

In the family a similar and still more central transformation took place. For it was in the late sixteenth and seventeenth centuries that, according to Ariès, the conjugal unit began to set itself off in sensibility from the surrounding society. It was in the same period that, according to J. Hajnal, Europeans first diverged from a marital pattern that they had maintained in common with the rest of the world and began to marry much later in life, under conditions of greater domestic isolation. And it was at the same time, too, that individuals began to stand forth distinctively from their families, especially at the critical junctures of birth, marriage, and death, as their families stood forth from the wider social fabric. Newborn children of the seventeenth century invariably received their own specific names, where siblings had shared forenames as late as the Elizabethan era. Young men and women assumed a significant initiative in their choice of a marriage partner, where they had submitted to the marital arrangements of their parents in an earlier

10. Walzer, *Revolution of the Saints,* 151–52; Thomas, *Religion and the Decline of Magic,* 639, 637; Larzer Ziff, *Puritanism in America: New Culture in a New World* (New York, 1973), 6, 14–15; cf. Rice, *Foundations of Early Modern Europe,* 147; Richard Slotkin, *Regeneration through Violence: The Mythology of the American Frontier, 1600–1860* (Middletown, Conn., 1973), 65–66; and Sacvan Bercovitch, *The Puritan Origins of the American Self* (New Haven, Conn., 1975), 110–11. In science, too, humans first imagined with Bacon and then achieved with Newton a mechanistic reduction of the teeming natural world of their medieval predecessors (E. A. Burtt, *The Metaphysical Foundations of Modern Physical Science,* 2d ed. rev. [Garden City, N.Y., 1954], 238–39). As the historian of the Royal Society reported proudly at mid-seventeenth century, English scientists had returned "to the primitive purity" of a "naked, natural way of speaking" and had succeeded in "bringing all things as near the mathematical plainness as they can" (Floyd W. Matson, *The Broken Image: Man, Science and Society* [New York, 1964], 26).

time. And mortals met their eternal fate alone and unaided at the advent of predestinarian Protestantism, where formerly they had been able to attach themselves to kinfolk by whose good works their souls could still be saved after death in the Catholic conception of purgatory.[11]

In the community as well, it was most momentously in the early modern era that the immemorial traditions came undone. English men and women experienced immense social dislocations under the Tudors and the first Stuarts. Population doubled in a little more than a century before the Civil War. The economy was transformed by crown confiscation and subsequent sale of monastic and chantry property, by an expansion of overseas commerce that made the cloth trade a national preoccupation, by enlargement of internal trade and specialized markets, by a dramatic reduction of interest rates, by the institutionalization of a money market, and above all by the creation of proto-capitalistic relations of production in agriculture. The tens of thousands of smallholders displaced by enclosure and its attendant alterations set in motion a geographic mobility generally apprehended as ominous and a social mobility nearly "unique in English history."[12]

The vagabonds, rogues, and roaring lads who stirred such anxiety in the England of Elizabeth and James were but the most visible embodiment of the throng that was loosed upon the land. Towns and villages were roiled by migrations of remarkable extent.[13] And such mobility

11. Ariès, *Centuries of Childhood;* J. Hajnal, "European Marriage Patterns in Perspective," in *Population in History: Essays in Historical Demography,* ed. D. V. Glass and D. E. C. Eversley (Chicago, 1965), 101–43; Daniel Scott Smith, "Child-Naming Patterns and Family Structure Change: Hingham, Massachusetts, 1640–1880" (paper delivered at the Clark University Conference on the Family and Social Structure, Worcester, Mass., April 1972), 7; Lawrence Stone, *The Crisis of the Aristocracy, 1558–1641* (Oxford, 1965), chap. 11; Hsu, "Kinship," 422–23.

12. Lawrence Stone, *The Causes of the English Revolution, 1529–1642* (London, 1972), 110, and see generally 58–117. See also Carl Bridenbaugh, *Vexed and Troubled Englishmen, 1590–1642* (New York, 1968).

13. E. E. Rich, "The Population of Elizabethan England," *Economic History Review,* 2d ser., 2 (1949): 247–65; Peter Laslett and John Harrison, "Clayworth and Cogenhoe," in *Historical Essays, 1600–1750: Presented to David Ogg,* ed. H. E. Bell and R. L. Ollard (London, 1963), 157–84; S. A. Peyton, "The Village Population in the Tudor Lay Subsidy Rolls," *English Historical Review* 30 (1915): 234–50; Julian Cornwall, "Evidence of Population Mobility in the Seventeenth Century," *Bulletin of the Institute of Historical Research* 40 (1967): 143–52; Peter Clark, "The Migrant in Kentish Towns, 1580–1640," in *Crisis and Order in English Towns, 1500–1700: Essays in Urban History,* ed. Peter Clark and Paul Slack (London, 1972), 117–54; Stone, *Causes of the English Revolution,* 110–11; Bridenbaugh, *Vexed and Troubled Englishmen,* 21–22; Alan Everitt, *Change in the Provinces: The Seventeenth Century* (Leicester, Eng., 1969); E. A. Wrigley, "A Simple Model of London's Importance in Changing English Society and Economy, 1650–1750," *Past and*

betokened even more extensive upheavals. Puritans, for example, set such high priority on dismantling the rituals and routines that helped sustain the medieval community that Keith Thomas has insisted on reckoning the "true significance" of Puritanism less in terms of its putative relation to capitalism than in its "implacable hostility to [the] more primitive society" of the Middle Ages. And Puritans were by no means alone in their antipathy to conventions of collective sentiment. They assailed those ceremonies of solidarity—the hagiography and festivals, the sports and dancing, the magic and taboos—with special vigor, but a wide spectrum of English society conspired in their dissolution. Many communal usages were already declining if not disappearing before the Marian exiles ever departed the realm. Many others waned without any apparent relation to the distinctive pressures of the movement the exiles ignited on their return.[14]

As ancient cords of kinship and community frayed, men and women began to counterpose things that had been better integrated for their parents and to schematize things that had been full of the stuff of life. As the depth and enduringness of primary relationships diminished, individuals began to depend both more and less than they had before on the old centers of the common life. And as they did, those centers could no longer hold so compellingly. The family could not remain an unconsidered matter of course when its members began to set themselves apart from it and, at the same time, make demands and place burdens upon it that it had never borne before. The community could not continue to engage its inhabitants as a matter of casual necessity when they began to refuse its social and economic confinements while, at the same time, clinging the more tenaciously to a mental image of it as a deliberate ideal.

From these beginnings the English would be impelled by contrapuntal forces of excess and insufficiency, exaggerated and attenuated fellowship. And this impulsion, with the disturbances and intensifications of

---

*Present* 37 (July 1967): 45–49. On the implications of such mobility for the ancient web of kinship and community, mediated as it was by marriage, see Bridenbaugh, *Vexed and Troubled Englishmen,* 35–36, 40–41, 153–54, 368, 373.

14. Keith Thomas, "History and Anthropology," *Past and Present* 24 (Apr. 1963): 3–24, quotation on 8. See also Charles Pythian-Adams, "Ceremony and the Citizen: The Communal Year at Coventry, 1450–1550," in *Crisis and Order in English Towns,* ed. Clark and Slack, 57–85; John Dolan, "Religious Festivities during the Reformation and Counter-Reformation: Challenge and Response," *Societas* 2 (1972): 95–120; Alan Macfarlane, *Witchcraft in Tudor and Stuart England: A Regional and Comparative Study* (London, 1970).

local life that accompanied it, is essential to an understanding of the emergence of American individuality and the conditions of American community.

Social psychologists have held that among persons for whom "doubt" has replaced "basic trust" in "the way of one's social group or in one's place in it," such doubt may "undermine the sense of one's own identity." They have suggested the salience, in the precipitation of what they call an "identity struggle," of a "sense of being expendable." [15] In early modern England, with its unemployed and underemployed masses, its conviction of overpopulation, its official complicity in the departure of its offscourings for the colonies, and its apprehension of declension and even of impending apocalypse, men and women might readily have received the impression that they were not needed and thereby found occasion for doubting their own identity.

In such situations of endangered identity people often project onto others the characteristic they fear may be their own: an "incompetence for civilized living" associated with their anxiety at being supernumerary in their society.[16] They are driven to define others as adversaries, as if to vindicate their own uncertain worth by assaults on those around them. Certainly many seemed so driven in a nation paranoid in its abhorrence of popery, fanatical in its execration of the French and Spanish, and, withal, sufficiently insatiable for contrariety to sustain a civil war for a dozen years and more.[17]

15. Lynd, *On Shame,* 46–47; Anthony F. C. Wallace and Raymond D. Fogelson, "The Identity Struggle," in *Intensive Family Therapy: Theoretical and Practical Aspects,* ed. Ivan Boszormenyi-Nagy and James L. Framo (New York, 1965), 396–97.

16. Wallace and Fogelson, "The Identity Struggle," 396–97. Wallace and Fogelson associate such phenomena with "technologic society" and insist that its attendant prejudices "have not (despite the cross-cultural ubiquity of ethnocentrism) been in any degree as savagely and indiscriminately destructive in nonindustrial societies as they have been in the technologic societies of the past four hundred years." They deny that there are any comparable confrontations of identity in most primitive groups; see 388. Hsu, too, has argued the affinity of early modern Europeans for religious persecution. He maintains that such abstract struggles may flare briefly in societies with denser kinship ties but that they are "neither long lasting nor widespread" in those settings ("Kinship," 412, 423).

17. Stone, *Causes of the English Revolution,* 121. Charles and Katherine George argue that indeed "the Protestant mind came into being" in England during the assault on Catholicism (George and George, *Protestant Mind,* 12–13). And see more generally William Haller, *The Elect Nation: The Meaning and Relevance of Foxe's "Book of Martyrs"* (New York, 1964); William M. Lamont, *Godly Rule: Politics and Religion, 1603–1660* (New York, 1969); William S. Maltby, *The Black Legend in England: The Development of Anti-Spanish Sentiment, 1558–1660* (Durham, N.C., 1971); Carol Z. Weiner, "The Beleaguered Isle: A Study of Elizabethan and Early Jacobean Anti-Catholicism," *Past and Present* 51 (May

In situations of disruption of basic trust people often express their fearfulness of life by exaggerated emphasis on morality and heightened hatred of "sin."[18] They embrace identities defined primarily by their aversion to iniquity, as if to salvage a satisfactory sense of self in circumstances in which that sense is imperiled. Assuredly, a host of men and women embraced such identities in seventeenth-century England. Their exquisite concern for the determination of the boundaries of sin betrayed the *ressentiment* implicit in their "disinterested tendency to inflict punishment."[19] Their fixation on salvation, damnation, and the separation of sheep from goats suggested their profound need to achieve a new basis for trust, in an eternal order if not a temporal one.

These stresses had their origins in the mother country before the first British ship ever anchored in the James, but they were felt most forcefully in the colonies. Modernization proceeded most unimpededly in America because the intricate webs of kinship and vicinage that were already disintegrating in England came quite apart in the New World. Traditional familial ideals and communal norms could be carried intact across the Atlantic and reconstituted in America from the models in the colonists' minds, but such deliberate recourse to tradition was, at bottom, the very antithesis of tradition. The rich particularity of the past could not be remade from models.

Indeed, the very effort to preserve traditional precepts and practices provoked innovation. The people who projected colonies and crossed an ocean to establish them may have acted defensively, in regressive determination to resist the centralizing initiatives of the Stuarts in England. Some of them—the Puritans who fled the alluring corruption of their native land, the would-be patroons of New York, the Catholics who envisioned a feudal retreat in Maryland, Shaftesbury and his gifted secretary who set forth the Fundamental Constitutions of Carolina— may have aimed to arrest the changes that were undermining older ways. But in their endeavors to defend that traditional insularity, they shattered the continuity with the past that was a hallmark of the English localism they sought to conserve. For the communities which could be

---

1971): 27–62. Weiner is especially sensitive to the counterposition of order and adventure in the fragile but strident nationalism of the time. For the ubiquity of the impulse to affirmation by negation see Christopher Hill, *Antichrist in Seventeenth-Century England* (London, 1971).

18. Lynd, *On Shame*, 47.

19. Svend Ranulf, *Moral Indignation and Middle Class Psychology* (Copenhagen, 1938), 1 and *passim*.

constructed on a wilderness coast were wholly new communities, without indigenous customs, without elders who had lived there all their lives, without ancient burying grounds or even any old buildings. Traditional ends had therefore to be achieved under novel circumstances by novel means. In the exigencies of existence three thousand miles from kings and archbishops, and in the cause of conserving ancient ideals, the colonists improvised a variety of new institutional arrangements unparalleled since the Norman conquest.[20]

Modernization also began most unobstructedly in America because a secure sense of social place could not be sustained in the strange land. Some people in some degree discovered their superfluousness in the mother country, but men and women in the colonies came face to face, inescapably, with the evidence of their own dispensability, simply by being where they were, an ocean apart from all they took to be civilized.[21]

A few of the colonists accepted that evidence and gave vent to an answering savagery in themselves, but most of them made other, more poignant adjustments to their inconsequence. A Marylander, pleading Lord Calvert's case in London, conceded that his patron's province was "not a place any way considerable or worth his Highness' trouble." A "simple cobbler" of Aggawam, patching "all the year long, gratis," resigned himself "never to be paid for his work" in the wilderness. A Puritan chronicler admitted the dismay of the first planters at their "perpetual banishment from their native soil," in a "desert's depth where wolves and bears abide." The proprietor of Pennsylvania confessed his own colony "a desert of original wild people . . . [and] wild beasts."[22]

20. T. H. Breen, "Persistent Localism: English Social Change and the Shaping of New England Institutions," *William and Mary Quarterly*, 3d ser., 32 (1975): 3–28. See also Philip J. Greven, Jr., "Historical Demography and Colonial America," *William and Mary Quarterly*, 3d ser., 24 (1967): 438–54, and Darrett B. Rutman, *American Puritanism: Faith and Practice* (Philadelphia, 1970), chaps. 2–3.

21. The evidence of the impact of this discovery is inferential and not equally extensive for all the colonists. The surviving sources inevitably reflect disproportionate articulateness about self and society and an incapacity to commit that articulateness to print that leaves the exposition that follows consistently overattentive to certain elites and sometimes overmindful of New England.

22. John Langford, *A Just and Cleere Refutation of a False and Scandalous Pamphlet Entituled Babylons Fall in Maryland . . .* (1655), in *Narratives of Early Maryland, 1633–1684,* ed. Clayton Colman Hall, (New York, 1910), 262; Theodore de la Guard [Nathaniel Ward], *The Simple Cobler of Aggawam in America . . .* (1647), in *Tracts and Other Papers Relating Principally to the Origin, Settlement, and Progress of the Colonies in North America . . .,* comp. Peter Force, (Washington, D.C., 1844 [orig. publ. London, 1713]), 3: no. 8 [1]; J. Franklin Jameson, ed., *Johnson's Wonder-Working Providence, 1628–1651* (New York,

And creole colonials betrayed still deeper doubts. Cotton Mather was merely one of the first among many to lust after English acclaim on a suspicion that American accolades did not count, offered as they were in a "wilderness, in the ends of the earth," whose brave beginnings had "come to nothing."[23]

Mather could hardly admit even to himself his grim apprehension that the American experiment had fallen into "outer darkness" in remote regions "which the unprofitable are there condemned unto." But English men and women at home could and did entertain such notions, in disparaging images of the New World that inevitably offered emigrants a disturbing impression of their own undesirability by the very fact of their departure for such places. A promotional tract for the Chesapeake colonies admitted that "the country [was] . . . reported to be an unhealthy place, a nest of rogues, whores, dissolute and rooking persons; a place of intolerable labor, bad usage and hard diet, etc." Friends of New England recognized that the reputation of the Puritan outposts quickly came to "stink everywhere." And a popular saying abroad in England suggested that South Carolina was proverbial for its unsavoriness; men and women in the mother country measured the distastefulness of their circumstances by whether they "would rather live and die in Carolina."[24]

---

1910), 53, 112; Gary B. Nash, *Quakers and Politics: Pennsylvania, 1681–1726* (Princeton, N.J., 1968), 162. See also John Pory to Sir Dudley Carleton, Sept. 30, 1619, in *The Elizabethans' America: A Collection of Early Reports by Englishmen on the New World,* ed. Louis B. Wright (Cambridge, Mass., 1965), 253–54. These and subsequent quotations are modernized.

23. Cotton Mather, *Magnalia Christi Americana; or, the Ecclesiastical History of New-England . . .* (Hartford, Conn., 1855), 1:26, 27. See also [Henry Hartwell, James Blair, and Edward Chilton], "An Account of the Present State and Government of Virginia," Massachusetts Historical Society, *Collections,* 1st ser., 5 (1798): 127; *The Prose Works of William Byrd of Westover: Narratives of a Colonial Virginian,* ed. Louis B. Wright (Cambridge, Mass., 1966), 19, 22–23, 345, 368. Three of the four narratives that were bestsellers in New England between 1680 and 1720 were captivity narratives, which Richard Slotkin takes to be paradigms "of the self-exile of the English Israel from England" (*Regeneration through Violence,* 94–96).

24. Mather, *Magnalia,* 1:27; John Hammond, *Leah and Rachel, or, the Two Fruitfull Sisters Virginia and Mary-land . . .* (1656), in *Narratives of Early Maryland,* ed. Hall, 284; George Downing to John Winthrop, August 26, 1645, Massachusetts Historical Society, *Collections,* 4th ser., 6 (1863): 537; Peter H. Wood, *Black Majority: Negroes in Colonial South Carolina from 1670 through the Stono Rebellion* (New York, 1974), 66–67. South Carolina's proverbial bad name persisted in England. As an eighteenth-century saying had it, "Whoever desires to die soon, just go to Carolina" (Louis B. Wright, *The Colonial Search for a Southern Eden* [University, Ala., 1953], 44). For Bermuda's reputation as "the

The effect of such conceptions was that an aura of outcast infelicity hung over the seaboard settlements, to color the migrants' ideas of their destinations before they came or, indeed, to discourage their coming. The colonies standing "not handsomely in England, very few of good conversation would adventure thither" to "join with such an indigent and sottish people as were reported to be in Virginia." And in truth, relatively few of the indigent and sottish would adventure there either. People chose to "beg, steal, rot in prison, and come to shameful deaths," to "stuff Newgate, Bridewell, and other jails with their carcasses, nay cleave to Tyburn itself," before they would cross the ocean. The awareness of such choices detracted still further from the image of America, and consequently of themselves, that colonists could hold.[25]

Men and women who came in the face of such forbidding knowledge had, or quickly acquired, other reasons as well for doubting that they were wanted or of worth. Some, such as the Puritans, Catholics, and Quakers, were derelicts of religious devotion, forced from England because "every corner" of the country "was filled with the fury of malignant adversaries." They had fled with "breast-breaking sobs" and "bowel-breaking affections" for friends and relatives left behind, and they clung to their attachment to England even in flight. It was, as one of them said, "for England's sake" that they were "going from England." A majority of the rest, such as younger sons or persons otherwise in "extreme misery" or "reduced to . . . poverty," were servants, forced to sell themselves into bondage to come to the colonies at all. The terms of their transplantation made plain that they had no attractive alternative in England. The often ruthless exploitation to which they were subjected in the New World disabused them of any hopes they might have held of a new and better home. Like the religious refugees who soon began to ask "how shall we go to England?" as well as "how shall we go to heaven?," many of those servants came to "cry out day and night, oh that they were in England without their limbs and would not care to

---

Devil's Islands," a "hideous and hated place" shunned by mariners "as they would shun the Devil himself," see Wright, ed., *Elizabethans' America*, 194, 196–97.

25. Hammond, *Leah and Rachel*, 287, 286, 281, 296. See also, for example, ibid., 283, 285, 299–300; "Extracts from the Annual Letters of the English Province of the Society of Jesus . . . ," in *Narratives of Early Maryland*, ed. Hall, 123; Wood, *Black Majority*, 133n; Samuel Wilson, *An Account of the Province of Carolina, in America* . . . (1682), in *Narratives of Early Carolina, 1650–1708*, ed. Alexander S. Salley, Jr., (New York, 1911), 164; John Archdale, *A New Description of that Fertile and Pleasant Province of Carolina* . . . (1707), in *Narratives of Early Carolina*, ed. Salley, 295.

lose any limb to be in England again, yea though they beg from door to door."[26]

And in fact many did return, or attempted to. The very first English settlement in North America, at Roanoke, failed because Ralph Lane refused to wait for a promised supply that was actually on its way and chose instead to put his entire expedition aboard Drake's ships and go home. The survivors among the first settlers of Virginia were under sail on the James when, by almost incredible coincidence, they met Lord De la Warr and were persuaded to remain. A few years later the Virginia Company sent its storied shipload of women because the young men of the plantation were staying only "to get something, and then to return for England." A few years after that, and after the demise of the company, the governing council of the colony also acknowledged that what settlers sought in Virginia was still, essentially, "a present crop, and their hasty return." More than one hundred of the first migrants to Massachusetts went back to the mother country within a year of the arrival of the Winthrop fleet, despite the desperate entreaties of their governor, and they were merely the beginners of what became a great remigration in the years of Cromwell's Commonwealth. And among the colonists of the Caribbean the very "mark of a successful . . . planter was his ability to escape from the island and retire grandly to England."[27]

26. Jameson, ed., *Johnson's Wonder-Working Providence*, 23, 51–52, 53; "Letters of the Society of Jesus," in *Narratives of Early Maryland*, ed. Hall, 118–19, 122; "Roger Clap's Memoirs," in *Chronicles of the First Planters of the Colony of Massachusetts Bay*, ed. Alexander Young (Boston, 1846), 354–55; Richard Frethorne to his parents, March 20, April 2, 3, 1623, in *The Old Dominion in the Seventeenth Century: A Documentary History of Virginia, 1606–1689*, ed. Warren M. Billings (Chapel Hill, N.C., 1975), 305. See also, for example, John Smith, *Advertisements For the unexperienced Planters of New-England, or any where . . .* (1631), in *Travels and Works of Captain John Smith: President of Virginia, and Admiral of New England, 1580–1631*, ed. Edward Arber and A. G. Bradley (Edinburgh, 1910), 2:954; Perry Miller and Thomas H. Johnson, eds., *The Puritans* (New York, 1938), 119, 122; Jameson, ed., *Johnson's Wonder-Working Providence*, 45; Wood, *Black Majority*, 54n; Billings, ed., *Old Dominion*, 140; and Edmund S. Morgan, "The First American Boom: Virginia 1618 to 1630," *William and Mary Quarterly*, 3d ser., 28 (1971): 169–98.

27. Edmund S. Morgan, *American Slavery, American Freedom: The Ordeal of Colonial Virginia* (New York, 1975), 41, 111, 112; Susan Kingsbury, ed., *The Records of the Virginia Company of London* (Washington, D.C., 1906), 1:256; "Dudley's Letter to the Countess of Lincoln," in *Chronicles of the First Planters of Massachusetts*, ed. Young, 315; Thomas Hutchinson, *The History of the Colony and Province of Massachusetts-Bay*, ed. Lawrence Shaw Mayo (Cambridge, Mass., 1936), 1:xxix; William Sachse, "The Migration of New Englanders to England, 1640–1660," *American Historical Review* 53 (1948): 251; Richard S. Dunn, *Sugar and Slaves: The Rise of the Planter Class in the English West Indies, 1624–1713* (Chapel Hill, N.C., 1972), 116 and, for quantitative data, 111. For the same

Nonetheless, we would miss much of the inner meaning of modernization if we were to take these sources of the sense of displacement too straightforwardly. For the self-diminution that attended the recognition of dispensability evoked its own contravention in other, more expansive ways in which men and women apprehended their situation. In religious terms, New Englanders took the lead. Their jeremiads lamented the unworthiness of their land, but they also took the Lord's afflictions to prove His continuing concern for its inhabitants, in circularities that were ultimately as self-serving as self-abasing. Jonathan Mitchell called his fellow colonists "a small, weak . . . and despised people," but he did so by deliberate analogy to the chosen people of the Bible who also suffered such oppression. Cotton Mather trembled for New England's fate, but his very trepidation impelled him to an opposite verge of compensatory consecration and sublime certainty of its glorious destiny. When he declared, in the introduction to the *Magnalia*, that "whether New England may live anywhere else or no, it must live in our history," he expressed exactly the depth of his doubt and the outlandishness of his aspiration. His ambivalence articulated at once his exaggerated anguish that the errand might have gone for naught in the wilderness and his equally exaggerated determination that it survive, inviolate, in the American imagination.[28]

In realms other than religion, other colonies were at least as presumptuous as New England. Extravagant derogation of the rude settlements was met, in the colonial promotional literature, by correspondingly extravagant inflation of New World excellences and opportunities. If the image of America as hell on earth disposed English men and women to scorn the plantations, the counterimages of the country as Canaan or even Eden must have carried people's minds to states of voluptuous anticipation. Almost every promotional tract held out prospects of gold, or silks, spices, and wines, or health and long life, or spiritual fulfillment, or peace, or a passage to India, in innumerable alluring combinations. One Virginia production of the seventeenth century actually advanced Sir Walter Ralegh's mystic conviction that God had placed His earthly paradise on the 35th parallel of north latitude, in

situation in Virginia by the second half of the seventeenth century see Morgan, *American Slavery, American Freedom*, 191, 200, 206.

28. Miller and Johnson, eds., *The Puritans*, 239; Mather, *Magnalia*, 1:27. See also Bercovitch, *Puritan Origins of the American Self*, chap. 4, esp. 132–34.

what was then part of Virginia. And like the assumption of God's cherishing faith in the jeremiads, the promulgation of these Edenic images in the promotional works offset the negative notions of the day without ever annulling them.[29]

In regard to servitude, too, the exploitation endured by inferiors was only one side of a disjunctive development of the institution in the New World. As much as servants became mere commodities in the colonies, they were also indispensable on the virgin continent, where labor was everywhere in short supply. Consequently, the ones who stayed and survived cultivated cunning in turning their advantageous situation to account and acquired a sense of self-importance and worth in the course of doing so. Masters in New England grumbled that servants learned "to live idly, and work when they list." Manor lords in New York complained of their tenants' "hopes of having land of their own and becoming independent of landlords." Planters in Virginia had to exempt white servants from the slavishness of their original legal lot and afford them the prerogatives of a racial upper class. As the younger Thomas Shepard explained, men and women of the most servile status came in America to "desire liberty."[30] Every colony was obliged ultimately to gratify that desire in some degree—by legislation, adjudication, or common custom—in order to attract inhabitants at all. In every colony there were "laboring men, who had not enough to bring them over, yet now worth scores, and some hundreds of pounds." And in some colonies, such as Pennsylvania and New York, rival publicists vied in promoting their own province as the "best poor man's country," in an odd conflation of poverty and prepotency that was itself indicative of the antipodal tensions of early American life.[31]

These antithetic images and experiences of indispensability and expendability, which jostled each other in uneasy irresolution, affected the dominant classes of colonial society, too. As if driven to exorcise the demons of their unnecessariness and prove that they did belong despite

29. Wright, *Search for a Southern Eden*, 37; see also Louis B. Wright, *The Dream of Prosperity in Colonial America* (New York, 1965).

30. Ziff, *Puritanism in America*, 86, 87; Patricia Bonomi, *A Factious People: Politics and Society in Colonial New York* (New York, 1971), 195; Oscar Handlin and Mary Handlin, "Origins of the Southern Labor System," *William and Mary Quarterly*, 3d ser., 7 (1950): 199–222; Edmund S. Morgan, "Slavery and Freedom: The American Paradox," *Journal of American History* 59 (1972): 5–29.

31. Jameson, ed., *Johnson's Wonder-Working Providence*, 212; James Lemon, *The Best Poor Man's Country: A Geographical Study of Early Southeastern Pennsylvania* (Baltimore, 1972), xiii, 229; Bonomi, *A Factious People*, 196. See also Wilson, *Account of Carolina*, 167.

their transplantation, the very men and women who had come most effectively to terms with the New World engaged in a prodigious variety of exaggerated affirmations of their Englishness. In the tropical islands of the Caribbean they wore English woolens and worsteds and put up lodgings that resembled London row houses. In the forest clearings of New England they perpetuated classical learning. And in the presence of marauding Powhatans in the Chesapeake they pursued an English gentry ideal so ardently that even in the declining days of the Virginia Company, when sickness, starvation, and death stalked the straggling settlements, the town cow-keeper and the wife of a collier still decked themselves out in modish silks.[32]

In their importunate desire for the amenities of the mother country, the colonists exhibited a disposition to conceive the world in dualistic terms, as though to redeem their own enigmatic identities by disparaging the identities of others, in the peculiar logic of negation and self-salvage imposed by the identity struggle. The early settlers were, as Winthrop Jordan has said, "especially inclined to discover attributes in savages which they found first but could not speak of in themselves." They were disposed to defend their civility by comparing their own skin color and social customs with those of the Indians and Africans. Yet the very comparison that spared them the strain of dwelling on the disparity between their own practices and those they had left behind, and the contraposition that sustained their psychic equilibrium by reassuring them of who they were when they were a long way from home, also compounded their dilemma. For those contrasts intensified their con-

---

32. Dunn, *Sugar and Slaves*, chap. 8; Kenneth A. Lockridge, *Literacy in Colonial New England: An Enquiry into the Social Context of Literacy in the Early Modern West* (New York, 1974); Robert Middlekauff, *Ancients and Axioms: Secondary Education in Eighteenth-Century New England* (New Haven, Conn., 1963); John Pory to Sir Dudley Carleton, September 30, 1619, in *Narratives of Early Virginia, 1606–1625,* ed. Lyon Gardiner Tyler, (New York, 1907), 284–85. A suggestive expression of this effort to imitate the English, or outdo them on their own terms, was the obsessive comparison the colonists forced between English and American flora and fauna, as if the settlers had to defend against a haunting fear that things American were offscourings of the earth as well as of England. For the first generations see Miller and Johnson, eds., *The Puritans,* 382; William Wood, *New Englands Prospect* (Boston, 1865), 14; Thomas Morton, *New English Canaan . . .* (1637), ed. Charles Francis Adams (Boston, 1883), 180–83, 185–90, 193, 194, 201–3; Jameson, ed., *Johnson's Wonder-Working Providence,* 91, 99, 210; Archdale, *New Description of Carolina,* 288. For the persistence of such fears to the end of the eighteenth century see Henry Steele Commager and Elmo Giordanetti, *Was America a Mistake?: An Eighteenth-Century Controversy* (New York, 1967), and Gordon S. Wood, ed., *The Rising Glory of America, 1760–1820* (New York, 1971), 14–16.

viction that they were poised on the edge of an abyss of barbarism. They reinforced their disjunctive definition of the colonial situation as one in which civilized virtue stood always in awful temptation of descending into savage vice.[33]

Inhabitants of the southern colonies yielded to the temptation most nearly, in exploiting their slaves, and at the same time resisted it most stridently, in drawing a dichotomous color line between themselves and the Africans. Whereas New World settlers from other European nations apprehended color categories in continua that reflected initial African diversity and subsequent racial interbreeding, the English who colonized America acknowledged only the polarized alternatives of white and black. Whereas Spaniards and Portuguese evolved elaborate vocabularies that recognized the complexity of racial realities, Virginians and Carolinians put themselves radically apart from their slaves. Drawing a line that denied all gradation or degree, they defied the abundant actuality of miscegenation and the evidence of the varied complexions before their eyes.[34]

Settlers of the northern as well as the southern colonies drew a clear line of demarcation between themselves and the other people they found tempting them to savagery, the Indians. Few frontier dwellers would have disputed Samuel Purchas's description of the indigenous inhabitants of the eastern woodlands as "bad people, having little of humanity but shape, ignorant of civility, or arts, or religion; more brutish than the beasts they hunt, more wild and unmanly than that unmanned wild country, which they range rather than inhabit." And the few who did see the natives differently could not defend their vision in the face of open strife between the two cultures and the consequent extinction of sympathy for the Indians. Virginians accepted the Indian

33. Winthrop D. Jordan, *White over Black: American Attitudes toward the Negro, 1550–1812* (Chapel Hill, N.C., 1968), 40, and see 97–98, 110, 119–20, 143–44, 193 for discussion of specific spheres—religion, law, community, and family—in which racial comparisons enabled the colonists to cling to their self-conception as Englishmen in otherwise unconvincing circumstances.

34. There was, to be sure, a more elaborate and complex set of color categories in the British West Indies than in the British colonies on the mainland; see, for example, Winthrop D. Jordan, "American Chiaroscuro: The Status and Definition of Mulattoes in the British Colonies," *William and Mary Quarterly*, 3d ser., 14 (1962): 183–200. But this is, in the exact sense of the phrase, the exception that proves the rule, since even in the British islands the intermediate categories were less elaborately and more grudgingly applied than in the French, Spanish, and Portuguese colonies. See, for example, Donald Horowitz, "Color Differentiation in the American Systems of Slavery," *Journal of Interdisciplinary History* 3 (1973): 509–42, esp. 518–20.

incursion of 1622 in grim exultancy, "because now we have just cause to destroy them by all means possible." New Englanders improved King Philip's provocations as a pretext "to extirpate the enemy in holy war." Indeed, almost the only relations with the Indians that New Englanders could even imagine were the antagonistic ones of war and captivity.[35]

New Englanders drew other lines as well. They drew them deliberately, pervasively, and at the highest levels of conscious culture, for they, preeminently among the settlers of early America, distilled dichotomies out of the traditional multiplicities of medieval pluralism. The logic of Ramus on which their formal thought depended was a logic that displaced the profuse categories of Aristotle and exalted instead "the doctrine of contraries." It postulated that every art and science fell "of itself into dichotomies," and accordingly it took the task of thought to be the successive bifurcation of its subject into "serried ranks of opposites" so as to trace that subject to its elemental units. John Cotton exemplified the letter of the method in the opening exposition of a sermon in which he explained that "all the men in the world are divided into two ranks, godly or ungodly, righteous or wicked; of wicked men two sorts, some are notoriously wicked, others are hypocrites; of hypocrites two sorts . . . some are washed swine, others are goats." Michael Wigglesworth exemplified the spirit that lay behind the letter in his simple resolution to wage "spiritual war against sin." And similar martial metaphors entered into innumerable Puritan preachings and utterly shaped such statements as Edward Johnson's *Wonder-Working Providence*, which set dichotomy at the heart of history just as others had established it at the center of logic. Johnson viewed all the modern history of Europe as a contest between men pursuing the reformation of religion and men opposing that pursuit. He saw the history of New England, in particular, as just such a series of battles between saints seeking "to batter down, root up, and quite destroy all heresies and errors" and the motley minions of Antichrist.[36]

35. Gary B. Nash, "The Image of the Indian in the Southern Colonial Mind," *William and Mary Quarterly*, 3d ser., 29 (1972): 222–23, 218–19; Slotkin, *Regeneration through Violence*, 83–195. See also Ziff, *Puritanism in America*, 171–72; Roy Harvey Pearce, *Savagism and Civilization: A Study of the Indian and the American Mind*, 2d rev. ed. (Baltimore, 1965); and Francis Jennings, *The Invasion of America: Indians, Colonialism, and the Cant of Conquest* (Chapel Hill, N.C., 1975).

36. Miller and Johnson, eds., *The Puritans*, 32–33; Miller, *New England Mind: The Seventeenth Century*, 127; Miller and Johnson, eds., *The Puritans*, 314; Edmund S. Morgan, ed., "The Diary of Michael Wigglesworth," Colonial Society of Massachusetts, *Publications* 35 (1951): 326; Jameson, ed., *Johnson's Wonder-Working Providence*, 189, and see also 269; Mather, *Magnalia*, 1:25–26.

Settlers west of the Connecticut were less relentlessly preoccupied with heresy and error, but English settlers everywhere understood themselves in absolute antitheses. Saved and damned, Christian and heathen, civilized and savage, white and black were counterpositions that came congenially and, indeed, compellingly to the colonists, at the Chesapeake as much as at Massachusetts Bay. And in such counterpositions, and the counteridentities they betokened, were the seeds of a new individuality and a new community alike.

Individual settlers, unable to accept fully their disordered experience in the New World, confined its complexity in disjunctions and then deliberately disdained one side of the disjunctions. They attained identity by denying the undisciplined and undifferentiated impulses that plagued them and by disowning the abundant opportunities that tempted them. Thomas Morton of Merry Mount caught their character in his offhand observation that "he that played Proteus (with the help of Priapus) put their noses out of joint." Virginians illustrated his insight—that the orthodox subordinated even their animus against phallic license to their abhorrence of unfixed identity—in their repeated resentment of men with more power than breeding and in their revulsion from the Indians as "most treacherous people" because "inconstant in everything." New Englanders were even more vehement. Nathaniel Ward raged revealingly against the Apocrypha in the Bible, foreigners in his country, counterfeit coins, and religious toleration as the four things his heart "naturally detested." All four were emblems of the adulteration of homogeneous substance; and Ward, who pronounced "polypiety" the "greatest impiety in the world," found "mixtures pernicious" and "power" only in "purity." [37]

In significant measure, individuals such as Ward came to know themselves by their negations. They forged their identities as one might make a silhouette, establishing a boundary about themselves and appearing as what was inside without having to say exactly what that was. In their logic they distinguished ideas "by setting them against their opposites." In their lives they discerned themselves by setting their assumptive civility against the unconditional abandon—the "license, sedition, and

---

37. Morton, *New English Canaan*, 281; John Pory, "A Report of the Manner of Proceeding in the General Assembly . . . 1619," in *Elizabethans' America*, ed. Wright, 243; William Strachey, *History of Travel into Virginia Britannia*, in *Elizabethans' America*, ed. Wright, 218; [Ward], *Simple Cobler*, 7. For Puritan detestation of the "mixed multitude" of the English parish before the great migration to New England see David D. Hall, *The Faithful Shepherd: A History of the New England Ministry in the Seventeenth Century* (Chapel Hill, N.C., 1972), 25.

fury" of the "inordinate soul," as the Virginia Company put it—that they ascribed to others. They achieved a sense of their own moral ideal by conjuring a contrast to "the Indian as a symbol of that . . . degradation to which the spiritual thralls of the wilderness are brought." They preserved an assurance of their religious aspiration by emphasizing, as Roger Williams noted of the New Englanders, that they were "no Jews, no Turks . . . nor Catholics," despite "their own formal dead faith," or by supposing, as Jordan suggests of the early Virginians, that they were not so "*totally* defective" as their African slaves, despite their own deficiencies of Christian piety.[38] And so they defined themselves less by the vitality of their affirmations than by the violence of their abjurations. Their apprehension of their individuality came to be encapsulated in such counteridentity and in the "identity work" by which they managed the modicum of their inclinations that they could accept and the rest that they rejected.[39]

The very counteridentifications that forced a more straitened and simplified fixing of individuals forced also a more deliberate fixing of the terms of their associations. For people's phobias did not sustain them, or enable them to solve the problem of their endangered identity, unless they could share those abhorrences with others. Individuals whose identity was established primarily by purification, as an integrity achieved by putting many inclinations aside, were individuals impelled to dissolve old tolerances and old ties of family and propinquity and consequently to search for "wider circles of solidarity."[40]

The search was most manifest among the Puritans of Massachusetts and Connecticut, for whom its result was, inevitably, to expose individuals to the strictures of those they embraced as brothers and sisters. That very attachment placed people's outward behavior under the ceaseless surveillance of such spiritual siblings and made the most inward experience, the vicissitudes of regeneration, subject to their scrutiny. Individuals could not count their own conversion complete or authentic until they had confessed its course to the satisfaction of their fellows.

The result of the search was also to impose upon men and women a

38. Miller and Johnson, eds., *The Puritans,* 33, 480; *A True Declaration of the estate of the Colonie in Virginia . . .* , in *Tracts,* comp. Force, 3: no. 1, 15; Slotkin, *Regeneration through Violence,* 86; Jordan, *White over Black,* 98.

39. On the concept of "identity work" see Anthony F. C. Wallace, "Identity Processes in Personality and in Culture," in *Cognition, Personality, and Clinical Psychology,* ed. Richard Jessor and Seymour Feshbach (San Francisco, 1967), 62–89.

40. Hsu, "Kinship," 421. On the notion of purified identity see Richard Sennett, *The Uses of Disorder: Personal Identity and City Life* (New York, 1970), esp. chap. 1.

range of reciprocal obligations of intrusion and examination into the affairs of such fellows. Once admitted to a congregation of visible saints, individuals had in their turn to hear the confessions of other candidates. They had to know themselves precisely in order to obtain a "standard of sanctity" by which to judge the experience of others and to carry on relations with their religious kinsmen. They had to display a daily "zeal for the morality of others" in order to uphold the social covenant on which they predicated the temporal prosperity of the community and in order to be confident of the covenant of grace on which their own eternal destiny depended. For their alacrity in overseeing the reformation of their neighbors was a test of the efficacy of their own conversion. "Whatever sins come within [the true convert's] reach," wrote Thomas Hooker, "he labors the removal of them, out of the families where he dwells, out of the plantations where he lives, out of the companies and occasions, with whom he hath occasion to meet and meddle at any time."[41]

The imperative to be their brother's and sister's keepers also provided Puritans with a way of alleviating their unease at the inevitable impurities of their community. For even in their expectation "that wicked men will be mixed with the godly," proper Puritans believed with Samuel Willard that, by a suitable surveillance, they could mingle with the multitudes and still preserve a sense of social purity. "When [the wicked] are not countenanced, but due testimony is born against them; when they are contemned in the places where they live, and a note of infamy and scandal is put upon them; this will not be charged on [the saints] for apostasy."[42]

Puritans were therefore driven to demand a close association with their godly brethren and prohibited any comparable tie to the ungodly. Exactly as believers, they faced always the "double requirement" of an "ardor of intimacy" within the fellowship and a fierce "heat of hostility" outside it, amid "the circling mass of enemies." Their communities were never merely places where babies were born and people died. The land they consecrated was God's country.[43]

Some of the most sophisticated students of Puritanism have recog-

41. George and George, *Protestant Mind,* 102–3; Morgan, ed., "Diary of Wigglesworth," 316–17. See also Edmund S. Morgan, *Visible Saints: The History of a Puritan Idea* (New York, 1963).

42. Miller and Johnson, eds., *The Puritans,* 374–75.

43. George and George, *Protestant Mind,* 103–4; Bercovitch, *Puritan Origins,* esp. chap. 4.

nized this power of the movement simultaneously to individuate and aggregate. Michael Walzer has observed the "constant tendency" of the saints to "turn the theology of salvation into a sociology" in which the very voluntarism of private allegiance led to "a collective discipline" that "created bonds in many ways more intensive than those of blood and nature." Perry Miller marked the concomitance between "a piety in which the individual was the end of creation" and "a social philosophy in which he was subordinate to the whole." Max Weber pointed to the propensity of Reformed religion to plunge men and women into "inner isolation" and, at the same time, "the undoubted superiority of Calvinism in social organization." [44]

Nonetheless, few of these dispositions and disjunctions were unique to the New England Puritans. Many of them were developed even more fully among the Quakers, [45] and most of them were evident in some measure in all the colonies. For early English Protestantism in its entirety was at once a renewal of the old tribal temper and a symptom of the decay of the common life of preceding centuries. It brought both a new scrupulousness in the reconnaissance of conduct and a new freedom from such scrutiny. And it subjected settlers of every plantation to more and, concurrently, less control than they had known in the land of their nativity. [46]

In all the colonies the first settlers were disproportionately composed of Englishmen impatient of conventional social ties and disproportionately disposed to set their own advantage before the public good. In

44. Walzer, *Revolution of the Saints*, 170; Miller, *New England Mind: The Seventeenth Century*, 462; Max Weber, *The Protestant Ethic and the Spirit of Capitalism* (New York, 1958), 108. See also Morgan, ed., "Diary of Wigglesworth," 315, for a characterization of an ideal-typical Puritan as a "selfish busybody."

45. Quakers legitimated "personal authoritative revelation" as the Puritans never did and at the same time secured an even more encompassing "system of discipline and church control" with a thoroughness the Puritans never managed (J. William Frost, *The Quaker Family in Colonial America: A Portrait of the Society of Friends* [New York, 1973], 49). A similar simultaneity shapes almost every account of colonial Quakerism; for example, see Richard Bauman, *For the Reputation of Truth: Politics, Religion, and Conflict among the Pennsylvania Quakers, 1750–1800* (Baltimore, 1971); Susan Forbes, "'As Many Candles Lighted': The New Garden Monthly Meeting 1718–1774" (Ph.D. diss., University of Pennsylvania, 1972); Sydney V. James, *A People among Peoples: Quaker Benevolence in Eighteenth-Century America* (Cambridge, Mass., 1963); and Frederick B. Tolles, *Meeting House and Counting House: The Quaker Merchants of Colonial Philadelphia, 1682–1763* (Chapel Hill, N.C., 1948).

46. George and George, *Protestant Mind*, 82–83, 84. See also Nelson, "Self-Images and Systems of Spiritual Direction," 70–71, for a comparable connection in early Lutheranism.

Massachusetts as much as in Virginia or Carolina, authorities had to contend with "self-love" that "forgot all duty" and with men who "neither feared God nor man." Indeed, such men often took their cues from the authorities themselves. Thomas Weston "pursued his own ends" assiduously in the Plymouth enterprise. Gov. George Yeardley gave an impression of being "wholly addicted to his private" in Virginia. And leading men and lesser men alike found "their own conceived necessity" a "warrant sufficient" to take up lands where they pleased and to plant crops as they pleased, even if their fellows implored and the laws enjoined otherwise.[47]

At the same time, such determined affirmations of personal liberty evoked equally determined assertions of social control. The imbalance of bachelors among the early settlers was offset by the assignment of such potentially reckless young men to reputable families in New England and by the confinement of such potentially dissolute young men to grinding servitude in Virginia. Enticements to self-interest were counteracted by exemplary penalties imposed on worldlings as different as Robert Keayne and Thomas Morton. And inclinations to go off from settled society—ultimately, to go off to the Indians—were fought with maledictions on the wilderness and grisly executions of recaptured renegades "to terrify the rest for attempting the like."[48]

Religious controls also evolved in the face of unprecedented freedom from religious sanctions. In every colony on the North American continent, religious and lay leaders became uneasy as farms spread scatteringly and the nearby woods whispered of the possibilities of privacy;[49]

47. William Bradford, *Of Plymouth Plantation, 1620–1647*, ed. Samuel Eliot Morison (New York, 1952), 54, 107, 254; "A True Declaration of the estate of the Colonie of Virginia . . . ," in *Tracts*, comp. Force, 3: no. 1, 18; Morgan, *American Slavery, American Freedom*, 123n.

48. Morgan, *American Slavery, American Freedom*, 74. Under Gov. Dale, some who tried to go off to the Indians were "appointed to be hanged, some burned, some to be broken upon wheels, others to be staked, and some to be shot to death" (Morgan, *American Slavery, American Freedom*, 74). And at least as revealing was the cautionary tale told by William Strachey of the fate that Englishmen might expect if they did succeed in getting to the Indians: "When [Powhatan] would punish any notorious enemy or trespasser, he causeth him to be tied to a tree, and with mussel-shells or reeds the executioner cutteth off his joints one after another, ever casting what is cut off into the fire; then doth he proceed with shells and reeds to case the skin from his head and face, after which they rip up his belly, tear out his bowels, and so burn him with the tree and all. Thus themselves reported that they executed an Englishman . . . whom the women enticed up from the barge unto their houses at a place called Appocant" (*History of Travel*, 209).

49. On the significance of scattered settlement for privacy see David H. Flaherty, *Privacy in Colonial New England* (Charlottesville, Va., 1972).

and in every colony an answering church discipline of a strikingly similar sort emerged. Quakers did not maim and kill to maintain their way, as New England Puritans sometimes did, but Quakers, Puritans, and Anglicans alike appointed ecclesiastical agents to pry into personal lives and attempt the repression of iniquity, under conditions of tribal exclusivity and congregational communalism. For without effective bonds of episcopal order, individual churches everywhere in British America functioned essentially by themselves. They were not enmeshed in national or papal hierarchies, and they were not organized as inclusive parishes. On the contrary, they were gathered by spiritual affinity out of much larger local populations. They reflected both the heightened individuality that led people to separate themselves from society at large and the augmented intensity of community life that was embodied in the very churches in which they set themselves off.[50]

Political controls also expanded and contracted concurrently, and expectations and assumptions of both individuals and the organized community underwent a simultaneous inflation. Government was notoriously harsh in almost all the early settlements, while the governed were notoriously unruly and even rebellious. Virginia oscillated incessantly between the libertinism of the first planters and the brutal leadership necessary to contain it. Governors imposed martial law on the populace or were "thrust out" for trying to impose it. The air rang with recriminations of "extreme choler and passion" and "tyrannical proceeding" on one side and "mutinous meetings" and "treason" on the other. "Giddy headed and turbulent persons" rose repeatedly against the "oppressions" of "men in authority and favor," burning Jamestown itself to the ground in Bacon's Rebellion; and men in authority responded as repeatedly and heatedly, executing the rebels for treason.[51]

50. Laymen gained control of all these churches, most completely, perhaps, among the Quakers and pietist sectarians and more completely, in many ways, in the officially Anglican South than in ostensibly Congregational New England, where ministers maintained occasional synods and rather regular consociations and asserted a sacerdotal authority that would have been inconceivable in the Quaker colonies and was literally laughable in Virginia. See Paul Lucas, *Valley of Discord: Church and Society along the Connecticut River, 1636–1725* (Hanover, N.H., 1976); Hall, *Faithful Shepherd;* and on the derision of such pretensions in Virginia, *Prose Works of Byrd,* ed. Wright, 344.
51. "The Thrusting Out of Sir John Harvey," in *Old Dominion,* ed. Billings, 252, 253, 255; "The Surry County Court's Verdict, January 6, 1673/74," ibid., 265; "Bacon's 'Manifesto,'" ibid., 278; see, generally, ibid., 236–87. Howard Mumford Jones, *O Strange New World: American Culture, The Formative Years* (New York, 1964), 277–78; Morgan, *American Slavery, American Freedom.* For a suggestive study of the extensive detachment of individuals from familial moorings in the early years of colonization, with implications

And though Virginia was perhaps the most sorely torn of all the colonies, similar cleavages appeared everywhere. In Massachusetts the public affairs of the first decades were occupied with a periodic sparring between magistrates insistent upon an extensive discretionary sphere and more popular forces adamant in their demand for legal guarantees of local rights and liberties. In New York political volatility was "chronic and inherent," and governors found their subjects so "contentious" and recalcitrant that one observer was "sure if the Roman Catholics have a place of purgatory, it's not so bad as [this] place is under my Lord's circumstance." In Carolina a succession of smaller "broils," as John Archdale called them, was punctuated by a number of serious collisions such as the one in which a "loose and extravagant spirit . . . got head in the government of James Colleton" and provoked "the common people" to choose representatives "to oppose whatsoever the governor requested." In Maryland an atmosphere of intrigue prevailed from the time of Baltimore's first instructions and exploded over the next two decades in "illegal executions and murders," "seditions and mutinies," and "malicious plots and conspiracies" on the part of both antagonists and adherents of the proprietor. In Ingle's rebellion and in the affair of the Parliamentary commissioners, the colony was twice "deflowered, by her own inhabitants, stripped, shorn and made deformed," even before the battle at the Severn in 1655.[52]

In all of these struggles the modernizing logic of polarization that shaped the fray was apparent in the pronouncements of the partisans. Lord Baltimore's opponents charged that he "ruled in Maryland in such an absolute way and authority, as no Christian prince or state in Europe exercises the like," yet they were so little daunted by his "absolute" power that they were able to resist it effectively for more than twenty years. Proponents granted that the Calverts claimed prerogatives "not . . . convenient for any one man to have in England," yet they added in the very next breath that the freemen of the colony also possessed polit-

---

for both collective instability and the necessity for oppressive authority, see Irene W. D. Hecht, "The Virginia Muster of 1624/5 as a Source for Demographic History," *William and Mary Quarterly*, 3d ser., 30 (1973): 65–92.

52. Bonomi, *A Factious People*, 138, 11; Archdale, *New Description of Carolina*, 282, 295; *Instructions 13 Novem: 1633 directed by the Right Hon[ora]ble Cecilius Lo: Baltimore and Lord of the Provinces of Mary Land and Avalon . . .* (1633), in *Narratives of Early Maryland*, ed. Hall, 16–17; *Virginia and Maryland, or The Lord Baltamore's printed CASE, uncased and answered. . . .* (1655), ibid., 201; "Letter of Governor Leonard Calvert to Lord Baltimore" (1638), ibid., 152; "Extract from a Letter of Captain Thomas Yong to Sir Toby Matthew" (1634), ibid., 56; Hammond, *Leah and Rachel*, ibid., 300.

ical privileges exceeding those current in the mother country. And even in Pennsylvania, where the Quaker leadership was preoccupied with peace, Isaac Norris was obliged to acknowledge that, from the first, the government was unable to attain to a middle ground "between arbitrary power and licentious popularity." [53]

Indeed, in their most idealistic envisionings of an appropriate public order in the New World, people seemed incapable of imagining a regime that did not augment at once the authoritarian and the libertarian tendencies of the time. The "true and absolute Lords proprietors" of Carolina might wish to "avoid erecting a numerous democracy" and set forth on that account Fundamental Constitutions that provided for a hereditary nobility and leet-men whose children would be leet-men "to all generations," but they also operated under a charter that promised the inhabitants "full and free license" in religious affairs and extensive rights in the political process. The proprietors of New Jersey might proclaim their lordly powers in the most "full and ample manner," but they also issued Concessions and Agreements that allowed their colonists "liberty of conscience," generous terms of landed settlement, and a representative assembly with decisive control over provincial taxation; and the purchasers of their privileges in West Jersey issued further Concessions and Agreements that renewed the assurance of "full liberty of religious faith and worship," offered elaborate protections against corruption of the electoral process, and guaranteed that representatives would "act nothing in that capacity but what shall tend to the fit service and behoof of those that send and employ them." William Penn's charter for Pennsylvania might confer upon him a "free, full, and absolute power" of superintendency over his province, but his Frames of Government made every inhabitant a member of the assembly for the first year of the venture, provided for annual elections of as many as five hundred representatives thereafter, and established a representation not only proportional to population but also rotated so that "all may be fitted for government, and have experience of the care and burden of it." In all these colonies, then, and in the others as well, the government grew more ambitious of control than the state was at home even as it afforded

---

53. *Virginia and Maryland*, 199, 191; *The Lord Baltemore's Case, Concerning the Province of Maryland* . . . (1653), in *Narratives of Early Maryland*, ed. Hall, 174; Nash, *Quakers and Politics*, 292–93. Nash depicted early Pennsylvania politics as "a make-believe world" in which "words became more important than actions," which is striking in the light of Hsu's point that, in the absence of a dense social web, people are more prone to be "pulled asunder by abstract issues" ("Kinship," 409; cf. 423).

its citizens a more effective participation in authority than they had at home. Discipline and autonomy developed apace.[54]

The coming apart of the old connectedness of self and society was simultaneously a coming into being of new unities of covenanted community and purified personality.[55] But the new unities betrayed their basis in the initial partitioning. Communities made excessive claims of concord for themselves and then fell into a dismayed sense of declension whenever they failed to sustain such ideological aspirations.[56] Individuals defined sanctified reaches of being for themselves and then found themselves drawn—even driven—to the very impurities they professed to have put aside. They did not cease to be susceptible to the terrors of the irrational merely because they distinguished themselves in terms of an exaggerated sanity. They did not divest themselves of carnal desire merely because they conceived themselves as civilized white people and projected their sensuality upon the "savage" blacks. They had to have their counterposed impurities, in order to complete themselves.[57] They had to have those they scorned—the blacks, the Indians, and all the idle, dissolute, and damned—to maintain the boundaries of their increas-

54. William MacDonald, ed., *Select Charters and Other Documents Illustrative of American History: 1606–1775* (New York, 1899), 122, 150, 151, 154, 123–25, 140, 142–43, 146, 176, 180–81, 186, 197, 202–3, 194, 201. Similar tensions appeared even earlier, as in George Donne's design for the reconstitution of Virginia, with its plea for stronger government *and* for a more sturdily self-reliant citizenry. These tensions persisted far into the eighteenth century, as in Benjamin Franklin's plan for a colony of Vandalia, with its provision for an appointed governor of feudal proclivities *and* for the happy mediocrity and republican simplicity that were hallmarks of his "Virtuous order." See T. H. Breen, "George Donne's 'Virginia Reviewed': A 1638 Plan to Reform Colonial Society," *William and Mary Quarterly*, 3d ser., 30 (1973): 449–66, and Paul W. Connor, *Poor Richard's Politicks: Benjamin Franklin and His New American Order* (New York, 1965), 143–44.

55. This may seem like an application of the Parsonian logic of functional differentiation; see Neil J. Smelser, *Social Change in the Industrial Revolution: An Application of Theory to the British Cotton Industry* (Chicago, 1959). But where that logic posits mere dispersion of a persistent set of functional imperatives, the argument of the present paragraph goes beyond such segmentation of old responses and responsibilities to the creation of responses and responsibilities quite new and unprecedented.

56. At the local level such sentiments often serve as evidence in studies such as the ones cited in n. 1 above. At the provincial level Bernard Bailyn has traced the structure and consequences for colonial politics of a comparable caesura of overinflated ambition and underdeveloped aptitude. See Bailyn, *The Origins of American Politics* (New York, 1968), chap. 2.

57. On the asymmetry of the civilized person's need for the idea of the "savage" and the lack on the part of the "savage" of any analogous need for the civilized see Stanley Diamond, ed., "Introduction: The Uses of the Primitive," in *Primitive Views of the World* (New York, 1969), v–xxix.

ingly brittle identities. Precisely because they found themselves, and in truth created themselves, in their counteridentities, they required for their very sense of selfhood the outcasts they purported to abhor.[58]

These oppositional notions of social and personal identity set the contexts within which the colonists of the seventeenth century moved. And these notions were given substance and force in the narrow nuclear families of the early modern era, which were at once the loci of the new lust for aversive classification and the crucibles of the new identity. Purified personality became possible under the aegis of their interdicts as it had never been possible amid the extended networks of traditional families. Guilt became important to people whose personalities were forged in such fear and denial as it had never been important amid the diffuse ties of traditional communities.

For guilt is an issue of boundaries. It is essentially a transgression. It can begin to be crucial only for people whose rage for categories and classifications is sufficiently strong to focus their psychic energies on barriers that might be violated. And just where the care of a previous era had been to ascertain the similitude of things, the intellectual enterprise of the early modern age was to discriminate the differentness of things.[59] In many ways it was from such concern for distinguishing, say, the saved from the damned or the civilized from the savage, and upon the structures of guilt that were built on that concern, that the modern idea of the self emerged.

Americans sensitive to such distinctions struggled unendingly

58. The notion of boundary maintenance is derived from Durkheim; for an instance of its application in a colonial setting see Kai T. Erikson, *Wayward Puritans: A Study in the Sociology of Deviance* (New York, 1966). Such dependence on counteridentities was sometimes a source of genuine dilemmas of identity. The settlers' emphasis on the heathenism of other races helped reassure them of their Christian character in the wilderness. It also obliged the settlers to convert the heathens and risk eradicating the very contrast on which they predicated that Christian conception of themselves (Michael Kammen, *People of Paradox: An Inquiry Concerning the Origins of American Civilization* [New York, 1972], 142).

The promotional efforts of the colonists often exaggerated the differences between the Old World and New World in order to attract immigrants. This dichotomous advertising often carried over into the self-justifications the colonists composed for themselves, as in Cotton Mather's celebration of "the wonders of the Christian religion, flying from the depravations of Europe to the American strand." But the gratification the colonists found in differentiating themselves from the Europeans by the opposition of innocence and corruption simultaneously jeopardized the identity they claimed as Europeans in opposition to the "innocent" denizens of the New World, the Indians (Martin E. Marty, "Reinterpreting American Religious History in Context," in *Reinterpretation in American Church History,* ed. Jerald C. Brauer [Chicago, 1968], 200–204).

59. Gerhart Piers and Milton B. Singer, *Shame and Guilt: A Psychoanalytic and Cultural Study* (Springfield, Ill., 1953), 11; Foucault, *Order of Things,* 42–43.

against what they took to be their own lower nature and thereby doomed themselves to ravages of guilt when they crossed the line between what they conceived to be spirituality and what they consigned to the sphere of sensualism. In the first decades in Virginia, for instance, John Rolfe underwent a "mighty war in [his] meditations" before convincing himself that he could marry Pocahontas with "an unspotted conscience." He knew that others would believe him to be acting from a "hungry appetite, to gorge [him]self with incontinency," and, more than that, he was uncertain in his own mind for a time whether he proceeded from an "unbridled desire of carnal affection." Indeed, even after he had persuaded himself that his marriage to the Indian princess would be a "godly labor" in converting the heathen, he still felt compelled to plead the "clearness of his conscience" and the "pious duties of a Christian" in his appeal for the approval of the governor. Earlier, other adventurers in the Virginia Company blamed the distress of the first settlers on "idleness and bestial sloth" and insisted that the colonists were "conscious and guilty . . . of their own demerit and laziness." A few years later, company officials attributed the massacre of 1622 to the vengeance of God upon the "enormous excesses of apparel and drinking" among the Virginians, "the cry whereof cannot but have gone up to heaven." And a few years after that, the burgesses enacted legislation establishing churchwardens to enforce moral regulations, lest the colony "answer before God for such evils and plagues wherewith almighty God may justly punish His people for neglecting" His "good and wholesome" commandments.[60]

In the first years of settlement in New England, the same anxieties arose from the same dichotomies. Men and women like Michael Wigglesworth searched their own "vile heart." People like Thomas Hooker discovered there their "inordinate and raging lusts." And like Thomas Shepard, they trembled at the discovery, for they could see "no wrath like this, to be governed by [their] own lusts for [their] own ends." They therefore cultivated the "strong exercises of conscience" that attended the accession of grace and enabled them to bow before their Lord and "bid farewell to all the world." And increasingly over the years, they

60. "John Rolfe Requests Permission to Marry Pocahontas (1614)," in *Old Dominion*, ed. Billings, 217–19; David Bertelson, *The Lazy South* (New York, 1967), 24. Perry Miller, *Errand into the Wilderness* (Cambridge, Mass., 1956), 120, 120n. See also Bertelson, *Lazy South*, 28; Miller, *Errand*, 109, 118–19, 126. For the persistence of such values to the end of the century see the analysis of Robert Beverley's *History and Present State of Virginia* (1705), a Virginia jeremiad, in Bertelson, *Lazy South*, 67–68.

came to seek such submissive dedication in dread of God's retribution if they failed to keep their covenants with Him. Their guilt-ridden recognition that they had in fact failed expressed itself obsessively in the jeremiads of the second generation and achieved its culminating articulation in the fulminations of the third, especially of Cotton Mather. Assailing the "torrent of wickedness" all about him, Mather demanded of his followers that they be always "full of self-abasing and self-abhorring reflections" by "loathing of [themselves] continually."[61]

Haltingly, and despite such derogations of self, colonists came to an awareness of their susceptibility to these compunctions of conscience, which carried them toward a new vision of individual freedom as atomism. For it is only in societies where such a vision obtains that "guilt, a separate, individual act that transgresses a barrier, attracts more attention than shame, a falling short of ideals," and it is only in such societies that men and women view their fellows so focally as threats to their own freedom. It is, in truth, "a special version of life which regards society as external to the individual."[62]

To this day, Americans remain heirs to that early modern sense of antagonism between self and society. With Calvin, they continue to counterpose self-love and the love of others, sanctions of guilt and sanctions of shame. And their very conception of such counterpositions, in which the society always encroaches on the self, is in its own right a reflection of the primacy among them of boundary maintenance. For on that conception guilt actually augments the autonomy of the self. The boundaries on which it is based not only define but also limit the individual's obligation to society. To the extent that he does not over-

61. Morgan, ed., "Diary of Wigglesworth," 328; Miller and Johnson, eds., *The Puritans,* 306; Michael McGiffert, ed., *God's Plot: The Paradoxes of Puritan Piety, Being the Autobiography and Journal of Thomas Shepard* (Amherst, Mass., 1972), 116; John Winthrop, "John Winthrop's Christian Experience," *Winthrop Papers* (Boston, 1929), 1:155–56; *Diary of Cotton Mather,* pt. 2, Massachusetts Historical Society, *Collections,* 7th ser., 8 (1911): 27, 69. By their disjunctions of spirituality and sensualism the New Englanders were drawn inevitably into the tangled paradoxes of polarity. Wigglesworth, for example, could scarcely sustain an unequivocal conception of himself for a single sentence in his diary. He would begin in disgust—"I am vile, I desire to loathe myself"—and then confess at once his countervailing and apparently invincible self-love— "(O that I could!)." Or, conversely, he would start from "pride"—"instead of admiring God I admire myself"—and then admit immediately his revulsion—"for this I loathe myself" (Morgan, ed., "Diary of Wigglesworth," 323, 327). And of course his professed self-love was unloving, his purported self-loathing proud and satisfied. See also McGiffert, ed., *God's Plot,* and Rutman, *American Puritanism,* 126.
62. Lynd, *On Shame,* 158–59.

step its limits, his society can make no claims upon him whose force he is inwardly driven to acknowledge. And so a process initiated in early modern Europe, in the erosion of an old integrity of clan and congregation, has persisted quite beyond that original fission and indeed persists today, in its ever more intensive elaboration of individuation and its ever more extensive exposure of the individual to the surveillance and sanctions of others.

TWO

# The Social Context of
# Democracy in Massachusetts

For more than a generation now, scholars have debated the extent of democracy in the old New England town. The debate began, of course, with Robert E. Brown, and it did not begin badly: Brown's work was a breath of fresh air in a stale discussion, substituting statistics for cynicism and adding figures to filiopietism. But what began decently degenerated, and findings that should have provoked larger questions only produced quibbles and counterquibbles over methodology and quantification. The discussion has not been entirely futile—few would now maintain the old claim that the franchise was very closely confined in provincial Massachusetts—but neither has its apparent potential been realized. We are, ultimately, as far from agreement as we ever were about whether eighteenth-century Massachusetts was democratic. Somehow, the discussion has stalled at the starting point; a promising avenue of inquiry has not developed beyond its initial promise.

Perhaps a part of that failure was implicit in Brown's initial formulation of the problem; but one man cannot do everything, and Brown did advance our consideration of the New England town as far as any one ever has. If he did not answer, or even ask, all the questions that might have been raised, other students could have done so. Brown's work made that possible. But since *Middle-Class Democracy and the Revolution in Massachusetts* (Ithaca, 1955) no comparable advances have been

From *William and Mary Quarterly*, 3d ser., 25 (1968): 523–44.

made. Indeed, the discussion seems to have stopped conceptually where Brown stopped, and one is forced to wonder not merely whether the right questions are being asked but whether any significant questions at all are being asked, other than those of how better to compute voting percentages. Certainly the terms of the debate have been, and are, inadequate to its resolution. Most obviously, figures on the franchise simply cannot serve to establish democracy. In our own time we have seen too many travesties on universal suffrage in too many nondemocratic regimes to continue to take seriously in and of itself such an abstract calculus. Yet on both sides the discussion of New England town-meeting democracy has often assumed that the franchise is a satisfactory index of democracy, and the recourse to the seeming solidity of the voting statistics has depended, if only implicitly, upon that dubious premise.

Even those few critics who have challenged the contention that the issue of eighteenth-century democracy could be settled by counting heads have generally acquiesced in the far more fundamental assumption that in one way or another the issue of the eighteenth century was what the Browns have declared it to be: "democracy or aristocracy?" But democracy and aristocracy are probably false alternatives in any case for provincial Massachusetts; and in this case they are surely so, because they have been made initial tools of inquiry instead of end terms.

Of course, the Browns have hardly been alone in their strategy of frontal assault. On the contrary, it is indicative of how thoroughly their work established the contours of subsequent study that others also rushed right into the issue of democracy without even a pause to ponder whether that issue was quite so readily accessible. Yet it would be admitted on most sides that democracy was hardly a value of such supreme salience to the men of provincial Massachusetts that it governed their conscious motives and aspirations; nor, after all, did it provide the framework for social structure in the towns of the province. In application to such a society, then, a concept such as democracy must always be recognized for just that: a concept of our own devising. It is not a datum that can be directly apprehended in all its immediacy; it is an abstraction—a rather elevated abstraction—that represents a covering judgment of the general tenor or tendency of social relations and institutions. As such, it can carry its own assurance of validity only if it proceeds out of, rather than precedes, analysis of the society to which it is applied. To rip it out of its social context is to risk exactly the disembodied discussion of democracy we have witnessed.

If we would study democracy in provincial Massachusetts, we cannot plunge headlong into that issue without sacrificing the context that conferred meaning on whatever degree of democracy did exist. Since democracy was incidental to the prime purposes of provincial society, we must first confront that society. Democracy, to the extent that it existed, was no isolated element in the organization of the political community, and problems of political participation and inclusion cannot be considered apart from the entire question of the nature of the provincial community. Even if most men in eighteenth-century Massachusetts could vote, that is only the beginning, not the end, of inquiry. What, then, was the *function* of a widely extended suffrage, and what was the function of voting itself in the conduct of the community? Who specifically was admitted to the franchise, and who was denied that privilege, and on what grounds? For ultimately, if we are to understand the towns that made the Revolution in Massachusetts, we must find out not only *whether* most men could vote but also *why*.

It is particularly imperative that we place provincial democracy in its social context because nothing else can plausibly account for its development. The founders of the settlement at Massachusetts Bay came with neither an inclusive ethos nor any larger notions of middle-class democracy. In 1630 a band of true believers had entered upon the wilderness, possessed of a conviction of absolute and invincible righteousness. Their leaders, in that first generation, proudly proclaimed that they "abhorred democracy," and, as Perry Miller maintained, "theirs was not an idle boast." [1] The spirit of the founders was set firmly against inclusion, with the very meaning of the migration dependent for many on an extension of the sphere of ecclesiastical exclusivity. The right of every church to keep out the unworthy was precisely the point of the Congregationalists' difference with the established church, and it was a right that could not be realized in England. [2] Yet, without any English prodding and within about a decade of the first settlements, the original ideals of exclusion had begun to break down at the local level. Until 1692 the colonial suffrage extended only to freemen, but by that time nonfreemen had been voting in town affairs for almost half a century. [3]

1. Perry Miller, *Orthodoxy in Massachusetts* (Boston, 1959), 37.
2. Edmund S. Morgan, *Visible Saints: The History of a Puritan Idea* (New York, 1963), esp. 10–12, 21.
3. The first break occurred in 1641 when the Body of Liberties made all men free to attend town meetings; an enactment of 1647 allowed them to vote. On the other hand, some restrictions on nonfreemen did remain. See Joel Parker, "The Origin, Organization, and Influence of the Towns of New England," Massachusetts Historical Society, *Proceedings* 9 (1866): 46.

The ability of the settlers to sustain suffrage restrictions at the colonial level so long after they were abandoned in the towns not only indicates the incomplete coincidence of intellectual currents and local conduct in early New England but also contradicts any contention that the pressures for democratic participation derived from Puritan theology or thought. The New England Puritans were pressed to the popularization of political authority only in grudging adjustment to the exigencies of their situation.

Their situation, quite simply, was one that left them stripped of any *other* sanctions than those of the group. The sea passage had cut the new settlement off from the full force of traditional authority, so that even the maintenance of law and order had to be managed in the absence of any customarily accepted agencies for its establishment or enforcement. Furthermore, as the seventeenth century waned and settlement dispersed, the preservation of public order devolved increasingly upon the local community. What was reluctantly admitted in the seventeenth century was openly acknowledged in the eighteenth, after the arrival of the new charter: The public peace could not be entrusted to Boston but would have to be separately secured in each town in the province. And though this devolution of effective authority to the local level resolved other difficulties, it only aggravated the problem of order, because the towns even more than the central government were without institutions and authorities sanctioned by tradition. Moreover, the towns had relatively limited instruments of enforcement, and they were demonstrably loath to use the coercive power they did possess.[4]

Nonetheless, order was obtained in the eighteenth-century town, and it was obtained by concord far more than by compulsion. Consensus governed the communities of provincial Massachusetts, and harmony and homogeneity were the regular—and required—realities of local life. Effective action necessitated a public opinion approaching if not attaining unanimity, and public policy was accordingly bent toward securing such unanimity. The result was, to be sure, a kind of govern-

4. Difficulties of enforcement are not easy to demonstrate in a few sentences, but they can be suggested, perhaps, by the ease of mob mobilization and by the extensive evasion of the office of constable, especially by the middling and upper classes of the community. Their readiness to pay fines rather than serve in the office was both symptomatic of and contributory to the structural weakness of the constabulary. There was, in other words, a formal legal system in the province without an autonomous instrument for its own enforcement. A more elaborate development of the general theme is in Michael Zuckerman, "The Massachusetts Town in the Eighteenth Century" (Ph.D. diss., Harvard University, 1967), esp. 118–26.

ment by common consent, but government by consent in eighteenth-century Massachusetts did not imply democracy in any more modern sense because it required far more than mere majoritarianism. Such majoritarianism implied a minority, and the towns could no more condone a competing minority by their norms and values than they could have constrained it by their police power. Neither conflict, dissent, nor any other structured pluralism ever obtained legitimacy in the towns of the Bay before the Revolution.[5]

Thus, authority found another form in provincial Massachusetts. Its instrument was the town meeting, which was no mere forum but the essential element in the delicate equipoise of peace and propriety that governed the New England town. In the absence of any satisfactory means of traditional or institutional coercion, the recalcitrant could not be compelled to adhere to the common course of action. Therefore, the common course of action had to be so shaped as to leave none recalcitrant—that was the vital function of the New England town meeting. To oversimplify perhaps, the town meeting solved the problem of enforcement by evading it. The meeting gave institutional expression to the imperatives of peace. In the meetings consensus was reached, and individual consent and group opinion were placed in the service of social conformity. There the men of the province established their agreements on policies and places, and there they legitimized those agreements so that subsequent deviation from those accords became socially illegitimate and personally immoral as well, meaning as it did the violation of a covenant or the breaking of a promise. In the town meetings men talked of politics, but ultimately they sought to establish moral community.

In the context of such a community, the significance of an extended franchise becomes quite clear: Governance by concord and concurrence required inclusiveness. In communities in which effective enforcement depended on the moral binding of decisions upon the men who made

5. The import of the argument sketched here and developed below must be understood. No full-scale defense of the consensus hypothesis will be attempted here, nor would one be possible in such a piece as this: An examination of such a narrow matter as electoral eligibility can hardly *prove* a set of propositions about so substantial a subject as the social organization of the New England town. A full-scale defense of the hypothesis assumed here is found in Zuckerman, "Massachusetts Town in the Eighteenth Century." What is in fact claimed here is, first, that this hypothesis in particular does illuminate many aspects of political "democracy" in the Massachusetts town of the eighteenth century and, second, that whatever failings may be found in this particular hypothesis, *some* kind of hypothesis is surely necessary to ground the discussion of democracy in the colony and establish it in a social context.

them, it was essential that most men be parties to such decisions. Not the principled notions of the New Englanders but the stern necessities of enforcement sustained town-meeting democracy in Massachusetts. The politics of consensus made a degree of democracy functional, even made it a functional imperative. Men were allowed to vote not out of any overweening attachment to democratic principles per se but simply because a wide canvass was convenient, if not indeed critical, in consolidating a consensus in the community.

Under this incentive to inclusion, most towns did set their suffrage almost as liberally as Brown claimed. To seek the social context of the suffrage, then, necessitates no major quarrel with Brown's figures on franchise democracy; what it may provide is an explanation for them. It also offers the possibility of accounting for more than just the figures. As soon as we see that the high degree of participation permitted in the politics of the provincial town was not an isolated phenomenon but rather an integral aspect of the conduct of the community, we are in a position to go beyond a disembodied study of electoral eligibility and a simple celebration of middle-class democracy in Massachusetts. We are in a position to convert polemics into problems and to press for answers.

In many communities, for example, a substantial and sometimes an overwhelming proportion of the people were *not* technically entitled to vote. Brown did not discuss some of these places, and the ones he did discuss were added to his evidence only with the special explanation that sometimes even the ineligible were admitted to the ballot box. But in the context of community such lapses would not necessarily invalidate his larger conclusions, nor would such ad hoc expedients be required; for the same imperatives impinged on towns where few were legally qualified as on the others, and the same results of wide political participation obtained because of the same sense that inclusiveness promoted peace while more rigorous methods threatened it. The town of Douglas, with only five qualified voters in its first years, flatly refused to be bound by a determination confined to those five, declaring its conviction "that the intent of no law can bind them to such ill consequences." Mendon, in its "infant state" in 1742, voted "to permit a considerable number of persons not qualified by law to vote . . . being induced thereto by an apprehension that it would be a means of preserving peace and unity amongst ourselves." Princeton, incorporated in 1760 with forty-three settlers but only fourteen eligible to vote according to provincial regulations, established a formal "agreement among themselves to overlook" those regulations, and the General Court upheld that agreement. "The poor freeholders" in the early days of Upton were also "allowed liberty to vote in town meeting," and it had produced "an encouraging harmony" in local affairs until 1746, when a few of the qualified voters, momentarily possessed of a majority of the ten in town, sought to upset the customary arrangements and limit the franchise as the law required. The rest of the town at once protested that "such a strenuous method of proceeding would endanger the peace of the town" and begged the General Court "to prevent the dismal damages that may follow" therefrom. The Court did exactly as it was asked, and at the new meeting the town reverted to its old form: "Everyone was admitted to vote, qualified or not."[6]

The principle that governed such universalism was not deliberate democracy; it was merely a recognition that the community could not be governed solely by the qualified voters if they were too few in number. Such a situation was most likely to occur in new communities, but it was not limited to them. Middleton had been established for almost a quarter of a century when it was conceded that in the local elections of 1752 "there was double the number of votes to the lawful voters." In a variety of towns and at other times, requirements for the franchise were also ignored and admission of the unqualified acknowledged explicitly.[7] Thomas Hutchinson's wry lament that "anything with the appearance of a man" was allowed the vote may have been excessive, but it was not wholly fabricated.[8] And even towns whose political procedures were more regular resorted to universalism in cases of conflict or of major issues. Fitchburg, for instance, voted in 1767 that "every freeholder be a votter in Chusing of a minestr," while twenty years earlier, in a bitterly contested election in Haverhill, "there was not any list of valuation read nor any list of non-voters nor any weighting of what name or nature whatsoever by which the selectmen did pretend to show who was qualified to vote in town affairs."[9]

6. Massachusetts Archives, State House, Boston, 115: 168, 169, 316–17, 319–20, 469–71, 864–65; 117: 647–49, 652; 118: 734–35a, 762; Francis E. Blake, *History of the Town of Princeton* (Princeton, Mass., 1915), 1:76–77.

7. Mass. Archives, 8:279, for others see ibid., 278; 49: 398–400; 50: 20–22, 25–26, 85–88, 89–90; 113: 270; 115: 36–37, 291; 116: 373–74; 117: 291–93, 302–5; 118: 23–24a.

8. Robert E. Brown, *Middle-Class Democracy and the Revolution in Massachusetts* (Ithaca, 1955), 60.

9. Walter A. Davis, comp., *The Old Records of the Town of Fitchburg Massachusetts 1764–1789* (Fitchburg, Mass., 1898), 39; Mass. Archives, 8: 273.

The question of inclusiveness itself sometimes came before a town, not always without challenge but generally with a democratic outcome. Dudley, more than a decade after the incorporation of the town, voted "that all the freeholder of sd town should be voters by a graet majorytie and all agreed to it." In Needham in 1750 it was also "put to vote whether it be the mind of the town to allow all freeholders in town to vote for a moderator," and there too the vote carried in the affirmative. And that verdict for inclusion was not even as revealing as the method by which that verdict was reached, for in voting *whether* to include all in the election, Needham *did* include all in the procedural issue. Every man did vote on the question of whether every man was to be allowed to vote.[10]

Of course, absolute inclusiveness never prevailed in provincial Massachusetts—women could not vote at all, and neither could anyone under twenty-one—and property and residence qualifications, introduced in 1692, were probably adhered to as often as they were ignored, so that even the participation of adult males was something less than universal. It was an important part of Brown's achievement to show that, in general, it was not *very much* less than universal, but, by the nature of his research strategy, he could go no further than that. If we are to penetrate to particulars—if we are to ask who was excluded, and why, and why the suffrage standards were what they were—we must consider not only numbers but also the conditions of community.

The men who were not allowed legitimately to vote with their fellow townsmen were commonly tenants or the sons of voters; as Brown discovered, it was these two groups against which the property requirement primarily operated. But where the controversialists seek to *excuse* these exclusions, or to magnify them, a broader perspective allows one to *explain* them, for against these two groups sanctions were available that were far more effective than those of the generalized community. Stringent property qualifications were clearly self-defeating in a society where consensus was the engine of enforcement, but overly generous qualifications were equally unnecessary. Where some men, such as tenants and dependent sons, could be privately coerced, liberality on their behalf, from the standpoint of social control, would have meant the commission of a sin of superfluity.

Similarly, almost nothing but disadvantage could have accrued from

10. *Town Records of Dudley, Massachusetts, 1732–1754* (Pawtucket, R.I., 1893), 1:106; Mass. Archives, 115: 616–17.

a loose residence requirement enabling men not truly members of the community to participate in its decision-making process, since voting qualifications in provincial Massachusetts were connected to the concept of community, not the concept of democracy. The extensions and contractions of the franchise were significant to the townsmen of the eighteenth century primarily as a means of consolidating communal consensus. All those whose acquiescence in public action was necessary were included, and all those whose concurrence could be compelled otherwise or dispensed with were excluded, often very emphatically. Sixty-six citizens of Watertown, for example, petitioned against the allowance of a single unqualified voter in a 1757 election because he was "well known to belong to the town of Lincoln." In many towns such as Sudbury the town clerk "very carefully warned those that were not legally qualified not to vote and prayed the selectmen to be very careful and watchful that nobody voted that was not legally qualified." [11] Even in disputes over specific qualifications, both sides often agreed on the principle of exclusion of the unqualified; contention occurred only over the application of that principle. [12]

Consciousness of voting qualifications colored the conduct of other town affairs as well as elections, as indeed was natural since the meaning of the franchise went so far beyond mere electoral democracy. Protests by men recently arrived in a town could be discredited, as they were in Haverhill in 1748, without any reference to the justice of the protest itself, simply by stating that "many of their petitioners are not qualified to vote in town affairs as may be seen by the selectmen's list of voters, and some of them were never known to reside in town or did we ever hear of them before we saw their petition." Similarly, in the creation of new communities qualification for the franchise could be crucial. Inhabitants of Bridgewater resisted their own inclusion in a precinct proposed by thirty-seven men dwelling in their vicinity by pointing out that "there is not above eleven or twelve that are qualified to vote in town meetings as the law directs." Many towns in their corporate capacity made much the same plea when confronted with an appeal for separation from the community. As Worcester once noted in such a case, more than half the petitioners were "not voters and one is a single Indian." [13]

11. Mass. Archives, 117: 302–5; 49: 361–62; see also ibid., 117: 300, 306–7, 647–49; Jeremiah L. Hanaford, *History of Princeton* (Worcester, Mass., 1852), 23.

12. See for example Mass. Archives, 115: 412–13, 463.

13. Ibid., 305–8, 144; "Early Records of the Town of Worcester," Worcester Society of Antiquity, *Collections* 2, no. 8 (1881), 42–43. See also Mass. Archives, 115: 392.

Such consciousness of qualifications sometimes appeared to be nothing more than an insistence on a "stake in society" in order to participate in the society's deliberations and decisions, but the stake-in-society concept, despite its popularity in the West and its convergence with certain conditions of public life in the province, was not precisely the notion that controlled those restrictions of the franchise that did persist after 1692. It was not out of any intrinsic attachment to that concept, but simply out of a fear that those without property were overly amenable to bribery or other such suasion, that the men of Massachusetts clung to their voting qualifications. As the Essex Result was to state the principle in 1778, "all the members of the state are qualified to make the election, unless they have not sufficient discretion, or are so situated as to have no wills of their own."[14] Participation in community decisions was the prerogative of independent men, of *all* a town's independent men, but, ideally, *only* of those. Indeed, it was precisely because of their independence that they had to be accorded a vote, since only by their participation did they bind themselves to concur in the community's chosen course of action. The town meeting was an instrument for enforcement, not—at least not intentionally—a school for democracy.

This logic of competence governed the exclusion of women and children and also accounted for the antipathy to voting by tenants. The basis of the prohibitions that were insisted upon was never so much an objection to poverty per se—the stake-in-society argument—as to the tenant's concomitant status of dependence, the pervasive assumption of which emerged clearly in a contested election in Haverhill in 1748. There the petitioners charged that a man had been "refused as a voter under pretense that he was a tenant and so not qualified, when the full reason was that he was a tenant to one of their [the selectmen's] opposers and so at all hazards to be suppressed," while another man, a tenant to one of the selectmen themselves, had been received as a voter though "rated at much less in the last year's taxes than he whom they refused." The protest was thus directed primarily against the abuses of the selectmen: That tenants would do as their landlords desired was simply taken for granted.[15] And naturally the same sort of assumption controlled the exclusion of sons still living with their parents. The voting age of

14. [Theophilus Parsons], *Result of the Convention of Delegates Holden at Ipswich* . . . (Newburyport, Mass., 1778), 28–29.
15. Mass. Archives, 115: 330–34, 414–13; 116: 276–77; 117: 84–86, 306–7; "Early Records of Worcester," Worcester Society of Antiquity, *Collections* 2, no. 6 (1881): 63.

twenty-one was the most rudimentary expression of this requirement of a will of one's own, but the legal age was not very firm at the edges. Like other laws of the province, it could not stand when it came up against local desires, and the age qualifications were often abrogated when unusual dependence or independence was demonstrable, as in the case of the eighteen-year-old who voted in a Sheffield election of 1751 because his father had died and he had become head of his family. As the town's elected representative could declare on that occasion, quite ignoring the legal age requirement, the lad "had a good right to vote, for his estate rested in him and that he was a town-born child and so was an inhabitant."[16]

Of course, the townsmen of the eighteenth century placed no premium on independence as such. Massachusetts townsmen were expected to be independent but not too independent; ultimately, they were supposed on their own to arrive at the same actions and commitments as their neighbors. Any *genuine* independence, excessive *or* insufficient, was denigrated if not altogether denied a place in the community. Thus, when a number of inhabitants of a gore of land near Charlton faced the threat of incorporation with the town, they submitted "one word of information" about the townsmen who had asked for that incorporation. The note said only:

| | |
|---|---|
| Baptist signers | —7 |
| Churchmen | —3 |
| Tenants | —4 |
| Neither tenants nor freeholders but intruders upon other men's property | —15 |

The whole of the petitioners in Charlton consisting of 35 in number.

In other words, tenants were tainted, but so too were all others who were their own men, such as squatters and those who dared to differ in religion. In denigrating them, the inhabitants of the gore drew no distinctions: Tenant and Baptist were equally offensive because equally outside of orthodoxy, beyond the confines of consensus.[17]

Ultimately almost *any* taint on membership in the homogeneous community was a potential basis for derogation. Some inhabitants of Rutland once even attempted to deny the validity of a town decision

16. Mass. Archives, 8: 278; for a comparable case in the opposite direction see ibid., 116: 668–69. Another basis for exclusion was insanity. For a revealing contretemps see ibid., 50: 85–88; 117: 295–97, 302–5.

17. Ibid., 117: 86, and see 84–85.

merely because many of its supporters were "such as were and are dissenters from the public worship of God in the old meeting-house." And though Rutland's religious orthodoxy was a bit exquisite even for eighteenth-century New England, it was so only in degree. For example, when Sutton opposed the erection of a new district out of parts of itself and several other towns in 1772, the town actually deducted the Anabaptists from the number of signatories to the application—Baptists simply did not count as full citizens. Worcester did the same thing and indeed went even further. Several of the signers of the petition for separation were not heads of families but mere "single persons, some of them transient ones," and so, said the town, were not to be "accounted as part of the number of families the petitioners say are within the limits of the proposed district." Whereas excessively reliable bonds confined the tenant, no reliable bonds at all attached a single man to the community, and either alternative evoked suspicion.[18]

Ultimately, however, the insistence on orthodoxy did not directly exclude any excessive number, and neither did the property and residence requirements disqualify any great proportion of the province's adult males. In the perspective of the English villages from which the New Englanders came, these very dimensions of disqualification may be better seen, in fact, as defining a broader qualification than had previously prevailed in English practice. Far more fundamentally, the criteria of exclusion were measures of the inclusiveness of the communities of early Massachusetts.

The most fundamental shift that had occurred was the one from property to residence as the irreducible basis of town citizenship. In England, several classes of property holders were "technically termed inhabitants even though they dwelt in another town"; property defined political citizenship, and only those who held the requisite property in the community directed its affairs. In provincial Massachusetts such stake-in-society notions never prevailed for reasons that had little to do with any abstract attachment to democracy or antipathy to absentee ownership. They never prevailed because the point of the town meeting was not so much the raising of a revenue as it was political government, especially the maintenance of law and order. In Massachusetts it was necessary to act only on the individuals living in each town, and it was imperative to act upon all of them. Of course, taxation as well as resi-

18. Ibid., 115: 741–42; 118: 613–16, 619; see also ibid., 116: 276–77. And others found more reasons to discredit any who stood outside communal orthodoxy. See ibid., 115: 393–96, 412–13, 596.

dence provided the basis for the ballot in Massachusetts, but that was of a piece with the residence requirement. As early as 1638 "every inhabitant of a town was declared liable for his proportion of the town's charges," in sharp contrast to the towns of England where only a few were so taxed.[19]

The democracy of the Massachusetts towns was, then, a democracy despite itself, a democracy without democrats. But it was still, so far as anything yet said is concerned, a democracy, at least in the simple sense of a widely diffused franchise. Such democracy is admitted—indeed, required—in the analysis advanced above; the objection urged against the defenders of that democracy is not that they are wrong but that they are right for the wrong reasons, or for no reasons at all. When they examine electoral eligibility apart from its social setting, and when they place franchise democracy at the center of provincial social organization instead of in the peripheral position it actually occupied, they do not condemn their findings to invalidity, only to sterility. They may be correct about the degree of diffusion of the vote, but they can go no further. Within their original terms, they cannot systematically study the purposes of participation, the relative importance of inclusiveness when it confronted competing values, the limits of eligibility and the reasons for them, or, more broadly, the particular texture of the electorate as against abstract statistics.

But if the analysis urged thus far has basically buttressed Brown's position by extending and explaining his statistics, that analysis also has another side. For when we see franchise democracy as a mere incident in the central quest for concord and concurrence among neighbors, we must also observe that the same concern for consensus that promoted wide participation also imposed very significant limitations on the democracy of the provincial community, limitations sufficiently serious to suggest that the democratic appellation itself may be anachronistic when applied to such a society.

For one thing, the ideal of "townsmen together"[20] implied the power of each town to control its own affairs, and that control not only

---

19. Edward Channing, "Town and County Government in the English Colonies of North America," *Johns Hopkins University Studies in Historical and Political Science,* 2d ser., 2, no. 10 (1884): 12, 32.

20. The phrase is from Conrad M. Arensberg, "American Communities," *American Anthropologist* 57 (1955): 1,150. For affirmations of that ideal as a consummatory value see Mass. Archives, 113: 616–17; 114: 645; 115: 282–83; 116: 527–28; 117: 563–65; 118: 122b–d.

extended to but also depended upon communal control of its membership. From the founding of the first towns communities retained the right to accept only those whom they wished, and that right persisted without challenge to the time of the Revolution. "Such whose dispositions do not suit us, whose society will be hurtful to us," were simply refused admission as enemies of harmony and homogeneity. Dedham's first covenant, "to keepe of from us all such, as ar contrarye minded. And receave onely such unto us as be such as may be probably of one harte," was typical. For inhabitancy was a matter of public rather than private concern, and among the original settlers it scarcely had to be argued that "if the place of our cohabitation be our own, then no man hath right to come in to us without our consent."[21] Consent meant the formal vote of the town or its selectmen, and none were admitted without one or the other. Not even inhabitants themselves could entertain outsiders—"strangers," they were called—without the permission of the town, and any who violated the rule were subject to penalties.[22] And of course the original thrust of congregational Puritanism to lodge disciplinary powers with the individual churches rather than with bishops also aimed at more local control of the membership of the local community.[23]

Most of these practices continued unabated into the eighteenth century. Swansea's "foundation settlement" of 1667 provided that "if any person denied any particular in the said agreement they should not be admitted an inhabitant in said town," and half a century later seventy-eight townsmen reaffirmed their commitment to the ancestral covenant. Cotton Mather's manual of 1726, *Ratio Disciplinae Fratrum Nov-Anglorum,* described a process of "mutual Conferences" by which men came to "a good understanding" that might be subscribed to by any applicant. And even in the crisis of the dissolution of a church, as at Bellingham in 1747, the congregation could not simply disperse to the nearest convenient towns. Each of the congregants, for all that he had

21. Sumner C. Powell, *Puritan Village* (Middletown, Conn., 1963), xviii; George L. Haskins, *Law and Authority in Early Massachusetts* (New York, 1960), 70; Josiah Benton, *Warning Out in New England* (Boston, 1911), 8. The early towns also forbade inhabitants to "sell or let their land or houses to strangers without the consent of the town"; see Benton, *Warning Out,* 18, 19, 23, 87, and William Weeden, *Economic and Social History of New England, 1620–1789* (Boston, 1891), 57.

22. Benton, *Warning Out,* 18, 33. And the fines were indeed established and enforced in the towns. See Myron Allen, *The History of Wenham* (Boston, 1860), 26, and Weeden, *Economic and Social History,* 79–80.

23. Morgan, *Visible Saints,* 10–12, 21.

already met the tests of church membership and partaken of communion, had to be accepted anew into the nearby churches and approved by their towns, and in 1754 Sunderland claimed that this right of prior approval was "always customary." [24]

Another customary instrument for the stringent control of access to the town that was also sustained throughout the provincial era was the practice of "warning out." Under this aegis, anyone who did secure entry to the town and was then deemed undesirable could be warned and, if necessary, lawfully ejected from the community. Such a policy was, in some part, a device to escape undue expenses in the support of paupers, but it was also, and more importantly, the product of the powerful communitarian assumptions of the early settlers, and those assumptions did not decline in the eighteenth century. William Weeden found the invocation of warning procedures so common that "the actual occurrences hardly need particular mention," and he concluded that "the old restrictions on the admission of freemen to the municipality, and on the sale of land to outsiders, do not appear to have been relaxed generally" as late as the era immediately preceding the imperial crisis. Town records such as Worcester's were studded with such warnings, from the time of the town's founding to the time of the Revolution itself. In other towns, too, penalties were still imposed for violation of the rules of inhabitancy.[25]

The result was that fundamental differences in values were rarely admitted within a town, while differences of race, nationality, or culture scarcely appeared east of the Hudson River before the Revolution. Massachusetts was more nearly restricted to white Anglo-Saxon Protestants than any other province in English America, with the possible exception of its New England neighbors, Connecticut and New Hampshire. Less than one percent of the quarter of a million Germans who came to the English colonies between 1690 and 1770 came to New England, and the proportion of Irish, Scotch, and Scotch-Irish was little larger. There

24. Mass. Archives, 113: 613–15; 115: 268, 272, 276; 49: 380–83; Cotton Mather, *Ratio Disciplinae Fratrum Nov-Anglorum* (Boston, 1726), pt. 3, 2. See also Mass. Archives, 116: 392–93; 117: 15–16. In one case, that of Medway (Mass. Archives, 49: 380–83), such consideration was not accorded.

25. Weeden, *Economic and Social History,* 519, 673; "Early Records of Worcester," Worcester Society of Antiquity, *Collections* 2, no. 6 (1881): 22–23, 102, 122–23; 2, no. 8: 19, 27, 57–58, 128; 4 (1882): 28, 47, 67, 85, 99, 137, 147, 148, 202, 223. For penalties in other towns, see *Town of Weston: Records of the First Precinct, 1746–1754 and of the Town, 1754–1803* (Boston, 1893), 61, 101, 108, 115, 126; Herman Mann, *Historical Annals of Dedham, from its Settlement in 1635 to 1847* (Dedham, Mass., 1847), 23, 25; Allen, *History of Wenham,* 26.

was no welcome whatsoever for French Catholics and very little encouragement, according to Governor Bellomont, even for the Huguenots.[26] Negroes never attained significant numbers at the Bay—by 1780 they accounted for only two percent of the population of the province and a bare one percent of all the Negroes in the Confederation—and the Indians, who once were significant, were on their way to extinction well before the Revolution broke out.[27] Committed to a conception of the social order that precluded pluralism, the townsmen of Massachusetts never made a place for those who were not of their own kind. The community they desired was an enclave of common believers, and to the best of their ability they secured such a society, rooted not only in ethnic and cultural homogeneity but also in common moral and economic ideas and practices. Thus, the character of the community became a critical—and non-democratic—condition of provincial democracy; for a wide franchise could be ventured only after a society that sought harmony had been made safe for such democracy. In that society it was possible to let men vote precisely because so many men were not allowed entry in the first place.

Thus, we can maintain the appearance of democracy only so long as we dwell on elections and elections alone, instead of the entire electoral process. As soon as we depart from that focus, the town meetings of Massachusetts fall short of any decent democratic standard. Wide participation did obtain, but it was premised on stringently controlled access to eligibility, so that open elections presupposed anterior constriction of the electorate. Similarly, most men could vote, but their voting was not designed to contribute to a decision among meaningful alternatives. The town meeting had one prime purpose, and it was not the provision of a neutral battleground for the clash of contending parties or interest groups. In fact, nothing could have been more remote from the minds of men who repeatedly affirmed, to the very end of the provincial period, that "harmony and unanimity" were what "they most heartily wish to enjoy in all their public concerns." Conflict occurred only rarely in these communities, where "prudent and amicable com-

26. On the Germans and Scotch-Irish see Clarence Ver Steeg, *The Formative Years, 1607–1763* (New York, 1964), 167–68. On the Huguenots see Charles W. Baird, *History of the Huguenot Emigration to America* (New York, 1885), 2:251–53; G. Elmore Reaman, *The Trail of the Huguenots in Europe, the United States, South Africa, and Canada* (London, 1964), 129.

27. On the Negro see Marvin Harris, *Patterns of Race in the Americas* (New York, 1964), 84. For some of the story of the extinction of the last Indian town in the province see Mass. Archives, 117: 690–91, 733–35.

position and agreement" were urged as preventives for "great and sharp disputes and contentions." When it did appear it was seen as an unnatural and undesirable deviation from the norm. Protests and contested elections almost invariably appealed to unity and concord as the values that had been violated; and in the absence of any socially sanctioned role for dissent, contention was generally surreptitious and scarcely ever sustained for long. The town meeting accordingly aimed at unanimity. Its function was the arrangement of agreement or, more often, the endorsement of agreements already arranged, and it existed for accommodation, not disputation.[28]

Yet democracy devoid of legitimate difference, dissent, and conflict is something less than democracy; and men who are finally to vote only as their neighbors vote have something less than the full range of democratic options. Government by mutual consent may have been a step in the direction of a deeper-going democracy, but it should not be confused with the real article. Democratic consent is predicated upon legitimate choice, while the town meetings of Massachusetts in the provincial era, called as they were to reach and register accords, were still in transition from assent to such consent. The evidence for such a conclusion exists in an abundance of votes from all over the province on all manner of matters "by the free and united consent of the whole" or "by a full and Unanimous Vote that they are Easie and satisfied With What they have Done."[29] Most men may have been eligible to vote, but their voting did not settle differences unless most men voted together. In fact, differences that voting could have settled had no defined place in the society, for that was not in the nature of town politics. Unanimity was expected ethically as well as empirically. Indeed, it was demanded as a matter of social decency, so that even the occasional cases of conflict were shaped by the canons of concord and consensus, with towns pleading for the preservation of "peace and unanimity" as "the only occasion of our petitioning."[30]

This demand for unanimity found its ultimate expression in rather frequent denials of one of the most elementary axioms of democratic theory, the principle of majority rule. A mere majority often com-

28. Mass. Archives, 118: 707–12, 715–17. The theme is omnipresent in the records of the towns and of such conflicts as did occur. See Zuckerman, "Massachusetts Town in the Eighteenth Century," especially chap. 3.

29. Mass. Archives, 118: 388–90; *Weston Records,* 11. See also Mass. Archives, 116: 446–47; 118: 715–17; "Records of Worcester," Worcester Society of Antiquity, *Collections* 2, no. 8, (1881): 43, 75; 4 (1882): 18, 173, 264–66.

30. Mass. Archives, 50: 30–31; 115: 479–80; 116: 709–10.

manded scant authority at the local level and scarcely even certified decisions as legitimate. In communities that provided no regular place for minorities a simple majority was not necessarily sufficient to dictate social policy, and many men such as the petitioners from the old part of Berwick were prepared to say so quite explicitly. Since its settlement some eighty or ninety years earlier, that town had grown until by 1748 the inhabitants of the newer parts easily outnumbered the "ancient settlers" and wished to establish a new meetinghouse in a place that the inhabitants of the older parts conceived injurious to their interest. Those who lived in the newer parts of town had the votes, but the "ancient settlers" were icily unimpressed nonetheless. Injury could not be justified "merely because a major vote of the town is or may be obtained to do it," the petitioners protested. They would suffer "great hurt and grievance" and "for no other reason than this: a major vote to do it, which is all the reason they have for the same." Equity, on the other hand, required a "just regard" for the old part of town and its inhabitants. They "ought" to retain their privileges despite their loss of numerical preponderance. And that principle was no mere moral fabrication of a desperate minority. Six years earlier the Massachusetts General Court had endorsed exactly the same position in a similar challenge to the prerogatives of numerical power by the "ancient part" of another town, and in the Berwick controversy the town majority itself tacitly conceded the principle upon which the old quarter depended. Accusing the old quarter of "gross mis-representation," the rest of the town now maintained that there had been a disingenuous confusion of geography and population. There could be no question as to the physical location of the old town, but, as to its inhabitants, "the greatest part of the ancient settlers and maintainers of the ministry do live to the northward of the old meetinghouse and have always kept the same in times of difficulty and danger." The newer townsmen, then, did not deny that ancient settlers were entitled to special consideration; they simply denied that the inhabitants of the old quarter were in fact the ancient settlers.[31]

Antiquity restricted majoritarianism elsewhere as well in demands of old settlers and in determinations of the General Court. In Lancaster as in Berwick, for example, a "standing part" could cite efforts to disrupt the old order, efforts that had been rejected by the Court as unreasonable, "and now though they have obtained a vote from the town the case still remains equally unreasonable." In other towns, too, a majority

31. Ibid., 115: 368–75, 377–78, 393–96.

changed nothing.[32] Consensus comprehended justice and history as well as the counting of a vote. In such a society a case could not be considered solely in its present aspects, as the original inhabitants of Lunenburg made quite clear. "What great discouragement must it needs give to any new settler," those old ones inquired,

to begin a settlement and go through the difficulties thereof, which are well known to such as have ever engaged in such service, if when, so soon as ever they shall through the blessing of heaven upon their diligence and industry have arrived to live in some measure peaceably and comfortably, if then, after all fatigues and hardships undergone, to be cut to pieces and deprived of charter privileges and rights, and instead of peace and good harmony, contention and confusion introduced, there will be no telling what to trust to.[33]

Nor was history the only resort for the repudiation of a majority. Other men offered other arguments, and some scarcely deigned to argue at all. In a contested election in Haverhill, for example, one side simply denied any authority at all to a majority of the moment. It was, they said, nothing but the creature of "a few designing men who have artfully drawn in the multitude and engaged them in their own cause." That, they argued, was simply "oppression." The merchants of Salem similarly refused to accept the hazards of populistic politics, though their refusal was rather more articulate. The town meeting had enacted a tax schedule more advantageous to the farmers than to themselves, and the merchants answered that they felt no force in that action, because "the major part of those who were present were [farmers], and the vote then passed was properly their vote and not the vote of the whole body of the town." That legitimacy and obligation attached only to a vote of the whole community was simply assumed by the merchants, as they sought a subtle separation of a town ballot—sheer majoritarianism—from a "vote of the whole body of the town"—a notion akin to the general will—for which the consent of every part of the population was requisite.[34]

Disdain for direct democracy emerged even more explicitly and sweepingly in a petition from the west precinct of Bridgewater in 1738. The precinct faced the prospect of the loss of its northern part due to a

32. Ibid., 114: 613–14; 113: 275–76; 116: 736–38.
33. Ibid., 117: 165–69. In this case, nonetheless, the General Court declined to accept the argument and thus afforded no special safeguard to the original settlers. For similar cases without the adverse action of the Court see ibid., 114: 286–88; 115: 729–30.
34. Ibid., 115: 330–34, 596.

town vote authorizing the northern inhabitants to seek separation as an independent town, and the precinct feared that the loss would be fatal. Accordingly, the parishioners prayed the General Court's intervention, and after briefly disputing the majority itself, the precinct allowed that, whether or not a majority in the town *had* been obtained, such a majority *could* be contrived. "We own it is easy for the two neighboring parishes joining with the petitioners to vote away our just rights and privileges and to lay heavy burdens upon us, which they would not be willing to touch with the ends of their fingers." Yet for all the formal validity of such a vote, the precinct would not have assented to it or felt it to be legitimate, "for we trust that your Excellency and Honors will not be governed by numbers but by reason and justice." Other men elsewhere urged the same argument; perhaps none caught the provincial paradox of legality without legitimacy any better than the precinct of Salem Village, soon to become the independent town of Danvers. After a recitation of the imposition it had suffered from the town of Salem for no reason but superior numbers, the village came to its indictment of the town: "we don't say but you have had a legal right to treat us so, but all judgment without mercy is tedious to the flesh." [35]

Typically in such cases, the defense against this indictment was not an invocation of majority rights but rather a denial of having employed them oppressively. Both sides, therefore, operated upon an identical assumption. One accused the other of taking advantage of its majority, the other retorted that it had done no such thing, but neither disputed the principle that majority disregard of a minority was indefensible. [36]

This principle was no mere pious protestation. In Kittery, for instance, the parent parish complained that the men who later became the third parish had "long kept us in very unhappy circumstances . . . counter-acting us in all our proceedings" until finally "we were obliged to come into an agreement with them for dividing the then-lower parish of Kittery into two separate parishes," yet it was conceded on both sides that the old inhabitants enjoyed an easy numerical supremacy. Had they been disposed to employ it, almost any amount of "counter-acting" could have been contained and ultimately quashed, so far as votes in public meeting were concerned. But the parish clearly did not rely upon simple majoritarian procedures. It was more than morality that made

35. Ibid., 114: 244–46, 244a, 786–88; also 117: 463–65.
36. Ibid., 115: 866, 872–75; 118: 388–90; 181: 133–34, 139.

consensus imperative; it was also the incapacity for coercion without widespread consent. It was the same incapacity that shaped a hundred other accommodations and abnegations across the province, that enabled some "aggrieved brethern" in Rehoboth to force the resignation of a minister, that paralyzed the town of Upton in the relocation of its meetinghouse. "All are agreed that it should be removed or a new one built," a town petition explained, "but cannot agree upon the place." In the absence of agreement they could see no way to act at all on their own account; there was never any thought of constructing a coalition within the town or contending for a majority.[37]

Ultimately almost every community in the province shared Upton's determination "to unite the people." Disputes, when they arose at all, were commonly concluded by "a full and amicable agreement" in which all parties "were in peace and fully satisfied," and the conflicts that did occur evoked no efforts at resolution in a majoritarian manner. "Mutual and general advantage" was the condition of town continuance in "one entire corporate body."[38] But that corporate ethos was something distant indeed from democracy, and electoral eligibility is, therefore, an unsatisfactory index even of political participation, let alone of any more meaningful democracy. Most men may have been able to vote in the eighteenth-century town, but the town's true politics were not transacted at the ballot box so much as at the tavern and all the other places, including the meeting itself, where men met and negotiated so that the vote might be a mere ratification, rather than a decision among significant alternatives. Alternatives were antithetical to the safe conduct of the community as it was conceived at the Bay, and so to cast a vote was only to participate in the consolidation of the community, not to make a choice among competing interests or ideals.

Accordingly, the claim for middle-class democracy in provincial Massachusetts simply cannot be sustained from the figures on electoral eligibility; relevant participation resided elsewhere than in the final, formal vote. And yet, ironically, local politics may have been democratic indeed, a least in the limited terms of political participation, since a politics of consensus required consultation with most of the inhabitants in

37. Ibid., 115: 872–75; 116: 276–77; 118: 207; George H. Tilton, *A History of Rehoboth, Massachusetts* (Boston, 1918), 106–7, 102.

38. Mass. Archives, 115: 461–62; 118: 526, 707–12; see also Samuel A. Bates, ed., *Records of the Town of Braintree, 1640 to 1793* (Randolph, Mass., 1886), 69–70.

order to assure accord. In little towns of two or three hundred adult males living in close, continuing contact, men may very well have shared widely a sense of the amenability of the political process to their own actions and attitudes, and the feeling of involvement may well have been quite general. But to find out we will have to go beyond counting heads or tallying the town treasurers' lists.

# THREE

# Pilgrims in the Wilderness: Community, Modernity, and the Maypole at Merry Mount

On the face of it, the tale of the Maypole at Merry Mount seems almost too trivial to take seriously. In all Plymouth Colony, where it begins, there were only about two hundred people at the time. At Thomas Morton's trading post there were seven. Morton eventually left Massachusetts without leaving a lasting trace, and Plymouth never amounted to much either. A generation later it still had but a thousand inhabitants, scuffling for a living on a stubborn shore. A generation after that, it faded from formal political existence altogether, in the imperial embrace of Massachusetts Bay.

On the face of it, as well, the tale seems too vulgar to bear any weight of interpretation. A comic-opera army under Miles Standish first arrested Morton by a ruse, then lost him by drunken ineptitude, then recovered him because the men at his post themselves proved "over-armed with drink." No one on either side displayed any discernible courage or tactical aptitude, and no one suffered any heroic hurt. The sole casualty was one of Morton's inebriated comrades, who "ran his own nose upon the point of a sword" held by a Pilgrim soldier and lost "a little of his hot blood." [1]

Yet American poets, playwrights, and novelists have always seen something immensely suggestive in this tawdry contretemps. Nathaniel Hawthorne thought that "the future complexion of New England was

From *New England Quarterly* 50 (1977): 255–77.
1. William Bradford, *Of Plymouth Plantation 1620–1647,* ed. Samuel Eliot Morison (New York, 1959), 209, 210. Spelling, in this and subsequent quotations, is modernized.

involved" in the struggle of "grizzly saints" and "gay sinners," and others have seen still more: a portent of the very fate of the nation implicit in the conflict.[2]

American historians have gone over this ground more gingerly than the poets, perhaps because the historical record is so thin. There are, essentially, only two accounts of the affair: those of Morton and Governor Bradford, the chief antagonists. Between them there is little agreement. But history often becomes engaging at exactly the point where, if we would approach the past at all, we must deal in inference more than in certainties. The defects of the record may be precisely our opportunity.

It is not difficult to establish the outlines of Morton's American career. He arrived in New England in 1625, as a minor partner of Captain Wollaston in a private colonizing venture. When Wollaston departed for Virginia with most of the company's men, whose terms of service he sold there, Morton persuaded the remaining few to stir themselves before they too were summoned. Together with them, he ousted the lieutenant left in the master's stead and took over the plantation, renaming it Merry Mount. He fell to "frisking" with the Indian women of the vicinity and carousing with the Indian men. He revived the roisterous English holidays of old. And, withal, he prospered in the fur trade, even to the point of out-maneuvering the Pilgrim traders themselves for the furs of the Kennebec. Then, in the spring of 1628, he was arrested by the Plymouth authorities and deported to England, ostensibly for selling guns to the Indians. A little more than a year later he returned, was arrested again under the auspices of the new colony at Massachusetts Bay, and was banished once more to England. Finally, over a decade after that, he came back again, was taken prisoner yet another time, and died shortly after his release from jail.[3]

In itself, such a recital hardly suggests anything remarkable. Hundreds of forgotten soldiers of fortune must have endured as much in an

---

2. Nathaniel Hawthorne, "The Maypole of Merry Mount," in *Twice-Told Tales* (Boston and New York, 1895), 78.

3. On Morton's career, see Charles Banks, "Thomas Morton of Merry Mount," Massachusetts Historical Society, *Proceedings* 58 (1924–1925): 147–92; Charles Francis Adams, Jr., "Thomas Morton of Merry-Mount," in Thomas Morton, *New English Canaan* (Boston, 1883), 1–98; and Charles Francis Adams, *Three Episodes of Massachusetts History* (Boston and New York, 1892), 162–250 and *passim*. For a nice explication of the rich punning implicit in the name Merry Mount, see Richard Slotkin, *Regeneration through Violence* (Middletown, Conn., 1973). The reference to "frisking" is in Bradford, *Plymouth Plantation*, 205.

age of European upheaval and ambition. But Morton was a remarkable man, and not merely because his learning and wit were beyond Pilgrim powers to fathom, nor even because he seems to have been the only man who ever flew falcons at quarry in colonial Massachusetts. The very savagery of his treatment at the hands of the Pilgrim fathers and the Puritan magistracy suggests that they knew all too well that in his freedom there was something extraordinary at stake.

The Pilgrims took Morton prisoner on charges they knew to be untenable at law. They "disposed of what he had at his plantation" before so much as sending him to England to stand trial. And not content with dispossessing him before indicting him, they tried to kill him under cover of judicial process. They left him for a month at the Isles of Shoals to await an outward-bound fishing vessel, alone in the chill spring of northern New England with only "the thin suit" on his back and only his bare hands with which to defend himself and forage for food.[4]

The Puritans proceeded even more eagerly and even less legally. Endicott and his advance guard cut down Morton's maypole before they secured their own settlement at Salem for the winter. Governor Winthrop and his assistants ordered Morton arrested at their first court in America, on a warrant so unlawful that evidence of its employment had to be kept out of the colony records, and found him guilty at their second court, on charges so specious that even a Puritan apologist called them "trumped up." The judges then sentenced him to be set in the stocks, stripped of his properties, imprisoned, and banished; and more, they delayed burning down his house until his departure, so that he had to see the spectacle as he sailed into exile.[5]

Morton did not venture again to New England for almost fifteen years. But in England he wrote a maliciously witty book about his misadventures, which the men of Massachusetts remembered. When he turned up in Boston in 1644—a mere shadow of himself, unable, on one account, to "procure the least respect" and reduced to living so "meanly" that he had to be "content to drink water"—the magistrates threw the book at him. For his temerity in complaining against their administration, in his tract and in an indiscreet letter they had saved for a decade against the possibility of his return, they ordered that he be fined prohibitively and imprisoned indefinitely, "that the country might be satisfied of the justice of our [former] proceeding against him." And

---

4. Morton, *New English Canaan*, 287, 289.
5. Adams, "Thomas Morton of Merry-Mount," 46 and, more generally, 45–47.

where the Pilgrims had failed, the Puritans succeeded in judicial execution. They kept him to his cell for a year, in irons, without a fire or bedding, and the dank New England winter did their dirty work for them. When he was released—because he had become "a charge to the country"—his health was broken and his death close at hand.[6]

# I

The essential questions, therefore, are what drove Pilgrims and Puritans alike to their venomous pursuit of the man? and what impelled them to the exaction of such condign punishment?

The answer that the Pilgrims offered was that Morton sold guns and powder to the Indians. Such traffic was sufficient reason to restrain him because, as they said, their own survival in the New World depended upon their ability to keep the natives cowed. Indians with European arms would be "a terror unto them."[7]

Yet the Pilgrim fathers need no more be taken at their own estimation than any other men. They were not above self-serving fabrication, they lied infamously to cover up their massacre of the Indians at Wessagusset in 1622, and it is at least an interesting coincidence that Morton was himself first taken captive by their forces at Wessagusset.

It must be mentioned, then, that the Indians got guns from the English, and the French and the Dutch, before they got any from Thomas Morton. They got them from coasting fishermen and traders, and they got them in great plenty. By the summer of 1627 there were guns among the Massachusetts Indians "both north and south all the land over."[8]

It must be added that the Indians continued to get guns long after Morton was gone. Bradford lamented in 1640 that they were "too well furnished with pieces by too much remissness," and others echoed his plaint a generation later. It was European cupidity that supplied the Indians with arms and ammunition, and the Pilgrim leaders knew it.

6. Edward Winslow to John Winthrop, Massachusetts Historical Society, *Collections*, 4th ser., 6 (1863): 175; John Winthrop, *The History of New England from 1630 to 1649* (Boston, 1825), 2:189, 192; Samuel Maverick to the Earl of Clarendon, New York Historical Society, *Collections*, 2 (1869): 40–41. See also Adams, *Three Episodes*, 343–51.

7. Bradford, *Plymouth Plantation*, 208 and, generally, 207–9.

8. Bradford to Sir Ferdinando Gorges, Massachusetts Historical Society, *Collections*, 1st ser., 3 (1794): 63–64.

They simply could not—or would not—assail the itinerant traders whose provisions were so welcome at their straggling settlement. They could not—or would not—search their own company for the few who put private advantage before public safety.[9]

It must also be said that when Morton returned to New England in 1629, reinstalled himself at his old estate, and resumed the fur trade without providing any arms to the natives, he was hounded as relentlessly and sentenced as summarily by the lords of Boston as he had been by the masters of Plymouth.

And more than all of that, it must be observed that the Indians were simply not the threat that the Pilgrims proclaimed. Even if they had been outfitted by Morton, they were little likely to have destroyed the English settlements. It was not their style. A decade later they had still not learned from the Europeans the art of total war. The Narragansetts who fought alongside the New Englanders against the Pequots were appalled by the ferocity of their allies. "It is naught, it is naught," they insisted. "It is too furious and slays too many men." The aims of extermination that the Pilgrims attributed to the natives were, at that early date, more nearly projections of English intentions than reflections of northern Indian realities.[10] The colony advertised its actions in the name of national security, but it stood in almost no immediate danger. Bradford betrayed as much when he maintained that, in apprehending Morton, his men had merely acceded to appeals for help from outlying inhabitants, since his own colonists "themselves had least cause of fear or hurt."[11] The truth would seem to be that the Pilgrims were not, and knew they were not, in the imminent jeopardy they professed. We must seek elsewhere for the sources of their agitation.

On first inspection, such sources appear to be obvious enough. Merry Mount flourished in the fur trade while Plymouth struggled unavailingly with its immense and mysteriously multiplying debt to the English merchants. Eight Undertakers had recently assumed that debt

9. Bradford to Winthrop, Massachusetts Historical Society, *Collections,* 4th ser., 6 (1863): 159; Nathaniel Morton, *New England's Memorial,* 6th ed. (Boston, 1855), 89–94, esp. 92.

10. John Underhill, *News from America,* Massachusetts Historical Society, *Collections,* 3d ser., 6 (1837): 27, and cf. 26. On the ideology and technology of warfare among the New England Indians, see, e.g., Patrick Malone, "Changing Military Technology among the Indians of Southern New England, 1600–1677," *American Quarterly* 25 (1973): 48–63; Gary Nash, *Red, White, and Black* (Englewood Cliffs, N.J., 1974), 84–85; Larzer Ziff, *Puritanism in America* (New York, 1973), 90–92.

11. Bradford, *Plymouth Plantation,* 209.

personally, in return for a six-year monopoly of the Indian trade; in some measure these leading men had to meet Morton's competition or go bankrupt. And upon his brief remigration to Massachusetts in 1629, Morton managed profits of "six and seven for one," while the traders under Salem's aegis were losing money. The disparity could hardly have diminished Endicott's animosity.[12]

Yet for all that, economic antagonism alone cannot explain the savagery of the saints. Endicott vented his fury on Merry Mount before Morton had even arrived again at his "nest." Bradford lost his composure at the merest recollection of his adversary, whereas he managed to accept with some equanimity the recession of his colony into the economic shade of the new giant to the north.[13]

Morton must, therefore, have touched the men of Plymouth and Boston very deeply. More even than he menaced their lives or livelihoods, he must somehow have threatened what they lived for. And in that regard there were immense dissimilitudes between the saints of Massachusetts and the rakes and roughnecks of Merry Mount, in their aspirations, assumptions, and ways of being.

## II

Among the most elemental of these was a striking divergence in their attitudes to the land itself. Morton found a fierce joy in ranging over its craggy hills and sailing its chilly waters. He exulted in its wildlife, insisting again and again that its fowl or fish or fruits were bigger or better or sweeter than those of the mother country. He even held its beaver superior to the golden fleece of antiquity. And in his evocations and exaggerations, he gave us almost the only natural history of New England that we have for the first half-century of its settlement.[14]

12. Bradford, *Plymouth Plantation,* 187, 194–96; Samuel Eliot Morison, *The Story of the "Old Colony" of New Plymouth, 1620–1692* (New York, 1956), 107–8; Morton, *New English Canaan,* 307–8.

13. Bradford, *Plymouth Plantation,* 206–8.

14. Morton, *New English Canaan,* 180–81, 182, 182–83, 185, 186, 187, 188, 189–90, 190, 193, 194, 201, 202–3, 203, 295. For similar comparisons with Virginia, see 225, 228–29, 231–32, 233, 264–66, 273–76.

The orthodox, on the other hand, either ignored their new environment—Winthrop confided in one of his first letters home that, "for the country itself, I can discern little difference between it and our own"—or disparaged it. Settlers grumbled that the water was "not wholesome," that the earth was "barren" and bore "no grass," and that the mosquitoes were unbearable. They were terrified by wolves and bears and convinced that they heard lions "roaring exceedingly" in the woods.[15] And they remained ill at ease for decades, complaining of their "hazardous . . . banishment" in "remote" parts after twenty or thirty years in the New World.[16]

Morton might conceive the land as a Canaan, but proper Pilgrims and Puritans never could. They knew too well that no earthly habitation could be, as he supposed, a "paradise." They felt too keenly that no country could be, as he declared, "nature's masterpiece." For they were certain that, in every country alike, men would suffer, sin, and die. Morton saw his domain as a setting of sensual splendor and delight. The people of Plymouth and Massachusetts Bay believed that nature everywhere was corrupt and had to be subdued.[17]

An almost identical conflict of convictions obtained in regard to the Indians. Morton sought the company of the natives because he found them more "full of humanity" and "more friendly" than the "precise separatists." He implied that the "infidels" were creatures of profound innocence, as Calvinists could not, and he asserted that they bore true "love toward the English," as the Christians would not.[18] For Pilgrims and Puritans ultimately preferred to meet the Indians in relations of hostility and conquest.

Morton made his distinctive identification evident by repudiating the convention that the writers of Plymouth and Boston all embraced, of a land unemployed if not empty—"fruitful and fit for habitation, being devoid of all civil inhabitants," as Bradford put it—before the advent of the English. He gave over the first third of his *New English Canaan* to the "Manners and Customs" of the aborigines; and even in

15. Winthrop, *History of New England,* 1:375; Bradford, *Plymouth Plantation,* 143–44; Morton, *New English Canaan,* 208n, 214n.

16. "Governor Bradford's Third Dialogue," Massachusetts Historical Society, *Proceedings,* 1st ser., 11 (1870): 461–62; see also, e.g., William Bradford, "Verses," ibid., 465, and Bradford, *Plymouth Plantation,* 62.

17. Morton, *New English Canaan,* 180, 109; see also 122, 179–80, 180–81, 230, 241–42.

18. Ibid., 123, 256, 273, 280, 115; see also, e.g., 137, 270, 289, 312, 313, 344.

his history itself, he proceeded initially from the perspective of the na-tives, where Bradford, Winthrop, and the other chroniclers of early New England began in the Old World.[19]

He also made his allegiance evident in his management of the trading station at Merry Mount. He gave the Indians salt, and taught them how to use it to preserve food for the winter, as gladly as he sold them guns and taught them how to use those. For his was a comprehensive relation of sharing with the Indians, not only a commercial interest specific to pieces and pelts. And his sharing extended to other intimacies. He and his men ate and drank with the Indians, spoke their language, and kept sexual company with them.

All of this was much too much for Bradford and his solemn band— or Winthrop and his—to tolerate. It stirred the very specter of instinc-tual abandon that they had hoped to exorcise in their movement to a new land. For if Morton and his cohorts could fall so easily into bar-barism, might not even saints slip? Who was to say that the demonic descent into primitivity that had occurred at Merry Mount could not happen elsewhere in New England?

Thus the very existence of the post challenged what Richard Slotkin has called the "psychological commitment" of the orthodox colonists "to maintain an English identity" and "to resist acculturation to the In-dian's world." It compelled such settlers to redouble their determination to avert all appearance of nativization and of the debasement of racial amalgamation that they took to be its inevitable symptom and symbolic seal.[20]

They did so by keeping their distance from the natives, psychically as well as strategically. Bradford believed the Indians a "cruel, barbarous, and most treacherous" people before he left Leyden, and he clung doggedly to that opinion to the end of his days.[21] His followers expected the worst of the woodland dwellers too, and they could not even conceive "how we should find or meet with any . . . except it be to do us a mischief." And Pilgrims and Puritans alike displayed a garrison mentality that led them to enclose their compounds "with a good strong pale" and to build forts "where they kept constant watch."[22]

19. Bradford, *Plymouth Plantation,* 25; Morton, *New English Canaan,* 115, 243–45.

20. Slotkin, *Regeneration through Violence,* 64.

21. Bradford, *Plymouth Plantation,* 26. See also 25, 62, 70, 83–84; Bradford, "Verses," 465–66, 467.

22. Dwight Heath, ed., *A Journal of the Pilgrims at Plymouth: Mourt's Relation* (New York, 1963), 35–36; Bradford, *Plymouth Plantation,* 96–97, 111. See also James Axtell,

These images of the native population that the men of Massachusetts held were, as Gary Nash has shrewdly observed, ways of "predicting the future, preparing for it, and justifying what one would do, even before one caused it to happen."[23] So the Pilgrims initiated relations with the Indians by stealing all the corn and seed they could carry away, robbing unattended wigwams, and desecrating a native grave. In a couple of years they massacred a number of preeminent Indian warriors, in an ambush so appalling that their beloved minister in Leyden was dismayed enough to protest, "necessity of this . . . I see not."[24] The Puritans came with warnings to be "wise as serpents" in dealing with the Indians and with instructions from the company to have every man "exercised in the use of arms." In a few years the Bay colonists launched a campaign to "conquer and subdue" the natives, a campaign that claimed hundreds of aboriginal lives.[25]

In the beginning and in the end, aggression was the method the Pilgrims and Puritans preferred in their transactions with the Indians. And on just that account, Morton's offense was that he met the natives in a different and more erotic mode. The authorities in the colonies were quite willing to concede that the savages would be uninhibited brutes,[26] but their sense of civilized identity was deeply disoriented by the discovery that such sensual excess could find an answering amorality among Englishmen. Morton forced upon them their most haunting anxieties, that immersion in the wilderness and association with the Indian would weaken the discipline they maintained so tenuously over their own impulses. For his debauchery was still another of his elemental differences with the magistracy of Massachusetts. The saints were as scandalized by his licentiousness as they were terrified by his having gone native.

There has been an effort in recent scholarship to exculpate the men and women of early Massachusetts of "puritanical" attitudes toward the pleasures of the flesh. But the effort has been basically misconceived. It has been founded on the fact that seventeenth-century Puritans did accept sexual desire within marriage, and it founders on the fact that such

"Through a Glass Darkly: Colonial Attitudes toward the Native Americans," *Essays from Sarah Lawrence Faculty* 2, no. 1 (Oct., 1973): 3–24.

23. Nash, *Red, White, and Black,* 40.

24. Bradford, *Plymouth Plantation,* 375; ibid., 65, 66; Alden Vaughan, *New England Frontier: Puritans and Indians, 1620 to 1675* (Boston, 1965), 66–67; Morton, *New English Canaan,* 170; George Willison, *Saints and Strangers* (New York, 1945), 223–24.

25. Alexander Young, ed., *Chronicles of the First Planters of the Colony of Massachusetts Bay* (Boston, 1846), 136, 156–57; Ziff, *Puritanism in America,* 90–92.

26. See, e.g., Bradford, "Verses," 466.

acceptance was merely one of the many strange fruits of a religious outlook that was, exactly as its critics always contended, inimical to the gratifications of the senses.

Puritans could not countenance carnal pleasure for its own sake any more than they could countenance art or anything else for its own sake. They believed that God had appointed the things of the earth only as instruments of His own glory, and they held that it was sinful to take such means as ends in themselves. "All experience" was, for them, "given of God" and had therefore to "have some reason behind it."[27]

So the saints emphasized relentlessly the purposefulness in their pastimes. And in the realm of eros the purpose was procreation alone. Massachusetts law made all coition outside wedlock a crime, often a capital crime, and Massachusetts morality made immodest passion impermissible even within the wedded state. For sexual expression had always to be limited to utility. Puritan handbooks warned against intemperate adventure in the marriage bed. They bid husband and helpmate be wary of "wanton speeches" and "foolish dalliance" with each other, insisting as they did that the man might "play the adulterer with his own wife . . . by inordinate affection and action."[28]

Thomas Hooker spoke from the heart of this antipathy to instinctual abandon when he said, "I know there is wild love and joy enough in the world, as there is wild thyme and other herbs, but we would have garden love and garden joy, of God's own planting." Winthrop similarly exhorted his son incessantly against "the lusts of youth, which are commonly covered under the name of recreations." And though the Pilgrims were never such eloquent moralists as the Puritans, they were only a little less careful of the heats of the flesh. They went out of their way to banish an adulterous minister who "satisfied his lust" on women yet "endeavored to hinder conception." They executed a man for bestiality—with "a mare, a cow, two goats, diverse sheep, two calves, and a turkey"—and they wondered all the while how such conduct was possible in a society where transgressions were "so much witnessed against, and so narrowly looked into."[29]

27.  Perry Miller, *The New England Mind: The Seventeenth Century* (Boston, 1961), 39; see also 41, 51–52, 179, 213, 257–59, 261; Charles H. and Katherine George, *The Protestant Mind of the English Reformation* (Princeton, N.J., 1961), 271–72; Max Weber, *The Protestant Ethic and the Spirit of Capitalism* (New York, 1958).

28.  George Haskins, *Law and Authority in Early Massachusetts* (New York, 1960), 145–51; George and George, *The Protestant Mind*, 272.

29.  Miller, *The New England Mind: The Seventeenth Century*, 48; Winthrop, *History of New England*, 1:338 and *passim*; Bradford, *Plymouth Plantation*, 166–69; George Lang-

Modern demographic evidence suggests that the Pilgrims well might have been inquisitive about the sexual affairs of others, since they were themselves so frequently self-denying. Extended intervals of abstinence marked the mature careers even of the married couples who were the only ones allowed a legitimate sexual outlet in Plymouth.[30] And among such men and women, it is easy to imagine that Morton and his concupiscent crew might have been more than a little provocative. They made no effort to be circumspect about their amorous escapades. They kept open house for Indian women. And they paraded their impertinence, as in Morton's advertisement for the beaver as an aphrodisiac "of such masculine virtue that if some of our ladies [in London] knew the benefit thereof, they would desire to have ships sent of purpose to trade for the tail alone."[31]

The men of Massachusetts could hardly have seen in such unsuppressed sensualism anything but the most terrifying portents of the collapse of European civility. And it was indeed in carnal terms that they conceived Morton's malefactions. The Pilgrims reacted extravagantly to the fertility rites of the May Day celebrations at Merry Mount. Endicott complained of the "profane and dissolute living" there, and he razed the offending Maypole. The Massachusetts Bay Company, still in London, directed the settling of "some good orders . . . to prevent a world of disorders, and many grievous sins and sinners." The magistrates, in Massachusetts, expressly prosecuted Morton as a "libertine," and Winthrop himself called for condemnation so that "the habitation of the wicked" would "no more appear in Israel."[32]

## III

Winthrop's concern that corruption not contaminate his holy land also hinted at other divergences between the saints and the traders, in religious beliefs and practices, in attitudes to festivity, and in conceptions of community. For the leaders of the Plymouth and Boston

don, *Pilgrim Colony: A History of New Plymouth from 1620 to 1691* (New Haven, Conn., 1966), 64.

30. John Demos, "Notes on Life in Plymouth Colony," *William and Mary Quarterly,* 3rd ser., 22 (1965): 270–71.

31. Morton, *New English Canaan,* 162; see also 205.

32. Young, *Chronicles of Massachusetts,* 83–84, 187–88; Adams, "Thomas Morton of Merry-Mount," 48; Winthrop, *History of New England,* 1:35n.

expeditions alike aspired to see their followers "knit together."[33] Bradford, maintaining again and again the imperative of mutual love, found parables everywhere of the success men might anticipate when they lived "compact together" and the abject failure they could expect when each "pursued his own ends" or followed the promptings of "self-love." He affirmed on exactly such account the necessity that "those that were . . . incorrigible" be "purged off" when "no other means would serve," and he urged an "exemplary punishment" for Morton.[34] The Puritans similarly strove to avoid contamination "by the evil conversation of any," and men such as Endicott never hesitated to make "one exemplary, that others might fear."[35]

It was as if the authorities sensed that others mocked them, that, as Hawthorne expressed it, "when a psalm was pealing from their place of worship, the echo which the forest sent them back seemed often like the chorus of a jolly catch, closing with a roar of laughter."[36] Just such a sense made the merest presence of Morton and his kind intolerable, and many men and women—no one has ever tallied exactly how many— were expelled from Massachusetts in its early decades by men who would admit neither laughter nor significant dissidence. For the rogues who inclined to sexual license, religious deviation, or insubordination represented the very specter that the saints dreaded, of degeneration into a savage Babel of controversy and indiscipline.

Plymouth drove off some of these miscreants, such as John Lyford, Roger Williams, and Samuel Gorton, for fomenting faction. It exiled others, such as a Mr. Fells and his maidservant, and "those that belonged unto" Fells, for fornicating and for keeping company with the fornicators.[37] Massachusetts Bay dispatched even more, for even more varied motives. The authorities in Boston also banished Williams and Gorton, and the Child petitioners, and Hutchinson, Wheelwright, and a host of their Antinomian adherents. They forced many "infected with Anabaptism" to remove from the colony. They turned back the Quakers, mutilated the ones who returned, and hanged the ones who re-

33. Bradford, *Plymouth Plantation*, 33; Perry Miller and Thomas Johnson, eds., *The Puritans* (New York, 1963), 198.
34. Bradford, *Plymouth Plantation*, 87, 107, 54, 18, 208; see also 33, 75, 76–78, 78–79, 116, 118–19, 133, 140–41, 149, 151–52, 160, 192.
35. Winthrop, *History of New England*, 1:348; Robert Wall, *Massachusetts Bay: The Crucial Decade* (New Haven, Conn., 1972), 143.
36. Hawthorne, "The Maypole of Merry Mount," 78.
37. Bradford, *Plymouth Plantation*, 192. Bradford, 146–69; Langdon, *Pilgrim Colony*, 63.

turned again. They shipped Christopher Gardiner to England because he kept two wives and got along too well with the Indians. They disfranchised John Underhill and urged him on to New Hampshire because he defended Anne Hutchinson and trusted enough in the free grace she promised to indulge in adultery.[38] And they sent off any number of others who would be quite unknown to history had they not been banished, for "contempt of authority" or for "scandalous invectives" against the established order.[39]

Indeed, Morton himself was brought to book for withholding a suitable subordination to duly constituted superiors. When Endicott gathered all the old planters within the company's patent in 1629 to tell them that they had to submit to his authority, and that "he that should refuse to subscribe, must pack," Morton did not subscribe. In less than a year, the Master of Revels was sent packing.[40]

At the time, Morton wondered why such submission was necessary in a land vast enough for enormous armies, where tens of thousands could coexist without needing even to "contend for room for their cattle." Since that time, at least a few historians have marveled too. Conjuring "an immeasurable wilderness," all but "unbroken . . . from the Penobscot to the Hudson," Charles Francis Adams pointed the essential paradox, that "that wilderness, though immeasurable to them, was not large enough for both." The company had formally instructed Endicott that "all must live under government and a like law," and Endicott was only too willing to carry out his instructions.[41]

And in the end all the inhabitants of Massachusetts, red as well as white, did indeed swear subjection to powers such as Salem's. Saints and strangers alike pledged a "due submission and obedience" in 1620. The Wampanoags offered obeisance in a 1621 treaty that established the supremacy of English law upon the land and laid unreciprocated obligations upon the Indians in three of its seven articles. Isolated adventur-

38. Winthrop, *History of New England,* 2:123–24. For Gorton, see Perry Miller, *Orthodoxy in Massachusetts 1630–1650* (Boston, 1959), 283–86; Wall, *The Crucial Decade,* 121–56. For Gardiner, see Winthrop, *History of New England,* 1:54–55; Thomas Prince, *Annals of New England,* Massachusetts Historical Society, *Collections,* 2d ser., 7, pt. 2 (1818): 27–28; Morton, *New English Canaan,* 338–42. For Underhill, see Slotkin, *Regeneration through Violence,* 70–71.

39. Nathaniel Shurtleff, ed., *Records of the Governor and Company of the Massachusetts Bay in New England* (Boston, 1853–1854), 1:86; Winthrop, *History of New England,* 1:56; Morton, *New English Canaan,* 316–20.

40. Morton, *New English Canaan,* 306.

41. Ibid., 306; Adams, *Three Episodes,* 182; Young, *Chronicles of Massachusetts,* 158.

ers were brought to heel, or banished, because the authorities did not feel it fit for men to live "so remote" from governance.[42]

Historians ordinarily apologize, at this point, that the insistence on orthodoxy in Massachusetts was nothing more than the common coin of the age. But in the New World, uniformity was neither the norm nor the operative ideal. Virginia allowed a great many "hundreds" or "particular plantations." Bermuda was largely colonized on the basis of such substantial land grants and the local immunities they conferred. Maryland provided havens for Catholics as well as Protestants. And a little later in the century, Carolina would be founded on a plan for plural jurisdictions and Pennsylvania conceived as a congeries of disparate communities in mutual toleration.

Even in Massachusetts, men such as Morton were willing to live and let live, though the invincible earnestness of the saints must have irritated him as much as his hedonism offended them. More than that, his outfitting of the Indians worked to preserve their hegemony over their accustomed hunting grounds intact, whereas the Pilgrims and Puritans, by opposing such supply, aimed to take control wholly into their own hands. And the Indians themselves also thought intuitively to divide sovereignty. So far from harboring thieves and runaway servants, as the English feared, they brought them back to the English settlements to be dealt with by English procedures.[43]

Only the powers at Plymouth and Boston sought a single law to rule all the land. Only they aimed at a single way of living. Avid for command, they imputed a lust to "domineer" to the Indians. Acutely tuned to aggressive modes, they chose to truck with those tribes by arms and by awe rather than by sex and strong liquor. Morton's methods of familiarity led to a "league of brotherhood" with the natives; the Pilgrims' operations at a distance tended as if inexorably to the Indian wars of the seventeenth century and to that time in the eighteenth century when Amherst would encourage his officers to spread smallpox among the Algonkians to put down the revolt of Pontiac.[44]

A similar sense of living apart, in relations only of dominion and deference, enabled leaders of the saints to treat other Englishmen too as "them that [were] without" and to oppress any whom they thus deemed

42. Bradford, *Plymouth Plantation*, 76; Axtell, "Through a Glass Darkly," 6; Morton, *New English Canaan*, 340.

43. Adams, *Three Episodes*, 78; Vaughan, *New England Frontier*, 43–44.

44. Bradford, *Plymouth Plantation*, 96–97; Morton, *New English Canaan*, 289; Francis Parkman, *The Conspiracy of Pontiac* (Boston, 1924), 2:44–46.

"carnal." For against those outside their circle of solidarity, "whatsoever could be thought . . . was urged." The Pilgrims thought nothing of neglecting the law in their arraignment of Morton, because they believed that any capitulation to his invulnerable legal position "would only make him far more haughty and insolent."[45]

Indeed, in their apprehension of the Deity Himself, in whom all attributes were theoretically in perfect parity, the Puritans still placed "more emphasis upon one attribute than upon any other—upon that of sovereignty." And on the assurance inherent in their derived deification of their own authority, the Massachusetts magistrates set themselves as moral wardens of the world, or at least as much of it as lay within their grasp. They could set the law aside because they saw themselves as instruments of divine policy. They never doubted their rectitude when they exchanged legal technicalities with Morton and lost. They merely changed tactics, since there was then "no way to take him but by force."[46]

The truth is that force was rarely far from the fore in the thoughts of the governing officials of New England. Convinced as they were of men's mortal depravity, they could hardly imagine a polity premised on trust. They took Indians to be perfidious and treacherous, and they took others much nearer to be unreliable besides. Bradford reflected endlessly on cases of betrayal and instances of evil returned for good. He reminded himself ceaselessly to place his hopes in God rather than in men. And he pointed as if in every tale the somber moral: "the uncertainty of all human things and what little cause there is of joying in them or trusting to them."[47]

Given those beliefs, men such as Bradford had to abjure most of the deepest sources and expressions of such joy and trust. As Max Weber observed, Puritans put "every purely emotional, that is not rationally motivated, personal relation . . . under the suspicion of idolatry of the flesh." Just as they distrusted sensuality for its own sake, so they scorned the mingling of souls merely for the sake of personal fulfillment, bringing friendship too before the bar of rational purpose.[48] And because

---

45. Morton, *New English Canaan*, 318; Bradford, *Plymouth Plantation*, 209.

46. Miller, *The New England Mind: The Seventeenth Century*, 14; Bradford, *Plymouth Plantation*, 209.

47. Bradford, *Plymouth Plantation*, 117; see also 10, 11, 11–12, 12–14, 30–31, 34–35, 46, 53–54, 61–63, 94, 107, 110, 118–19, 119, 124–25, 135–36, 147–51, 152–53, 170, 177, 180, 199–200.

48. Weber, *The Protestant Ethic*, 224.

they could allow no relations among men but rationally purposive ones, they spurned the ceremonies and celebrations in which men had long linked themselves to one another in affective communion. Puritans in the mother country railed endlessly against the revelries of "merrie olde England" as popish motes in God's eye. Puritans in New England wasted no time in abolishing such rituals. When a band of young men tried to mark the Christmas holidays in 1621, Bradford informed them that their frivolities were "against his conscience" and confined them to their quarters for private devotion. "Since that time," as he recalled in serene satisfaction, "nothing hath been attempted that way, at least openly."[49]

Anthropologists and even a few historians are now acutely aware of the role of ritual in binding a group together.[50] In a very real sense, the decay of the medieval English community can be traced by the attrition of its traditional festivals. So Morton's Maypole was no insignificant annoyance in the Puritan view. The merriment of which it was a token was itself emblematic of a much more portentous clash of consciousness.

Puritan antagonism to festivity was as much at the center of the saints' differences with Morton as divergent attitudes and interests regarding trade, land, Indians, or the flesh. Morton himself never fully understood how hugely his revival of the orgies of the May grated on Puritanical sensibilities. He spoke of his saturnalia as merely a "harmless mirth made by young men," and he scoffed at the Separatists for "troubling their brains more than reason would require about things that are indifferent."[51] But even he knew that his difficulties in Massachusetts dated from the day he hoisted the Maypole,[52] while we in retrospect may see how superbly that shaft symbolized at once the phallic eroticism, the interracial amity, and the attachment to ancient festivities that so infuriated the Pilgrims and—because it afforded a beacon for coasting traders—the commercial rivalry that so threatened Pilgrim business interests.

Since the Pilgrims and Puritans could not, finally, place their trust in friends and neighbors, and since they could allow themselves so little of the social cement that shared ritual might have provided, they could

49. Bradford, *Plymouth Plantation*, 97.
50. See, e.g., Keith Thomas, "History and Anthropology," *Past and Present* 24 (1963): 3–24.
51. Morton, *New English Canaan*, 280.
52. Ibid., 278.

hardly maintain the social solidarity for which they yearned. They sought communal unity more strongly—more rationally, more ideologically—than it had ever been sought in England, but they denied themselves the mundane relations by which such assent and attachment are secured. Inevitably, then, they suspected that their communities could be held together only by authority, so that the maintenance of authority became—at least in the eyes of the authorities—a means of clinging to the only control that could be attained in a world where nothing and no one could be counted on.

In such a context, offenses against authority were the most dire of all; and Morton's offenses were manifold. He rejected the jurisdiction of Plymouth and bested its officials in their epistolary exchange of legal niceties. He disdained the suzerainty of the Massachusetts Bay Company when Endicott called all the old settlers to submission. He made a mockery of the magisterial pretensions of both colonies in the book for which he was imprisoned in 1644.

In fact, he acquired his eminence in the first place by instigating insurrection against the deputy left in charge at Mount Wollaston, thus beginning his American career by dismantling the master–servant dyad on which so much of Massachusetts' social structure was founded. He instituted his own administration of the trading post by abandoning the assumptions of hierarchy and offering instead to "converse, plant, trade, and live together as equals" with the men there. And he managed this casual democracy among comrades in the teeth of the insistence of Puritan potentates that "God almighty in His most holy and wise providence" had ordained that a few men be "high and eminent in power and dignity" while the mass of men were "mean and in subjection."[53]

The pillars of the Puritan settlements held steadfastly to precepts of order and authority and assumptions that only "wild creatures" would "ordinarily love the liberty of the woods." They could not conceive of freedom except on terms of submission to masters and participation in the common fate. So men and women on their own were indigestible elements in the Massachusetts craw. As Winthrop would one day declare, those who "lived under no government . . . grew very offensive."[54]

The magistrates therefore allowed only such freedom as was itself a

53. Bradford, *Plymouth Plantation*, 204–5; Miller and Johnson, eds., *The Puritans*, 195.

54. Alan Heimert, "Puritanism, the Wilderness, and the Frontier," *New England Quarterly* 26 (1953): 369n; Winthrop, *History of New England*, 2:84.

means of social control. The Mayflower Compact was, as Bradford admitted, an expedient to avert individual autonomy. It was drafted only because, by "discontented and mutinous speeches," a few of the "strangers" aboard the ship let slip that "when they came ashore they would use their liberty, for none had power to command them." Winthrop's speech aboard the *Arbella,* and the social covenants with which the Puritans established their civil and ecclesiastical regime in the New World, served similarly to bind potential isolates to the authority of magistracy and ministerium. For the founders of New England could comprehend no social order but a solidary one and no way to uphold it but by a sovereignty as absolute as their Lord's.[55]

Morton's ultimate offense, then, was simply to insist upon his own liberty, because in early Massachusetts there was no place for such a man. Inhabitants were not permitted to live alone or even to dwell very far from the center of settlement. They participated in politics only as a privilege conferred by the neighbors to whom they applied for freemanship. They labored largely as servants, subject to all the obligations of their station, in an economy regulated for the public weal. They could not so much as sell their houses or lands without the approval of the community.[56]

In such a society, unbridled pursuit of personal advantage was unthinkable. Or rather, it was thought upon and therefore suppressed the more stridently for being so tempting. Merry Mount provoked the saints precisely because they themselves were not immune to its appeal, precisely because they struggled ambivalently with the heady desires its indiscipline epitomized.

## IV

Thomas Morton was a man whose like New England would not soon see again. And in this as in so much else, New England was aberrant among the American settlements. Men such as Morton were far more evident in other colonies.

55. Bradford, *Plymouth Plantation,* 75–76; Miller and Johnson, eds., *The Puritans,* 195–199; Michael Zuckerman, *Peaceable Kingdoms: New England Towns in the Eighteenth Century* (New York, 1970), 54–55.
56. Edmund Morgan, *The Puritan Family* (New York, 1966), 27, 145–46; Morison, *The Story of the "Old Colony,"* 96, 149; Langdon, *Pilgrim Colony,* 147–50.

Yet in spite of all that, and in spite even of their denials of their own disposition to be free, the Pilgrims and Puritans were agents of a freedom more radical in certain respects than any that Morton represented. They were agents of an unprecedented liberation from tradition.

It was Morton, after all, who bore the culture of the mother country most nearly in colonial New England. It was he who tried to maintain the rituals of the English heritage, he who preached the latitudinarian notions of the English church, he who preserved the bawdy, ebullient spirit of the Elizabethans. And it was just because he did that he drew upon himself the fury of the masters of Massachusetts, who found his lush prose inscrutable, his sensual adventurism abhorrent, and his festivities almost demoniacal.

In their determination to set themselves apart from a ritual patrimony they found appalling, the Puritans launched upon a course destined to conclude in atomism. But of that they were not aware; and by their very entry into the dialectic of severance from the traditional community, their position became more equivocal at each successive lurch to freedom. For exactly as their antipathy to the irrational ties of ceremony and sentiment dissolved community, it also frustrated their own deep need for the support of fellows.

The Puritans' yearning for communal unity was strong, in some part, because their community itself was so fragile. It was bound primarily by bonds of ideology, abstraction, and formal authority, and its thinness and artificiality not only attenuated demands for cohesion but also, at the same time, vastly exaggerated them. Just because the Puritans could sense the corporate solidarity they craved slipping always away from them, they had to bolster it by the most exemplary suppression of all who assailed it too visibly. The inner tendency of Puritanism was fissive. Its outward history was accordingly a chronicle of efforts to arrest that tendency.

But such propensities could not, in the end, be countermanded everywhere. And even as the Pilgrims and Puritans strove to secure orthodoxy and obedience in the symbolically strategic realms of religion and politics, they began to be driven to change in areas they supposed less central. Bit by bit, in Plymouth as much as at the Bay, colonial authorities extended the sphere of private initiative in the economy and its attendant pattern of settlement, because "they saw not how peace would be preserved without so doing."[57]

---

57. Bradford, *Plymouth Plantation*, 187.

In time, the economic enterprise and geographic mobility they thereby condoned would be the ideological undoing of the social order they hoped to uphold. A new pace of dislocation in the mundane relations of daily life would emerge—alongside a continuing conformism of religious and political ideas—and eventually erode the old ideal of close communal control itself. There would still be scant emotional or instinctual freedom in the norms of the nineteenth century, and meager scope for fundamental dissidence in politics or religion in its actual practices, but Americans by then would hardly notice. For the mass of them would conflate freedom for economic endeavor and residential relocation with freedom itself.

# FOUR

# The Family Life of William Byrd

William Byrd was not a callous man, nor an impassive one. He was certainly not crazy. Yet, in the spring of 1710, as his little boy lay dying, he displayed an indifference that is baffling if not bizarre.

For more than three weeks, while his son's fate hung in perilous suspension, Byrd scarcely troubled to try to turn the course of the fatal fever. He hardly bothered to treat the child himself, though he diagnosed and dosed friends and veritable strangers on half a dozen occasions during the same days. He did not call in another local medical expert for almost a week, though he often sought such assistance more speedily when his slaves were sick. And he never asked the man back again, though the erratic oscillations of the illness invited expertise to the very end.[1]

Instead, he simply pursued his ordinary businesses and pleasures. At one point, undeterred by driving rains that left him "wet to the skin," he abandoned the boy for a couple of days of visiting with friends and outlying overseers. At another point, undisturbed by a fleeting thought of his "affliction," he passed his day in playing billiards, gossiping with

From *Perspectives in American History* 12 (1979): 253–311.

1. *The Secret Diary of William Byrd of Westover 1709–1712,* ed. Louis Wright and Marion Tinling (Richmond, Va., 1941), May 12–June 3, 1710. For the three times Byrd treated his son, May 12, 26, 30; for the six times he treated others, May 18, 19, 22, 27, June 2; for his one appeal for outside assistance, May 17; a neighboring woman did come a couple of times, on May 18 and May 27, apparently quite on her own intiative, but Byrd neither consulted her nor followed any directives from her. Unless otherwise indicated, all dates refer to entries in Byrd's diaries.

guests, eating berries, and preparing medicine for a neighbor's gout. At no point did he ever stay up with the child at night or even seem to worry much whether the lad would live or die.[2]

On the day before the fateful one, Byrd looked after an ailing retainer rather than his own firstborn son. On the last evening of the boy's life, Byrd gave up his customary stroll around the plantation to entertain guests rather than to spend a few final hours with his child. On the morning that his son died, Byrd received the news with resignation rather than any discernible distress or grief. "God gives and God takes away," he reasoned; "blessed be the name of God."[3]

Beyond that moment of laconic lamentation, Byrd scarcely seemed affected at all. He did notice that his wife was "much afflicted" and did wish that she might have "submitted . . . better" to the divine design. But then he simply resumed his regular rounds, as if nothing out of the ordinary had happened. He attended to dinner for his house guests. He rued the recurrence of his week-old bellyache. He watched the weather and walked in the garden when the skies cleared in the evening. And he went to bed that night with "good thoughts, and good humor."[4]

The day after the boy's death, Byrd was concerned primarily with his own unsettled stomach. He studied his symptoms closely and recorded his unsuccessful treatment earnestly. He busied himself with letters from his fellow planters. And he never experienced any rush of heavy-heartedness or any flood of feeling. He hardly departed, indeed, from his daily routine, except that he kept an eye on his wife to be sure that she was not unduly moved.[5]

On the day of the funeral, he still remained untouched by any sentiment of calamity. He did refrain from his regular reading in Greek, but only "because [he] prepared to receive company." He did note carefully

---

2. May 15–16, 22, 1710. See also May 25, a week before his boy's death, when all Byrd could think about was his own discomfort in the heat of the Virginia spring.

3. June 2, 3, 1710.

4. June 3, 1710.

5. June 4, 1710. Over the next ten days he monitored his wife's melancholia, noting with approval the occasions when she "kept within the bounds of submission"; see June 5–14, 1710. As for Byrd's bellyache, John Walzer shrewdly suspects that it was a somatic symptom of grief for the lost child ("A Period of Ambivalence: Eighteenth-Century American Childhood," in *The History of Childhood*, ed. Lloyd de Mause [New York, 1974], 359–60). But Walzer may be too clever in his interpretation. Byrd's "gripes" began almost a week before his son died—see May 29 and 31 and June 1 and 2—and even if they were indeed related to the boy's dying, it would seem merely the more significant that Byrd himself was either too obtuse to make the connection or too determined to display unconcern (to himself, in a diary no one else was to see) to acknowledge it.

who came to the ceremony, what he "gave them" to eat and drink, and how late his visitors stayed. He did detail his ministrations to "two of the new negroes" who were "taken sick." But he did not register any emotion at all. Insofar as he reacted to the funeral, he reacted to it as a social occasion. His concern was for the figure he cut, not for the loss he had suffered. The death of his only son belonged, for him, to the sphere of public life, not to the realm of family feelings.[6]

Byrd's indifference to the death of his young child is difficult to assess because it is difficult even to comprehend. By twentieth-century standards of domestic sensibility, his behavior seems to suggest an elemental emotional insufficiency in Byrd rather than any intriguing problems in his conduct. Yet, just because it does, it calls in question the applicability of our standards to Byrd and his fellow planters. So far as we know, none of them found him unfeeling. None of them indicted his disregard of his dying child or even considered him unmindful of the boy. If we would make sense of their acceptance of his actions, we must, by an effort of historical imagination, enlarge our apprehension of expired possibilities so as to see that colonial Americans may have lived within a different framework of familial feeling from our own.

Our most brilliant imagining of such outworn ways is Philippe Ariès's splendid study of European sensibility, *Centuries of Childhood*.[7] In arresting and often ingenious detail, Ariès shows that, prior to early modern times, an extensive interpenetration of public and private spheres prevailed in Western society. Medieval people did not distinguish as we do between the cloistered hearth and the bustling marketplace, nor differentiate as we do between domestic security and civic uncertainty. They pursued their tasks and their gratifications amid the promiscuous minglings of the community, and they raised their children amid its motley throngs as well. Children entered early into a relatively undifferentiated adult life. By the age of six or seven, they were assigned small adult roles and responsibilities, given small adult clothes, admitted to adult games, and made privy to adult jokes. Parents neither pampered them nor held them under loving surveillance, and no one ever mistook them for vessels of innocence and infirmity to be sheltered from the buffetings of a brutal world.

In the very teeth of such indifference and unconcern, Ariès argues, a

6. June 6, 1710.
7. Philippe Ariès, *Centuries of Childhood: A Social History of Family Life* (New York, 1962).

new idea arose among a new elite: the conception of childhood as a distinct stage of life, to be treasured in its own right and for its own sake. At first, this idea appealed only to a few strategic sectors of the population. Later, as it gained ground and even became prescriptive for people whose ancestors would have found it unthinkable, its power became profound and its consequences beyond calculation. When men and women withdrew from the entanglements of the complex community to the privacy of the simple family, to sequester their little ones from the corruptions of the wider world, they forged the modern middle class.

The grandest significances of *Centuries of Childhood* lie in its subtle delineation of the ways in which differentiation of children from elders and isolation of the nuclear family from its social context heralded the specializations and segregations that are at the very center of modernity. But the fascinations of the study lie as fully in its imaginative evocation of the very different modes of the late middle ages. Those fascinations are all the more arresting for their curious capacity to illuminate the family mores and mentality of people who lived hundreds of years later, in the supposed citadels of the new society.

A few scholars have argued that Ariès's account of premodern social sentiment is entirely too imaginative. They have suggested that the medieval heedlessness that he contrasts with the bourgeois passion for order is more nearly an idealized flight of his own fancy than an accurate rendering of historical reality.[8] Yet, in the case of William Byrd, at least, Ariès's reconstruction of premodern sensibility is very far from fiction. Its insights are as applicable to life at Westover in the early eighteenth century as to life in Lyon in the sixteenth century or in Winchester in the fifteenth.

This persistence of premodern modes is remarkable, for Virginia has seemed to many scholars a prime example of the Tocquevillian maxim that America was "born modern." Virginians crossed the Atlantic with as little of the intellectual baggage of earlier epochs as colonists anywhere in the New World. Virginians embarked on a course of exploitative capitalism with as much alacrity, and as little resistance, as settlers anywhere on two continents. So Virginians might have been expected to shed ties to remoter kinsmen and neighbors as well, in favor of the narrow nuclear unit generally held to be the paradigmatic family form of modernity.

---

8. For a fine summary of such second thoughts, see Richard Vann, "The Youth of *Centuries of Childhood*," *History and Theory* 21 (1982): 279–97.

Nevertheless, for the likes of William Byrd, a century of abounding prosperity in the Old Dominion did not in fact foster the development of domestic privatism. Pioneer census takers and tax assessors did assume a nuclear norm in arranging their rolls. Courts took a similar norm for granted in apportioning inheritances, and churches in allocating pews. But they had always done so, in Europe as well as in America. The vast majority of Western households had long been nuclear in their formal composition. The emergence of the middle-class family was less a matter of law and demography than of new feelings infused into older social forms. Medieval families maintained their traditionally communal outlook though they domiciled themselves apart from their fellow villagers. Medieval parents rarely cherished their children, though they generally ate and slept alone with them. In much the same manner William Byrd accepted many conjugal ascriptions and discharged many parental duties without ever appearing to desire intimacy or isolation with his wife and children. His practices and priorities suggest the laggardly advent of a modern familistic sensibility along the James. They also suggest that, for at least a decade, we have been mistaking a deviant family style for the dominant one in early America.

Most accounts of the colonial family have been accounts of the institution in New England, where many of the inhabitants were bearers of an English Puritan ethic of marital affection and possessive privatism characterized by Lawrence Stone as highly unusual in late Elizabethan times.[9] Most of the remaining studies of colonial domesticity have been studies of the Quakers, who were even more absorbed in intense mutual caring and expressive family attachments than the Puritans.[10]

Most of the American colonists, on the other hand, lived outside the orbits of Boston and Philadelphia. We know very little about the family life of these people, and the little we do know pertains more to its external contours than its inner impulses. Yet even the external evidence is sufficient to indicate that settlers in the middle, southern, and Caribbean colonies established their families under very different circum-

9. Lawrence Stone, *The Crisis of the Aristocracy, 1558–1641* (Oxford, 1965), chap. 11, esp. 610–12, 662–64, 669–71.

10. J. William Frost, *The Quaker Family in Colonial America: A Portrait of the Society of Friends* (New York, 1973); Robert Wells, "A Demographic Analysis of Some Middle-Colonies Quaker Families of the Eighteenth Century" (Ph.D. diss., Princeton University, 1969), and "Family Size and Fertility Control in Eighteenth-Century America: A Study of Quaker History," *Population Studies* 25 (1971): 73–82; and esp. Barry Levy, "The Light in the Valley: The Chester and Welsh Tract Quaker Communities and the Delaware Valley, 1681–1750" (Ph.D. diss., University of Pennsylvania, 1976), and "'Tender Plants': Quaker Farmers and Children in the Delaware Valley, 1681–1750," *Journal of Family History* 3 (1978): 116–35.

stances from those prevailing among the relative few who followed the familial precepts of Puritanism or Quakerism. The great majority of Americans lived and died, moved and married, birthed and bequeathed, according to conventions quite unlike those that have been normative in recent scholarship.[11]

By himself, Byrd cannot convince us of such differences. He was hardly even a typical Virginian, let alone a man representative of provincial America at large. But he was never a man at odds with his society or alienated from it. He accepted his situation and was comfortable within

11.  Recent studies of the Quakers take cognizance of, and even vaunt, the distinctiveness of the colonial Quaker family. But much of the literature on the colonial New England family bids, implicitly or explicitly, to be taken as exemplary of all of colonial America, and that pretension simply cannot be sustained, in regard to sex ratios, marriage ages, fertility and family size, mobility, inheritance, and mortality. See, e.g., Stephanie Wolf, *Urban Village: Population, Community, and Family Structure in Germantown, Pennsylvania, 1683–1800* (Princeton, N.J., 1976), chaps. 7–8; Irene Hecht, "The Virginia Muster of 1624/5 as a Source for Demographic History," *William and Mary Quarterly* 30 (1973): 65–92; Edmund S. Morgan, *American Slavery, American Freedom: The Ordeal of Colonial Virginia* (New York, 1975); James Deen, "Patterns of Testation: Four Tidewater Counties in Colonial Virginia," *American Journal of Legal History* 16 (1972): 154–76; Darrett and Anita Rutman, "Of Agues and Fevers: Malaria in the Early Chesapeake," *William and Mary Quarterly* 33 (1976): 31–60; Daniel B. Smith, "Mortality and Family in the Colonial Chesapeake," *Journal of Interdisciplinary History* 8 (1978): 403–27; Scott Wilds, "The Unification of Lowland South Carolina in the Eighteenth Century: A Demographic Perspective from St. Thomas Parish" (typescript, Department of American Civilization, University of Pennsylvania, 1976); Richard Dunn, *Sugar and Slaves: The Rise of the Planter Class in the English West Indies, 1624–1713* (Chapel Hill, N.C., 1972), chaps. 8–9; Patricia Molen, "Population and Social Patterns in Barbados in the Early Eighteenth Century," *William and Mary Quarterly* 28 (1971): 287–300. There is a suggestive similarity in the pretension to typicality of the New England family studies to a slightly earlier stage in the evolution of early American community studies. In that phase, almost every one of the seminal studies was of New England, and conclusions based on those towns were mistaken for representative renderings of collective life in the colonies. But over the course of the last quarter-century we have come to see that the leap from a few places east of the Hudson River to the whole of English America was unwarranted and massively misleading. The town patterns of colonial New England have not proven extensible as models to the rest of the New World, and recent historians have therefore realized the necessity of alternative models that might encompass a majority rather than an aberrant minority of settlements. See, e.g., James Henretta, "The Morphology of New England Society in the Colonial Period," *Journal of Interdisciplinary History* 2 (1971): 379–98, and Jack Greene, "Autonomy and Stability: New England and the British Colonial Experience in Early Modern America," *Journal of Social History* 8 (1974): 171–94. A few of those historians have even attempted to go beyond mere redress of the regional balance to a reconfiguration of our very conception of the colonial community. See Darrett Rutman, "The Social Web: A Prospectus for the Study of the Early American Community," in *Insights and Parallels: Problems and Issues of American Social History,* ed. William O'Neill (Minneapolis, 1973), 57–89, and Richard Beeman, "The New Social History and the Search for 'Community' in Colonial America," *American Quarterly* 29 (1977): 422–43.

it.[12] In any event he was one of the very few colonial Americans who left much evidence of their private behavior and beliefs. His extensive personal papers promise us some purchase on the quality of social life where the demographic data are silent.

William Byrd was an accomplished writer in a dozen genres, but his diaries are in many ways his most revealing expression of himself. Composed in code and intended only for his own eyes, they remained unknown until relatively recently, and they remain largely unrecovered to this day.[13]

Because he trusted that no one else would ever see them, we can approach them without worrying about the ambiguities of audience that complicate interpretation of his other writings. Whereas his Histories of the Dividing Line were altered to appease the shifting circles of friends who had access to the manuscripts, and his letters varied greatly in style and substance to suit his successive correspondents, his diaries display a notable consistency of direction and design.[14]

12. For concurrence in this judgment, see Lewis Simpson, "Review Essay: William Byrd and the South," *Early American Literature* 7 (1972): 187–95, and cf. Byrd's sustained acceptance of his provincial position in his diaries. For a diametrically different view, drawn heavily from a few of the letters, see Kenneth Lynn, *Mark Twain and Southwestern Humor* (Boston, 1959), chap. 1.

13. *The Secret Diary*, ed. Wright and Tinling; [William Byrd], *The London Diary (1717–1721) and Other Writings*, ed. Louis Wright and Marion Tinling (New York, 1958); *Another Secret Diary of William Byrd of Westover, 1739–1741, with Letters and Literary Exercises, 1696–1726*, ed. Maude Woodfin (Richmond, Va., 1942). These three fragments are the only ones that have come to light of what seems to have been a secret journal kept by Byrd throughout his adult life. All three have been examined for this study, but only the two earlier ones are taken up here. By the time of the final fragment, Byrd was a very old man by contemporary Virginia standards and barely three years from his deathbed. His diary displays a much diminished level of activity of all sorts; even its editor concedes that his "more strenuous years were behind him," and his child-rearing years were well past. See *Another Secret Diary*, ed. Woodfin, xli.

14. Byrd's regularity in recording his daily affairs is not something to be taken for granted in diarists. Samuel Pepys, for one, frequently fell days behind and then caught up in a single sitting—see *The Diary of Samuel Pepys*, ed. Robert Latham and William Matthews (Berkeley, 1970), 1:143 (May 17, 1660); 2:19 (January 20, 1661), 52 (March 9, 1661)—and in any case made his entries in intricate and erratic combinations of compositional modes ranging from the most direct registration to the most elaborate recasting from rough notes—see 1:xcvii–cxiii. And indeed, such regularity is not a quality to be prized for all purposes. As Latham points out, in his important distinction between "literary immediacy" and "historical immediacy," many of Pepys's pieces composed at some remove from events have a higher capacity to project the reader into the action they describe than many of the items drafted on the spot (1:cv–cvi). The only argument to be urged here is the one Michael Barton makes in his recent analysis of the uses of personal documents in historical study, that diaries such as Byrd's have the advantage of being less "the products of a special sort of evaluative process" for their being written regularly and

Their consistency is marred primarily by the gaps between the diary fragments that have been found. The last of the three segments now known resumes eighteen years after the end of the second and gives us a Byrd distinctly diminished in energy as his own demise draws near; and even setting that one aside, we still confront substantial discontinuities in the other, earlier portions. In the first of them, Byrd begins as a man in his mid-thirties, married for six years with a daughter almost two. During the three and a half years of this fragment, he fathers his first son and, less than a year later, loses him. In the second portion, Byrd is a widower in his mid-forties, with daughters ten and two years old at the outset. During an almost identical span of three and a half years, he lives in London, looks for a wealthy wife, fails to find one, returns to Virginia without his daughters, and resumes his affairs at Westover.

Over the years of the first two fragments, then, we see Byrd in Virginia and England and Virginia again. We observe him in the prime of his life and a little past it, wed and widowed, with infants and young children and a daughter entering adolescence and without any children to attend to at all. Much is hidden from our view and much that we might wish to know we cannot, unless more of the little octavo notebooks should turn up. But many things in these fragments reward analysis.

Among these, none is more revealing than Byrd's unconcern for his children, his perennial disinclination to do and feel and care for them. Ariès has taught us to take attitudes toward children as touchstones for entire constellations of familial and social values. He has shown how we may mark the late medieval mode by the "gay indifference" of parents to their offspring and the early modern attitude by the determination of mothers and fathers to withdraw their young from the promiscuous concourse of public life to the purer precincts of the family's own secluded privacy.[15]

By such benchmarks, Byrd's relationship to his children was unmistakably premodern. He neither cherished them nor took any apparent pleasure in them. He did not conceive of them as developing individuals with distinctive personalities to be cultivated. He did not imagine them

---

unreconstructedly. See "The Character of Civil War Soldiers: A Comparative Analysis of the Language of Moral Evaluation in Diaries" (Ph.D. diss., University of Pennsylvania, 1974), 110, and, more generally, chaps. 2–4.

15. Ariès, *Centuries of Childhood*, 406.

as vessels of pristine purity to be protected. He did not even treasure them as extensions of his own familial line.[16] He simply ignored them. They appeared in his diaries essentially as medical objects, beneath notice except when sick, and infrequently at that.

For months at a time, in the earliest diary, his little daughter and his newborn son disappeared from sight.[17] All told, from the early months of 1709 to the autumn of 1712, he mentioned them barely twice a month. He did not discuss his son at all from the day of the christening to the time the boy's fatal illness began, eight months later. Apart from her ailments, he did not discuss his daughter much more; and, at that, almost half his nonmedical references to her were but passing allusions to times when she tagged along with her mother or joined her father in activities in which her participation was insignificant. On the one evening when Byrd wrote of sharing a meal with her, he recalled revealingly that he had "dined by [him]self" and dismissed his companion as "nobody but the child."[18] On two of the six occasions when he accorded her any consequence in her own right, he complained that she had disturbed him in the night. On three others, he took issue with the way his wife fed or disciplined her. On one occasion alone, he actually "played with the girl," though even then he expressed no pleasure at having done so.[19]

Indeed, he was so remote from his daughter that he designated her by name less than a dozen times in the entire diary, while referring to her as "my daughter" or "the child" literally dozens of times. Aside from

16. It is notorious that Byrd's daughter Evelyn, and not his son William Byrd III, was his darling when the children were grown older. But even as infants and young children, Evelyn was favored over the ill-fated Parke by their father. She and not her brother was the one Byrd called occasionally by name. She was the one he worried over in sickness and the one on whose behalf he intervened in disciplinary disputes. See, e.g., July 16, 1709; January 12, 24, May 21, 23, 24, 25, 26, August 4, 5, September 1, December 17, 1710; June 23, 1711; February 9, 1712.

17. For periods of two and three months without a single reference to the children, see the weeks after April 17, September 28, 1709; February 12, 1710; February 24, May 19, November 20, 1711. For still longer sequences of four and five months with but an isolated allusion or two, see April 17–September 6, 1709; January 24–May 12, 1710; May 19–October 6, 1711; and March 17–August 20, 1712.

18. February 12, 1710; June 23, August 26, October 6, 23, 1711; March 4, 17, May 1, August 20, 1712. The dinner was on March 17, 1712. When Byrd and his daughter drank syllabub together, on June 23, 1711, it was the only occasion of congenial sharing between father and child in his diary.

19. For annoyances at night, Jaunary 24, 1710; May 1, 1711. For disciplinary issues, January 13, May 21, 1710; January 18, 1712. (Byrd's report that he was "out of humor with [his] wife for forcing Evie to eat against her will"—May 21, 1710—was his only allusion to a child's "will" in the diary.) For play, February 9, 1712.

the single instance of the boy's christening, he never spoke of his son by name at all. He simply called him "the child" or "the boy." [20]

The infrequent occasions when Byrd did recognize the presence of his children were concentrated heavily in a few sieges of sickness. Almost a third of all his references to his offspring over three and a half years occurred in the single span of three weeks when both of them were bedridden and the boy finally died. Well over two-thirds of all Byrd's acknowledgments of their existence appeared during that period of affliction and four other spells that were generally briefer still. For their ailments constituted their principal claim upon his attention. Sicknesses, therapeutic regimens, recoveries, and, in the son's case, death accounted for more than six out of every seven references to them in the diary. [21]

Nonetheless, not even the illnesses of his children ever engaged Byrd's attention compellingly. He went away for long stretches, sometimes weeks on end, when one or the other of them was sick in bed, and he did not let their precarious condition distract him from more powerful interests when he did stay home during their illnesses. In the midst of the distemper that took his son's life, he bought slaves, sold glass, fetched his wine from Williamsburg, conversed with friends, and instructed overseers exactly as he did in less perilous seasons. Indeed, he discovered himself in "good thoughts, and good humor," to the very eve of his boy's death, and he found himself in equally fine mental fettle in the days that followed the burial. When he did at last descend to

20. Byrd's most common designations for his son were "the child" (14 times) and "the boy" (7 times). Others were "my son," "our son," "our child," "my boy," and "my child," in descending order. His preferred appellations for his daughter were "my daughter" (42 times) and "the child" (35 times). Others were "Evie," "my child," "my girl," "our daughter," "my daughter Evelyn," and "our child," in descending order. All told, he spoke of his daughter by name 11 times, his son just once. He called his daughter his own ("my") 55 times and divided her with his wife ("our") only 3 times, whereas he called his son his own just 10 times and shared him with his wife 6. Moreover, his daughter was left in unclaimed limbo ("the") only about a third of the time (35 of 104 references), while his son was similarly stranded almost twice as commonly (21 of 38 references).

21. Over the entirety of the 1709–1712 diary, Byrd referred to his children 150 times. Of these references, 47—or 31.3 percent—occurred between May 12 and June 4, 1710. 105—or 70 percent—occurred during that span and four others of less serious sickness: July 31–August 9, 1710; November 3–7, 1710; December 15, 1710–January 14, 1711; and February 20–24, 1711. Over the 43 months of the diary, Byrd referred to his children on 99 different days, or 2.3 days a month. (Excluding merely the two most extensive sieges of sickness, May 12–June 4, 1710, and December 15, 1710–January 14, 1711, he referred to them 61 times, or 1.5 days a month.) Of the 150 total references to the children, 129—or 86 percent—were to their illnesses.

"indifferent thoughts" and declare himself "out of humor extremely," he had long since ceased to think about the child. His sour mood was due solely to a series of business disappointments and plantation mishaps he had suffered, not to any sudden sense of bereavement.[22]

His remoteness from his daughter was comparable to his aloofness from his son, but it was more blatant in the second surviving fragment of the diary, when he kept her at a discreet distance while he lived in London and then left her in the metropolis when he returned to Westover.

Though she was barely ten years old when he had her sent to London, Byrd did not allow her to settle in his own household. He deposited her with a landlady far enough from his own lodgings not to interfere with his attentions to ladies of great estate and women of easy virtue. He never expressed any regrets at leaving his little girl to live apart from him, and he never made any sustained effort to be with her even when her need for him was greatest.

When he heard that she was "indisposed" with what "they feared . . . would be a smallpox," he went fully a week, without a word about her in the interim, before he paid her a perfunctory visit. When he learned that she had the measles, he did not go to look after her, or even to comfort her, for three days. When, a few months later, he found her "bad of a pain in the head," and again showing symptoms of smallpox, he stayed with her only briefly before resuming his regular rounds at the coffeehouse, the theater, the haunts of loose women, and the alehouse.[23]

Byrd was still more distant from his younger daughter, born after the end of the first surviving segment of the diaries and only two years old at the commencement of the second. For the first year and a half of the London portion of that log, he kept her an ocean away from him, in Virginia. While she was there, he never sent a single letter evincing any curiosity about her development or any concern about her health.

22. For the trip to Williamsburg, September 11–14, 1709. For trips abroad while his children were abed, April 14–May 7, 1709; May 15–16, 1710; February 5–9, 1711; on the last of these, Byrd's wife went as well. For business as usual in the midst of sickness, see, e.g., May 12–June 3, 1710, esp. May 22, 26. For his good spirits while his son languished, May 13–June 2, 1710; on two of the only three nights he found his humor "indifferent" during those three weeks—May 20 and May 28—it was clearly because of difficulties with his overseer and distress over the breaking of his dam, not on account of any anxiety about his boy. For his failure to fall to mourning, June 3–24, 1710; quotations on June 24.

23. June 17–24, 1718; August 1–11, 1718; January 8, 1719. On January 27, 1719, he did return a mere two days after discovering his daughter with a cold on January 25.

When he had her sent to London, he did not change his ways. He did not see fit to meet her when she arrived, leaving that inconvenience to her prospective landlady. He did not get around to greeting her for almost two weeks, and then only when a friend brought her to his quarters unbidden. He simply did not believe it incumbent upon him to go to his anxious young child. She stirred neither his sympathy nor his sense of parental responsibility. Even when he learned that she was sick, he still ignored her plight; and when he saw her at last, he only noted blandly that she seemed "much better than [he] had heard." Despite what must have been her bewilderment and agitation in a starkly strange world all but empty of friendly faces, Byrd made time to visit her just once more in the next two months.[24]

When he saw her again, she had already "been very bad [i.e., sick] but was better." When he went to her once more, she had actually recovered from smallpox without his taking any interest in her fate. When he visited her the following time, he had been off for more than a month in the country. On his departure he had not dreamed of taking his town-bound children along with him, and on his return he had been in no hurry to see how the children had fared in his absence, though he discovered time enough for an evening at his favorite whorehouse on each of his first days home.[25]

Over the duration of the London diary, Byrd saw his older daughter less than once a week and his younger one less than once a month, for no more than an hour on an ordinary call. The rest of the time he consigned them to their own devices, strangers, utterly alone, and all but abandoned. By way of comparison, he made almost twice as many visits and appointments over the same span with a succession of mistresses and lusty ladies of the stews.[26]

Moreover, when he went back to Westover, he left his two young

24. April 17, 29, May 5, 1719. All told, Byrd spent three hours with her in her first two and a half months in London.

25. July 2, 14, September 7, 8, 1719. As it happened, when Byrd did finally visit his older daughter, after a week of other, more compelling projects and pleasures, he learned that his younger daughter was sick. Characteristically, he was neither disturbed nor moved to any action by the news. See September 13, 1709.

26. Byrd paid 81 visits to his older girl in 2 years and 8 visits to his younger child in a bit more than 8 months. Of visits for which it is possible to tell how long he stayed, 28 were for more than 1 hour, 48 for an hour, and 8 for less than an hour. He also paid 160 calls on female consorts, or almost exactly twice as many as on his favorite child; and that tally includes only his duly arranged assignations, not the multitude of casual pickups he made in the parks and by the ways. He never begrudged the hours he lingered with such companions or, indeed, the occasions he "lay all night" with them.

girls behind in London. He ceased to see them and, for all intents and purposes, even to think about them for the remaining year and a half of the diary. Indeed, on the one occasion when they intruded on his indifference, they still scarcely dented it. They sent him a letter, which he received in April 1721 with the brief notation that they "were well, thank God." And that was all. To the first word he had had from his own only children in the fifteen months since he had left them alone in the metropolis, he could muster no more response than he managed dozens of times over when he returned home to his servants and slaves after a few days away.[27]

If Byrd was not as callously inattentive to his wife as he was with his children, he was still no doting husband to his fiery and free-spirited spouse. Their relationship may seem to be cast more nearly in the modern mold, but the semblance is deceptive. It arises only because the battle of the sexes has remained a Western perennial, while neglect of one's brood has become peculiar and even pathological.

The battle of the sexes was fought on a distinctly different terrain for distinctly different stakes in Byrd's Virginia than in our own day, and the differences depended, in many ways, on the insensitivity to children that Byrd displayed so steadily. For, as Ariès has argued, the core of the modern familial configuration is the isolation of cherished children in narrowly nuclear families of loving intrusiveness and control. Where there is no such concern for youngsters and no such surveillance, there are, in effect, no modern children. And where there are no modern children, there can be no modern marital partners either. Byrd's relations with his wife were therefore little more meaningfully modern, little more dependent upon an ethic of domestic isolation, than his relations with his sons and daughters.

Most elementally, he was not at home on any consistent basis. In addition to day trips to his outlying plantations and his incessant visiting with neighbors, Byrd was away from hearth and home and laid his head on a strange bed—sometimes with a strange bedfellow—almost one night out of every three from 1709 to 1712. The proportion is striking in its own right, and still more so because it differs surprisingly little from the proportion in 1720–1721, when he had no wife and children at Westover to draw him home. The similarity suggests that his comings and goings were to a considerable extent independent of any imagined marital responsibilities. For William Byrd, other motives

27. April 14, 1721.

weighed more heavily than the pressures and pleasures of connubi-ality.[28]

Even when he was home, or when his wife was with him in his trav-els, he hardly held his mate steadily in his heart and mind. Taking all the days of the first fragments of the diary together, he failed to record any-thing about her on almost three-fifths of them. On two-thirds of the days that he mentioned her, he mentioned her only once.[29]

More revealingly, his limited attentiveness was seldom loving or con-siderate, or otherwise appreciative or affectionate. He recorded warm or cordial attitudes toward his wife less than once a month over the many months of the diary; his friendly feelings accounted for less than one twentieth of all his references to her.[30] Further, his expressions of fond concern were almost wholly dissociated from his notations of sexual re-lations with her. On only four occasions in nearly four years did he enter an expression of compassion or affection for her on the same day that he recorded intercourse with her.[31]

His sexual life with his wife was impressive in its spontaneity and range of settings—their celebrated coupling on the billiard table was by no means unique in its ingenuity—but it was marked by only the most perfunctory exhibitions of human connectedness or emotional intensity. Except on the rarest occasions, Byrd scarcely seemed to notice his wife's response to him. His continuing care was for whether he performed "with vigor." The flat affect of his deposition that he "rogered [his] wife in the morning and also wrote a letter to England and settled several accounts" conveys exactly the dead-level parity on which he often placed his sexual intimacies with his wife and his conduct of the most mundane daily business.[32]

---

28. For 1709–1712, Byrd was away 28.8 percent of the time (377 nights out of 1,309). For 1720–1721, he was away 38.7 percent of the nights (165 out of 426). For the two periods together, he was away 31.2 percent of the time.

29. He mentioned her 562 of 1,309 days, or 42.9 percent of them. He mentioned her more than once 201 of the 562 days, or 35.8 percent of them.

30. Of 850 references to his wife, 42—4.9 percent—were fond, joyous, or generally kind.

31. The 4 days were November 3, December 26, 1711; January 1, April 3, 1712. There were 94 other days when he had sex with his wife without expressing affection for her or did or said something affectionate without having sex.

32. May 2, 1712. For rare instances of Byrd's attention to his wife's feelings in their sexual unions, see November 4, 1710; April 30, May 16, 1711. It should be added that even Byrd's expressions for sexual intercourse—"rogered," "gave a flourish"—which seem so piquant if not charming to us, were essentially stereotypical to him. They were virtually the only two locutions he ever used.

Even if we combine the two realms of relations with his wife as Byrd rarely did, they accounted for fewer than one-eighth of all his references to her and fewer by far than his references to their quarrels. On more than one of every five days on which Byrd mentioned his wife at all, he recorded a row with her. Of her impingements upon him, almost half again as many revolved around their battles as around their fondlings and fondnesses.[33]

Yet neither such squabbles nor their occasional intimacies constituted the substance of the Byrds' marriage, which was never love or hate so much as sheer sustenance of life and health. Far oftener than he declared his affection for his wife or made love to her, oftener even than he bickered with her, Byrd simply watched over her in her illnesses. Matter-of-fact requirements of maintenance accounted for more than three times as many of his attentions to her as the pleasures of sexual and emotional companionship and more than twice as many as the trials of quarrelsome confrontation.[34]

Even his concern for his wife's physical condition expressed no consistent solicitude or compassion for her. As often as not, his very recognitions of her ailments betrayed his failure of feelings for her or his inability to respond sensitively to her situation. A couple months after she gave birth to their first son, when she was still "much incommoded with her term which came away in great abundance," he and his friends were "very merry" far into the night. Several months before the projected end of her next pregnancy, when she was "very sick and peevish in her breeding," he departed for four days of traipsing around the neighboring plantations and remarked dully on his return that she "was indisposed and had been ever since [he] went from home." A month later, a week after she had miscarried and only a few days after they had had a "mortal quarrel," he went off to Williamsburg. A year later he did the same thing again. While his wife was "abed" and afraid of another miscarriage, he forsook her for five days at the capital, where he did his business at the Council, dined with the governor and other Virginia gentlemen, recorded what he ate with some relish, and generally made

33. In addition to his 42 references to their fondnesses, Byrd made 60 references to their sexual congresses, another 7.1 percent of all his references to his wife. (As a matter of prurient interest, that was not much more than one mating a month.) As against those 102 occasions, Byrd bickered with his wife 146 times on 117 different days. Thus, their contention occasioned 17.2 percent of all his references to her on 20.8 percent of all the days he referred to her.

34. Sickness was the substance of 336 of Byrd's allusions to his wife, or 39.5 percent of them, on 235 days, or 41.8 percent of all the days he discussed his wife in any fashion.

himself "merry," without ever thinking of his mate and her precarious pregnancy until he went back to Westover.[35]

Beyond these recurrent lapses of sympathy, Byrd's diary affords access to what he did feel as well as to what he did not, and to what he thought as well as to what he did. For at the end of every day, in formulaic fashion, he took systematic stock of his sentiments. Under the three headings of "health," "thoughts," and "humor," he reviewed his reactions to the events of the day and assessed his general state of mind.

His assessments revealed, again and again, the deep disconnectedness of his conduct and consciousness from his dealings with his wife. On days when he had been "out of humor" with her, for example, he went to bed with good thoughts and humor as if in deliberate demonstration of her irrelevance to his disposition.[36] On a day when they had had "a terrible quarrel" and she had given him "abundance of bad words," acted like "a mad woman," and "endeavored to strangle herself," he still settled down to sleep in good spirits, oblivious to their earlier contretemps. On an evening at Westover when he had kissed another woman on the bed until his wife "was uneasy about it and cried as soon as the company was gone," he was able to acknowledge, "the lust [he] had for another man's wife" without in the least impairing his own good temper.[37]

When his wife was "out of order all day with a headache," or bothered by "great pains in her belly," or merely "melancholy," he was equally insensitive to her distress and in a good humor all his own.[38] When she miscarried, he still slept a sleep of equanimity.[39] Even when every member of his immediate family gave him grounds for baleful feelings—when he was "out of humor" with his wife, when his daughter was "in a great fever," and when his son was sick and dying—he could yet dissociate his own mood from the affairs of his family and discern in himself both good thoughts and good humor.[40]

35. November 17, 1709; May 26, 31, 1711; July 4–7, 1711; July 20–24, 1712. For still other instances, see June 11–14, 1711; April 24, September 20, 1712.

36. E.g., May 21, 1709; September 1, 24, October 12, 1710.

37. March 2, 1712; November 2, 1709.

38. May 30, 1709; February 9, 1710; May 4, 1711; see also January 9, 1712. Conversely, when Byrd had a bad headache and his wife cared for him "with a great deal of tenderness," her affection was insufficient to alter his state of mind. He still had "very indifferent thoughts." See September 6, 1711.

39. June 25, 1711. See also June 28, 1711; August 26, 1712.

40. May 21, 1710. See also March 16, 1710, when his wife was "out of order [i.e., sick] and melancholy" and an older relative, a "Mrs. Byrd," died, yet he still had good thoughts and humor. It is not always easy to know what world William Byrd lived in. It

If Byrd was not always so sublimely unmindful of his domestic situation, it is nonetheless difficult to define areas where it made much of a difference in his nightly inventories. Through thick and thin alike, he detached his inmost feelings from his relations with his wife. He had good thoughts and humor on ninety-five percent of the days when they had intercourse, but he also had good thoughts and humor on ninety-five percent of the days when they didn't have it. In fact, he found his spiritual estate equally excellent on ninety percent of the days when he quarreled with her; and if that proportion was a little lower than when they made love, it was also a little higher than when they were kind or affectionate toward each other in nonsexual contexts.[41]

Taken together, Byrd's mental assessments are chiefly notable for their disconnectedness from his daily domestic travails. His wife and children were never the fulcrum of his emotional existence. More often than not, they did not even impinge upon it.

If his immediate family was not focal for Byrd, we confront the intriguing question of what was pivotal in its stead. But we must not pose that question too quickly, for it blinks the antecedent issue of what Byrd meant by family in the first place. Just because he did not set the nuclear family as near the center of his affective life as we do does not mean that he undervalued the family. He may simply have defined it differently.

When we look at Byrd's actual use of the word "family," and his responses to those close to him by consanguinity and coresidence, it is clear that his conception of the institution was indeed different from our own. His attachments were never confined within the sealing circle of spouse and fledglings. On the contrary, they were diffused far and wide

---

was sometimes as strangely, intensely private as—what will be argued shortly—it was sociable and neighborly.

41. Byrd had good thoughts and good humor on 57 of the 60 days on which he "rogered" his wife, or exactly 95 percent of them. He had similar good spirits on 864 of the 913 days he was at home on his plantation, or 94.6 percent of them, though those days represented an indiscriminate mixture of seasons of sickness and health, setbacks and successes, and aggravations and satisfactions, while the days he gave his wife a "flourish" were obviously days in which at least one sort of marital satisfaction was maximized. He had good thoughts and humor on 105 of the 117 days on which he squabbled with his wife, or 89.7 percent of them, and on 33 of the 37 days on which he was tender with her and monitored his mood, or 89.2 percent of them. These figures and all the preceding ones on his humors are derived solely from the 1709–1712 diary, not only because Byrd had no helpmate over the course of the 1717–1721 journal but also because he had given up such spiritual scorekeeping by then.

among a heterogeneous plantation community, conceived in its entirety as his family and explicitly so described.

For every mention of his family in which Byrd meant merely himself, his wife, and his children, there were a dozen references in which he comprehended his retainers, servants, and slaves. His lady and his little ones were a part of his family, but never its preemptive or even its principal part. As he explained to the Earl of Orrery:

I have a large family of my own. . . . Like one of the patriarchs, I have my flocks and my herds, my bond-men and bond-women. . . . I must take care to keep all my people to their duty, to set all the springs in motion, and to make everyone draw his equal share to carry the machine forward. But then 'tis an amusement in this silent country.[42]

When he "recommended [his] family to God almighty" or "committ[ed his] family to the divine protection" before journeying away from Westover, he referred to everyone around the plantation, not just his mate and their offspring.[43] When he returned from such sojourns to find "several of [his] family sick, and his daughter among them," or his "family well, thank God, only Sue had lost her child," he barely even conceded a privileged position to his wife and progeny among the dwellers on the estate.[44] When he persisted in such usage after his wife was dead and his daughters left behind in London—when he still "committed [his] family to the protection of God" before going off on a trip, and still "found all the family well, thank God," on his return—he proved that immediate kin were neither sufficient nor even necessary for his notion of family.[45]

The flocks comprised within his conception of family were an ex-

42. Byrd to Charles Boyle, Earl of Orrery, July 5, 1726, in Marion Tinling, ed., *The Correspondence of the Three William Byrds of Westover, Virginia 1684–1776* (Charlottesville, Va., 1977), 355.

43. February 28, April 18, September 11, October 15, 1709; March 29, April 17, June 22, September 5, October 9, 16, November 8, 1710; April 15, July 4, October 1, 16, November 14, 1711; January 22, February 19, March 30, 1712.

44. September 16, 1710; September 22, 1711. See also November 26, 1709; April 17, September 7, November 4, 22, December 14, 21, 1710; January 11, February 27, October 1, 1711; February 19, 21, August 27, September 11, 1712.

45. April 24, May 13, 1720. See also April 19, June 1, 3, July 29, August 30, October 13, November 1, 23, 1720; February 19, 28, March 25, April 16, May 14, 1721. Byrd's expansive usage seems to have been shared. He spoke similarly of other planters' "families"—see February 28, 1711; September 11, 1712; November 15, 24, 1720—and other planters spoke with a comparable inclusiveness about his—see January 7, 1711.

ceedingly motley lot. They included children of the gentry in residence at Westover, overseers and other managerial agents, and artisans of all sorts. In a very real sense they included the slaves as well, even such refractory ones as Redskin Peter, for whose malingering Byrd reserved some remarkably cruel cures but for whose recovery from serious sickness he prayed "in particular."[46]

Altogether, ninety-one members of this expansively extended family appeared in their own identifiable individuality in the first fragment of the diary alone.[47] Twenty-seven turned up at least ten times, twenty-one at least twenty times, and half a dozen at least fifty times.[48] Twenty-two different overseers served at the plantation. Seventeen artisans stayed on for a while, including a tailor, a shoemaker, a stonecutter, a brickmaker, a plasterer and painter, a boatwright, a carpenter, a joiner, a "wire man," and a "coaler." All of them and a host of others namelessly embraced in Byrd's recurrent references to his "people" were encompassed within his family and treated accordingly.[49]

Overseers had almost unlimited access to Byrd's attention and a fair measure of mutuality besides. He conferred with them about his affairs. He shared confidences with them about theirs. He had them to dinner when he ate with his fellow planters. He heard them out when they "came [to him] with a heavy heart and cried." He allowed them to dispute their differences with him and to "justify" themselves against ac-

46. February 16, 19, 1712; for brutal corrective measures, see January 11, 22, May 12, 1712. In a not entirely fanciful sense, Byrd's idea of his family even stretched to include his horses and cattle; see February 28, 1710, and September 22, 1711.

47. Byrd distinguished all but about a dozen of them directly by name. The rest appeared unequivocally enough; e.g., "the negro shoemaker," "the Frenchman," or "the old joiner."

48. There were even four—Tom, Grills, Mumford, and Mrs. Dunn—whom he mentioned more than 100 times, and another—Bannister—whom he mentioned on 94 occasions. The very variety of the 27 who appeared 10 times or more indicated the range and richness of the plantation community. Nine of them—Tom Turpin, Tom, Grills, Mumford, John Bannister, Mr. M–r–s–l, Joe Wilkinson, Tom Osborne, and Tom Randolph— were major domos, overseers, or suboverseers. Another—John Grills—was Byrd's personal secretary, and another—Daniel Wilkinson—his personal attendant. Two—George Smith and the boatmaker—were artisans. One was a doctor, one a nurse. One—Isham— was a Randolph scion living at Westover to learn French. One—Billy Wilkins—was the son of a lesser planter nearby. Three—Tom L–s–n, Ben O–d–s–n, and mulatto Jacky— were servants. Six—Anaka, Eugene, Jenny, Moll, Indian Peter, and Prue—were slaves.

49. In the year and a few months of the Virginia portion of the later diary, Byrd had at least a dozen other overseers, besides those still in his service from a decade earlier, and several sorts of artisans—a gardener, a well-digger, and a miller—he had not had in the previous years.

cusations. He even bowed before their arguments on occasion, and he was contrite with those whom he realized that he had wronged.[50]

Artisans also had their familiarities and entitlements. Byrd went for walks about the plantation with them, tended them when they fell ill, often treated them to a bottle of rum when they finished a job. He allowed them leave to receive relatives and others as guests at Westover. And they asserted prerogatives all their own that he honored because they did not abide with him if he did not abide by them. A boatwright who was asked to make a sawhorse reminded Byrd that such work "was not his business." A personal attendant who was bidden to go in the sloop "denied" the demand and Byrd "took him at his word." A workman who "was affronted that [Byrd] gave him pone instead of English bread for breakfast" simply "took his horse and rode away." A gardener who was offended that Byrd paid him less than his due actually "sent [Byrd] back a pistole and went away in the night."[51]

Household staff maintained an even sturdier sense of their own dignity and privileges. A nurse who stayed out all night at a wedding, "contrary to her mistress' orders," was ready to give Byrd "as good as [he] brought" when he flew into "a passion" at her behavior, willing to take a beating for the satisfaction of being "impudent to her mistress," and able to defy her master when he subsequently "commanded" her not to complain of her treatment to a neighbor.[52] A servant of another sort, Byrd's "mistress Annie Carter," never really served him at all in that ca-

50. March 2, 1712; March 28, 1710; June 7, October 11, 29, 1720; March 8, April 1, 22, 28, May 8, 1721; July 10, August 3, December 6, 1709; January 23, 1710; April 14, September 7, 1711. May 28, 1710. September 7, 1709; January 24, 1710; June 12, 1720. September 6, 30, 1710; March 15, 1721. Byrd even entered into his overseers' immediate familial affairs, authorizing their excursions home to parents and even himself visiting across the river with a man's mother; see August 11, 1709; January 20, February 2, 1710; June 17, July 15, 29, December 29, 1711; June 28, 1712; October 30, December 6, 1720; February 19, April 17, 1721.

51. March 4, 1720; March 22, 23, 24, June 2, 3, September 6, 1720; April 11, 1720; May 21, 1720; March 12, 1711; July 12, 1709; March 2, 1711; December 30, 1720; see also July 2, 1709 (and, for that matter, March 23, 1712: overseers also left in righteous indignation). Revealingly, Byrd never tried to rationalize his departures from customary canons of fair dealing and never tried to penalize his artisans when they returned and resumed the work after making their point.

52. May 13, 19, 20, 1709; see also February 22, 1709. It should be added that the nurse "met with no comfort" when she did complain to Mr. Harrison, but it should also be added that Byrd did not pursue this subsequent defiance and did not in any way contemplate dismissing her from her position for it. When she was finally fired, it was for stealing from the wine cellar, and it was two years later; see April 30, May 4, 1710.

pacity, except in trifling ways and on her own terms. Over the course of a year and a half at Westover, she refused unfalteringly to do anything more than "feel about [his] person" or permit him to masturbate with her. He "asked" her "to come to bed with" him, but he did not coerce her and "she would not be prevailed with." He "persuaded" her, "but she did not consent." He begged her merely "to let [him] feel her, but she would not" allow him even that liberty when she was disinclined. And he both recognized her right to refuse him and respected her moral personality. When she withheld her favors, he observed in all earnestness that she was "to be commended." Indeed, he went further and added, "God be praised." [53]

Similarly, slaves had rights that Byrd was bound, or at least elected, to respect. He protected their perquisites and "scolded" an overseer "for stealing [their] potatoes." They in turn presumed upon such protection and complained against mistreatment with every confidence of being heard. When they submitted "a petition" because they were denied their small beer, Byrd "did them right." When they were refused "what was ordered them," the superior who refused it was whipped. [54] For the chain of command was not as significant to Byrd as the contentment of his plantation community. He spent endless hours with his slaves. He "discoursed," "talked," or "walked and visited" with them almost nightly when he was at Westover. He "looked after" them during the day and "gave audience" to them after supper. And he gave them more than such attentions and audiences. He was responsive to their endeavors and rewarded them for "a good day's work" with "a dram in the evening" or

53. May 22, November 1, 1720; December 25, 1720; February 19, 23, 26, 1721 (she did, on a few occasions, allow him to kiss her: see February 18, 21, March 12, May 9, 1721); March 9, 1721; August 9, 1720; September 4, 1720. See also December 25, 26, 27, 1720; on the last of these days Byrd "resolved to forbear Annie by God's grace," but he was not entirely up to his resolution; see February 18, 19, 21, 23, 26, March 9, 12, May 9, 1721. For Byrd, at least, sexual gratification must surely have been one of the recommendations of the married state in Virginia, since he seems to have done little more than masturbate with Annie in all the sixteen months of the duration of his journal in the Old Dominion in this bachelor phase of his life. The abounding bagnios of London were nowhere to be found in the provincial capital, and neither were the complaisant ladies of St. James Park. When in Williamsburg, he was unfailingly reduced to frustration. "I endeavored to pick up a whore but could not find one" (November 18, 1720). "I walked after two women but in vain" (December 3, 1720). "I walked a little to pick up a woman and found none" (December 9, 1720). "I took a walk to meet some women but I met none so I went home" (May 2, 1721).

54. September 19, 1720; February 20, May 12, 1709; July 8, 1710; March 30, 1720; April 9, 1712.

"a bowl of punch." He dispensed with requirements of specific merit and simply granted them gifts of cherries, mutton, rum, and cider.[55] Beyond such bounties, he allowed them the more precious indulgence of time: time without work when the weather turned foul, time for holiday frivolity and merriment, time simply to relax or pursue their own pleasures.[56] On Sundays, he often "invited nobody home [after church] because we would not make our people work too much on a Sunday" or simply so "that our servants might have some leisure."[57]

He was capable of a degree of awareness of his servants' feelings, a measure of sharing in their feelings, and a modicum of feeling for them. He knew when his people "grieved" at the death of a particular slave. He himself took communion especially "devoutly" on the day after another died. He acknowledged his error when convinced that he had accused his bondsmen wrongly, and he felt the same furtive regret on realizing that he had treated a slave unjustly as he felt on finding that he had misjudged his overseers.[58] And more than this, he seems to have accorded his hands an acceptance in an ultimate sense, difficult to demonstrate, which is usually reserved for people who comprise the unalterable core of a family. With a few house servants in particular—the young boy Eugene, the maids Anaka and Jenny, and the cook Moll—he meted out punishment after punishment in vain attempts to extract

55. April 2, June 30, July 4, 1720; see also May 9, 10, 15, 1712; September 30, 1720; March 9, 1721. January 1, August 31, 1712; May 19, 20, June 11, 18, 21, July 2, 9, 13, 14, 16, 24, 25, 26, August 7, 15, September 3, 11, 13, 15, October 8, 1720; February 19, 1721. Slaves also sent presents to Byrd in reciprocal gratuitousness; see April 14, December 29, 1720.

56. December 25, 1709; January 26, 30, May 17, December 26, 1711; March 24, May 9, 10, 17, 1712; June 21, 1720. It was possible for slaves to bargain with Byrd over such holidays, and even to win, as one did when he argued that "it was not fortunate to work on this [Childermas] day" (December 28, 1720). But Byrd never went so far as the governor, who "made a bargain with his servants, that if they would forbear to drink upon the Queen's birthday," when the governor was giving a grand ball, "they might be drunk" the day after. In the event, "they observed their contract and did their business very well and got very drunk." See February 7, 1711.

57. July 23, August 20, 1710; see also December 24, 25, 1710; May 27, 1711; April 15, 1720. Byrd also tried inviting no one home so that his people could themselves go to church, but he did not repeat that experiment; see July 9, 1710.

58. January 2, 1711; December 25, 1710; August 27, 1709; August 22, 1710; May 1, 1711; April 12, 1712. When Byrd forgave Anaka on May 1, 1711, and excused her from all punishment, he did so "on [his] wife's and sister's persuasion"; and in several other instances as well, he and his wife had bitter differences of opinion over the discipline of slaves. Such disputes plainly implied that all parties agreed that the slaves had enough moral personality to be worth such concern and moral reconsideration, and they preclude as well the possibility that such discipline was merely a matter of hierarchical or impersonal administration. See July 15, 1710; December 31, 1711; March 2, May 22, 1712.

more conscientious performances of their duties from them, yet he never for a moment considered replacing them. In the final analysis, their incompetence was immaterial to their standing within the family, for better or for worse.[59]

In many ways, slaves, servants, artisans, and overseers all had a place within the Westover family comparable to that reserved by Byrd for his own wife and children. For the family as he conceived it was always founded on the household—or, better, the estate—and not the home. Its orientation was public far more than private. It existed in a rush of social roles and relations and not in a hush of intimacy and autonomy. Its members learned to live in it by participating in its actual practices and not by mastering its abstract preachments or manipulating the tangled triads of the narrow nuclear family.

Family feeling entailed for Byrd an inclusive concern for everyone on the plantation, in the house and the quarters alike, and that concern was especially evident in his preoccupation with sickness and dying. He prescribed the same medications for his slaves as for himself, his wife, his children, and his friends. He sent for expert medical advice and assistance as speedily for his "sick people" as for his own kin. He dispatched servants to such specialists even more readily than the members of his own immediate family who fell ill.[60] He incorporated his servitors in his family community in more intensely personal ways as well. He spoke of ailing slaves as his "family" or "children" exactly as he spoke of his own kindred. He begged divine protection for his endangered slaves in the very same terms in which he asked it for his gentry peers and his own flesh and blood. He rejoiced when his lowliest laborers recovered in the same language that he applied to the recovery of his overseers or his children. He lamented in the identical accents of sublime fatalism when "a negro woman" at one of his outlying plantations died as when his own son succumbed before his very eyes at Westover.[61]

59. For Eugene, see February 8, June 9, 10, November 30, December 1, 3, 16, 1709; August 31, 1710; October 23, December 31, 1711; September 18, 1712. For Anaka, see February 22, April 17, September 19, 22, 1709; April 30, 1711; January 3, April 12, 1712. For Jenny, see March 30, September 3, 16, December 1, 1709; August 31, 1710; February 27, October 11, 1711; March 2, 1712. For Moll, see May 23, July 31, 1709; March 16, 20, May 20, June 10, August 22, 1711; April 9, 1712.

60. December 27, 1711; September 12, 1712. January 7, July 7, October 4, 5, December 4, 8, 1711; February 17, 19, June 27, 1712; cf. May 12–17, 1710. February 25, 1711.

61. January 7, 17, March 7, May 5, September 7, 9, 16, December 14, 21, 1710; January 7, 11, 12, 1711. April 15, 1711; cf. May 15, 1710. January 22, 23, 24, May 4, 1711; March 6, 1711. May 28, 1711; June 3, 1710.

If anything, Byrd sometimes went beyond even-handed impartiality to a greater solicitude for his slaves than for his immediate family. When an Indian slave was sick and his wife "indisposed," he prayed for the Indian "in particular" and his wife not at all when he went off to Williamsburg. When a house maid was merely "taken sick," he attended her more closely and treated her more carefully than he did his own wife when she miscarried at about the same time.[62] When some slaves were "sick" and his daughter "very sick," he "tended" the slaves "diligently" all day and ignored his little girl entirely. When a number of slaves and his wife and child were all afflicted, he brought the local medical expert in for the slaves alone, administered the recommended medicaments solely to the slaves, and spent the afternoon doing "nothing but mind[ing]" the slaves.[63]

These ministrations might possibly be discounted as simple reflexes of self-interest. Slaves were valuable property, and Byrd knew their worth as well as the next man. Indeed, he was not above explicit calculations of their exact value. Referring to a neighbor's retinue, he noted coolly that "several . . . were sick" and "a young fellow worth £100" already lost.[64]

Such cynical interpretations of his conduct, however, do not explain why, when he tried to read one afternoon, he was unable to concentrate "because poor C–l–y was so very ill," or why, at the actual or impending loss of a servant, he experienced unmistakable anguish. Another man's "young fellow" might have been just a capital asset. His own people were far more significant to him, and he endured their diseases and deaths far more achingly. "These poor people suffer for my sins," he grieved, as twelve of his slaves lay sick. "God is pleased to afflict me with His judgment for my sins," he lamented again a few days later, as one of them approached his last hours. For it was in deep and dire conviction of his complicity in their ills that Byrd implored forgiveness for "all [his] offenses" so that his flocks might be "restore[d] . . . to their health if it [were] consistent with His holy will." He never doubted the absolute

62. February 18, 19, 1712; February 14, 20, 1710. On the very day on which he spent half the morning medicating and observing the slave, moreover, he allowed himself only the barest breath of perturbation that his wife, less than a week after her miscarriage, was "not very well." And his reactions to the recoveries of his maid and his wife were also suggestive: Of his wife, he noted that she "was better, thank God," on February 16; about his servant, he expressed an identical satisfaction twice, on February 23 and again on February 26.
63. January 9, 1711; January 7, 1711; June 2, 1710.
64. February 28, 1711.

reality of his responsibility for his people nor ever felt for a moment absolved from implication in their fate.[65]

At the same time, and with the same certitude, he believed that they would be reciprocally responsible for him and implicated in his fortunes. He did not hesitate to leave his sick daughter in their hands through the night, while he and his wife slept. He did not tremble to leave himself to their attendance at the height of the most severe sickness he suffered over the seven years of the first two fragments of the diaries. He did not even wrest responsibility for vigilance from them on the night that his son died. He simply slumbered while they sat watch, and he left it to them to call him when the boy was "just ready to die."[66]

Byrd also relied upon his wider Westover family to serve him wholeheartedly in all manner of nonmedical matters. He trusted his people to tell him "how everything was" on the plantation when he "inquired." He did not hesitate to go off with his wife for days at a time and leave the place wholly to their care. Indeed, even when his wife stayed home while he went away, he preferred to put his affairs in their hands rather than hers. He simply "took leave" of her when he departed. He "left orders with [his] family what to do."[67]

His faith in his own expansive family exceeded in several circumstances the importance that he attached to such central considerations in provincial Virginia as class and race. He was willing to take the word

65. March 7, 1710. January 2, 1711; cf. August 4, 1710, for an identical inability to "keep [his] mind steady" when his daughter was ill. December 29, 1710; January 2, 1711; December 29, 1710. If anything, it was his economic adversities from which Byrd was able to stand aloof in stoic equanimity. "God's will be done" was all he said when he learned he had lost sixty hogsheads of tobacco on April 21, 1711. "The Lord gives and the Lord has taken away—blessed be the name of the Lord" was the way he expressed his acceptance of still larger losses on May 6 and July 10, 1709. It is worth noting that he received his own son's death more nearly as he learned of the destruction of his cargoes than as he watched the wasting of his plantation hands.

66. May 24, 1710; July 9, 1711; June 3, 1710. Other fathers did sometimes sit up through the night with sick children, their own or those of neighbors, so Byrd's disinclination to do so cannot be accounted a simple resultant of the boundaries of the paternal role of that time. See, e.g., *The Diary of Colonel Landon Carter of Sabine Hall, 1752–1778,* ed. Jack Greene (Charlottesville, Va., 1965), 193, and *The Diary of Robert Rose,* ed. Ralph Fall (Verona, Va., 1977), 19. Rose's wife did stay up with their son one night when Rose would not, but that cannot have been because Rose contemned such solicitude as women's work, since on another occasion he attended a neighbor while she was lying in (see 14, 26).

67. February 20, 1709; December 26, 1711. October 1–5, 1711; he was equally unperturbed to return from extended expeditions alone to find his wife gone visiting and the plantation entirely under the management of the hands; see October 9, 1711. September 22, 1712; April 17, 1710; see also April 16, 1709; March 7, November 14, 1711.

of his own overseers, for example, against the insinuations of his planter peers and neighbors. He was prepared to presume his slaves' fidelity to the plantation rather than to their own race when he dispatched them after a runaway. He did not doubt their affections when he called on them to come to his wife's aid in a "great quarrel" with one of their own in which his wife "got the worst" until "by the help of the family" her antagonist "was overcome and soundly whipped."[68]

In the crucible of such family feeling, other allegiances and assumptions often melted almost away. Distinctions of color virtually vanished when a dear friend of Byrd's wife, herself the wife of an established white minister, was annexed to Byrd's "people" by her service with them. Byrd boasted that his "people attended [him] very well . . . particularly Mrs. Dunn," when he was seriously ill. Distinctions of class nearly disappeared when low-born white servants were assimilated to the status of their betters by membership in the plantation family. Byrd looked on indulgently as his eligible cousin courted the impertinent (white) nurse on the plantation.[69]

Distinctions that could not be boiled off so readily were still reduced. Class and color differentials did often shape the discipline of transgressors, but, just about as often, they did not. White overseers and artisans might be "scolded" where black field hands and house servants would be whipped, but the overseers and other whites had their whippings too, and slaves sometimes got off with reproofs.[70] Even the most privileged members of the plantation family, the children of other affluent planters sent for a while to Westover, met with measures as stern and unsparing as the meanest slave. Young Ned Randolph, for one, complained "that he was starved." Byrd resented his censure and retorted that the lad "ran about without [his] knowing anything of it" and "would not come" when called. He reported the boy's behavior to his father, who promptly "threatened" his son "if he should dare" to carry on in such fashion and thus left the lad on notice that a child of one of

68. October 12, 1711; June 9, 10, 24, 25, 28, 1709; February 27, 1711.

69. July 9, 1711; January 17, 1711; for a temporary dissolution, at least, of the distinctions of color and class alike, see June 18, 1712. Where Byrd was all but unconcerned by these transgressions of the lines of caste and class, he was deeply disturbed by infringements *within* those lines of his own standards of marital and extramarital morality; see June 17, 1710; June 30, 1712.

70. For mere scoldings of overseers, see, e.g., March 28, April 5, July 11, August 13, 1709; January 13, September 7, 1710; February 19, December 1, 1711; May 13, 1712; April 17, May 15, September 19, 1720; March 15, 1721. For actual and threatened whippings of overseers and other white servants, see, e.g., May 13, June 27, 1709; June 17, 1710; February 25, May 31, September 5, 1711; February 20, November 23, 1720.

the great clans of Virginia was to be fed like the servants, forced to report in like them, and subject to being summoned like them. Young Will Eppes was similarly bound over to Byrd and then dismissed within a matter of months because Byrd "would keep nobody that would not follow orders."[71] Other youths were actually subject to corporal punishment for their failings. Byrd "beat Billy Wilkins for telling a lie" and had him "whipped for not writing well." He beat his own niece Suky "for not learning to read." He whipped his nephew Billy "extremely" because the youngster "would not learn his books." He marked his principled approbation of such strenuous corrections when he hailed as "well done" the flogging of a gentleman's "refractory" son by the planter with whom the boy was boarding.[72]

These similarities of treatment, and these blurrings of the status prerogatives of gentry children, overseers, artisans, and slaves of all sorts, insinuated themselves into the very words in which Byrd discussed such matters. An irreducible imprecision always governed his family language, reflecting as it did the imprecision of social boundaries within his wider family itself.

He spoke of his "boys" when he referred to slaves whom he beat because they were going to burn his hogshead staves, and identically of his "boys" when he meant the white youngsters whom he was teaching to sing psalms, and identically again of his "boys" when he designated his neighbors' and relatives' children whose time he "settled . . . so that they might have leisure to improve themselves at night." And of course he called his own son his "boy" as well.[73]

Similarly, he sometimes called his white mistress Annie his "girl," as he sometimes called his daughter and also the slaves in the quarters.[74]

71. May 16, June 7, 1709; April 11, August 14, 1711. The dismissal of the Eppes youth was especially indicative of the strength of Byrd's convictions because, in those very days, Byrd was dealing regularly with Colonel Eppes in his capacity as commander of the militia in the crisis of an unexpected French invasion. See August 15–23, 1711. Military emergency conferred no more immunity from the rigors of servile discipline on young Eppes than simple family connection did.

72. March 3, July 25, 1712; February 1, 1711; July 14, 1710; September 27, 1711. See also October 8, 1710; January 11, 1711; May 31, August 21, 1712. With another of his nephews, almost uniquely, Byrd consistently contented himself with "gentle words," "quarrels," "scolds," and "displeasures"; see February 14, March 3, 4, 27, April 3, May 7, 15, 1720. But Byrd also gladly offered the young man his ship's passage to England to be rid of him; see June 18, 1720.

73. April 5, 1712; January 25, 1711; September 6, 1712. See also August 5, 1709; May 7, December 24, 30, 1710; January 11, June 9, 1711; May 3, September 13, 1712; March 25, August 3, September 14, 1720.

74. December 14, 18, 1719; February 14, 1720. December 31, 1710; January 14, 1711; January 12, 1712.

At other times he referred to Annie as his "maid," the same term he occasionally applied to both his white servants and his black house slaves.[75] Blood family and social family were indistinct in name because they were indistinct in fact.

In dealing with his more distant relatives, Byrd's nomenclature was still more confusing and less consistent. On the one hand, he moved in many ways to bring his remoter relatives verbally closer to him. He called his sister Mary's husband James his "brother Duke" and, though she had been dead for decades, his sister Ursula's husband Robert his "brother Beverley." He addressed his wife's sister Frances as his own "sister Custis" and her husband John as his "brother Custis" or sometimes simply as his "brother."[76] He embraced his wife's parents as his own "father Parke" and "mother Parke." He assumed his wife's more distant relations as his own as well, making "cousins," "aunts," and "uncles" out of her connection with the Ludwell clan. In all these usages, he aggrandized his blood family and tightened its members' ties.[77]

On the other hand, he was sometimes less than punctilious about kinship terminology in ways that did not bring remote relatives closer at all. He called his nephew John Brayne his "cousin Brayne" and his niece Susan Brayne his "cousin Suky Brayne." He did not even assign another nephew to any kinship category at all. He just called him "Billy Beverley," as though to concede that if he could not call him cousin, he had no other familial classification for him.[78]

The centrality of cousinage also shaped his thinking of the widow of his once-dear friend Benjamin Harrison as his "cousin Harrison" and of her son as his "cousin Ben," though in fact they were no blood relatives

75. December 27, 1719; January 12, 13, September 12, 1720. December 14, 27, 1719; May 23, 1720. April 10, September 22, December 24, 1709; February 20, 23, 26, 1710; April 3, 5, September 12, 1712; April 4, 1720. For the one time Byrd called Annie his "mistress," see November 1, 1720.

76. E.g., among many, September 17, 19, 1720; March 26, 1720; February 28, November 19, 20, 1709; April 11, 14, 27, 30, 1709; May 2, 1709. Occasionally Byrd did define an in-law through his wife, as when he spoke of his wife's sister as "her sister"; see May 1, November 3, 1709; November 3, 6, 1711; April 25, 1712.

77. E.g., April 1, 8, 19, 1709; November 3, 1709; February 15, 1720; October 21, 28, 1720; February 10, April 27, May 6, November 1, 1720; May 3, November 1, 2, 1720; November 3, April 30, 1709. In a very different kind of aggrandizement of his "blood" family, Byrd also called his fellow members of the Virginia Council his "brothers"; see April 18, December 24, 1711.

78. February 14, 20, 23, March 13, 15, 16, 18, 27, 31; April 3, May 7, 1720; March 18, 19, 20, 22, 23, April 6, 1721; April 22, October 25, 1711; December 14, 1720.

to him whatsoever.[79] Besides brothers, sisters, parents, and children, Byrd's kinship universe contained only one category of any consequence, the category of cousins. He required no others because he used that one so vaguely and expansively that it became all-encompassing.

Finer distinctions were unimportant to Byrd because he was never concerned to place people scrupulously. His was a communal family, and he seemed almost deliberately to draw distant relatives closer by calling them all cousins while setting his own children off at some remove by calling them only "the child" or "the boy." People had their places in his family, but he felt no need to dwell on them or draw out their hierarchical possibilities. If anything, he attempted to exaggerate attachments that might have been more fragile while attenuating those that were inherently more privileged. For the family's internal differentiations never dominated his notions of it. On the contrary, its integration engrossed his attention. The effective interpenetration of its multitudinous members and their social roles and responsibilities elicited his best energies and afforded him a fair measure of his finest "amusement."

If his family's internal differentiation concerned Byrd comparatively little, its external differentiation from the wider society of provincial Virginia occupied him hardly at all. His family was not an institution sharply set apart from the contagions and contaminations of the community but rather an assemblage of individuals intricately intertwined with the community. Byrd's family network was not a fortress designed to hold a hostile world at bay but rather a sprawling and spatially discontinuous domain open to, interspersed with, and elaborately enmeshed in its environment.

Just as Byrd's kinship categories were unsteady at best, so his applications of them to his kinfolk themselves were cavalierly inconstant. He occupied himself as little about the boundaries between blood relatives and boon companions as he did about the lines of demarcation between constituencies within his own plantation family.

He did refer consistently to a few relatives by their family titles. He never called Mrs. John Custis or Mrs. James Duke anything but "sister," and he hardly ever called Mr. Duke anything but "brother." But he set other relatives as unfailingly beyond his family pale. He never accorded his cousin William Bassett or his nephew Billy Brayne their kin cognomens, and he hardly ever spoke of Philip Ludwell as his "uncle." More often than he exhibited even such contradictory consistencies of usage,

79. February 14, June 2, November 13, 1720; February 16, 1720.

he showed himself unconcerned for consistency of any kind. He divided his designations of a number of other individuals almost randomly between the civil and the familial spheres, and, still more suggestively, he split his stylings vacillatingly within the very same families. His Philip Ludwell was almost always a "Colonel," but the colonel's wife and daughter were "aunt" and "cousin" about a third of the time each. His "sister Custis" was always family, but her husband was Byrd's "brother Custis" only half the time. His Billy Brayne was never a "cousin," but Billy's sister Suky and brother John had that appellation two and three times as often as not. Byrd never declared William Bassett a kinsman at all, and he counted the colonel's wife a "cousin" only a couple of times, but he claimed their daughters as "cousins" in nearly half his allusions to them.[80]

Byrd did not always keep his kindred straight because he did not ever hold kinship supremely significant in the first place. His preoccupation was always with his wider world. His family, as he forged it at Westover, was essentially a microcosm of the greater community, teemingly peopled with apprentices, artisans, servants, and slaves as well as friends, flunkies, and veritable strangers. Insofar as he could not bring all the affairs of Chesapeake society within his walls and marches, he went out willingly from their confines. At home and abroad, he was an utterly public man, happy in company and happier still amid "abundance of company."[81]

At home he was hardly ever without such company. From 1709 to

80. Mrs. Custis was "sister" all 83 times she was mentioned, and Mrs. Duke all 19 times; Mr. Duke was "brother" 35 out of 40 times. William Bassett had his civil or military titles all 76 times he was discussed, Billy Brayne was neither a nephew nor a cousin in 8 references, and Philip Ludwell had an avuncular label only twice in 167 references. John Custis was kin in 63 allusions and merely "Mr." or "John" in 61; others such as Byrd's father-in-law, his cousin Mrs. Grymes, and his cousins Bassett were spoken of almost as equivocally. While Philip Ludwell was almost invariably a "Colonel," the women of his menage were cast as kindred 4 of 14 times each. While Billy Brayne was never a cousin, Suky was in 9 of 14 instances and John in 16 of 22. While Colonel Bassett was never a cousin and Mrs. Bassett was a cousin only 2 of 13 times, the Bassett girls were within the family compass 6 of the 13 times. While Mrs. Grymes counted as a cousin 2 of 5 times, her husband counted so only 2 of 26. All tallies are for the two fragments combined. (And even in that there was further inconstancy, at least in a few striking cases. John Custis was a brother to Byrd in 63 of 93 references in 1709–1712 but not once in 31 in 1720–1721. Colonel Ludwell's wife had a kin title only an eighth of the time in the first fragment but half the time in the second. Suky Brayne was a cousin only once in 5 allusions from 1709 to 1712 but in 8 of 9 from 1720 to 1721. The Bassett girls were always called by their proper names in the earlier segment but accorded the kin referent 6 of 7 times in the latter one.)

81. April 12, 1712.

1712 he had visitors almost two days out of every three. Month in and month out for the better part of four years, he entertained at least fifty people a month at his plantation or his quarters in Williamsburg. From the time of his return in 1720 until the middle of the following year, he still received guests at least every other day and still fed or bedded more than forty men and women a month, though he no longer had his wife's help in the management of the household.[82]

Such numbers scarcely satisfied his needs. He "desired" his guests, again and again, to remain for meals. He "persuaded" them to tarry for the night. He was glad when they were "so kind as to stay." And he was genuinely distressed when they "threatened" to leave or actually went.[83]

Once he had maliciously sweet solace when his "company went away," since "soon after there came a great gust of wind and rain to punish them for not staying." More often he had others still staying on to comfort him for his losses. People did stay for days and even weeks at a time at Westover, and an unremitting parade trooped through for shorter periods. Doctors and ministers remained while they tended members of the family who were seriously sick. Women of the neigh-

82. From 1709 to 1712, Byrd received 49.7 visitors a month on 19.9 days a month. From 1720 to 1721, he had 40.9 visits on 16.1 days a month. For the two periods together, he entertained 47.5 guests on 19.0 days a month. And these figures do not include Byrd's own overseers, servants, and slaves when they came in from the outlying plantations, nor his friends and the children of his friends whom he installed in long-term residence, nor artisans attached to his operations. (They do count artisans on specific short-term employment on the days they were explicitly cited in the diary; but even such a procedure understates the extent of their visitation, since such artisans stayed until their task was complete, often a month or more, but were ordinarily recorded only on their arrival and/or departure.) The figures do not, indeed, count anyone except on days he or she was specifically mentioned, though on literally dozens of days people were demonstrably at Westover even if they were not actually named. (For the most egregious example, see May 24–June 17, 1712.) The figures also discount many groups of guests referred to in the diary merely as "many" or "abundance" or the like; all such indeterminable references were tallied as 3 visitor units, even when such locutions clearly pointed to much larger numbers. In other words, these figures underrepresent in half a dozen ways the actual extent of entertaining that Byrd undertook.

83. For his entreaties to stay, and satisfaction when they did, see March 4, September 22, October 4, December 3, 1709; February 10, May 24, September 26, December 22, 1710; February 16, April 13, July 2, October 11, 12, November 11, 1711; January 6, 9, February 8, May 5, 16, September 3, 1712; February 27, 1721. For his regrets over those who "would not" extend their stay, see March 26, May 16, 30, June 3, 16, July 2, August 10, 29, September 20, October 4, 1709; June 13, August 1, 25, October 13, 1710; January 30, February 16, 21, March 16, May 9, 11, 13, 18, June 5, August 20, 28, 31, September 24, October 9, November 11, 1711; February 10, 17, 18, 29, March 12, April 2, 4, 5, May 6, 26, June 5, 7, 25, July 8, August 1, 29, 31, 1712; March 25, August 3, 12, October 11, November 6, 1720; February 27, March 5, 1721.

borhood were put up while they took charge of deliveries and miscarriages. Friends from far away stopped on the way to or from funerals and court days. Fellow churchgoers came back from services for dinner. Men with business dealings dropped in. Even the Indians of the area passed through and found food and drink freely given.[84]

In the midst of all this bustling to and fro by others, Byrd also made time for his own inveterate visiting. From 1709 to 1712 he availed himself of hospitality on at least one of every three days and from 1720 to 1721 almost two days of every three. Since in each period he made a couple stops on each day out, he visited about twenty-five homes a month in addition to welcoming forty or fifty guests at Westover every thirty days.[85]

Day after day after day, he maintained his hectic social schedule. Week in and week out, unabatingly, for five years, he spent six days of every seven in visiting or being visited.[86] He participated in a system of supercharged sociability that sometimes seemed to run of its own momentum. For Byrd and his fellow planters, incessant visiting was a way of life that could proceed in occasional cases of necessity without one or the other party to the visitation. Guests arrived and settled themselves at Westover when the Byrds themselves were not even there. One man waited for four days while Byrd and his wife were off at the capital; he simply made himself comfortable until his hosts returned. Another stayed with Mrs. Byrd for a similar stretch while her husband alone went away to Williamsburg. Yet another guest was actually left behind to take charge of the estate while his putative host rode off for a day's social engagements.[87]

Such assumptions of accessibility and responsibility ran the other way as well. When Byrd and a few of his friends found no one at home

84. For the retribution by drenching storm, see March 19, 1710. For entertainments of Indians, see July 24, August 13, 1709; March 11, 1712; March 23, 24, 1721. The other sorts of visits occurred too commonly to cite specifically. For the rare occasions on which Byrd confessed any reservations about the constant crowds, see June 24, 1709; August 15, 1710; January 10, 1712.

85. From 1709 to 1712 Byrd made 20.5 visits on 11.3 different days a month. Through 1720–1721 he made 37.1 visits on 18.6 different days a month. Over the entire time he averaged 24.2 visits on 13.1 different days each month.

86. From 1709 to 1712 he averaged 4.6 days a month neither visiting nor visited; from 1720 to 1721, 3.7. For the two stretches together, he averaged 4.4 days a month, or almost exactly one day a week, without his customary company.

87. May 7, 1709; June 7–13, 1712; September 16, 1710; see also June 11, 1709; October 12, December 14, 1710; September 10, 11, 14, October 22, 1711; February 5, 16, March 5, April 3, June 16, September 11, 1712.

at the Harrisons, they simply let themselves in and "had some victuals." When Byrd missed Drury Smith at his militia captain's plantation, he similarly entered, "stayed about two hours," and "ate some cold beef for dinner."[88]

Byrd simply put no premium on privacy and displayed no desire for domestic intimacy. Even amid the multitudes already about his estate, he stood ready to take in more. He took the sons and daughters of his social peers who sought to serve for a while at Westover. He took the relatives of the gentry who had fallen on hard times, such as a sister of Mr. Digges who "had nobody to take care of her." He took his own hapless kin, such as his marginally mad uncle and his orphaned nephews. He took a feckless friend of his wife whose husband "threatened to kill her, and abused her extremely." He even attempted to take in total strangers. He promised "a poor woman" whose name he did not know that he would "endeavor to cure" her daughter of her "vapors" if the woman would let the girl "come and stay [at Westover] for two months."[89]

Byrd's engrossment in such social relations was so consuming as to make him indifferent to his wife's desires and, indeed, to her needs. Even when she was "not well" he left her to go visit others. Once he forsook her to go gallivanting off to a Mrs. Cocke. Another time, when his wife was recuperating from a miscarriage, he abandoned her to the occasional ministrations of a few women of the neighborhood while he went visiting, played billiards, and ate abundantly. Yet another time, when she had been sick and he had been gone for five days, he did feel a touch of contrition, but it did not deter him from dallying on the way home for some additional business, an inspection of a salt works, and a stop "by the way" to discuss politics and patronage with another planter.[90]

88. July 4, 1710; March 27, 1712; see also December 19, 21, 1710; August 24, September 18, November 14, 1711; and, for identical practices a generation later, see *Diary of Robert Rose,* ed. Fall, 23, 27, 38, 39, 41, 52, 68, 74, 86.

89. April 11, June 7, 1709; January 4, 15, 31, February 10, 11, March 7, 10, 1710; February 24, April 11, August 14, 1711. March 10, 1711. February 10, 11, June 28, 1710. March 31, 1711. June 14, 1710. See also April 12, 1710; August 14, 1711.

90. May 14, 1710; April 24, 1712; February 14–16, 1710; March 30–April 3, 1712. See also March 15, 1710; May 31, 1711; February 18–22, July 20–24, 1712. When his wife was well, Byrd did little better. He still waited lengthily on another lady living on the plantation, rather than return to his wife at once, when he came back from an extended stay in Williamsburg; and when he did finally get around to his mate, their reunion provoked only an argument. See October 12, 1710. And when it was not just the abandoned wife of a local minister but the governor himself who was available, Byrd could not even

Similarly, when his first son was born, Byrd was off within five days of the event for a bout of politics, card playing, drinking, and excessive eating in the capital. Not even the birth of a male heir, nor for that matter the boy's subsequent death, could distract him from his true passions. During the course of his son's fatal illness, Byrd never once went out of his customary social way as he did over and over again when his fellow planter Benjamin Harrison was dying. For the last three weeks of his neighbor's life, Byrd looked after him every single day. He sent medications and even a partridge when his friend asked for it. He arranged to stay up to watch with him through the night, three or four times, as he never did at all with his own child. When Harrison finally died, Byrd was moved to pronounce a spontaneous tribute, as he was never impelled to express any laments for his own son.[91]

Though Byrd had no other friends as close as Colonel Harrison, he still went out of his ordinary course for any number of other neighbors. When Colonel Randolph was sick Byrd "let the Colonel know anything [he] had was at his service." When Colonel Hill was incapacitated, Byrd "offered to bring the Colonel's tobacco from York River." Indeed, when Bland was in danger, Byrd was unable to "forbear crying to see [his] friend so bad," though he had never shed a tear over his son's mortal peril.[92]

Just as Byrd extended himself for his friends and neighbors, he watched anxiously to see if they did the same for him. When he himself was ill, he was relieved as well as pleased when "everybody was so kind as to ask after" him. He cared about their caring. He was affected mightily when the doctor who attended him in one illness insisted that he did

---

be bothered to quarrel with his wife. For the four days of an executive visit at Westover, Byrd entertained to the lavish best of his ability without ever once bestowing a thought on his helpmate in all that time. See March 24–27, 1711.

91. March 22–April 10, 1710. For that matter, Byrd was more immediately and, to all appearances, emotionally involved in the similarly protracted dying of his servant, old Ben O–d–s–n, than in the decline and death of his child; see July 15–August 15, 1709. Even the seventeenth-century English diarist John Evelyn, who was otherwise as preoccupied with public affairs and as laconic about his private life as Byrd, acknowledged an "inexpressible grief and affliction" at the loss of his little boy and launched into a long and tender recollection of the lad's brief life. See *The Diary of John Evelyn*, ed. William Bray (London, 1907), 1:327–30. And even Landon Carter, who shared something of Byrd's fatalistic resignation to divine design, allowed himself a loving lamentation for his "dear little daughter Susannah" after her passing (see *Diary of Landon Carter*, ed. Greene, 220, 221–22).

92. May 27, June 29, 1710; April 4, 1720. See also April 10, May 2, 17, August 22, 1710; February 11, 1712.

so "out of pure friendship and not as a doctor," neglecting "a great deal of other business" to be with Byrd incessantly for five days, and he was "amazed" when the man "took nothing for all his trouble" besides. On the other hand, he was visibly disconcerted when another medical man "came to the next house" when Byrd's little girl was ailing "but would not be so kind as to call to see the child." When the man did appear on the following day, Byrd was bothered less by the jeopardy in which his daughter had been than by the breach of neighborly relations.[93]

Failures of friendship touched Byrd as derelictions of duty toward his immediate family were powerless to do. He did not dismiss insignificant slights. He worried when someone was "very sullen against" him or "not kind to [his] people." He was "out of humor" when his neighbors behaved badly toward him or believed ill of him. When his steer strayed into an adjacent corn field, he killed the animal "rather than keep anything injurious to my neighbor," and he sent part of the carcass "to make amends." When the parson sent to him for "a pint of canary" for a bad case of "the gripes," he dispatched it, "notwithstanding [he had] but a little, because [he] should be glad if [he] were in his condition to receive such a kindness from another."[94]

Byrd's overweening concern for such social exchange even affected his conduct of more crucial affairs. On receiving word one morning that sixty Virginians had been killed by Indians, he heard the news with uncharacteristic impassivity. When, as military commander of the county, he received orders from the governor to proceed to an immediate rendezvous, he delayed his departure for a full day. He "could not go till tomorrow because [he] had invited company to dine." Confronted with

93. October 4, 1711; see also July 9, 12, August 19, 1711. July 8, 9, 13, 1711. August 4, 5, 1710.

94. April 24, 1711; July 9, 1709; August 2, 1711; August 17, 1709. June 3, 4, 1711. March 25, 1709. Byrd sent gifts such as he gave the parson with exceeding frequency. They ranged from pomegranates to pigeons and from medical potions for poor women to a panther for the governor. See, e.g., March 26, April 3, 7, 9, 15, May 18, 22, 30, June 20, July 18, 22, 28, October 6, 9, 14, 28, November 6, 8, December 23, 1710; January 16, February 12, April 14, May 10, 11, 13, 19, 21, 31, June 14, 16, July 26, August 1, 14, 25, September 1, 19, 20, November 1, 11, 29, 1711; January 19, 29, February 4, 5, 8, 9, March 2, April 10, September 9, 1712. At the same time, he also received gifts from others—watermelons and wax and wine, sturgeon and crab, spices and dessert knives, and more—and he registered them delightedly as tokens of esteem and fellow-feeling. See, e.g., February 17, March 21, June 17, 20, August 6, 10, October 6, November 3, 14, December 8, 9, 1710; February 24, March 2, July 20, August 7, 29, September 1, 13, 15, 20, 24, 1711; March 5, 31, May 13, July 11, 24, August 2, 1712. The exchange of gifts altogether dwarfed the occasional borrowings back and forth between planters; see, e.g., December 4, 1711; June 24, August 30, 1712.

a choice between responding promptly to the most catastrophic Indian massacre of his generation and serving dinner to a few promising "young men" of the province, he chose to serve his dinner.[95]

Less dramatically, but perhaps more powerfully, Byrd disclosed his predilections and priorities when he returned from his long stay in London in February 1720. He had not been home for fully five years. He had not canvassed the state of his plantation in all that time, nor walked its once-familiar fields, nor spoken with his "flocks." Yet when his ship touched shore after almost two months at sea, he did not start straight for home. Visiting and receiving visitors as he went, he made his way to Williamsburg. He spent several days there, renewing old acquaintances and refreshing old alliances. He wended a dawdling course up the James, enjoying the hospitality of friends and favored guests. Altogether, he was in Virginia for nine days of politicking and neighboring before he set eyes on his own acres at Westover.[96]

Westover was simply not, for him, a sanctuary from the stress and strife of the world beyond. On the contrary, it was in the wider world that he felt most at home and most at one with himself. When he was visiting, he experienced good thoughts and good humor more steadily than when he was on his own ground.[97] It was in the wider world that he carried himself most cordially as well. In a few areas to the north of the Chesapeake, the family was already becoming what it would eventually be, at least as an ideal, throughout the modern West: an institution in which aggression was inhibited if not interdicted.[98] But on the banks of the James, the family was still, for Byrd and his fellow settlers at Westover, the terrain where all sorts of aggressions were disinhibited. Within the narrow nuclear group, the master and his mistress quarreled interminably and often incandescently. In the wider family, even more flagrant aggressions occurred, such as scoldings, beatings, and, on occasion, brandings. Only in his social engagements—in the endless rounds of comings and goings in which Virginians of Byrd's class

95. October 7, 1711.
96. February 4–13, 1720.
97. He had good thoughts and good humor 315 of 326 nights, or 96.6 percent of the time, and he never had a single night abroad that was marked by both bad thoughts and bad humor. He was in good spirits a little less, 94.6 percent of the time, at home, and he had both bad thoughts and bad humor together half a dozen times there. (The one place he fell into foul moods with fair frequency was on his own outlying plantations, where he had bad thoughts or bad humor six nights of 27, or 22.2 percent of the time.)
98. John Demos, *A Little Commonwealth: Family Life in Plymouth Colony* (New York, 1970).

passed their days—was he at his mildest and most gracious. Only at home amid company and away amid company did he flourish most fully.

Many questions remain. Why was Byrd driven to expand his immediate family into a considerable community? Why was that plantation community still insufficient, so that he had always to be busying himself with additional guests at Westover? Why were even such guests insufficient, so that he had always to be off visiting and obsessively courting more company? What impelled him always outward, to satiate his craving for company?

These are not the questions ordinarily raised about the familial mores of Southern planters. Conventional questions and controversies about early Southern families have generally reflected the debate over the appropriateness of feudalism and bourgeois modernism as models of the Southern past, a debate that has long dominated discussion of early Southern society itself.

Those disposed to see the South as a unique region have usually emphasized the feudal aspect. On Bertram Wyatt-Brown's reading, for example, Southerners held hierarchical assumptions and harbored dynastic ambitions that savored of the courts of Castile and the castles of Aquitaine. They possessed a peculiarly "family-centered" culture, in which an intense consciousness of far-flung kindred afforded them their "main source of personal security, advancement, and assistance," and a distinctively "ascriptive" one, in which birth and bloodlines provided them their primary "values by which to judge others." [99]

Contrarily, those inclined to draw other than regional dividing lines have customarily asserted the essential modernity of the early South and its dominant family systems. In Philip Greven's account, for example, "genteel" colonists maintained middle-class ideals and aspirations that suggest the suburbs of Long Island in the twentieth century. They cultivated families "notable for the intensity of their affection and love" and "remarkable" for the "preoccupation" of their members with one another. "Above all else," according to Greven, "genteel parents adored their children from infancy on." They "cherished and fostered a sense of domesticity and intimacy" almost wholly contained "within the walls

99. Bertram Wyatt-Brown, "The Ideal Typology and Ante-Bellum Southern History: A Testing of a New Approach," *Societas* 5 (1975): 1–29; quotations at 4. For another recent version, see Eugene Genovese, *Roll, Jordan, Roll: The World the Slaves Made* (New York, 1974). Needless to say, all these invocations of feudal forms are far indeed from the family ethos and communitarian context Ariès attributes to the late Middle Ages.

of the household." They defined domestic unity in terms of an "image of the 'family circle' . . . self-consciously set apart from the world in which they lived," a "one secure place where peace, harmony, and love reigned."[100]

Neither Greven's nor Wyatt-Brown's analysis illuminates the family life or family values of William Byrd. So far from displaying any abiding concern for distant kin, Byrd could hardly keep his relatives straight and rarely even tried. So far from projecting grand dynastic plans, he always preferred his daughter to his sons. He never exhibited any notable affection or love for the members of his immediate family, nor did he ever appear to adore his offspring from infancy on. He was not preoccupied with his wife and children, he did not seek intimacy with them, and he certainly did not set a narrow nuclear group apart from the wider world or prefer the family circle to larger spheres.[101]

What is more, he was by no means alone. Other surviving personal testimonies of the provincial South square substantially with Byrd's and, taken together, indicate that the pattern of his family life was anything but aberrant.

In regard to his incessant visiting and entertaining, for instance, it is clear that almost every other early Virginian of whom we have any record was occupied in a similar sociability. Twenty years before Byrd be-

100. Philip Greven, *The Protestant Temperament: Patterns of Child-Rearing, Religious Experience, and the Self in Early America* (New York, 1977); quotations at 265–70. For another, earlier version, see Edmund S. Morgan, *Virginians at Home: Family Life in the Eighteenth Century* (Williamsburg, Va., 1952).

101. In fairness to Wyatt-Brown, it should be conceded that he wrote primarily about anti-bellum Southern society and not the colonial era. In fairness to Greven, it should be said that he chose to write rather more about the "genteel" of the North than of the South. But Greven did take Byrd as a prime example of his 'genteel' mode. Byrd is, in fact, his primary evidence that the "genteel" were "far more at ease with their sensuality and with sensual experience" than other colonists; and Byrd is his best example of a gentleman of "powerful sexual appetites" who was "almost always able to satisfy them" (see *The Protestant Temperament*, 313–14). But if Byrd's London days do testify to a remarkable concupiscence, his Virginia years can only be construed as testimony to a still more extraordinary frustration. As shown already, he coupled barely once a month with his wife from 1709 to 1712 and fornicated not at all, with Annie or anyone else, from the beginning of 1720 to mid-May of 1721. Greven simply misreads Byrd's relationship with Annie when he says she "usually served to gratify his sexual needs." And so far from feeling no guilt over his unsuccessful advances to Annie, Byrd experienced immense misgivings, hailed her refusals of his importunities as deeply moral, prayed God's forgiveness for his own "uncleanness" in the affair, and pledged himself repeatedly to desist. Greven also suggests that the "genteel" endured no distress about masturbation (see 317), but Byrd almost unfailingly called that act "unclean," and it occasioned four of the only six nights he had "bad thoughts" while away visiting in the entire 1709–1712 diary; see April 21, 1710; October 29, 1711; March 12, April 1, 1712.

gan his diary, the French traveler Durand reported that people around the Chesapeake spent "most of their time visiting each other" rather than rusticating in domestic isolation. "When a man has fifty acres of ground, two menservants, a maid, and some cattle," the Frenchman found, "neither he nor his wife do anything but visit among their neighbors."[102] When a man had much greater assets, he moved among his neighbors still more grandly. William Fitzhugh could accommodate a troop of twenty travelers quite "royally," even when they descended on him without a word in advance of their arrival. He gave them food and fine wines, beds for the night, and "fiddlers, a jester, a tight-rope dancer, [and] an acrobat" for their amusement besides.[103]

Twenty-seven years after Byrd died (in 1744), the other great Virginia diarist of the eighteenth century, Landon Carter, recorded a still more lavish affair, a "three days' festival" to which he invited "all [his] neighborhood." Besides such extravagant entertainments, he reckoned his "many comers and goers fed" among the regular expenses of his household.[104]

Robert Rose, a clergyman on the Northern Neck and later in Albemarle, was abroad more often than Byrd. One year he spent more nights visiting with others than under his own roof. Over a half-dozen years around the middle of the century, he devoted an absolute majority of the substantive entries in his diary to his social calls and callers.[105] This was all the more striking since he began his journal explicitly to keep "an account of the most precious talent almighty God has entrusted with man, Time." In his eyes, an endless succession of social exchanges was evidently a worthy employment of God's gift.[106]

George Washington also defined his diaries as a means of taking

102. Gilbert Chinard, ed., *A Huguenot Exile in Virginia* (New York, 1934), 111. For other instances of the inveterate conviviality of ordinary folk, see 128–29, 135–36, 139.

103. Ibid., 158. It is revealing that the details of the event come from the dazzled Durand, while Fitzhugh himself was much more diffident about it all. See Richard Beale Davis, ed., *William Fitzhugh and his Chesapeake World 1676–1701* (Chapel Hill, 1963), 245–46.

104. *Diary of Landon Carter*, ed. Greene, 533, 534.

105. Altogether, Rose entered 4,276 items in the diary; excluding 896 that pertained purely to the weather, 1,795 of the remaining 3,380 referred to his visiting and his receiving of visitors. (Of the rest, 354 referred to his business interests, 318 to his religious and pastoral duties, 269 to disease and death, and 231 to his servants and slaves and the management of his estate.) For the computation of his nights at home and away, see Richard Dunn's review of the diary, in the *Virginia Magazine of History and Biography* 87 (1979): 361–63.

106. *Diary of Robert Rose*, ed. Fall, 3; see also 26 for the genuine moral revulsion that an act of inhospitality had the power to arouse in Rose.

stock of "where and how [his] time [was] spent" and also proceeded to fill them primarily with social engagements. In his Barbados log of 1751–1752, he entered little more than his invitations from the planters there. In his Mount Vernon journals of 1760 and afterwards, he reduced his record so nearly to a "mere chronicling of dinner guests" that a recent editor of the volumes was impelled to worry that "at times the reader may feel that he has got hold of an eighteenth-century guest book rather than a diary."[107]

All these crowded social calendars at once reflected and sustained an unconcern for close family attachment deriving from a common social pattern. When Washington's aging mother asked him to allow her to move in with him at Mount Vernon, he rebuffed her because the plantation was too much like "a well-resorted tavern" to provide her with the "calmness and serenity" that he was sure she required in her waning years. When his wife managed to have dinner alone with him one day, he marked the moment as the "first instance" in which they had shared such conjugal intimacy in two years.[108]

Just as Washington never considered curbing the constant "sitting up of company" that kept him from Martha and his mother, Robert Rose never gave a moment's thought to curtailing the travels that left him little time for his wife and children. He set down at least a dozen refer-

107. *The Diaries of George Washington,* ed. Donald Jackson (Charlottesville, 1976), 1:xvii–xviii. South of Virginia, similar practices and priorities prevailed. Francis Le Jau, a Carolina contemporary of Byrd's, kept "a constant correspondence of visiting"; see *The Carolina Chronicle of Dr. Francis Le Jau 1706–1717,* ed. Frank Klingberg (Berkeley, 1956), 69. Eliza Lucas Pinckney, a little later, acknowledged her own rather constant social rounds, at a time when she was as much the manager of her three plantations in the low country as Byrd ever was of his five or ten along the James, and indeed maintained that "visiting [was] the great and almost only amusement" in Charleston. See *The Letterbook of Eliza Lucas Pinckney 1739–1762,* ed. Elise Pinckney (Chapel Hill, 1972), 7–8, 34–35, 39, 51, 60–61; the quotation is at 181. As if to prove Pinckney's observation accurate, Ann Manigault was keeping a diary at the time and devoting two-thirds of all the entries to just such dinners and entertainments. In fact, she was still apportioning a third of her items to her own comings and goings and those of her family and friends two decades later, when her health was broken and she was bedridden for weeks at a time. See Mabel Webber, ed., "Extracts from the Journal of Mrs. Ann Manigault, 1754–1781," *South Carolina Historical Magazine* 20 (1919); 57–63, 128–41, 204–12, 256–59; 21 (1920): 10–23, 59–72, 112–20.

108. *Diaries of George Washington,* ed. Jackson, 1:xxv. Both these episodes occurred in the 1780s, but they were not simply products of Washington's post-Revolutionary celebrity. In his 1760 diary, he made only a handful of references to his wife and stepchildren, and those only when they were sick, though he had only married the year before. See 1:211–83.

ences to his hospitality for every mention of his immediate family,[109] and he was often as callously inconsiderate of his family as Byrd ever was when their needs conflicted with his own desire to be out in the wider world. Rose disappeared for the day when his two-year-old boy came down with a fever. He went away again a few days later when the child suffered an inauspicious relapse. He set off on a four-day jaunt the day after his three-year-old son developed a "violent cough, a wheezing rattling in his throat, and a very great agitation in his lungs." He deposited his pregnant wife with her parents when she was approaching her term, vanishing for weeks of visiting, and did not return to learn the outcome of her crisis until days after the event. Indeed, as if to make his priorities unmistakably plain, he "sat up all night" with sick neighbors and their children. He had never done the same for his own wife and children when they might have welcomed his affectionate attention.[110]

Among all the Virginians of the eighteenth century who left extensive personal evidence, only Landon Carter concerned himself as ardently with his children as with his social rounds. It is surely suggestive that, among them all, only Carter considered himself unappreciated and unfulfilled.[111] Yet, for all his alienation from his fellow Virginians, he

---

109. Over the 54 months of the diary, Rose referred to his wife a mere 35 times and his children only 89 times (a figure that is the more striking since he had eight children during the years of the diary). At that, more than half of the occasions on which he acknowledged his children were periods of their illness. Rose also alluded to other relatives only 69 times, though he had many of them, including five brothers in Virginia or contemplating migration there. All told, he allowed little more than 5 percent of his non-weather entries to his family, either in the narrow nuclear sense or in an inclusive kindred conception. He took notice of his servants and slaves more often than he mentioned either his wife or his children; and here too his priorities paralleled Byrd's. From 1709 to 1712, Byrd acknowledged his children 150 times, his wife 850 times, and his servants, slaves, and overseers 1,142 times. Cf. Greven, *Protestant Temperament,* 274, where it is maintained that the presence of servants and slaves was "rarely noted in the letters and occasional diaries that were written by genteel women and men."

110. *Diary of Robert Rose,* ed. Fall, 14, 11, 15–16, 19, 67; see also 66. For the same preference for sociability at the expense of immediate family, in Carolina as at the Chesapeake and in lower social strata as in higher, see John Lawson's assertion that there were "very few housekeepers" in North Carolina who did not "give away more provisions to coasters and guests who come to see them than they expend amongst their own families" (*A New Voyage to Carolina,* ed. Hugh Lefler [Chapel Hill, 1967], 70).

111. Carter's attendance on his own children was unremitting in the early years of the diary, though largely because they suffered so steadily from fevers and agues. For his own, not altogether loving, assessment of the time he was thereby entangled with them, see *Diary of Landon Carter,* ed. Greene, 194: "It is necessary that man should be acquainted with affliction and 'tis certainly nothing short of it to be confined a whole year in tending

maintained a domestic establishment comparable in most respects to Byrd's. For all his attendance on his progeny, Carter never conceived of his family as "narrow in scope and limited in size." In the same encompassing way as Byrd, he always included his servants and slaves as members of his plantation "family."[112] For all his unease among his neighbors, he never sought to set his household "self-consciously . . . apart from the world." He received a multitude of visitors, and he received them with unfeigned liberality.[113] For all his emotional entanglement with his offspring, he never managed to win their "affection and respect" or to achieve "a pleasurable and valued intimacy between the generations." He meddled interminably in his children's affairs, provoked them repeatedly to rebellion, and responded to their every resentment in kind. He, his scions, and his scion's scions lived together only on terms of rampant animosity and barely bridled aggression.[114]

Elsewhere in the Old Dominion, men and women held still more closely to the configuration of family life evident in Byrd's diaries. The disinhibition of aggression between parents and children so palpable at Carter's Sabine Hall was as openly accepted in other homes, and extended to relations between husbands and wives besides. When Sarah Harrison married Commissary James Blair, she refused to promise him the obedience required by Anglican ritual, yet the minister proceeded with the ceremony and pronounced the couple man and wife. When the crew that drew the dividing line between Virginia and Carolina came upon an "exceedingly noisy" stream, all hands agreed as if by inspiration that it should be called Matrimony Creek. When Byrd's own brother-

---

one's sick children." For his sense of aberrancy among his neighbors and peers, see the splendid introductory essay by Jack Greene, 3–61.

112. Greven, *Protestant Temperament*, 268; *Diary of Landon Carter*, ed. Greene, 127, 217, 359, 363, 383–84, 447, 461, 527, 534. Carter did distinguish on rare occasions between his "indoors family" and "those without," or again between his "out and in family," but even his inside family took in an extensive complement of house servants and slaves; see 168, 170.

113. Greven, *Protestant Temperament*, 266; *Diary of Landon Carter*, ed. Greene, e.g. 130, 137, 140, 141, 142, 143.

114. Greven, *Protestant Temperament*, 268, 266; *Diary of Landon Carter*, ed. Greene, 185, 250, 310, 314–15, 316, 352, 359–60, 369, 371, 391, 407, 436–37, 447–48, 482, 485, 488, 489, 491, 492, 505, 508, 511, 514, 518, 522, 523, 527, 528, 533–34, 553, 577–78. It should be pointed out that Greven distinguishes uneasily between the gentry and the "genteel" and does not count Carter among the "genteel." But that merely makes the convergences between Carter's "moderate" family constellation and Byrd's "genteel" one all the more intriguing.

in-law reached the end of his days, he ordered the inscription on his gravestone to read:

> Under this marble tomb lies the body
> of the Hon. JOHN CUSTIS, Esq.
>
> \*   \*   \*   \*
>
> Age 71 years, and yet lived but seven years,
> which was the space of time he kept
> a bachelor's home at Arlington
> on the Eastern Shore of Virginia[115]

Similarly, the inclusion of servants and slaves in the familial unit was commonplace. Robert Rose could have been quoting from one of the Westover diaries when he returned home from a four-week excursion and recorded his "family in health, two Negroes excepted."[116] The dispatch of children to distant places was unobjectionable if not normal. William Fitzhugh hardly held off longer than Byrd before putting his children an ocean away from him.[117]

The preference for the hubbub of relentless sociability to the calm of hearth and home was virtually universal. Indeed, no one pretended otherwise. Fitzhugh, complaining of the "absolute necessity of business" that called him "abroad so often," occasionally proclaimed his determination to "have some leisure at home." But even as he vented an apparent longing for domestic ease, he was promising friends that they would

115. Morgan, *Virginians at Home*, 47–48; *The Prose Works of William Byrd of Westover*, ed. Louis Wright (Cambridge, 1966), 123, 256; Marshall Fishwick, "The Pepys of the Old Dominion," *American Heritage 11* (December 1959): 118. See also, e.g., Morgan, *Virginians at Home*, 30, 45; Byrd, *Another Secret Diary*, ed. Woodfin, 62.

116. *Diary of Robert Rose*, ed. Fall, 21; see also 16, 19. The usage was actually as old as the earliest decade of settlement in Virginia—see Alexander Brown, ed., *The Genesis of the United States* (Boston, 1890), 797–98—and it persisted to the end of the colonial era in the other Southern settlements as well—see *The Journal of Peter Gordon 1732–1735*, ed. E. Merton Coulter (Athens, Ga., 1963), 29–30; James Habersham to Willet Taylor, April 2, 1764, in *The Letters of the Hon. James Habersham*, Georgia Historical Society, *Collections*, 6 (1904): 22–23; and esp. William Drayton to Peter Manigault, November 16, 1754, in the Manigault Family Papers (South Caroliniana Library, Columbia, S.C.), for sentiments quite comparable to Byrd's most exotic in tending to attach even domestic animals to the "family."

117. Davis, *Fitzhugh and his Chesapeake World*, 194, 273. Eliza Lucas Pinckney, like Byrd, was abandoned by her father (as were her younger brothers) and abandoned her own boys in turn; Pinckney, *Letterbook of Eliza Lucas Pinckney*, ed. Pinckney, x, xi, xii, xv, xxii, xxiii, 5, 13–14, 16. But, unlike Byrd, she was both deeply attached to her father and convincingly distressed at her separation from her sons; see xvi, xxii, 5–6, 7, 21–22, 87–88, 118–19, 121, 122, 125–26, 133, 140, 145, 181, 183.

be "among the first whom when I get time I intend to visit." He never aspired simply to stay at home. He merely meant to go abroad for pleasure as freely as for business. Likewise, Rose often registered the discomforts and perils of his ceaseless wanderings. But in the process of bemoaning them, he accorded them a compelling power that he rarely discovered in the contentments of domesticity. On the roads and rivers, he itemized his every encounter and accomplishment. On his own plantation, he frequently ran four or five days together under the single dull entry "at home," which epitomized the emotional inconsequence to him of the time when he was confined to his conjugal family.[118]

It was not just one gentlemen on the James who craved company inordinately. If we can come to any comprehension of Byrd's intense cultivation of sociality, we may illuminate the sentiments of other colonists around the Chesapeake and farther south over the course of a century and more.

In that endeavor, it is tempting to speculate that the density of Byrd's social life in Virginia was a response to its inherent thinness. It is seductive to suppose that he was constrained to create a community, and sustain it day after unabating day by his frenetic activity, because there would have been none otherwise.

In London, Byrd could hold himself subtly separate from society. It existed indigenously and exercised its watch over people without his complicity. In Virginia, however, he could not hold himself aloof. Social life did not run on of its own accord. Community had to be consciously constructed and purposefully fostered or scarcely exist at all.

In such divergent circumstances, even ostensibly similar activities were subtly different. When Byrd visited incessantly along the James, he was at work. His pleasures had about them an aura of purpose. But when he visited incessantly along the Thames, he was simply at loose ends. His pleasures only betrayed his aimlessness.[119]

118. Davis, *Fitzhugh and his Chesapeake World,* 103; *Diary of Robert Rose,* ed. Fall, 62 and *passim.*

119. The argument here and below turns almost exactly on its head the ingenious argument advanced by David Bertelson in *The Lazy South* (New York, 1967). But where that exposition of colonial Southern dissociation from all sense of social purpose cannot account for the easy acceptance of self and society that pervades Byrd's Virginia journals and the compulsive frenzy that dogs his London days, the conception of a colonial Southerner's dissociation from such a sense in his Mother Country can. In addition, it can illuminate Byrd's remarkable excursion into sexual adventurism in the metropolis, since such a Don Juanish departure from the Virginian colonial character may then be understood as

Among the sophisticates of the great city, awash in a ceaseless whirl of playgoing and coffeehouse rounds and parties at the Spanish ambassador's, he found himself disconnected from any circle of authentic intimacy and assured acceptance. On almost a quarter of his visits to the mansions that he frequented, he was informed by the servants that their masters were "from home"; and there were days when he had to resume his forlorn rounds four, five, once even nine times before finding anyone to admit him.[120] Over the two years of the London segment of his diary, he neither developed any sense of anchored attachments nor showed any feelings of steady affections. Even when he courted an eligible widow or believed himself in love with a fine lady, he did not desist from patronizing his favorite prostitutes or kissing his chambermaid until he "polluted" himself.[121] When he went to receptions and stayed for hours, he knew that there was "nobody [he] liked" there. When he went to masquerades and did not reach home till five in the morning, he realized that he was "but indifferently diverted." He simply had no connections of consequence to London life.[122]

Despite his dalliances with insight, however, he went on with his relentless social rounds. Indeed, he visited more frequently in London than he ever did along the James. He sought society far more furiously where he was aware of its banality than he did where he recorded no such reservations.[123]

The disparity between his behavior in the Old World and the New was doubtless due in some degree to his detachment from social moor-

---

the sexual aspect of a more general fever for futile activity in the absence of any shaping social purpose.

120. He failed to gain admission on 356 of his 1,497 visits, or 23.8 percent of them. For days more difficult than most, see January 17, 27, February 22, March 26, May 12, 31, 1718; February 13, 25, May 26, 1719. For the day he met with nine rebuffs in succession, see December 30, 1717.

121. For Byrd's divertissements while paying court to the widow Pierson, see March 3–July 7, 1719. For his persistence with mistresses and maids even in the midst of his proclaimed passion for Mary Smith, see December 22, 1717–June 7, 1718. For allusions to his having "polluted" himself or otherwise "committed uncleanness" with such women and others encountered even more casually, see February 7, 21, 24, April 17, 26, May 1, 8, 1718.

122. January 15, December 16, 1718. See also, e.g., January 16, 17, 21, March 20, April 14, May 25, 28, 1718; January 12, 27, February 27, March 16, April 1, 22, October 17, 20, 1719.

123. During the two years of the London journals, he paid 1,497 calls, or 62.4 a month. During the five years of the diaries when he was in Virginia, he made 1,402 visits, or 24.6 a month. Even in the more strictly comparable circumstances of 1720–1721, he made but 520 visits, or 37.1 a month.

ings that might have conferred meaning on action in the metropolis. His very distance from all sense of social efficacy drove him to throw himself more madly into mere activity and, at the same time, sharpened his awareness of the disjointed dullness of his days.

Yet his detachment itself depended on differences in European and American social development that issued in an even more revealing disparity between his conduct in England and his carriage while at Westover. For though he did not disparage collective efforts in Virginia as he criticized corporate enterprises in London, he did judge individuals at home as he never did abroad. In England, a communal structure was already set. It was less necessary to probe men's personal qualities than to comprehend their places within the social system that substantially defined their roles. In Virginia, society was shallower and shakier. A social network had still to be solidified. It was risky to reflect invidiously on the collective enterprise and imperative to gauge the character of individuals, since the capacity and inclinations of the actor mattered more than the rudimentary role that he played.[124]

In effect, Byrd was constrained by the very stability of the English community to skim along selfishly on its surface in London, whereas he was driven by the very fragility of the social structure in Virginia to participate sympathetically in the framing of its foundations. The superficial security of anciently established ways was unattainable in the settlements of the Chesapeake, where a common life remained to be built and life itself remained problematic.[125]

124. For 1709–1712 and 1720–1721, Byrd made comments about individuals that could be construed as personal assessments of character or conduct 23.6 times a month; for 1717–1719, he made such comments only 11.5 times a month. For a few of the racier or more penetrating Virginia remarks, see September 15, November 11, 1709; June 16, September 12, 23, November 28, 1710; February 6, April 1, September 23, October 12, November 3, 1711; January 25, February 3, March 29, July 20, 1712. For the insipidity of the London references, almost any one will serve.

125. A generation later, as he moved westward to Albemarle County, Robert Rose assumed a similar responsibility "to do my neighbors a pleasure before I have got necessaries for myself" (see *Diary of Robert Rose*, ed. Fall, 50). And further south, other settlers did the same. Le Jau's "constant correspondence of visiting" was deliberately dedicated to a larger "endeavor to keep [his] neighbors at peace," and it was explicitly undertaken in concert with Carolinians engaged in the same endeavor. Eliza Lucas Pinckney's endless exchange of letters with friends was expressive in a different way of a similar "sense of responsibility for community welfare." And Levi Sheftall's very diary itself was an instrument of community-maintenance for the Jews of early Savannah. See Klingberg, *Chronicle of Le Jau*, 69; Pinckney, *Letterbook of Eliza Lucas Pinckney*, ed. Pinckney, 4; Levi Sheftall diary, 1733–1808, in the Sheftall Family Papers, Keith Read Collection (University of Georgia Library, Athens, Ga.), esp. the frontispiece.

Indeed, it was symptomatic of the disparate directions of his endeavor on the two continents that Byrd virtually abandoned his American obsession with disease and dying when he was in England. He did not make medical observations in London nearly as often as at Westover, and he scarcely thought of death at all.[126] Even when he did acknowledge dangers, he did so as an impotent victim or an irresponsible onlooker. He neither did any doctoring of the ill nor took any interest in how it was done. He hardly took the trouble to follow the progress of the infirm or to comfort the convalescent. When he found a friend "very sick," he simply proceeded to the next stop on his social circuit. Affliction impinged on him only as it disrupted his entertainments.[127]

In Virginia, Byrd was rarely so passive or self-centered in matters of life and death. He was incorrigibly curious about the sick, earnestly engaged in curing them, and absorbedly concerned in their fate. He struggled ardently to enlarge his pharmacological repertory. He gathered an extensive store of medications and dispensed them freely to all who sought his aid. He cultivated the company of doctors, learned from them, and applied his learning for the benefit of family, slaves, friends, and neighbors.[128]

Insofar as he dealt with disease and death at all in London, Byrd attended primarily to his own health. Relatively few of his medical references paid any regard to the suffering and dying that surrounded him. But at Westover and in his travels about the Tidewater, he expended the preponderance of his concern on others. Less than a fifth of his allusions

126. In London, Byrd made 214 medical references on 166 different days, or 8.9 such references a month on 6.9 different days a month. In Virginia, he made 2,116 medical references on 972 different days, or 37.1 references a month—more than four times as many as in London—on 17.1 days a month—two and a half times as many. In London, he mentioned death only 5 times in two years, or less than once very four months. In Virginia, he mentioned it 386 times, or 6.8 times a month. Death thus accounted for only 2.4 percent of the relatively meager attention Byrd paid to all manner of ailments in London, while it represented 18.6 percent of all his allusions to illness in Virginia.

127. May 12, 1718; see also, e.g., December 10, 1718, and January 3, 1719.

128. For Byrd's efforts in pharmacology, see especially his devotion of almost two months, after buying the books and medical cabinet of a deceased doctor, to ordering and mastering the man's "closet," February 8–March 25, 1710. For his own stock of medications (which ranged from grisly things such as Spanish flies to less heroic ones like sage and a bottle of sack) and his dispensation of it, see, e.g., March 1, 15, May 18, 19, June 14, August 20, September 2, 7, 8, 26, November 6, 1710; February 18, April 10, June 7, July 29, August 14, September 28, October 22, 1711; March 8, August 5, 12, 31, September 1, 2, 7, 9, 20, 25, 1712. For his sustained ministrations to colonists of all statuses, see (to take only the examples of a single year) March 1–6, May 25–31, September 12–16, September 24–October 1, November 26–December 2, December 19–22, 1720.

to illness were self-absorbed in Virginia, as against three-fifths in England.[129]

As Byrd shifted in medical matters from private preoccupations in the metropolis to solicitude for his fellow colonists along the James, so he moved more generally. With his servants, friends, and fellow planters of the Chesapeake he had an unspoken understanding of relatedness— relatedness of his own deliberate contrivance and determined maintenance—that he never enjoyed with his worldly peers in England. He had toward his own people and the community that they precariously constituted a sense of responsibility that he could scarcely even have imagined across the Atlantic. In London he looked after his own business and pursued his personal pleasures. Society went on well enough with or without him. But on his American plantations, he acted unceasingly to knit his neighbors together and to articulate their ties.

By his boundless exchanges of hospitality and by the priority that he gave to his public life over his more narrowly domestic affairs, he helped to forge a fellowship. By his indifference to the values of isolation and intimacy, and by his continuing concern for an extraordinary range of people, he helped to develop something of the social density and communal consciousness that those who remained in the Mother Country simply inherited. Ironically, then, the only place where he ever enacted the individualism that America purportedly promoted was England, where a social infrastructure was already in place, leaving him free to pursue his private gratifications as he never could in the New World.

129. During the days of the London diary, 136 of his 214 medical references—63.6 percent—were to his own infirmities. During his days in Virginia, only 406 of 2,116— 19.2 percent—were similarly self-centered, while 80.8 percent were attentive to others.

# FIVE

# The Selling of the Self:
# From Franklin to Barnum

Each of them straddled his century like a colossus. Each was born near its beginning—one in 1706, the other in 1801—and each lived almost to its end—one to 1790, the other to 1891. Each of them began in obscurity, each had half a century of celebrity, and each died acclaimed as the representative American of his age.

Benjamin Franklin was the embodiment of the Enlightenment. David Hume pronounced him "the first philosopher and indeed the first great man of letters for whom we are beholden to America." The Parisians lionized him while he lived among them and lamented him when he died far from them; his fame in France was so extraordinary that the National Assembly proclaimed a period of national mourning when word of his death reached the continent. Even caustic John Adams conceded enviously that "his reputation was more universal than that of Leibniz or Newton, Frederick or Voltaire, and his character more beloved or esteemed than any or all of them."[1]

Phineas Taylor Barnum was the most celebrated American of the nineteenth century. His own posters modestly hailed him as the "hero about whose name clusters so much of romantic interest and whose brilliant deeds are themes of poetry and prose." Others praised him more

---

An earlier version of this essay was read at the National Conference on Jonathan Edwards and Benjamin Franklin, Yale University, February 22–24, 1990.

1. Ormond Seavey, *Becoming Benjamin Franklin: The* Autobiography *and the Life* (University Park, Pa., 1988), 180, 76, 217; Gilbert Chinard, "The Apotheosis of Benjamin Franklin, Paris, 1790–1791." *Proceedings of the American Philosophical Society* 99 (1955): 440–73.

effusively. American presidents anointed him the most admired American in the world. Europeans saw in him the symbol of an era of unprecedented amusements for the masses. Upon his death the London *Times* grieved his passing and called him "an almost classical figure." The French press paid him homage as "the character of our century": a "great benefactor of humanity," an "incomparable," whose "name is immortal."[2]

Thomas Carlyle took Franklin for "the father of all the Yankees." Barnum implicitly acknowledged that paternity, patterning his autobiography unmistakably upon Franklin's and dedicating it to "the universal Yankee nation, of which I am proud to be one." American copywriters would one day salute Franklin as the "Patron Saint of Advertising." Memorialists marked Barnum's death by crowning him "king of advertising." Balzac celebrated Franklin as the inventor of the lightning rod, the republic, and the hoax. Barnum built his national notoriety on a succession of scams and flimflams long before he launched the circuses by which Americans still know his name.[3]

These convergences were more than merely casual. They were but a few of the commonalities and uncanny coincidences in the careers and concerns of the two men. Since those commonalities and coincidences spanned almost two full centuries of American history, it would seem plausible to propose that they issued from deep continuities in our character and that they reveal persisting preoccupations and perplexities in our collective life.

Franklin wrote the most popular and influential American autobiography of all time. Barnum wrote the best-selling American autobiography of the nineteenth century. And they both told a tale of ascent from humble origins through discouragements and hardships to inspiring triumphs. Each account was damned by a fastidious few as the confession of a con artist—the preachment of "our wise prophet of chicanery," as William Carlos Williams denounced Franklin's narrative, "a perfect pattern-book for would-be Yankees and 'cute' businessmen," as others assailed Barnum's—and each was discovered by the multitudes "as evidences of the American genius."[4]

2. Neil Harris, *Humbug: The Art of P. T. Barnum* (Boston, 1973), inside jacket, 281, 280.

3. Esmond Wright, ed., *Benjamin Franklin: A Profile* (New York, 1970), ix; Phineas T. Barnum, *The Life of P. T. Barnum* (New York, 1855), ii; Esmond Wright, *Franklin of Philadelphia* (Cambridge, Mass., 1986), 12; Harris, *Humbug*, 280; Wright, *Franklin of Philadelphia*, 355.

4. Frank Luther Mott, *Golden Multitudes: The Story of Best-Sellers in the United States* (New York, 1947); William Carlos Williams, *In the American Grain* (1925; reprint, New

Franklin and Barnum alike went forth to forge, in the smithies of their operations if not of their souls, the uncreated conscience of their country. And they both did so by empowering ordinary people as ordinary people had never been empowered before. Franklin devoted himself to the calculation of their increase with a demographic sophistication unsurpassed in his era. He rejoiced in them as a rising people and he cherished their happy mediocrity. He offered them the story of his own advancement as a talisman of the future he had plotted for them all. Barnum too took his own tale emblematically, as at once an object lesson and a tribute to the middling masses. He was a populist in his artistry as in his politics. He insisted again and again that "what gave pleasure to democratic audiences was good" and that "standards were fixed by the entertained, not the entertainer." His hoaxes did not infuriate the groups he gulled because, as Constance Rourke realized, "a hoax is an elaborate form of attention." Barnum's humbugs delighted the multitudes they deluded because no one else "had ever taken the pains to delude them on so preposterous a scale before."[5]

On the conventional understanding of their careers and their writings, both Franklin and Barnum exemplified the opportunity that America afforded people who were not born to privilege to seek their own aggrandizement on their own initiative. Both predicated their endeavors on distinctively American conditions of competitive enterprise, and both thereby promoted the materialistic individualism at the core of American culture.

There is much to be said for this conventional understanding. Both Franklin and Barnum took for granted the salience of self-interest among human motives. Both expected people to act on calculations of private advantage. Both moved in milieus of deceit and disappointment, and both became connoisseurs of conniving. Both presented their youth and early manhood as an insistent saga of sharp practice and chicane, in "a world where mutual hostility [was] the norm" and a wary attentiveness to one's own ends a necessity. As early as 1731, Franklin recorded his conclusion that "the great affairs of the world" were "car-

---

York, 1956), 156; A. H. Saxon, ed., *Selected Letters of P. T. Barnum* (New York, 1983), xiii; Constance Rourke, *Trumpets of Jubilee* (New York, 1927), 369.

5. For Franklin, see almost any of the recent accounts: e.g., Wright, *Franklin of Philadelphia;* Seavey, *Becoming Benjamin Franklin;* Herbert Leibowitz, *Fabricating Lives: Explorations in American Autobiography* (New York, 1989); R. Jackson Wilson, *Figures of Speech: American Writers and the Literary Marketplace, from Benjamin Franklin to Emily Dickinson* (New York, 1989). For Barnum, see Harris, *Humbug,* 79, 229–30; Rourke, *Trumpets of Jubilee,* 393.

ried on and effected by parties," that parties were actuated by "their present general interest," that each man within each party harbored simultaneously "his particular private interest," that "as soon as a party . . . gained its general point" each member became "intent upon his particular interest," and that few in public life sought the common good, "whatever they may pretend."[6]

But despite its undeniable force, there are distinct difficulties with this conventional understanding as well. Even as Franklin came to a keen appreciation of American egoism and articulated the logic of its eventual ascendancy, for example, he remained convinced that "men are naturally benevolent as well as selfish." His autobiography is in many ways his account of the means by which he heightened his own disposition to benevolence, weaning himself as he did from the gratifications of aggression and from his youthful delight in defeating others. As a boy in Boston, he proceeded by "abrupt contradiction and positive argumentation." In his maturity in Philadelphia, he saw that there was no point in "obtaining victories that neither my self nor my cause . . . deserved" and that "the chief ends of conversation" were information, pleasure, and persuasion, not the temporary titillation of triumph. He cultivated a "modest diffidence" that served him better than contentiousness or Socratic method ever had when he "had occasion to inculcate [his] opinions and persuade men into measures" that he was "engaged in promoting."[7]

Barnum never affected such modesty, but he did otherwise behave in much the same manner. Even as he insisted that he was "always looking out for the main chance" and that others too were "very apt to think of self first" in cases of "conflicting interests," he remained steadfast in his commitment to the common weal. Indeed, his commitment was the more striking because it was not nearly so necessary to him as a comparable commitment had been to Franklin.[8]

Franklin lived in a society still hedged about by patronage and its prerogatives. He made his way by ingratiating himself with his betters and securing their sponsorship. He had therefore to master or mask his aggression in order to achieve influence and advancement. He had, as he explained in his account of the founding of the subscription library,

6. Seavey, *Becoming Benjamin Franklin,* 116–17; Benjamin Franklin, *The Autobiography of Benjamin Franklin,* ed. Leonard Labaree et al. (New Haven, Conn., 1964), 161.
7. John Updike, "Many Bens," *New Yorker* 64 (February 22, 1988): 115; Franklin, *Autobiography,* 64–65.
8. Barnum, *Life,* 21, 29.

to submerge his own ego and subordinate his own celebrity to attain success. He had to accept "the impropriety of presenting one's self as the proposer of any useful project that might be supposed to raise one's reputation in the smallest degree above that of one's neighbors, when one has need of their assistance to accomplish that project."[9]

Barnum never had to suppress his ambition. He never even had to muffle his avidity to vanquish all rivals. He lived in an era of unbridled competition among men who acknowledged no betters. He came of age amid the liberal scramble and the capitalist clamor that Franklin only forecast.

Yet perceptive contemporaries caught the cunning and the irony in Barnum's recurring acclamations of self-interest and his pervasive presumption of the priority of the public good. As a reviewer of the autobiography observed, the great impresario frequently ascribed his actions to selfish motives when more charitable interpretations of his behavior were equally plausible. "He seems to fear," the reviewer wrote, "that he shall be suspected of having sometimes acted without an eye to the main chance."[10]

In a country without an entitled elite, everyone was under suspicion, because, in a country of "confidence men and painted women," everyone had a hustle. One way to dispel such suspicion was to affect honesty by conceding cunning. Aware that he had to move in the maze of appearances and realities that Franklin had heralded, Barnum disarmed doubt by anticipating his doubters. Knowing that he worked in a "wilderness of mirrors," he operated intuitively on a principle Charles Dickens enunciated explicitly. Americans would "strain at a gnat in the way of truthfulness" but "swallow a whole caravan of camels if they be laden with unworthy doubts and mean suspicions."[11]

Dickens insisted that a "universal distrust" among citizens of the new nation led them to impute mean motives to the most just and generous conduct. Tocqueville, earlier, caught a comparable characteristic of democratic society. Americans explained "almost all the actions of their lives" on the basis of self-interest, though in their actual relations with one another they often gave way to "those disinterested and spontaneous impulses that are natural to man." Tocqueville took this discrep-

9. Franklin, *Autobiography*, 143.

10. Harris, *Humbug*, 213.

11. Karen Halttunen, *Confidence Men and Painted Women: A Study of Middle-Class Culture in America, 1839–1870* (New Haven, Conn., 1982); Octavio Paz, *The Labyrinth of Solitude: Life and Thought in Mexico* (New York, 1961), 21; Harris, *Humbug*, 312.

ancy as a tribute to the power of American culture, or custom as he called it. Democrats "seldom admit that they yield to emotions of [a magnanimous] kind; they are more anxious to do honor to their philosophy than to themselves." But Barnum put no such stock in an abstract ethic of egoism. He was as willing to have recourse to the rhetoric of self-regard as to any other to claim credibility for himself. In that sense, the very rhetoric of self-regard was just another persuasive ploy, a humbug, as it were.[12]

Certainly Barnum believed himself a better man than his image allowed. "The fact is," he once told Thomas Wentworth Higginson, "I am not, nor never was, half so cute nor cunning nor *deep* as many persons suppose. I generally speak right out, just as I think, and have neither time nor inclination to indulge in duplicity." Barnum did pity those who underestimated the deviousness of men, but he also scorned those who overestimated it. "The man who believed everything and everyone to be humbugs" was "the greatest humbug of all," just as the man who wanted "something for nothing" was "sure to be cheated" and indeed "deserve[d] to be."[13]

Barnum bewailed the "blindness" of "the man who coins his brain and blood into gold" and "wastes all of his time and thought upon the almighty dollar." More than that, he often held himself to standards of integrity and concern for the common good that he ruefully regretted others did not share. In his campaign for Congress in 1867, he refused to "fight fire with fire" when he heard that his opponent was buying votes. As he admonished one supporter, there were "no circumstances" under which he would permit "a dollar of [his] to be used to purchase a vote or to induce a voter to act contrary to his honest convictions." He would lose the election sooner than "debauch and degrade" "the noble privilege of the free elective franchise."[14]

In his business dealings he did not demand the rectitude that he did in politics, but he did, again, differ from many with whom he dealt. He apologized for his own circus partners when they declined to preserve prize specimens and donate them to museums as he did, because they were "intent only on pushing the show to a profit" and did not "see dollars in our dead animals." He refunded "every cent" of the investments he secured for a fire extinguisher he hoped to market in America, as he had pledged he would if it failed a public test, though its failure

12. Harris, *Humbug*, 71, 214.
13. Saxon, ed., *Letters*, 87; Harris, *Humbug*, 217, 54–55.
14. Saxon, ed., *Letters*, 94, 153–55.

was, at the outside, only partial. He simply was not "governed by the system of morals which [was] too prevalent in the trading community." He "could have withheld the pledge" in the first place or construed the results of the test more accommodatingly afterward. He could have "put many thousands of dollars in the treasury" of his enterprise. But, "being a mere showman," as he said sardonically, he was "actuated by somewhat different principles." [15]

Being a showman, Barnum did take as his most minimal principle the promotion of his shows. In the dense thickets of semblance and substance of nineteenth-century America, he concentrated first on the management of impressions. He had learned by bitter "experiences in life" that "real merit [did] not always succeed as well as 'humbug,'" so he devoted "a large part of his daily existence" to an unabashed manipulation of public opinion. In the retrospect of his long career, he concluded that he was "indebted to the press of the United States" for "almost every dollar" he possessed and "every success as an amusement manager" he had "ever achieved." As he summed up his "universal plan" for his partner and successor, James Bailey, an essential item was "to advertise freely and without fear." Advertising was "the first, second, and third elements of 'success.'" [16]

Nonetheless, Barnum never mistook the necessity of advertising for its sufficiency. Despite his special sensitivity to promotion, he still made plain to James Bailey that an integral aspect of his "methods" was "to get the best of everything and the most of it." Despite his occasional conviction that people had only to "put on the appearance of business, and generally the reality [would] follow," he still swore that his own exhibitions always gave his patrons "more than [their] admission was worth" to them. The humbugs—the "little 'clap-trap' . . . and puffing advertisements"—were merely "skyrockets" to "attract attention and give notoriety" to the "wonderful, instructive, and amusing" enticements that he offered. Beyond that, Barnum declared his disbelief "that any amount of advertising . . . would make a spurious article permanently successful." It was possible to make money from the public only by "giving a full equivalent therefor," in amusement and in edification. [17]

Franklin was, of course, entangled in similar brambles of images and actualities a century before. Recent revisionists of his legend have been

---

15. Ibid., 233, 276; Barnum, *Life*, 380–81.

16. Barnum, *Life*, 381; Saxon, ed., *Letters*, xviii, 332, 159.

17. Saxon, ed., *Letters*, 332; Barnum, *Life*, 396, 400, 225; Saxon, ed., *Letters*, 103; Barnum, *Life*, 225; Saxon, ed., *Letters*, 103. See also Harris, *Humbug*, 54–55, 214–15.

quick to point out how "typically" he settled for "an indulgent appearance of virtue rather than the exacting reality," and in some regards they are surely right. Franklin himself admitted as much in his account of his efforts to attain humility (to "imitate Jesus and Socrates," as he put it in his initial plan, as if to capitulate before he began). But if Franklin conceded that he could "boast" of success only in acquiring the appearance of humility, that is not yet to say that his every virtue was only an apparent one. With virtues he accorded more consequence than humility, he mastered himself as well as the arcane arts of self-promotion. He rose not only by "the conscious and calculated display of diligence" but also by diligence itself. As he said, he "took care . . . to be *in reality* industrious and frugal" as well as "to avoid all *appearances* to the contrary." [18]

When Franklin paraded his paper home in a wheelbarrow, clanking noisily over the cobblestone streets as he went, he did indeed demonstrate devotion to his business with a brilliant flourish, but he did not engage in an exercise in empty ostentation. Lest anyone suppose otherwise, he gave the very next lines of his story to a striking contrast of his conduct with that of his chief rival, David Harry. Harry was a fellow apprentice similarly seeking to set himself up as a printer. He had patrons more able and influential than Franklin's. But he had none of Franklin's awareness of the importance of his "credit and character as a tradesman," and he had none of Franklin's commitment to his calling, either. He "was very proud, dressed like a gentleman, lived expensively, [and] took much diversion and pleasure abroad." More than all that, though, he "ran in debt, and neglected his business." It was because he mismanaged his interest as well as his image that "all business left him." [19]

The issue that Franklin intended in this contrast was not simply an issue of industry and application, or even of success and self-advancement. It was, rather, an issue of a certain sort of integrity. Poor Richard intimated it when he pronounced honesty the best policy. It was also an issue of a certain sort of utility. Franklin acknowledged it when he remembered, more than half a century later, the rebuke he received from his father for a youthful "scrape." Franklin and a few "playfellows" had stolen stones set aside for a new house to build themselves a fishing wharf. They were "discovered," "complained of," and "cor-

18. Leibowitz, *Fabricating Lives*, 34; Franklin, *Autobiography*, 150, 159; Seavey, *Becoming Benjamin Franklin*, 62–63; Franklin, *Autobiography*, 125–26.
19. Franklin, *Autobiography*, 125–26.

rected by [their] fathers"; and though the son "pleaded the usefulness of the work" his father convinced him "that nothing was useful which was not honest." Franklin chose to recall the contretemps as a cautionary tale. He meant his father's injunction to mark the boundary between unalloyed self-interest, however rationalized, and what Tocqueville would one day call self-interest rightly understood. He meant his boyish violation of that boundary to teach others as it taught him the priority of ethics to interest. A "projecting public spirit" had to be "justly conducted." Honesty and utility alike had to be measured by authentic community service.[20]

Franklin did not doubt that he could do well while doing good. In some of his most sanguine formulations of the relation between benevolence and self-seeking, he maintained that the two were, in the long run, inseparable. In those formulations, his most essential insight was, as John Updike said, his recognition of the close connection between virtue and happiness. Franklin himself averred the "doctrine" that it was "everyone's interest to be virtuous, who wished to be happy," in this world as in the next. He had Poor Richard put it even more pithily: "When you're good to others, you are best to yourself."[21]

In no way, then, can Franklin properly be understood as an unabashed advocate of the unbridled utilitarian individualism of which some have seen him a supreme symbol. Even in his most profit-motivated aspect, the Philadelphian did not set any sharp distinction between private pursuits and a self-conscious consideration of the public welfare. Indeed, he did not see the self as a solitary entity. Individuals did not act alone, and they did not succeed or even survive on their own. Poor Richard spoke for Franklin in his pungent challenge, "He that drinks his cider alone, let him catch his horse alone."[22]

Franklin almost invariably organized his endeavors in concert with others. The Union Fire Company, the Pennsylvania Hospital, the College of Philadelphia, and a multitude of other civic improvements that he initiated were cooperative ventures, deliberately formed to diffuse

20. Ibid., 54.
21. Updike, "Many Bens," 112–13.
22. Wright, *Franklin of Philadelphia*, 80–81. For Franklin as the prototypal figure of utilitarian individualism, see Robert Bellah, et al., *Habits of the Heart: Individualism and Commitment in American Life* (Berkeley, 1985), 32–33. For more classic statements in the same vein, see Max Weber, *The Protestant Ethic and the Spirit of Capitalism* (New York, 1930), *passim;* D. H. Lawrence, *Studies in Classic American Literature* (1922; reprint, Garden City, N.Y., n.d.), 19–31.

credit for their accomplishments. And they were all patterned on his first "club for mutual improvement," the Junto.[23]

The Junto was an association of his "ingenious acquaintance," but it was much more to him than a mere convenience at a time when he had neither wealth nor influence and consequently had to begin, as Carl Van Doren said, "where he could." It was his "benevolent lobby for the benefit of Philadelphia, and now and then for the advantage of Benjamin Franklin." Exactly because it was, he kept it alive long after he had outgrown his original need to promote his "interests in business by more extensive recommendation." A decade and more after he had given up his printing business entirely, he still prized the Junto's "power of doing good" for the public and its "atmosphere of camaraderie and companionship." Indeed, a decade and more after he had given up the Junto itself, he still held it close to his heart. When he brought his memoirs to their culmination and conclusion, as he supposed, in 1771, he ended not with his marriage to Deborah Read, an essentially private enterprise, but with the Junto and its launching of the Library Company, his "first project of a public nature."[24]

Barnum was equally keen to be seen as—and truly to be—public-spirited. He often expressed his scorn for mere moneymaking. He generally disdained the lucrative schemes and speculations that were set before him. He consistently conceived his own civic promotions in East Bridgeport as "profitable philanthropy."[25]

Even in his relentless recital of the sharp dealings and swindles of his Yankee youth, Barnum set at the strategic center a much more somber recollection of his grandmother. He was only fifteen at the time she called her grandchildren to her deathbed and took their hands in hers to speak with them, but decades later her awesome plea that they "live good lives and be of benefit to their fellow men" was still "vivid" in his thoughts. Her prayer "especially to remember that I could in no way so effectually prove my love to God, as in loving all my fellow beings," left him "affected to tears" and "completely overcome."[26]

The example of her husband Phineas Taylor—a man who would "go further, wait longer, work harder, and contrive deeper" to play a practi-

23. Franklin, *Autobiography*, 116.
24. Ibid.; Carl Van Doren, *Benjamin Franklin* (New York, 1938), 73, 75, 77; Franklin, *Autobiography*, 170–71; Wright, ed., *Benjamin Franklin*, xx; Seavey, *Becoming Benjamin Franklin*, 65–66; Franklin, *Autobiography*, 130–31.
25. Barnum, *Life*, 384–85. Cf. Harris, *Humbug*, 150, 180–81; Saxon, ed., *Letters*, xvi–xvii; Rourke, *Trumpets of Jubilee*, 406–7, 410, 413, 414.
26. Barnum, *Life*, 61–62.

cal joke than anyone he ever knew—certainly touched the teenager more, in his quotidian conduct, than her own dying exhortation did. But Barnum ultimately found his religious faith under her aegis, and in very real ways he lived his later life and wrote his autobiography under her impress as well. The tension between her consummate Christian *caritas* and her husband's irresistible aggressive energy remained with Barnum the rest of his days. Indeed, it embodied itself in his two greatest promotions.[27]

Tom Thumb and Jenny Lind each represented a profound impulsion of the showman's spirit. The midget incarnated the insouciance of old Phineas Taylor, and Barnum relished his diminutive ward's talent for tweaking the pretensions of the rich and powerful. The "Swedish nightingale" resurrected the virtues of his maternal grandmother, and Barnum rejoiced in the great diva's invincible altruism. If anything, he gave himself more wholeheartedly to her. While he initially engaged Tom Thumb for next to nothing, and had no idea of the endearing child's gift for witty repartee, he risked unprecedented sums on Jenny Lind and risked them precisely because of her reputation for goodness. He "never would have dared" make the offer he made to entice her to America for her splendid soprano alone. In truth, he hired her without ever hearing her sing. He knew her notoriety "as a great musical *artiste*," but he knew also, and far more decisively, "her character for extraordinary benevolence and generosity." It was that "peculiarity in her disposition"—Clara Schumann called her "the warmest, noblest being" she had ever encountered among musicians—that convinced Barnum that he could promote her in America. And it was the materialization of that nobility, and the joys it afforded him, that Barnum later maintained "alone would have paid me for my labors during the entire musical campaign."[28]

---

27. Ibid., 10. Barnum proudly proclaimed himself "a chip of the old block" in his own avidity to victimize others. He saw himself as his maternal grandfather's "counterpart," not just as his namesake. "Nothing that I can conceive of," he said of his practical jokes, "delights me so much as playing off one of those dangerous things." On the other hand, Barnum also recognized that the tension that controlled his career could be encompassed in the tutelage of his maternal grandparents. It was surely no accident that, in the later versions of his memoirs, he moved the deathbed scene to the opening of Chapter 2, where it presided over that chapter as his grandfather always presided over Chapter 1. See P. T. Barnum, *Struggles and Triumphs; or, Forty Years' Recollections of P. T. Barnum* (Hartford, Conn., 1869), and P. T. Barnum, *Struggles and Triumphs; or, Sixty Years' Recollections of P. T. Barnum* (Buffalo, N.Y., 1889).

28. Barnum, *Life,* 307; Harris, *Humbug,* 115–16; Barnum, *Life,* 330–31; see also 328, 333. Strikingly, Barnum told a story about Franklin in his autobiography, a story he

Barnum was grateful to the small towns of Connecticut that had taught him to be wary of gullibility and to take advantage of opportunity, but he never sentimentalized those towns and he never for a moment supposed them ideal societies. He recognized that their inchoate capitalism would make some men rich but would never make the mass of humanity happy. He understood that their undilute individualism served private ambition better than it promoted social sympathy and that without such social sympathy Americans were indeed condemned to lives of quiet desperation. "With the most universal means of happiness ever known among any people," he insisted, "we are unhappy."[29]

He appreciated his own benevolence primarily as the alleviation of such evident unhappiness, through his museums and circuses. Far more than his East Bridgeport improvements and his charities, those spectacles provided Americans the "relaxations and enjoyments" they required as respite from the "severe and drudging practicalness," the "dry and technical ideas of duty," and the "sordid love of acquisition" so prevalent in mid-Victorian America. When Barnum solicited favorable notices from the newspapers, therefore, he asked them on his conviction that the museum was "doing good for the community in which we live." When he contemplated retirement, he concluded that he could not "abandon the show business"—though he was certainly wealthy enough to do it "if *cash* was [his] only reward"—because he wished "to *elevate* traveling exhibitions" to make them "an important power for good." Even when disastrous fires destroyed his museums and circuses and he had every incentive to spend his remaining days in sumptuous indulgence, he took up each time the daunting task of rebuilding his collections, for the sake, as he said, of his hundreds of employees and of the masses to whom he had "so long catered." Maintaining that he was not in the show business "alone to make money," he pronounced the provision of "recreation for the public good" his persistent "mission."[30]

Just as Franklin did, Barnum called happiness rather than accumulation "the true aim of life." Against the grain of Victorian values, the incomparable showman urged an acceptance of hedonic gratification. Though he made a multitude of more conventional contributions to

---

professed to have heard while touring in France. The story is not a success story of a young man rising in the world but a benevolence story, told to him by a descendant of the recipient of Franklin's largesse. Barnum's Franklin "always felt a duty and pleasure in relieving his fellow men" (*Life*, 289–90).

29.  Harris, *Humbug*, 214; Barnum, *Life*, 399.

30.  Barnum, *Life*, 399; Saxon, ed., *Letters*, 116–17, 208; Harris, *Humbug*, 170–71, 271. See also Harris, *Humbug*, 79, 217; Saxon, ed., *Letters*, xv.

more conventional causes, he always considered his entertainments his grandest philanthropies. They ministered as nothing else in nineteenth-century America did to people's deep need for fun and frolic.[31]

Franklin's philanthropy was more direct than Barnum's, in principle and in practice. Franklin did sometimes entangle his projects of a public nature with his own private interests, but more often he placed social service before personal advantage. In the Junto, new members undergoing initiation "had to stand up with their hands on their breasts and say they loved mankind in general." In his own daily schedule, Franklin began each morning by asking, "What good shall I do this day?" and ended each evening by inquiring, "What good have I done today?" Even in the midst of his ironic plan for moral perfection, he paused to pray that the Deity would "accept my kind offices to Thy other children as the only return in my power for Thy continual favors to me." And in the creed that he composed, he maintained in much the same way that "the most acceptable service of God is doing good to man." In a more acerbic version of the same sentiment, he had Poor Richard observe that "serving God is doing good to man, but praying is thought an easier service, and therefore more generally chosen."[32]

Benevolence was the divine thing, even if the more difficult. Franklin was enough a realist to accept indulgently the ways of ordinary men and women. At the same time, he was enough a humanitarian to hold himself to a more strenuous standard. He simply believed himself a better man than many of his brethren, though he recognized readily that there were others as concerned for the common weal as he was. When he set down his observations on his reading of history in 1731, he did say that parties were driven by their general interests and individuals within those parties by their particular private ambitions, but he did not on that account subside into cynicism. On the contrary, he held that even if most people could not rise above partisan perspectives, a "good and wise" minority could. He therefore proposed a "United Party for Virtue," which would form "the virtuous and good men of all nations" into "a regular body" that would "act for the good of mankind." His analysis of human nature pointed to the prevalence of selfish pride; his project pointed to the mobilization of mutuality.[33]

From his first civic endeavors to his final contributions to the na-

31. Barnum, *Life*, 399. See also Harris, *Humbug*, 33, 37–38, 79, 217; Rourke, *Trumpets of Jubilee*, 407–10.
32. Van Doren, *Franklin*, 78; Franklin, *Autobiography*, 154, 153, 162; Leibowitz, *Fabricating Lives*, 63.
33. Franklin, *Autobiography*, 161–63.

tional cause, Franklin not only sought a virtuous fusion of public and private interests but also presumed the ultimate priority of the claims of public life. Early in his political career, when he floated his Proposals Relating to the Education of Youth in Pennsylvania, he treated "true merit" as "the great aim and end of all learning," and he defined such merit as "an inclination joined with an ability to serve mankind, one's country, friends, and family." More even than he meant to establish the College of Philadelphia on a foundation of applied knowledge, as is conventionally asserted, he sought to set it on a bedrock of altruism and concern for the general welfare. His innovative insistence on allowing a prominent place in the college's curriculum to the study of history arose out of his conviction that it would "fix in the minds of youth deep impressions of the beauty and usefulness of virtue [and] public spirit."[34]

Late in his life, when he drew upon the experience of his years at the Constitutional Convention, his commitment to the common good had deepened and his aversion to unvarnished self-interest had hardened. He proposed that the officials of the new government serve without salaried compensation at all, for "the pleasure of doing good and serving their country" and for the respect that would attend their office. Such gratifications seemed intelligible and indeed plausible incentives to Franklin, "sufficient motives with some minds to give up a great portion of their time to the public." Mere "pecuniary satisfaction," on the other hand, seemed to him a "mean inducement" that would only lead to corruption.[35]

Franklin lived as he lectured. So far from epitomizing the irrational energies of the spirit of capitalism, as Max Weber averred, he quit his business forever at forty-two. So far from laboring relentlessly, he gave up his leather apron for a life of "leisure . . . for philosophical studies and amusements." So far from seeking insatiably after wealth, he turned his press over to his foreman and settled a sort of pension on himself that netted him less than half what his foreman made over the term of their arrangement. And despite his diminished income, he found himself delighted to be done with "the little cares and fatigues of business." He had never valued industry and frugality as intrinsic ends, only as extrinsic means to an independence that would enable him to be done with the ascetic regimen by which he had risen. He loved his leisure—indeed, his laziness—and he loved too the opportunity it afforded him of producing "something for the common benefit of mankind." He re-

34. Seavey, *Becoming Benjamin Franklin*, 162–63.
35. Wright, *Franklin of Philadelphia*, 341.

joiced that he had hardly retired when "the public," suddenly "considering [him] a man of leisure, laid hold of [him] for their purposes." As he told friends and family alike, he much preferred to "have it said, 'He lived usefully,' than 'He died rich.' "[36]

Even in his prime, he refused emoluments that might easily have been his. When he assumed the postmastership, he vowed that he would not use it against other comers as his old rival Bradford had used it against him, and he was as good as his word. When he developed his famous stove, he disdained to patent it or, indeed, to profit from it. When he invented his lightning rod and his clockworks, he likewise allowed anyone interested in doing so to manufacture and distribute them. Throughout his mechanical and scientific career, he denounced monopolistic exploitation of innovations and promoted open exchange of information in order to better the human condition.[37]

As he grew older, Franklin grew even more willing to sacrifice his own purse to what he took to be the public interest. When he won a princely sum in a lottery for the support of an association to defend the province of Pennsylvania in King George's War, he turned all of his winnings over to the associators. When he learned that the British general Braddock could not convince the governors of Virginia and Maryland to supply the horses and wagons that the western campaign required in the French and Indian War, he took the pretext of his postmastership to obtain hundreds of horses and wagons by pledging £1000 of his own money to their owners and drivers. When he left Philadelphia to take up the Pennsylvania agency in England, he persuaded a leading London physician to prepare a pamphlet on methods of smallpox inoculation that could be administered easily in the home, had 1,500 copies printed at his own expense, and sent them to Philadelphia for free distribution there.[38]

As the imperial crisis deepened, he offered his fortune in its entirety to avert the rupture he dreaded. When he heard of the Boston Tea Party, he pledged every penny that he was worth to compensate the East India Company for its losses if Parliament would repeal the taxes the colonists resented. And once the die of revolution was cast, he gave of himself even more utterly. When he led the commissioners of the Continental

36. Franklin, *Autobiography*, 196; Wright, *Franklin of Philadelphia*, 52; Franklin, *Autobiography*, 196; Wright, *Franklin of Philadelphia*, 56.

37. Leibowitz, *Fabricating Lives*, 47–48; Wright, *Franklin of Philadelphia*, 5, 60, 64, 66, 127.

38. Wright, *Franklin of Philadelphia*, 78, 96, 127.

Congress on their expedition to Canada to try to convince the Canadians to join the thirteen colonies in their break with Britain, he was already an old man several months past his seventieth birthday. Yet he endured all the hardships of the grueling journey that the younger men did—sailing on open boats through the snow and ice of early April, sleeping in the woods, riding over rugged roads, nearing exhaustion, his legs swollen with dropsy—on an errand that availed the commissioners and their cause nothing. When he was appointed commissioner to France later in the same year of 1776, he was confronted with the objections of his dearest sister, who implored him not to go. Yet he accepted the assignment, as if to indicate that he would seal the significance of a life of public service by doing so. Before he left, he lent the Congress several thousand pounds and assured Benjamin Rush that the Revolution could "have [him] for what [it] pleased." [39]

Barnum was never so ready to put himself so utterly at his country's disposal, but he was willing and able to subordinate his pursuit of private economic interests to what he took to be the public good. Like Franklin, he had higher priorities than money and more than a little contempt for those who did not. Like Franklin, he sought a sufficiency and, once he had it, turned his energies to the service of society. Like Franklin, he conceived his career in such terms, dividing his autobiography into an early portion devoted to his youthful peccadilloes and the education in human nature that they afforded him, and a later portion detailing the tiresome twin triumphs of respectability and responsibility. [40]

Once he attained his first great successes, Barnum moved his family to Bridgeport, Connecticut, and became a veritable Franklin of his adoptive hometown. He promoted public improvements of every sort, in the authentic expectation that the community was "destined" to be the principal city of the state "in size and opulence." Especially in its eastern precinct, he laid out parks, planted the streets with trees, and had two bridges erected at his own expense. He built a coach factory to lease to a company of coach makers. He subsidized housing for workingmen. He even established a clock company of his own, in association with an illustrious firm in New Haven, in his expansive effort to "open

39. Ibid., 228, 239–42, 254–55.

40. For Barnum's scorn for people who thought only of their own purse and profits, see, e.g., Barnum, *Life,* 274, 380–82, 389–91; Saxon, ed., *Letters,* 31, 93, 94, 233, 276.

the way for new industries and new homes," so as to "be of service to his fellow men."[41]

As his civic endeavors matured, he served stints as park commissioner, as head of the water company, as chief executive officer of the hospital, as president of the bank (in which, he was at pains to point out, he "had no interest whatever" beyond the "public benefit" that it provided because "more banking capital was needed in Bridgeport"), and even as mayor. He donated land and money alike to create urban amenities such as a seaside park on Long Island Sound and a handsome cemetery that is "today the one remaining truly beautiful locale in all Bridgeport." He was an early supporter of the public library, and indeed he held the first card it ever issued.[42]

Beyond Bridgeport, Barnum served two terms in the Connecticut legislature, where he quarreled with Copperheads, assaulted the railroads as "enemies to public welfare" and "engines of political corruption," and labored largely "to do justice to the Negro." On one occasion, he set out upon a twenty-minute address to the assembly urging enfranchisement of African-Americans, warmed to the task when he encountered "interruptions from the other side of the house," and wound up speaking on the subject for an hour and three-quarters. His performance won him wide publicity and praise in the press, but it emanated, as he assured colleagues in private correspondence, from heartfelt conviction that his position was "the *only* just and truly democratic one."[43]

Barnum was an ardent abolitionist long before the Civil War and a passionate patriot once the war was declared. In the early months of the struggle, at the advanced age of fifty-one, he was militant. Once he led a loyal gang of Bridgeport toughs to a neighboring town to break up a Copperhead meeting. Another time, he stirred up a mob to sack the offices of the local Copperhead newspaper. As the conflict wore on, he

---

41. Harris, *Humbug*, 150. Harris dismissed Barnum's protestations of public interest derisively, maintaining that the canny promoter just "brought in" benevolence because "it was not enough" for him "simply to admit he wanted more money." But Harris cannot explain on his cynical interpretation why the canny promoter kept pouring money into the failing clock company long after anyone seeking merely to make "more money" would have cut his losses. Harris cannot explain why Barnum imperiled his entire fortune, and lost his museum for a time, for the sake of a business that never made as much as his show businesses did. Harris cannot even explain why Barnum felt the need to blend benevolence and pursuit of profit in his presentation of himself.

42. Saxon, ed., *Letters*, xvi; Barnum, *Life*, 382.

43. Harris, *Humbug*, 188; Saxon, ed., *Letters*, 133–35.

called the Confederacy the "d——dest barbarous, mean, and causeless rebellion ever known" and declared his own willingness "to be reduced to the last shirt and the last dollar—yes, and the *very* last drop of blood—in case that will help preserve this nation." He never actually sacrificed so much, but he did spurn opportunities for profitable engagements in England during the war because he was "shocked and disappointed" to see England "taking sides with the slaveholders."[44]

Ultimately, Franklin and Barnum both gave themselves so utterly to the public that commentators have questioned whether they had any interior existence at all. Neil Harris wondered if Barnum even "had a notion of privacy, so completely did he define his own needs and reactions in public terms." Harris admitted the possibility that Barnum simply kept his private side "carefully shielded," but beyond that he would not go. When he spoke of Barnum's "inner life," he added the cautious qualification, "if it existed." Constance Rourke was not so archly circumspect. "In a strict sense," she asserted, Barnum "had no private life." He lived "in the midst of crowds, in public; at times it seemed he was the public."[45]

Students of Franklin have voiced similar suspicions and drawn comparable conclusions. Herbert Leibowitz noticed that Franklin's autobiography "contains no intimations of neurotic behavior, no dreams or nightmares, no crises of spirit, scarcely any inwardness." Leibowitz found himself "tempted to say that [Franklin] appears to be the only person in American history without an unconscious." Esmond Wright also remarked Franklin's impenetrable exteriority, and his "root . . .

---

44. Saxon, ed., *Letters,* 113, 114, 120. Barnum was outspoken, and willing to put his money where his mouth was, on several of the most controversial issues of his day. He was an early and earnest supporter of the antebellum women's movements. He published Lucy Stone's lectures on women's rights in his widely circulated newspaper, and he asked her to speak on the subject at his church (because "they ought to hear it") and to stay with him at his house when she did. He espoused the cause of wage-working women and contributed substantially to the Working Women's Protective Union (Saxon, ed., *Letters,* 68–71, 86–87, 123–24, 167, 249). Barnum became a convert to teetotalism when Rev. Chapin convinced him that even moderate drinking was hurtful to the self or to others and should be given up for the self or "for the sake of your suffering fellow-beings." After he took the pledge (and destroyed his champagne collection), Barnum traveled extensively to lecture on temperance, often for weeks at a time and always at his own expense. At one point he spent almost a full month on the circuit in Wisconsin in the very midst of the Jenny Lind tour. He was willing to set aside his own interests "to benefit my fellow man" and to carry "happiness to the bosom of many a family" (Barnum, *Life,* 360).

45. Harris, *Humbug,* 4–5; Rourke, *Trumpets of Jubilee,* 371.

conviction that the individual is only truly himself in a gregarious, not a solitary, setting." Ormond Seavey concurred that if we would "understand Franklin's self we cannot separate him from the larger public." Indeed, Seavey went an essential step further. "If we accept the premise that the strongest feelings point to the deepest parts of the self, we must look for them in Franklin's public rather than his private life."[46]

Franklin simply "had no intimate friend" to whom he exposed his "inner spirit." He did make a few attempts, in his youth, to maintain close ties with select companions such as Collins and Ralph, but in the half-dozen decades after he returned from London and lost his patron, the merchant Thomas Denham, to "distemper," he had not a single soulmate nor even any steady circle of comrades in whom he could confide. As Seavey saw, his autobiography presents him in a succession of introductions to people he had not previously known—governors, employers, merchants, and many more—rather than in a recurrence of conditions in which he was long and well known. Franklin meant to be a benefactor to his community and indeed to all humankind, but he meant to do his good works at a distance, in the aggregate and in the abstract. He held himself aloof from extended familiarities with his associates, his "gregariousness notwithstanding." He could still recall, at a half-century remove, his father's comment that "nothing was more common than for those who loved one another at a distance, to find many causes of dislike when they came together." And he echoed his father's observation in Poor Richard's blunt maxim, "Fish and visitors stink in three days."[47]

Franklin would not entangle himself abidingly with others. He abandoned Boston and all his American kindred without ever betraying "a sense of something lost or left behind." Unencumbered by his past, he was free to invent himself anew, again and again. Untrammeled by any enduring commitments, he was at liberty to be always the disengaged spectator of his social relations. He could recall without evident anger and, in truth, with wry amusement the disappointments he had suffered

46. Leibowitz, *Fabricating Lives*, 29–30; Wright, *Franklin of Philadelphia*, 80; Seavey, *Becoming Benjamin Franklin*, 101.

47. John Griffith, "Franklin's Sanity and the Man behind the Masks," in *The Oldest Revolutionary: Essays on Benjamin Franklin*, ed. J. A. Leo Lemay (Philadelphia, 1976), 126; Franklin, *Autobiography*, 107; Seavey, *Becoming Benjamin Franklin*, 10, 118; William Hedges, "From Franklin to Emerson," in *The Oldest Revolutionary*, ed. Lemay, 151; Kenneth Silverman, "Introduction," in Benjamin Franklin, *The Autobiography and Other Writings*, ed. Kenneth Silverman (New York, 1986), xv.

at the hands of people he presumed his friends, because he was never unduly involved emotionally in his attachments to others to begin with.[48]

Barnum too held himself apart from those with whom he worked and, necessarily, lived. In his museum he saw his employees every day. On the road, touring, he saw them incessantly, day and night. Yet he made no effort to come close to them. He described them as "the South African savages" or "those dirty, lazy, and lousy Gipseys." He encapsulated his attitude to any number of the men and women who made his acts in a little outburst against some "d——n Indians": "They are a lazy, shiftless set of brutes—though they will draw." And he did not confine his attitude to foreigners, either. He talked of Tom Thumb's Yankee parents as "crazy" and "absolutely deranged with [their] golden success." He rebuked them when they had the temerity to be "inquisitive about the business" and brought them back "down to the old level," where he vowed to "keep them." As he expostulated to another showman, he could "do business with blockheads and brutes when there [was] money enough to be made by it," but he could not "be tempted by money to associate with them or allow them to rule."[49]

With his fellow showmen, Barnum rarely deigned to reveal more of his feelings than he did with the performers he hired. He wrote letters by the thousands, but he exposed nearly nothing of his personal sentiments in any of them. When he wrote to Moses Kimball, his closest confidant among the impresarios and adventurers in the mass entertainment melee of his day, he wrote almost entirely about gate receipts, contracts, and the latest scams. Even when he wrote to his own partners, he trusted nothing to them but entrepreneurial affairs, though he always marked those letters "Private." Just because he effaced his emotions, he quite collapsed the distinction between the private and the public realm. He could bid a college president campaigning for a major contribution from him, "In lower corner of all envelopes addressed to me, always please write 'strictly personal,'" yet after that ingratiating invitation exchange dozens of letters with the man and never discuss anything but business.[50]

Virtually nothing moved Barnum to open himself in strictly personal ways. "Loss of life in his enormous companies hardly touched him."

48. Seavey, *Becoming Benjamin Franklin*, 27.
49. Saxon, ed., *Letters,* 110, 24, 22, 31.
50. Ibid., 262, 310, 237. For the only exceptions with Kimball—and those paltry enough—see 16, 34, 35, 70, 76.

Friends such as Horace Greeley went to their tragedies without a word from him. Companions such as the Cary sisters died without any evident reaction from him. "His life was," as Rourke remarked, "in the circus."[51]

Neither Barnum nor Franklin was markedly more intimate with family than with friends. Both men were away from home as often as they were there. Both plainly put their business and their public ambitions before their wives and children. And both were actually off in Europe, pursuing that business and those ambitions, unconcerned to return, while their wives lay dying at home.

Franklin fled from his family of origin when he was still a stripling. He risked a lasting rift with his father when he left, he declined to send word of his whereabouts for months after he was gone, and he seems to have suffered not a pang. In the retrospect of a half-century, he did not even count his flight from home among his "errata." After he established himself in Philadelphia, he made no notable effort to reconnect with his kindred in Boston, and he did not dream of arranging regular reunions. So far from staying in touch, he would let his letters even to his sister Jane lapse for years, leaving her to suspect that he "dropped from mind those who were out of sight."[52]

He did write to his wife Deborah more regularly, but primarily because they had business together and he was away from her so often: five years in London, then ten more after a brief interlude back home. He expressed no more regret to be apart from her than he had ever expressed passion to be with her; and he made mock of the institution of marriage in half a dozen literary genres—in the salty aphorisms of Poor Richard, the insinuating satire of Polly Baker, the randy irreverence of the Old Mistresses Apologue, and more—because he was so minimally involved, emotionally, in his own marriage. Ensconced on Craven Street in London, he read her increasingly more urgent importunities to return to Philadelphia to be with her in her last languishing years, and he was unmoved.

He did, perhaps, for a while, feel more warmly toward his son. He did, certainly, address the opening of his memoirs to the young man. But he abandoned that trifling pretense before the ink was dry on the first paragraph, and he never resumed it again. Even before he broke with William, irreconcilably, over the issue of American independence,

51. Rourke, *Trumpets of Jubilee,* 422–23.
52. Silverman, "Introduction," xv.

their relations had grown steadily more strained. Even before he disinherited William in anger, and indeed in seething rage, he had disinherited him to a degree in cool calculation, warning the young man not to expect much at his father's death because his father meant to spend most of his modest fortune on his own gratification.[53]

Little as Franklin devoted himself to his family or delineated its life lovingly, he did still see some of his relations—his father, for example, and his brother, and his wife—sharply enough to render them in sketches that at least intimated their individuality in his autobiography. Barnum never conceived any of his kinfolk, except perhaps his grandfather, with any comparable clarity. His wives, his parents, his brothers and sisters, and his own children were all "indistinct" figures in his personal narrative. As Neil Harris said, the only thing we know about a number of them are their dates of birth and death. And almost the only things we know about the rest are the "conventional pieties" in which he swathed them, obscuring whatever personality they possessed. "Whether his married life was happy or unhappy, whether he was disappointed in or proud of any of his children, whether he maintained relationships with his sisters or brothers, he did not bother to disclose."[54]

Barnum did not even bother to dissemble his indifference to domesticity. He lived the larger part of his life on the road because he liked it better than being with his family. Though he inveighed publicly against "the privations, vexations, and uncertainties of a tour," he admitted privately that he had "less troubles" traveling "than when [he] was at home." Once, "in a fit of very *desperation*," he fled for foreign shores because he was convinced that he would have had to be "confined in an *insane retreat*" if he had remained with his wife. But even when he was not driven to such extremity, he still knew that, off the show circuit, there was "nothing to do."[55]

No obligations, no comforts, no enticements could keep him at home. He stayed away when he was just wedded, when his wives were pregnant, and when his children were newborn. He stayed away when his wives were ill and when they were dying. He was in Germany buying wild animals while his first wife was on her deathbed and in England on a similar errand while his second wife was lying at a point of "life

53. As for his daughter Sally, Franklin essentially forfeited his fatherhood, consigning her upbringing to her mother when he went to live in London.
54. Harris, *Humbug*, 14.
55. Barnum, *Life*, 211; Saxon, ed., *Letters*, 35, 225.

and death." And at that he was less interested in his wife's precarious health than in his circus. He begged his partner, James Bailey, to inform him at once, by cable, whether "the Philadelphia business [the acquisition of Adam Forepaugh's circus] is to be completed," and then he asked Bailey to tell him as well, by letter, if there was any news from "Mrs. Barnum's doctor." He promised Bailey that he would be back "*before the show opens,* even if I have to leave my wife behind."[56]

By his own account, he always left his wives behind. No matter how often he vowed "to spend [his] days in the bosom of [his] family," no matter how earnestly he "re-resolved that [he] would never again be an itinerant showman," no matter how "determined" he was that "no pecuniary temptation should again induce [him] to forego the enjoyments only to be secured in the circle of home," he never gave up gadding about. From the day he joined his first traveling circus in 1836 to the day he finished his first four years of touring with Tom Thumb, he was, as he said, "a straggler from home most of the time for thirteen years." And from the day he declared himself done with such straggling, he began looking for new promotions to take on the road. He was still traveling with the circus when he was eighty, in the last year of his life.[57]

Barnum did pronounce panegyrics to "home sweet home" in his autobiography. But they had no substance. They were empty words, and he knew it. He put them in quotation marks, as if to underline the irony. He did introduce the concluding chapter of his memoirs with pledges that he felt "more deeply interested" in his family and homestead "than in all other things combined," that his wife and children were "dearer to him than all things else in the world," and that he would therefore devote his final chapter to them. But he could not carry such pledges off, and indeed he did not even try. He permitted himself a couple of pages of insipid platitudes about domestic pleasures, and then he returned in the remaining twenty-five pages of that last chapter to the public endeavors that absorbed him.[58]

Neil Harris took Barnum's twaddle about home and family seriously enough to argue that it set the great trickster apart from the other touring picaros of the period, who made no secret of their satisfaction with life on the road. Discounting the rest of the showman's unruly rejection of the precepts of the Protestant ethic, Harris held that Barnum's vacuous Victorian sentimentality betrayed after all his yearning for the tra-

56. Saxon, ed., *Letters,* 319.
57. Barnum, *Life,* 295, 213, 295.
58. Ibid., 203, 379, chap. 14.

ditional Yankee tokens of success: "a fine home, servants, a carriage, local respect."[59]

But where other men of that era, under the sway of emergent ideals of domesticity, sought home, servants, and a carriage to enhance the amenity of their family life, Barnum sought those things almost solely to enhance the impression he made in public. If they had been gratifying in their own right, he would not have abandoned them so routinely for the enticements of adventure abroad. If they had even mattered to him intrinsically, he would not have been indifferent to their destruction. One after another, his houses burned to the ground. Each time, he learned of his loss without lamentation. Each time, he busied himself building a new one quite unlike the ones that had burned before.[60]

The plain truth was that Barnum's houses were not homes. They were, as he himself admitted, devices for display. He deliberately designed his first great house, Iranistan, with " 'an eye for business.' " He spent $150,000 on its onion spires, its Arabian Nights facade, its soaring fountains, its opulent gardens, and its rosewood and marble interiors, because he thought "that a pile of buildings of a novel order might indirectly serve as an advertisement of [his] various enterprises." Indeed, he defended his extravagance on his Asiatic palace precisely because it would pay for itself as a promotion.[61]

Rather than resenting or resisting the absorption of his personal residence into his public representation, Barnum abetted it, by reproducing the minareted pleasure dome of Iranistan on his business stationery. Rather than seeking domestic seclusion, he went out of his way to augment the invasion of his private life by publicity. When he disbanded a wild animal caravan, he kept one elephant from the show as "a capital advertisement for [his] American Museum." He put it to work on his farm in Bridgeport, in a field where he knew it could be seen from the railroad tracks. And lest anyone miss the outlandish spectacle, he furnished the creature's keeper "with a time-table of the road, with special instructions to be busily engaged in his work whenever passenger trains . . . were passing through."[62]

Such staging was, of course, what Barnum did for a living. But Franklin was scarcely less engaged in the arrangement of his public poses, scarcely less preoccupied with what Erving Goffman once called

59. Harris, *Humbug*, 30.
60. Ibid., 155.
61. Barnum, *Life*, 401–3; Harris, *Humbug*, 104.
62. Harris, *Humbug*, 104, 147. See also 192.

facework. When he discovered the Socratic method, he was so "charmed with it" that he "dropped" his argumentative demeanor and "put on the humble enquirer and doubter." Beliefs and the rhetorical modes in which they were embodied were like fashions in which to strike "poses" for Franklin. They could be "tried out" and tossed off (as, soon enough, he tossed off his Socratic style). They were, in Seavey's fine phrase, "attire for a self which [had] no required dress."[63]

As if instinctively, Franklin knew that "one does not dress for private company as for a public ball." He donned guises and doffed them, as circumstances demanded. He put manners on and took them off, according to the situation in which he found himself, and he did the same with morals as he did with manners. His project for moral perfection made ethical action "a style of dress which the self must put on to make its way in the world." It was, as its author understood from the first, as much an affectation as an aspiration. And just because it was, it could be abandoned "as a kind of foppery" as soon as it threatened to "make [him] ridiculous" in other people's eyes.[64]

Esmond Wright worried that Franklin made himself "increasingly obscure" by his consciousness of costume and his delight in his dramatic management of effects. He wondered if there was "a more real man behind the myriad personae" and if "the man himself" existed "independently of his images of himself." He feared that we might never find out "what [was] fact and what [was] fiction" in the man's multitudinous representations of himself.[65]

But Franklin himself was never bothered by his proliferating public images. If anything, he contributed to their compounding. He sat for more portraits than any other person of his period, and he composed himself differently for almost every one of them. Like Lord Chesterfield in his own time, he conceived the management of masks as "both a pleasure and a necessity for the continuance of civil harmony." Like a number of novelists and social scientists of our time—Musil and Mead and Goffman, for just a few examples—he presumed that we are the roles we play and the style with which we play them.[66]

Wright was reaching for such a presumption when he concluded that

63. Erving Goffman, *Interaction Ritual: Essays on Face-to-Face Behavior* (Garden City, N.Y., 1967), 5–45; Franklin, *Autobiography*, 64; Seavey, *Becoming Benjamin Franklin*, 26.

64. Franklin, *Autobiography*, 56–57; Seavey, *Becoming Benjamin Franklin*, 79; Franklin, *Autobiography*, 156.

65. Wright, *Franklin of Philadelphia*, 9–10.

66. Seavey, *Becoming Benjamin Franklin*, 43.

Franklin finally "became the parts he played." But Franklin did not *become* those parts. He *was* his roles. Wright clung to an ontology that still predicated a reality behind appearances. Franklin let it go. His life and his account of his life alike affirmed the reality of appearances. The very independence he prized was predicated on "society and the concealment of identity it required." The self-consciousness he sought was won in dramatic encounters in public places, not in isolation from such civic contexts. At a time when Jean-Jacques Rousseau, his brilliant Continental contemporary, was imploring readers to fly from the superficialities of social conventions to the deeper realities of the self in solitude, Franklin insisted on the significance of such conventions and the sufficiency of appearances adroitly managed.[67]

Franklin rarely resisted "his histrionic talent for trying on and discarding selves." He "relished playing a repertoire of roles," and he drew sustenance from the range of roles he played. As Poor Richard said, "What one relishes, nourishes." Carl Van Doren was correct when he pronounced Franklin less a unitary personality than a veritable committee, "a harmonious human multitude" (just as Constance Rourke was right when she called Barnum "an amused conglomerate"). Franklin's extended apprenticeship in the crafts of common experience enabled him to adapt fluently to disparate situations, and his overflowing intelligence obliged him to treat such disparate situations as challenges to be joyfully mastered. Herman Melville was right when he concluded that Franklin had "carefully weighed the world" and could consequently "act any part in it."[68]

Just as small-town Connecticut could not contain Barnum, so Boston could not hold Franklin. It was too earnest, too plodding, and too homogeneous. Philadelphia afforded Franklin a far more expansive field of play, though it was still smaller than the older settlement when he arrived in 1723. The Quaker city had been founded on pluralistic principles rather than under authoritarian, intolerant Puritan auspices. It had from its earliest days a diversity of ethnic, religious, and economic groups that demanded acute attentiveness to difference rather than an overriding regard to orthodoxy. Boston was hospitable to a certain species of hedgehog, Philadelphia to all sorts of foxes. Boston was about

67. Wright, *Franklin of Philadelphia*, 10; Seavey, *Becoming Benjamin Franklin*, 40.

68. Leibowitz, *Fabricating Lives*, 48, 33; Van Doren, *Franklin*, 782; Rourke, *Trumpets of Jubilee*, 371; Herman Melville, *Israel Potter: His Fifty Years of Exile* (Evanston and Chicago, 1982), 48.

integrity, Philadelphia about style. One could not be a cultural anthropologist in Boston.

Franklin reveled in manipulating masks, in attempting postures and personae he had never tried, in creating himself and re-creating himself again and again. Though he is conventionally taken for an avatar of American individualism, he ultimately individuated himself very little and revealed himself still less. He disdained the quest for self in the sense of authenticity and integrity. He bent his being to accommodate the claims of others more than to assert himself. His essential Americanness inhered in his mastery of the fronts and facades that in profound ways *are* American culture.

He experimented playfully with everything, with callings and careers, with beliefs and values, with old women and new nations, with words and deeds, with his identity and indeed with his very name. He was by turns a "Water-American," who would not touch "muddling liquor" and considered "sotting with beer all day" a "detestable custom," and a bon vivant who wrote drinking songs and kept five different kinds of champagne in his wine cellar. He could by turns set temperance above all other virtues and rely on rum to induce Indians to negotiate, advise against drinking "to elevation" and toast to intoxication to get a reluctant governor to supply his province's defense. He could follow a "vegetable diet" for years, convinced that eating "animal food" was "a kind of unprovoked murder," and then give it all up in an instant on the trifling enticement of an aroma of cod "hot out of the frying pan." He could counsel thrift and frugality, dispensing maxims to the masses about pennies saved and pennies earned, and then succumb to the temptations of "luxury," first with a 23 shilling silver spoon and China bowl, soon enough with "several hundred pounds" worth of plate and porcelain. More than that, he could accustom himself to such amenities of elegance for decades and then all at once in Paris fulfill the French legend of the "good Quaker" by ostentatiously putting on "the plain dress of Friends."[69]

Offering provisional personae as he did for the delectation of his diverse constituencies and communities, he was always prepared to proceed "in spite of principle" or, at any rate, to allow the claims of "incli-

---

69. Franklin, *Autobiography*, 99–101; Leibowitz, *Fabricating Lives*, 56–57; Franklin, *Autobiography*, 149; Leibowitz, *Fabricating Lives*, 56–57; Franklin, *Autobiography*, 63, 87–88, 145; Frederick Tolles, "Benjamin Franklin's Business Mentors: The Philadelphia Quaker Merchants," *William and Mary Quarterly*, 3d ser., 4 (1947): 67.

nation" alongside those of "principle." He left the preachments that might have defined a coherent character to Poor Richard, while he himself "went his own merry lenient way." He forgave his transgressions against his own injunctions "with amused nonchalance," and he disdained to take his absolutions any more seriously than he took his injunctions. When he abandoned his vegetarian ethics, he reported but did not defend his specious rationalization of the act. He merely marked the convenience of being "a reasonable creature, since it enables one to find or make a reason for everything one has a mind to do."[70]

It was no accident, then, that Franklin never found a unifying frame for his career, in his life or in his art. He did fantasize finding one. He confided to George Whitefield his notion that life, "like a dramatic piece," should "finish handsomely." He was, at fifty, "in the last act," and he was casting about for "something fit to end with." But he never achieved the fixity and finality he fancied. He never even achieved the esthetic stance or style that could intimate compellingly his occasional aspiration to complete the circle and establish the consistency of his character.[71]

His writings ranged over a dozen genres. His autobiography itself was composed in four disconnected segments addressed to different audiences and ends. He was simply not the same man in 1784, or 1788, or 1790, as he had been in 1771, and the discordancies in the form of the separate segments reflected alterations in the substance of his ideas and intentions. The only thread of continuity that ran through the disparate parts of the narrative—its Addisonian style—revealed in its own way Franklin's incapacity for constancy. The boy in Boston had indeed taken *The Spectator* as an ideal. The mature stylist in London and Philadelphia did not. As Seavey said, Franklin's prose never had "the static, lapidary quality" of his metropolitan model. "Tone and distance [were] always in motion" in the American, keeping him "from being imprisoned in an attitude." Franklin's voice as much as his behavior reflected his refusal of integrity and his determination to preserve plenitude rather than consummate commitment.[72]

It was no accident, either, that Franklin wrote so routinely in styles that were not his own and under names that were not his own. He was, as Updike said, "an inveterate impersonator." His very earliest surviving

70. Franklin, *Autobiography,* 145, 87; Leibowitz, *Fabricating Lives,* 49; Franklin, *Autobiography,* 87–88.

71. Griffith, "Franklin's Sanity," 125.

72. Seavey, *Becoming Benjamin Franklin,* 123.

writings were submitted under the pseudonym of Silence Dogood, the widow of a country minister. His most widely read works were published under the pseudonym of Richard Saunders, the Poor Richard of the almanacs. Franklin delighted in such simulations of other identities. He wrote so casually and so constantly in such characters that, to this day, scholars still quarrel over the extent of his canon. He wrote so frequently in personae remote from his own that their disputes may never be definitively resolved.[73]

When he was a stripling of sixteen, Franklin wrote as an aging widow. When he was a respectable pillar of his community, he wrote as a disreputable woman facing trial for bearing her fifth illegitimate child. When he was middle-aged, he wrote in the modes of youthful folly and elderly wisdom. When he was an impetuous youth he wrote of restraint, and when he was (presumably) too old to be in earnest, he wrote of passion. Again and again, he got outside himself. Again and again, he imagined the other. Updike was struck by "the androgyny of [his] imagination, from the speech of Polly Baker to his literary gallantries among the ladies of Paris." Leibowitz found it equally telling that, when he described his delayed marriage to Deborah Read, Franklin "imagine[d] her perspective."[74]

These abilities to assume roles without being consumed in or by them, to fit his psyche to circumstances with flair and fine humor, to try the other's point of view and allow the other's ethical authenticity, made Franklin whole, in one special sense. They enabled him to connect his convictions about public life with his perspectives on personal relations. They allowed him to integrate his conceptions of political economy with his predilections in private affairs.

In effect, these capacities to maintain a measure of disengagement from immediate personal interests extended the dominion of benevolence beyond the civil sphere into more personal realms. These competences to disavow a degree of enmeshment in present passions made disinterestedness a central category of social as well as political experience. People who could get inside the skin if not the soul of others were not people for whom private concerns were pervasive or even primary.

73. Updike, "Many Bens," 106; J. A. Leo Lemay, *The Canon of Benjamin Franklin, 1722–1776: New Attributions and Reconsiderations* (Newark, Del., 1986).
74. Updike, "Many Bens," 114 (although, for a treatment of the speech of Polly Baker that emphasizes its closeness to Franklin's own outlook, see J. A. Leo Lemay, "The Text, Rhetorical Strategies, and Themes of 'The Speech of Miss Polly Baker,'" in *The Oldest Revolutionary*, ed. Lemay, 91–120); Leibowitz, *Fabricating Lives*, 43.

Barnum similarly set the opinions of others before his own. So far from seeing the lone individual as a source of cultural authority, he "insisted again and again" that aggregates were the appropriate arbiters of American taste and that "what pleased the American masses was, by definition, good." The advertising that was the crux of his every operation precluded all possibility of prideful self-assertion. It presupposed that popular wishes were always right. It obliged the showman to abdicate his own judgments and preferences in deep and genuine deference to the desires of his audiences. And it found its justification exactly in the satisfaction of those democratic needs and desires. Barnum "never made the mistake of assuming that all men reflected his tastes and proclivities." He understood himself as a servant of the public, not as a molder of mass opinion and assuredly not as his own man.[75]

Both Franklin and Barnum have been taken for salesmen of the self and of selfishness. Nothing could be further from the truth, at least in the simplistic and ahistorical sense ordinarily asserted. In actuality, both men set civic and public obligations before private entitlements. Both understood themselves as disinterested and indeed benevolent. More than that, both these putative paragons of privatism were utterly public men. Both these assumptive avatars of individualism were people without any evident inner life. Perhaps, like Moses, they pointed to a promised land of private priorities. They never themselves entered it. Perhaps, like the prophets of old, they forecast the future. They never themselves knew it.

75. Harris, *Humbug*, 79, 86.

SIX

# The Power of Blackness: Thomas Jefferson and the Revolution in St. Domingue

Victorious rebels rarely maintain their revolutionary fervor after they secure their own ascendancy. So the Americans were hardly remarkable in their departure, after the Peace of Paris, from the principles for which they had battled the British.

From the northern frontier of New England to the southern seaport of Charleston, newly ensconced officials of the states and of the nation crushed uprisings premised on the political ideals of '76. Aspirations to liberty were subordinated to demands for order, local inclinations were overmastered by central imperatives, and legitimate suspicion of power gave way to an insistence upon its prerogatives. Emergent elites proceeded upon values they had once pledged their "lives, . . . fortunes, and . . . sacred honor" to oppose.[1]

The alterations were everywhere. The counterrevolution advanced on every front. But nowhere—not in the federal Constitution of 1787, not even in the Alien and Sedition Acts of 1798—did the abandonment

An earlier version of this essay appeared as "The Color of Counterrevolution: Thomas Jefferson and the Rebellion in San Domingo," in *The Languages of Revolution,* ed. Loretta Valtz Mannucci, Quaderno 2 of the Milan Group in Early United States History (Milan: Istituto di Studi Storici, 1989), 83–107.

1. See, e.g., Gordon Wood, *The Creation of the American Republic, 1776–1787* (Chapel Hill, N.C., 1969); David Szatmary, *Shays' Rebellion: The Making of an Agrarian Insurrection* (Amherst, Mass., 1980); Thomas Slaughter, *The Whiskey Rebellion: Frontier Epilogue to the American Revolution* (New York, 1986); Pauline Maier, "The Charleston Mob and the Evolution of Popular Politics in Revolutionary South Carolina, 1765–1784," *Perspectives in American History* 4 (1970): 173–98; Michael Zuckerman, "Thermidor in America: The Aftermath of Independence in the South," *Prospects* 8 (1983): 349–68.

of Revolutionary precepts appear more poignantly than in the realm of race. And nowhere in the realm of race—not in the retreats of the evangelical churches, not even in the notorious three-fifths clause of the Constitution—did the Thermidorean impulse appear more compellingly, and compulsively, than in the American response to the rising of people of color in St. Domingue.[2]

The San Domingan revolution is a minor episode at best, now, in the cavalcade of American history. It has been consigned to insignificance because it does not serve that saga well. But that revolution, and the American reaction to it, were not insignificant at all in their own time, or for decades after. In their practical effects, they altered irrevocably the pattern of American commerce and the direction of American development. In their impact on the imagination, they haunted American minds until at least the Civil War and poisoned American principles far longer than that. As Winthrop Jordan put it, "To trace the spread of Negro rebellion in the New World and to examine American responses to what they saw as a mounting tide of danger is to watch the drastic erosion of the ideology of the American Revolution."[3]

St. Domingue at the end of the eighteenth century was not the squalid, sordid place it became under a succession of appalling dictatorships in subsequent centuries. Or in any case it was not solely so. The island was a charnel house, to be sure, and a gruesome early grave for the great majority of its preponderant population of colored slaves; but it was also a vast mansion of extravagant wealth and indulgence—the "pearl of the Antilles," in the parlance of the time—for its white and mulatto people of privilege. As C. L. R. James said, "On no portion of the globe did its surface in proportion to its dimensions yield so much wealth as the colony of St. Domingue."[4]

2. A brief note on terminology may be helpful, even if my usage is, in the end, arbitrary. I call the colony St. Domingue because that is what the French, who held it from 1697 to 1803, called it. The colony occupied the western third of the island, which the aboriginals called Haiti and the Spaniards, following Columbus, named Espanola, or Hispaniola; the eastern two-thirds of the island remained in Spanish hands and was called Santo Domingo. The Americans from whose perspective I write never did come to any invariant nomenclature. They called the colony St. Domingo more often than anything else, but they also called it San Domingo and a variety of contractions, expansions, and elaborations of these terms. They rarely called it St. Domingue. After independence in 1804, the people of the former French colony reclaimed for their own portion of the island the name the natives had once used for its entirety: Haiti. Santo Domingo is now the Dominican Republic.

3. Winthrop Jordan, *White over Black: American Attitudes toward the Negro, 1550–1812* (Chapel Hill, N.C., 1968), 375.

4. C. L. R. James, *The Black Jacobins: Toussaint L'Ouverture and the San Domingan Revolution*, 2d ed., rev. (New York, 1963), 45–46.

The sudden, stupendous prosperity of the French West Indies in general, and of St. Domingue in particular, may be beyond our modern capacity to credit. It may be intimated, however, by way of a comparison with the British islands in the area. The major British outposts in the Antilles—Barbados in the seventeenth century, Jamaica in the eighteenth—were always more valuable by far to the mother country than the mainland colonies that would one day declare their independence. Yet even the lesser colonies of the Caribbean were more advantageous economically to England than the great colonies of the continent. In the six decades before the imperial rupture, Britain brought in from diminutive Montserrat three times what it did from voluptuous Pennsylvania. The empire took from tiny Nevis twice what it did from mighty New York, and more than triple what it did from all New England. The sugar societies of the island were so surpassingly affluent and prodigal that their tens of thousands imported more from the metropolis than the millions on the mainland ever did. British merchants exported as much to Barbados and Antigua as to New York, more to Montserrat and Nevis than to Pennsylvania.[5]

And as the island jewels of the English empire outshone its continental clods on every mercantilist calculation, so the French holdings in the Antilles eclipsed those of the English. The French West Indian possessions were larger, their soil more fertile and less exhausted, and their costs of production therefore considerably lower. Some of the figures in the plaintive submissions of Barbadian and Jamaican planters to the British Board of Trade were probably exaggerated for effect, but the fundamental superiority of the French plantations was unchallenged. French sugar invaded British markets in Europe and sold at half the price for which it sold in England. Two-thirds of the sugar and coffee consumed in the United States came from the French West Indies, and with good reason. Molasses from St. Domingue was cheaper in Philadelphia than molasses from Jamaica on the plantation.[6]

St. Domingue was an unlikely location for such staggering prosperity. It occupied but the smaller western portion of the modest island of Hispaniola. Columbus had made an uncomfortable landfall on its northwest coast in 1492, when his flagship foundered there. He had left a little detachment at the point of the wreck and advanced with the main

5. Roger Kennedy, *Orders from France* (New York, 1989).

6. Eric Williams, *Capitalism and Slavery* (London, 1964), 113–14; Rayford Logan, *The Diplomatic Relations of the United States with Haiti, 1776–1891* (Chapel Hill, N.C., 1941), 29–30; Ludwell Lee Montague, *Haiti and the United States 1714–1938* (Durham, N.C., 1940), 30.

body of his men to the eastern end of the island, where they found gold. Thereafter, the Spaniards left the unpropitious western precinct almost untouched, because they could not see how to cultivate its "ubiquitous mountains" or its "uncountable valleys and chasms." To the time they ceded it to the French in 1697, it was still scarcely more than a haven for buccaneers.[7]

Yet this fragment of an island, that had seemed so unpromising to the end of the seventeenth century, enjoyed an economic boom unrivaled in the Western world in the eighteenth. The estimates of the actual magnitudes of its explosive expansion vary widely, but they all point to an astounding affluence. By the outbreak of the French Revolution, St. Domingue alone accounted for more than a third of France's foreign trade.[8] On a land area less than a sixth the size of Virginia—most of it uncultivable—the colony sustained a slave population more than two-thirds the slave population of the entire United States.[9] With barely fifty thousand free people and those half-million slaves, the colony exported more sugar than all the British colonies taken together, and vast quantities of cotton, tobacco, indigo, and cocoa of the best quality besides.[10] The planters of the San Domingan plains were the world's principal coffee growers, and they made immense amounts of cocoa and rum. Their production exceeded that of all the colonies of Spain. Their export and import trades doubled those of the other French colonies combined and dwarfed those of the far more populous American mainland.[11]

7. Selden Rodman, *Haiti: The Black Republic* (New York, 1961), 1–2.

8. Julius Scott, "The Common Wind: Currents of Afro-American Communication in the Era of the Haitian Revolution," (Ph.D. diss., Duke University, 1986), 13–14. For other estimates of one-third, see Montague, *Haiti and the United States*, 5, and Thomas Ott, *The Haitian Revolution 1789–1804* (Knoxville, Tenn., 1973), 6. For an estimate of two-thirds, see James, *Black Jacobins*, 49–50.

9. Montague, *Haiti and the United States*, 5–6. David Geggus has calculated that the mean size of a sugar estate in St. Domingue was 177 slaves over the period 1745–1792, and the number was rising steadily to 209 in the years 1790–1792. Only a fourth of his sample estates had less than 100 slaves, and only 10 percent of all slaves were on such estates. Twenty-five percent of all slaves were on estates with more than 300 slaves, and two-thirds were on estates with 170 or more (David Geggus, "Sugar and Coffee Cultivation in Saint Domingue and the Shaping of the Slave Labor Force," paper presented to the conference on Culture and Cultivation, University of Maryland, April 1989, 3, 21).

10. Montague, *Haiti and the United States*, 5; Williams, *Capitalism and Slavery*, 122–23; James, *Black Jacobins*, 45–46.

11. Rodman, *Haiti*, 6; Scott, "The Common Wind," 13–14; David Nicholls, *From Dessalines to Duvalier: Race, Colour and National Independence in Haiti* (Cambridge, England, 1979), 19.

St. Domingue was "the market of the New World," with "a position of importance unsurpassed in the history of European colonialism." On its agriculture depended the livelihoods of anywhere from two to six million Frenchmen and the prosperity of entire cities as disparate as Bordeaux and Boston. To its ports, annually, sailed a greater number of ships than plied the trade lanes of Marseilles. In its great harbor of Cap Français, on any given day, were about twenty-five hundred seamen. St. Domingue's officially registered commerce with France alone was equal to the total trade of the United States with all the world in 1790, and that commerce was merely a fraction of the colony's dealings, licit and illicit, with the Atlantic trading nations.[12]

Even before the boom of the 1780s, French visitors who were in a position to know claimed that Cap Français could be compared for size and commerce to the flourishing French center of Lyon. In the 1780s, production in the colony doubled, and Le Cap burgeoned with it. Estimates again vary, but a recent one places the port's population at fifty thousand (three-quarters of them slaves) in 1791.[13] If that estimate is accurate, "the Paris of the Indies" was substantially larger than Philadelphia, then easily the largest city in the United States, and larger than Boston would be for at least another generation.[14] The city supported a royal society of the arts and sciences, a museum, botanical gardens, an academy of agriculture, a number of newspapers, and a playhouse that seated two thousand. The San Domingans' passion for the stage far exceeded anything evident in Philadelphia, let alone New York or lesser American centers, and the seafarers' craving for booze and betting did too. One observer in Cap Français in the 1770s counted no less than fifteen hundred of the drinking and gambling joints known as "cabarets" and "billiards."[15]

12. James, *Black Jacobins,* 49–50; Alfred Hunt, *Haiti's Influence on Antebellum America: Slumbering Volcano in the Caribbean* (Baton Rouge, La., 1988), 9; Logan, *Diplomatic Relations,* 3, 6; Montague, *Haiti and the United States,* 29–30; Scott, "The Common Wind," 60–61.

13. Logan, *Diplomatic Relations,* 4; James, *Black Jacobins,* 50, 55; Ott, *The Haitian Revolution,* 7. Hunt, *Haiti's Influence,* 21, advances a more modest estimate of 12,000, three-quarters of them slaves. Scott, "The Common Wind," 28, says that official figures for 1788 show 12,151 in the city itself, but he adds that this figure does not include "the tens of thousands of people living on plantations in the immediate highlands, whose lives were intimately connected to the city."

14. Hunt, *Haiti's Influence,* 21; U.S. Bureau of the Census, *U.S. Census of Population: 1960* (Washington, D.C., 1961), 1 (pt. A):1–66.

15. Ott, *The Haitian Revolution,* 11; Hunt, *Haiti's Influence,* 67; Scott, "The Common Wind," 66.

All of this activity made St. Domingue an irresistible magnet for American traders. In 1790, merchants of the young republic had more than five hundred ships on routes to Le Cap, Port-au-Prince, Môle St. Nicolas, and other San Domingan ports. By some reckonings, France herself had fewer than that.[16] In the decade after 1790, despite the devastations of war, the number of American ships regularly sailing in the trade rose to six hundred and more, while the number of French vessels braving the British blockade fell precipitately. Before Jefferson became president, the value of the American exchange with St. Domingue was perhaps seven times the value of the French commerce with the island. Before Jefferson imposed his embargo against all American shipping to the black republic, the United States was St. Domingue's most important economic partner. And the island was almost equally significant to the United States. With a population of little more than half a million people, ninety percent of them slaves, she stood second only to Great Britain in the foreign commerce of America in 1790, taking at least a tenth of all American exports in that year.[17]

This vast commerce was the foundation of the prosperity of New England and of the more abounding success of the Middle Atlantic region. John Adams even thought it "made . . . the southern provinces what they are." Americans everywhere saw the French islands as natural outlets and entrepôts. Americans everywhere resisted restrictions on the trade, insisting that their people and their standard of living depended on it. And when the revolution in St. Domingue erupted in 1791— when the slaves rose in murderous rage against their masters, and the flames of the smoldering plantations filled the sky over Cap Français— Americans everywhere found the danger of disruption of exchange impossible to ignore.[18]

But alongside the immense enticements of the Antillean traffic, Americans also took other interests into consideration. One constellation of such interests was ideological and, in truth, spiritual. The United

16. Logan, *Diplomatic Relations*, 30; Ott, *The Haitian Revolution*, 6. On another estimate, France would have had somewhat more ships in the trade than the United States; see James, *Black Jacobins*, 49–50. France surely had less by 1797.

17. Logan, *Diplomatic Relations*, 60; Ott, *The Haitian Revolution*, 142; Nicholls, *Dessalines to Duvalier*, 37; Montague, *Haiti and the United States*, 32; Scott, "The Common Wind," 83–4; John Coatsworth, "American Trade with European Colonies in the Caribbean and South America, 1790–1812," *William and Mary Quarterly*, 3d ser., 24 (1967): 243–66.

18. Montague, *Haiti and the United States*, 29–30; Scott, "The Common Wind," 82–83.

States was an outlaw if not an outcast among the nations of the Western world in 1791. It was a democracy in an era still dominated by aristocracies, a republic in an age still ruled by monarchs. Its revolutionary inception made those traditional dynasts intensely uneasy. Its isolation and its awareness of their uneasy animosity made it immensely edgy.

The San Domingan upheaval seemed to some Americans an uncanny echo of their own insurgency against England and an encouraging portent of the future. The rising that began on that fiery, fateful night of August 22, 1791, was the most unequivocally democratic of all the revolutions of that age of democratic revolutions. It mobilized disprivileged and enslaved masses in a remarkable resistance to tyranny. It began by seeking nothing more than a measure of self-determination, a sort of dominion status within a wider French empire, and it ended by achieving an autonomy it had not initially even envisioned, let alone sought. It was impelled to independence with the utmost reluctance, by the recalcitrance of the metropolis itself. Ultimately, it attached itself to the most elevated ideals of liberty and equality. And it was led almost from first to last by a veritable father of his country, Toussaint L'Ouverture.[19]

In all these ways the San Domingan revolution invited a comparison to which more than a few Americans were not averse. As Winthrop Jordan observed, "Americans had recently been rebels, were noted in the world as such, and knew it." As a Pennsylvania legislator put it at the time, "It would be inconsistent on the part of a free nation to take measures against a people who had availed themselves of the only means they had to throw off the yoke of the most atrocious slavery; if one treats the insurrection of the negroes as rebellion, what name can be given to that insurrection of Americans which secured their independence?"[20]

But another configuration of interests was material as well as ideological. Most Americans did differentiate between the two insurrections, precisely because the West Indian one was an "insurrection of the negroes." Most Americans, as Jordan also observed, were disinclined to "admit the exactness of the parallel" between their own revolt and that

19. Roger Buckley, ed., *The Haitian Journal of Lieutenant Howard, York Hussars, 1796–1798* (Knoxville, Tenn., 1985), xv; James, *Black Jacobins, passim;* Eugene Genovese, *From Rebellion to Revolution: Afro-American Slave Revolts in the Making of the Modern World* (Baton Rouge, La., 1979), esp. 88, 90; George Tyson, ed., *Toussaint L'Ouverture* (Englewood Cliffs, N.J., 1973).

20. Jordan, *White over Black,* 378.

of the blacks. In a world in which they were almost alone in their experiment in republican government, they still did not rush to propose
toasts to St. Domingue "expressive of our love for our sister republic,"
as they did for France. In a hemisphere in which they were literally
alone, before 1791, in their overthrow of European colonial dominion,
they still did not rush to erect equestrian statues of Toussaint, as they
did of Washington and as they would of any number of later white Latin
American liberators. The triumph of indomitable blacks, even in the
very causes they claimed as their own and in which they found their
own distinctive identity, did not inspire Americans to celebration. It
filled them with dread.[21]

The fear was especially vivid, of course, and the language of anxiety
especially livid, in the Southern states. By 1793, the French minister to
the United States found the planters "terrified" by developments on
Hispaniola. "Any number of slave plots, real and imagined, were
blamed on what happened in St. Domingue." Indeed, even before white
refugees brought lurid tales of black atrocities to Southerners who
waited for them with bated breath, those Southerners could conjure all
the enormities they required in their own imaginations.[22] Soon enough,
Southerners were bracing themselves against a black San Domingan invasion of the South. Soon enough, they were demanding defeat of the
insurgents who had "already crushed all the fair fruits of European culture, and in a few years . . . will convert these beautiful plantations into
an African wilderness." And soon enough, they were issuing more than
mere addresses and demands.[23]

In their fevered imagination of Toussaint's navy and of their own
slaves' eagerness for conspiracies of bloody vengeance, planter-
dominated legislatures and local councils formed numerous new regi-
ments and called out still more numerous local militias. Every single
state south of the Mason-Dixon line passed laws to prevent the entry of
slaves and free Negroes from the French West Indies. South Carolina
was so caught up in the hysteria that it forbade the disembarkation of
any "man of color" who had ever been or might ever be a resident of
any of the French islands. And the Southern governments dealt only a
little less rigorously with blacks already resident. Every slave state en-

21.  Ibid.; Charles Biddle, *Autobiography of Charles Biddle, Vice-President of the Supreme
Executive Council of Pennsylvania, 1754–1821* (Philadelphia, 1883), 253; Buckley, ed.,
*Haitian Journal*, xix.
22.  Hunt, *Haiti's Influence*, 115; Ott, *The Haitian Revolution*, 53–54.
23.  Hunt, *Haiti's Influence*, 133.

acted a myriad of repressive measures to curb the minimal freedoms they had previously permitted people of color.[24]

For Southern leaders, at least, the revolution in St. Domingue that took its rise from the Declaration of the Rights of Man became the occasion for a repudiation of the very rights for which American colonists had contended a few years earlier. The spectre of race war led planters in particular to a hardening antagonism to all discussion of emancipation and an augmenting insistence on the incapacity of blacks for civilization. The spectacle of former slaves in seats of power made Southern political leaders averse to all that they thought carried the contamination of liberty. "It was in the 1790s and the early 1800s that the South began to erect its intellectual blockade against potentially dangerous doctrines."[25]

The rise of a revolutionary republic in St. Domingue thus "helped forge an ideology" in America that "differed significantly from the humanistic traditions of Western civilization," in its denial of the humanity of blacks, and that departed decisively from the Revolutionary rhetoric of American patriots, in its refusal of the natural rights of African-Americans in bondage. Terms that were still talismans of enlightenment in St. Domingue became tokens of anathema in the American South.[26]

The revulsion from revolution went beyond extortion of consensus on racial issues and beyond even the rejection of freedom of thought itself in regard to race and all that race reached. It conditioned a more comprehensive Southern sense of disquietude. As they never had before 1791, slaveholders saw themselves living "on the edge of a precipice," where "a single false slip" could cause their ruination. The "immense scene of slaughter" in the West Indies haunted their thoughts, even as they "came increasingly to feel that slavery was a closed subject, entirely unsuitable for frank discussion."[27]

To avert all allusion to race and the reduction of persons to property, slaveowners and their sympathizers had to collude in a quarantine of the very ideas and ideals upon which they had won their own independence in their own rebellion. They had to abandon the universalistic language with which they had waged their fight for freedom. They had to revert

24. Ott, *The Haitian Revolution,* 122, 195; Hunt, *Haiti's Influence,* 107, 108; Montague, *Haiti and the United States,* 35.

25. Hunt, *Haiti's Influence,* 114.

26. Ibid., 2–3, 107.

27. Ibid., 107, 111; Clement Eaton, *The Freedom-of-Thought Struggle in the Old South* (New York, 1964), 89–117; Hunt, *Haiti's Influence,* 124; Jordan, *White over Black,* 384.

to a particularism that undermined the faith that had animated their endeavor and informed their identity.

In the flood tide of the spirit of '76, Tom Paine insisted that the ethos of the American Revolution was "not the concern of a day, a year, or an age; posterity are virtually involved in the contest, and will be more or less affected even to the end of time." Thomas Jefferson declared certain "truths to be self-evident" and proclaimed "inalienable rights" deriving from "the laws of nature and of nature's God." And on the eve of the eruption of black militance, almost a decade after the Franco-American triumph at Yorktown, Jefferson looked back on the revolution he and his fellows had wrought and saw that it was good. He took pride in the "thought that, while we are securing the rights of ourselves and our posterity, we are pointing out the way to struggling nations who wish like us to emerge from their tyrannies also."[28]

Before the conflagration in the Caribbean, Jefferson and many other American Revolutionaries welcomed the widening of rebellion against oppression. They trusted that their example would prove infectious, and they anticipated eagerly the contagion of liberation. Indeed, they could hardly have done otherwise. As Jordan said, "denial of the universal applicability of natural rights would have deprived their Revolution of its broader meaning and of its claim upon the attention of the world." Rejection of the generality of rights would have diminished the significance of their achievement and reduced the country it created to a passing provincial aberration.[29]

Yet by 1797 Jefferson was ready to relinquish such pretensions to world-historical significance sooner than see the principles on which such pretensions rested be a basis for Southern slaveowners' vulnerability. "If something is not done, and soon done," he warned, "we shall be the murderers of our own children." The *philosophe* who had contemplated recurrent revolution with equanimity in the dazzling deductions of his correspondence now shrank in horror from "the revolutionary storm . . . sweeping the globe." The democrat who had descanted on the beneficence of the blood of tyrants as a nutrient for the tree of liberty now trembled that "the day which begins our combustion must

---

28. Thomas Paine, *Common Sense,* in *The Complete Writings of Thomas Paine,* ed. Philip Foner (New York, 1945), 17; Thomas Jefferson, *The Declaration of Independence,* in *The Portable Thomas Jefferson,* ed. Merrill Peterson (New York, 1975), 235; Jordan, *White over Black,* 386.

29. Jordan, *White over Black,* 386, 387.

be near at hand; and only a single spark is wanting to make that day tomorrow." [30]

Jefferson was not alone in his retreat from the universalistic promise of the Revolution to the particularistic protections of a less lofty language. Other Americans—especially other white Southerners—also abandoned their radical ideology when they saw, in the maelstrom and massacres of St. Domingue, its "inherent implications." And in the attrition of their ideology, there was more than a mere "crystallization" of racial antagonism. There was an ebbing of revolutionary commitment itself. The combustions in the Caribbean "helped produce a novel hesitancy about revolutions in general." [31]

In and of themselves, such phenomena would not be unduly intriguing. Revolutions generally develop Thermidorean dynamics. Our understanding of the politics of the early republic has always followed the trajectory of the recession of Revolutionary ideals. Much of our most sophisticated contemporary scholarship continues in the same vein. When Thomas Slaughter sets the Federalists' resurgent devotion to order against the persisting faith in freedom of the Jeffersonian frontiersmen, his account accords with our expectations. We are accustomed to assign the new nation's disavowal of its Revolutionary heritage to the Federalists rather than to the Jeffersonians. [32]

Nonetheless, in St. Domingue it was the Federalists who held far more closely to the faith of the founders and the Jeffersonian Republicans who tried far more tenaciously to tether and traduce the will of a people. It was the Federalists who were keen to aid the oppressed in their effort at independence and the Republicans who resisted that effort. It was the Federalists who fostered freedom and the Republicans who attempted the restoration of a colonial regime and, indeed, the reimposition of slavery itself.

Republicans, of course, discounted all this. They castigated their Federalist foes as counter-Revolutionaries. Or, at best, they characterized their Federalist adversaries as aristocratically inclined conservatives. And their characterization has come to us across the centuries as received wisdom. Though Federalists resented these accusations and as-

30. Ibid., 386; Jefferson to James Madison, January 30, 1787, in *Portable Jefferson,* ed. Peterson, 416–17; Jefferson to William Stevens Smith, November 13, 1787, in *The Papers of Thomas Jefferson,* ed. Julian Boyd (Princeton, N.J., 1950–), 12:356–57.

31. Jordan, *White over Black,* 402, 387; see also Zuckerman, "Thermidor in America."

32. Slaughter, *The Whiskey Rebellion.*

sessments and insisted that they carried the Revolutionary flame as honorably as their Republican rivals, they were powerless to make their professions credible to contemporaries or to subsequent scholars.

Nonetheless, at the ideological crisis of their age, the point where Revolutionary principles were put most profoundly to the test, those accused aristocrats showed themselves able to accept another democratic revolution in the New World as the self-styled party of the people could not. They accepted ideas of natural rights that, in the end, appalled Jefferson and his followers. In conviction and in conduct, in abstract ideal and in the immediate application of power alike, they came to terms with the San Domingan demonstration of black competence and black capacity for command as the Republicans never did. In the realm of race, the Federalists clung to the ideological inheritance of the Revolution far more firmly than the Jeffersonians.

And since race intertwined, ultimately, with everything else the Revolutionaries believed themselves to be about, reexamination of American reactions to the triumph of the colonized over their colonizers in St. Domingue presents some tantalizing possibilities. It suggests that in important ways the Federalists were correct in their futile defense of themselves. It suggests too that Jefferson was correct after all in his fatuous inaugural pronouncement that they were "all republicans" and "all federalists." They all shared, authentically, in the language and logic of the Revolution. They all found it impossible, one way or another, to live within that language and logic. Fatefully for America, the Republicans who dominated the course of the country's development found it impossible with regard to the question of color.[33]

Despite the dictates of mercantilist theory and the demands of Bordeaux and its sister cities in the West Indian trade, Americans held the

---

33. Jefferson, First Inaugural Address, in *Portable Jefferson,* ed. Peterson, 292. For other intimations of the authenticity of Federalist republicanism, see, e.g., Joyce Appleby, "The American Heritage: The Heirs and the Disinherited," *Journal of American History* 74 (1987): 798, 801; Linda Kerber, "Making Republicanism Useful," *Yale Law Journal* 97 (1988): 1,666; John Murrin, "The Great Inversion, or Court versus Country: A Comparison of the Revolution Settlements in England (1688–1721) and America (1776–1816)," in *Three British Revolutions: 1641, 1688, 1776,* ed. J. G. A. Pocock (Princeton, N.J., 1980), 368–453; M. C. Baseler, "Immigration Policies in Eighteenth-Century America," (Ph.D. diss., Harvard University, 1991). For a close study of blacks and whites in New York and an explicit finding of far easier relations between the races, in regard to work and residence alike, in 1800 than in the succeeding generation, see Shane White, *Somewhat More Independent: The End of Slavery in New York City, 1770–1810* (Athens, Ga., 1991), esp. 168–69, 207–9.

lion's share of the business of supplying St. Domingue on the eve of its eruption. The French island needed provisions, lumber, and horses that neither France itself nor its American dependencies could muster, and the French planters had no home market for their rum and molasses because the mother country forbade importation of those commodities in order to protect its own brandy distillers. As early as the second decade of the eighteenth century, American merchants were defying the design of the French Monopoly if not the letter of the navigation laws in order to deal directly with St. Domingue and the other French colonies in the Caribbean. By the time Britain imposed the Molasses Act of 1733, smuggling was so settled a mode of enterprise that it could not be controlled by laws. It could only be contained by converting it into legitimate commerce, in the 1767 decree that made Môle St. Nicolas a free port for certain goods. By 1797, exchange with America was so vital to St. Domingue that Toussaint demanded of the French commissioners a halt to all privateering against the vessels of the United States, and the very cultivators in the fields insisted—by boycotts and rebellions—on positive protection of American shipping by the French authorities.[34]

Under such circumstances, it is easy enough to interpret Federalist support for the San Domingan revolution cynically, as an acquiescence in the importunities of the merchant element in the party and as a priority on the preservation of its lucrative traffic in the Caribbean. It is easy enough, in other words, to interpret the Federalists as the Jeffersonians did, as men possessed of the souls of shopkeepers, pursuing business as usual, without regard for political principle.

Certainly a succession of Federalist officials did seek to promote the nation's commercial relationship with the French colony without worrying overmuch which elements were in power on the island. Certainly Federalists did put a priority on the encouragement of trade. And probably Federalists did see Toussaint as an instrument by which they could dissociate the jewel of the Antilles from the French and their Monopoly. When the black general took command of the molasses, many Americans moved easily to align their material interests with his military and political ones.[35]

But Federalist attachment to Toussaint was more than a crass calcu-

34. Montague, *Haiti and the United States*, 29–30; Logan, *Diplomatic Relations*, 6; Ott, *The Haitian Revolution*, 89.

35. Ott, *The Haitian Revolution*, 54; Hunt, *Haiti's Influence*, 84–85; Montague, *Haiti and the United States*, 35–36.

lation of purse and profit. Federalists remained steadfast in their support of the black leader through a decade of the most disparate circumstances. They lent little aid or comfort to the British while His Majesty's forces mounted a savage four-year-long assault on the island, though American interests in trade lay manifestly more with monarchical Britain than with incendiary St. Domingue. Then, after the English gave up their ill-fated onslaught, they plainly favored Toussaint and his black followers over the French and over the mulatto and white interests on the island as well. Finally, after Jefferson became president, they persisted in sustaining and supplying the infant black republic in defiance of his implacable malice toward it. They had traded with St. Domingue before 1801, when returns were easy and abundant, and they continued to send their ships after that time, when the work was difficult and dangerous and the prospect of profit dubious. They did assuredly own slaves, and they did in all likelihood harbor their own racial prejudices; but they did also believe in their Revolutionary declamations of republican self-determination, and they did think that Toussaint and his movement embodied those ideals.

For all their putative conservatism, they were comfortable enough with developments in St. Domingue to prod Toussaint to proclaim the colony's independence from the French. They would have had him follow their own unruly revolutionary example long before he himself was prepared to do so. And they accepted coolly the demonstration his success would inevitably afford of black fitness for freedom. It was in the authentic language and spirit of '76 that Federalists like Theodore Dwight declared the St. Domingue upheavals the righteous risings of "oppressed human nature" against "a succession of unjust and contradictory measures." It was in the pristine passion of the Americans' own struggle for autonomy that he applauded the blacks' overthrow of "their tyrannical masters" and their establishment of themselves on the "firm pillars of freedom and independence."[36]

Moreover, the Federalist government spoke in the same accents as private individuals and acted even more audaciously than it spoke. In June 1798, at the outset of the quasi-war with France, Congress authorized a trade embargo against the great European power and all her imperial dependencies. But even as the Congressmen acted, officials in Washington were instructing the American consul in Cap Français to invite an advance from Toussaint before the embargo imperiled his po-

36. Hunt, *Haiti's Influence*, 152–53.

sition. The black ruler responded with an offer to protect American shipping if commerce between the United States and his country were reinstated. Then, before Congress could even take up the offer, Secretary of State Pickering decided to construe the terms of the embargo as inapplicable to St. Domingue to begin with. The act interdicted relations with "places under the acknowledged power of France," and Pickering chose to treat Toussaint rather than the French as the effective authority of the island, in virtual promulgation of San Domingan independence. By the time Congress officially lifted the embargo, in February 1799, Pickering had already appointed Edward Stevens as consul-general to St. Domingue with explicit instructions to encourage the blacks officially to declare their separation from France.[37]

Edward Stevens was not merely an exceptionally able man on whom Pickering and his president, John Adams, bestowed exceptional diplomatic powers. He was also a close friend and, quite likely, a half-brother of Alexander Hamilton. Since Pickering was Hamilton's man at the Department of State, Stevens could hardly have been more powerfully placed to implement high Federalist policies and predilections.[38]

From the first, Stevens won Toussaint's trust. Soon he was so close a confidant to the rebel commander that he was able to engineer an informal tripartite treaty between Toussaint and the British agent Thomas Maitland. The agreement gave the black Jacobin free access to American supplies in return for his abandonment of the privateering and shipping he had previously authorized. Stevens was not openly a party to this arrangement, "but in Toussaint's eyes he was the real negotiator, and his influence had more to do with the result than all the ships and sailors at Maitland's disposal."[39]

Toussaint L'Ouverture was nobody's fool. He saw into schemes and situations with preternatural insight, held his counsel with consummate cunning, and kept his country aloof from entangling obligations with inordinate skill. Yet Stevens won him over so swiftly and so totally that, in concluding the tripartite convention, "Toussaint threw himself into the arms of the United States."[40]

Toussaint's judgment was vindicated when Stevens placed both the

37. Henry Adams, *History of the United States of America during the First Administration of Thomas Jefferson* (1889; reprint New York, 1921), 1:384–85; Charles Tansill, *The United States and Santo Domingo, 1798–1873: A Chapter in Caribbean Diplomacy* (Baltimore, 1938), 15; Ott, *The Haitian Revolution*, 108.

38. Adams, *History*, 1:384–86; Kennedy, *Orders from France*, 146–49.

39. Adams, *History*, 1:384–85.

40. Ibid.

promised supplies and also American naval support itself at the general's disposal during his struggles with Rigaud in the climactic civil war of 1799. Rigaud was a mulatto who had risen to power in South Province as Toussaint himself had come to control in the north and west. He was allied more closely than Toussaint with both the old propertied classes of the island and the old colonial regime. And he offered commercial concessions to the United States as generous as those that Toussaint proposed. It would have been by far the most expedient course for the Adams administration to remain neutral in the battle between the blacks and the mulattoes. It would also have been fatal to Toussaint's cause.[41]

Stevens did not pursue that course. In defiance of all incentives to prudence, all inclinations to conciliate the good will of the French, all imperatives to placate the British, whose own most precious colony was poised nervously across the Jamaica Channel, Stevens and his secretary of state stood unbudging in their support of the former slaves.

The Federalists were not abolitionists. Even people like Pickering regretted emancipation as an "evil." But they also accepted it as a *fait accompli,* recoiling from any effort at a restoration of slavery such as the French or their ally Rigaud might attempt. He "confidently reckon[ed] on the independence of St. Domingue" under Toussaint's dominion, and he would help "crush" Rigaud and his forces "if they resist the will of T——t."[42]

Stevens himself never even intimated the passing regret that Pickering professed. His attachment to Toussaint was unwavering and indispensable. He provided the materiel that enabled the black commander to undertake the crucial siege of Rigaud's stronghold at Jacmel, and he ordered the naval assistance that allowed the siege to succeed. At a critical juncture, when the British had intercepted the black fleet and kept it from its mission at Jacmel, Stevens called in a small flotilla of American warships to carry blacks to the southern front, destroy Rigaud's marauding barges, and bombard mulatto positions. The American vessels maintained their blockade of the port until its evacuation enabled Toussaint to push his entire campaign to a successful conclusion.[43]

The operations at Jacmel were the first armed intervention the United States ever attempted in a foreign civil war. Yet Stevens never hesitated for lack of legitimate precedent, and neither did his Federalist superiors at home. The secretary of the navy himself ordered the offen-

41. Tansill, *United States and Santo Domingo,* 16.
42. Logan, *Diplomatic Relations,* 84.
43. Ibid., 102, 104; Ott, *The Haitian Revolution,* 112–13, 114; Montague, *Haiti and the United States,* 41.

sive against Rigaud's barges and declared his determination to see Toussaint defeat the French protégé. He even told one captain, "You cannot be too attentive to the cultivation of a good understanding" with Toussaint and the ex-slaves under his command. And the government instructed American captains more generally to take no action that might "disturb the harmony" between San Domingan rebels and "the people of the United States."[44]

Under the Federalists, that harmony was no mere nicety of diplomatic discourse, either. As long as the Federalists were in power, "a great proportion of the inhabitants of the United States" anticipated relations of amity with the black republicans rather than the restoration of colonial controls over them. More than that, they anticipated such relations "with pleasure." Federalist merchants in particular expressed enthusiasm for the rebel regime, especially after Toussaint extended conciliatory offers to whites to help in rebuilding the island and reconstructing its economy; to Talleyrand, it seemed that they were "all devoted" to the former slave. And Federalist officials and party stalwarts routinely referred to the insurgent leader as the "amiable and respectable Toussaint."[45]

Indeed, Federalists often subordinated obvious considerations of opportunity and advantage to attachments of ideological affinity and personal regard. The president himself understood all along that, on any calculus of conventional interest, independence was "the worst and most dangerous condition [the French colonies could] be in for the United States." As late as the middle of 1799, he remained resolved "to do nothing without the consent, concert, and cooperation of the British government" in the West Indies, because "a good understanding with the English" was "of more importance to us than the trade of San Domingo." Yet Hamilton, Pickering, and a host of others including Adams's own son John Quincy Adams, favored a "free and independent" St. Domingue. And before long the president did too, for reasons that were never primarily prudential.[46]

44. Logan, *Diplomatic Relations*, 103, 101; Tansill, *United States and Santo Domingo*, 75, 73. The captains caught the spirit of their civilian superiors, vying with one another to please Toussaint. In that effort they disregarded orders, violated Anglo-American treaties, convoyed San Domingan vessels through the British blockade under false pretenses, and otherwise bent and broke rules and exceeded proprieties in Toussaint's service. And in Le Cap, Stevens approved these ploys. See Tansill, *United States and Santo Domingo*, 74; Logan, *Diplomatic Relations*, 101–10.

45. Hunt, *Haiti's Influence*, 33–34; Logan, *Diplomatic Relations*, 127; John Miller, *The Wolf by the Ears: Thomas Jefferson and Slavery* (New York, 1977), 134.

46. Tansill, *United States and Santo Domingo*, 52–53; Logan, *Diplomatic Relations*, 85–86; Tansill, *United States and Santo Domingo*, 68, 69, 13–14; Logan, *Diplomatic Re-*

Despite their alleged and often authentic Anglophilia, Federalists were willing to defy England in order to seek their own ends in the Caribbean basin. John Adams may have pronounced accord with England "the thing [he had] most at heart," but he left the actual formulation of American policy in St. Domingue solely to his secretary of state. Pickering proceeded to extort from the British legate, Thomas Maitland, a series of "Points on which there is an understanding," and on almost every significant point the American made the Briton give up articles that the War Office and Foreign Office had insisted strongly upon. Though her quasi-war with France was raging and the United States had to have cordial relations with England on that account, Pickering and his fellow Federalists stuck to their guns and succeeded. Soon enough the Francophilic Jeffersonians would be bowing lamely before Napoleon and his emissaries, even when far more vital American interests were at stake.[47]

In the San Domingan civil war, Toussaint sensed sufficient sympathy from America, and indeed from Adams, that on Stevens's urging he wrote directly to the president begging aid. And Adams delivered it, allowing trade and then approving the clearance of American vessels for Cap Français and Port-au-Prince. By the time Rigaud fled for France, the Federalists were even willing to jeopardize Anglo-American relations for their new friendship. In 1800 they proclaimed the opening of all ports in St. Domingue to American commerce, violating as they did the accord they had made with Maitland the year before. Adams himself conveyed his "satisfaction to learn that General Toussaint continues in his friendly dispositions to the United States," though the deepening of the connection was provoking British seizures of American ships trading with the newly opened ports.[48]

Toussaint's attachment to the United States was gratifying rather than grating or embarrassing to the Federalists. The *de facto* independence to which they incited the black leader, years before he was ready

---

*lations*, 82. John Adams was actually a good deal more diffident than his rhetoric suggested. He went on to say that his "opinion" was "liable to so much uncertainty, that no great dependence can be placed upon it" (Tansill, *United States and Santo Domingo*, 85–86).

47. Tansill, *United States and Santo Domingo*, 69, 53, 55. A month later, the Americans actually won Maitland's agreement to an arrangement by which Edward Stevens would "superintend" British trade with St. Domingue, since Toussaint was so much closer to the United States than to Great Britain while the Federalists were in power (ibid., 58).

48. James, *Black Jacobins*, 227–28; Montague, *Haiti and the United States*, 39–40; Logan, *Diplomatic Relations*, 110–11; Tansill, *United States and Santo Domingo*, 76.

to announce it openly, was built on a bedrock of amicable relations between the two societies. And Federalists did not shy from such ties.
Edward Stevens had Toussaint's "unbounded" confidence and helped
him set economic policy for his country. Alexander Hamilton was asked
to devise a plan of government for the embryonic nation and threw
himself willingly into the work. Before the election of 1800, it was not
uncommon for St. Domingue blacks to refer to Americans as "good
whites." Before the passing of Federalist power, Toussaint pledged that
the persons and property of American citizens would "at all times and
under all circumstances be considered as sacred." [49]

Many Federalists went further still. Prominent leaders of the party
such as Alexander Hamilton, John Jay, and Benjamin Franklin joined
the earliest abolition societies.[50] Officeholders and opinion leaders of
the party expressed their sentiments almost as unmistakably. Throughout the 1790s, Federalists fumed that slaveholding in and of itself dis-
qualified men for leadership in a free society. Their animus against slavery and the power it provided autocratic planters was, as Linda Kerber
said, a consuming passion for them in the period of the San Domingan
revolution. It was also an authentic "part of their heritage from the Revolutionary generation." [51]

In Washington, Federalist senators debating the Breckenridge bill
spoke out openly against the expansion of slavery as Republicans never
dared. One called slavery "a serious evil" and declared his desire to
"check it wherever I have authority." Another called it "a curse." A third
pledged "to prevent, as far as possible, the horrid evil of slavery—and
thereby avoid the fate of St. Domingo." Even in the South, Federalists
kept the founders' faith in natural rights as Jeffersonians rarely did. In
Virginia, Federalists with but a single exception in the Burgesses opposed the three-fifths clause and the confinement of the suffrage to
white freemen. And though the partisans of Hamilton did not always
rise to such heights of principle, they did set themselves apart unmistakably from their Republican rivals. Everywhere in America, free blacks

49. Tansill, *United States and Santo Domingo,* 13–14, 33, 52; Adams, *History,* 1:385–
86; James, *Black Jacobins,* 245; Ott, *The Haitian Revolution,* 126, 131–32; Tansill, *United
States and Santo Domingo,* 72.

50. Thomas Jefferson never joined an anti-slavery society, early or late. Even in
France, amid his beloved *philosophes,* he deliberately declined an invitation to membership
in *Les Amis des Noirs.* See David Brion Davis, *The Problem of Slavery in the Age of Revolution,
1770–1823* (Ithaca, N.Y., 1975), 94, 172, 176.

51. Linda Kerber, *Federalists in Dissent: Imagery and Ideology in Jeffersonian America*
(Ithaca, N.Y., 1970), 23–66; quotation at 58.

reckoned the Republicans "the party of racism and oppression" and voted for the Federalists.[52]

Federalists maintained cordial relations with St. Domingue's black revolutionaries when such relations were profitable. They also remained friends of the slave revolution and of the embattled republic it birthed when such relations became problematic and perhaps provocative of their own government's ire. Before 1801, they promoted trade with the rebels, selling arms, ammunition, and essential supplies on a scale that made America the principal outfitter of Toussaint's army. After 1801 and Jefferson's accession to the reins of government, the United States ceased to support San Domingan independence. The harbor at Le Cap emptied of American vessels so swiftly that Toussaint was moved to ask sarcastically "if the change in administrations had destroyed all the American ships."[53] But despite the difficulties, private merchants, preponderantly Federalists, continued to convoy supplies to Toussaint and his successors. There was money in it, to be sure, but they believed in what they were doing as well.[54]

In the spring of 1802, many merchants expressed openly their eagerness to see Toussaint emerge victorious against the French invasionary forces with which their own president was in collaboration. A little later, they lodged open protests against the campaign of wanton butchery and brutality waged by the leader of the French expedition; and they backed their words with actions, declining his bids for provisions though he offered them twice what the San Domingans did. In 1805, a large fleet of American vessels returned from the island—now the independent republic of Haiti, unrecognized by Jefferson's government in Washington—to a grand banquet in honor of its safe return in New York. Before such luminous Federalist leaders as Rufus King and a host of city and state officials, a toast was proffered to the voyage in unabashed defiance of Jeffersonian policy and in unmistakable evocation of Revolutionary values: "To the government of Haiti, founded on the only legitimate basis of all authority—the people's choice. May it be as durable as its principles are pure."[55]

52. Ibid., 39–43; Davis, *Problem of Slavery,* 134.

53. Buckley, ed., *Haitian Journal,* 179; Ott, *The Haitian Revolution,* 131–32; Tansill, *United States and Santo Domingo,* 83.

54. James, *Black Jacobins,* 304–5, 366, 370; Logan, *Diplomatic Relations,* 132, 150.

55. Logan, *Diplomatic Relations,* 135–36, 137; Tansill, *United States and Santo Domingo,* 106; Logan, *Diplomatic Relations,* 173. As late as the 1830s, white working-class organizations continued to drink toasts to the "pure Republicanism" of the Haitian government. See Eric Foner, *Politics and Ideology in the Age of the Civil War* (New York, 1980), 61.

Federalists supported the provisioning of the popular government of Haiti to the bitter end. They urged diplomatic recognition of Dessalines and his newly independent nation, while Jefferson and his followers remained adamant in their determination to "establish a quarantine against the contagion of servile revolt." Federalists still had the votes to defeat a general embargo in 1805, but Jefferson controlled the next Congress handily. The Virginian made his confinement of the contagion of liberty "an administration measure" and pushed it through on almost purely partisan lines. At least twenty of the twenty-one votes for the embargo in the Senate were cast by Republicans, at least seven of the eight votes against it by Federalists; and the House vote of ninety-three to twenty-six was marked by an identical "division along party lines."[56]

These partisan divisions were ironically revealing. They showed the Federalists—conventionally considered the conservatives of the age—able to abide intimations of black competence for participation in the comity of nations, able to make their peace with a multiracial world, able to come to terms with a continuing contagion of liberty and eruption of revolution. They showed the Jeffersonian Republicans—the self-styled democrats of the day, and on some accounts the radicals—unable to extend their democratic doctrines beyond their own kind, unable to embrace in practice the Revolutionary rights they enshrined in principle, unable to accept the universalistic import of the Rights of Man when those rights threatened to reach beyond the provincial pale they silently presupposed.

Race was at the root of all these ironies. Race drove all these Jeffersonian retreats. Race overrode all other considerations for Jefferson whenever it was salient at all, and race was centrally salient in St. Domingue.

Others have, of course, implied as much. Such acute and sensitive scholars as Winthrop Jordan and David Brion Davis have made powerfully apparent the torments that the great Virginian endured in the tension of his "central dilemma": that "he hated slavery but thought Negroes inferior to white men."[57]

---

56. Montague, *Haiti and the United States,* 45; Logan, *Diplomatic Relations,* 177–78.
57. Jordan, *White over Black,* 429. Here and throughout this essay, I discount the subtleties of skin pigmentation and the complexities of Jefferson's attitudes to other races. I use "race" and "color," as Jefferson generally used them, to refer quite starkly to Africans and their offspring in America. In that usage I invoke, as Jefferson did, a wide range of "racial" attributes that went well beyond the question of color but were for Jefferson inseparable from color.

But I mean to take their insights somewhat further than they are inclined to do. I mean to suggest that Jefferson was a man intellectually undone by his negrophobia and that he was ultimately prepared to abandon all else in which he believed—and believed passionately—sooner than surrender his racial repugnances.

In other words, I mean to say that Jefferson was not as torn as he is taken to be, even by those who have studied him most closely and iconoclastically. I mean to insist that he was not as confined by his culture as his apologists have often claimed and that he was certainly not simply a sufferer of the constraints of his situation. In regard to race as in regard to so much else, he was a leader. He led the Southern retreat from the implications of the Revolution he himself rationalized in the Declaration of Independence. He was the foremost racist of his era in America. And St. Domingue constituted the crisis in which all this came clear. St. Domingue represented the moment of truth when a rhetoric grown ever more evasive and insincere became its own reality in the crucible of power.

It did not have to turn out that way. Thomas Jefferson was America's preeminent *philosophe*. His emotional and intellectual investment in his identity as a Revolutionary and as an ardent exponent of the Rights of Man was perhaps the most intense of any American of his generation. He was profoundly conscious of history and of his place in it, and he knew that that place rested upon his country's steadfast adherence to its own universalistic principles. Anything less reduced the American Revolution to a mere provincial flare, devoid of world-historical significance. Yet the claims of white pride and the immensity of his aversion to blacks overmastered identity itself for Jefferson.

When the Jacobin revolution first broke upon St. Domingue, Jefferson monitored developments on the island with cold clarity. As secretary of state, he could see a multitude of opportunities to advance America's interests in the insurrection. He anticipated that the planters of the colony would take the occasion of its unsettlement and their own newfound power in the assembly to seek an end to the French Monopoly, and he instructed his agents accordingly to encourage the deputies to demand free trade with the United States. He timed payments on the French debt so as to induce the French minister to support this demand. He calibrated the amounts he paid with an exquisite exactitude, affording the French authorities on the island just enough to enable them to resist a British attack but not so much as to arouse undue jealousy in Bordeaux or Paris. He was not above discreet threats (in the name of a "moral law" that licensed trade between neighbors) that if the European powers did not "avoid oppression," their failures of "policy" and "justice" might "tempt" America and St. Domingue "to act together." He was not even above plans for direct American military intervention to protect national interests in the West Indian trade.[58]

In other words, Jefferson had no difficulty in dealing with St. Domingue as long as whites controlled the colony. He could contemplate alliance with the local planters against the metropolis. He could conceive of infringing on French colonial prerogatives and even of risking war for the sake of American commerce with the French Caribbean. He did not hesitate to indulge his penchant for the provocative rhetoric of republicanism, exulting that the small planters—the "patriots"—had gained control of the assembly and dreaming that the great planters— the "aristocrats"—might be deported to the United States and dispersed among the Indians to be educated in liberty and equality.[59]

Before Toussaint and his black troops seized the San Domingan uprising and made it their own, Jefferson's policies were virtually indistinguishable from Hamilton's. They both planned to take all possible advantage of the insurgency short of seeing the colony fall into British hands. They both meant to avail themselves of France's difficulties to exact additional commercial privileges for their own countrymen. Jefferson could see past his Francophilia as easily as Hamilton his Anglophilia, before the convolutions of color clouded his vision. It was his own negrophobia that Jefferson could never transcend or even come to coherent terms with.[60]

The smoke had barely blackened the sky over Cap Français before Jefferson turned against the San Domingan revolution. The slaves had barely begun their revolt against their masters before Jefferson abandoned all fond thoughts of depositing haughty planters among the Indians to resocialize them to republican manners. The news of the sack of Le Cap "upset all calculations" and "necessitated an entirely new policy." Confronted with a real revolution rather than an agreeable shift within the elite, the sage of Monticello bent all his sympathy to the planter-fugitives, whose situation suddenly seemed to him to "call . . . aloud for pity and charity."[61]

58. Logan, *Diplomatic Relations*, 37; Montague, *Haiti and the United States*, 33–34; Logan, *Diplomatic Relations*, 38.

59. Montague, *Haiti and the United States*, 34–35.

60. Logan, *Diplomatic Relations*, 39.

61. Ibid., 38; Montague, *Haiti and the United States*, 34–35.

Just as the swiftness of Jefferson's conversion from contempt to concern for the planters revealed the superficiality of his swipe at their privilege and pride and the depth of his identification with them, so the ease with which he leaped to prognoses of impending cataclysm betrayed the bias of his deepest anxieties. From the day he first learned of the turn of events in St. Domingue, he broadcast his conviction that the whites would be utterly expelled from the French West Indies. And since such expulsion never did occur in the other French islands and occurred in St. Domingue only after a decade of deliberate multiracial development was undone by Napoleon's relentless prosecution of race war and Jefferson's own collusion in the campaign, the Virginian's phobic prophecy reveals much more about the bent of his own mind than about the actuality of affairs.[62]

Jefferson was never able to imagine a multiracial society that would endure on the basis of equity. As early as 1781, in his *Notes on the State of Virginia,* he expressed his sense that it was impossible to "retain and incorporate" free blacks "into the state." As late as 1821, in his *Autobiography,* he clung to the same conviction that "nothing is more certainly written in the book of fate than that the two races, equally free, cannot live in the same government." If the slaves were ever freed, he predicted, "all the whites south of the Potomac and Ohio" would necessarily "evacuate their States." The "most fortunate" would be those able to "do it first." The laggards would be left to endure the merciless retribution of the freedmen, in the racial Armageddon that would inevitably ensue.[63]

From first to last, Jefferson heard firebells in the night. "Deep-rooted prejudices entertained by the whites; ten thousand recollections by the blacks, of the injuries they have sustained; new provocations; the real distinctions which nature has made; and many other circumstances, will . . . produce convulsions which will probably never end but in the extinction of one or the other race." Jefferson was especially sensitive to

62. Montague, *Haiti and the United States,* 34–35; Tansill, *United States and Santo Domingo,* 10. Jefferson's reaction to the agreement that Stevens negotiated with Maitland was similarly revealing. Though the agreement gave Great Britain and the United States a veritable monopoly on the lucrative commerce of the colony, Jefferson simply could not see the economic bonanza in his obsession with the racial aspect. As he wrote to Madison early in 1799, the trade would bring "black crews, and supercargoes and missionaries . . . into the southern states," and "if this combustion can be introduced among us under any veil whatever, we have to fear it" (Scott, "The Common Wind," 299).

63. Thomas Jefferson, *Notes on the State of Virginia,* in *Portable Jefferson,* ed. Peterson, 186; Miller, *The Wolf by the Ears,* 278, 218.

the spectre of such genocidal convulsions because he never doubted the drive of the bondsmen to be free. Their "moral sense" was the one consequential element of humanity he allowed them equally with whites, the one point of parity he conceded them amid their multitudinous inferiorities. He did not believe them capable of delicacy in love or depth in grief—he doubted their capacity for poetry, for mathematics, and indeed for reason itself at any pitch comparable to whites—but he did not deceive himself as his Southern successors would that blacks were docile or contented with their lot.[64]

St. Domingue's insurrection did not, therefore, surprise him. It simply gave vivid reality to visions of bloody racial vengeance that had long occupied his mind. The apocalypse of color that seemed to him to have overrun the island was the divine rebuke he had long dreaded. As he once confessed, he could only "tremble" when he reflected "that God is just: that his justice cannot sleep forever: that . . . a revolution of the wheel of fortune, an exchange of situation, is among possible events: that it may become probable by supernatural interference! The Almighty has no attribute which can take side with us in such a contest."[65]

Even while the French commissioners still commanded the colony, even before Toussaint had seized its scepter, Jefferson declared himself "daily more and more convinced" of the conquest of St. Domingue and of "all the West India islands" by "people of color." In 1797 he predicted that "the revolutionary storm, now sweeping the globe, will be upon us" in orgies of racial massacre. It was therefore "high time" to "foresee the bloody scenes which our children, certainly, and possibly ourselves," would "have to wade through," and to "try to avert" such scenes.[66]

64. Jefferson, *Notes,* 186; Jordan, *White over Black,* 439–40. For Jefferson's notorious comparison of blacks and whites, see Jefferson, *Notes,* 186–93. For a brilliant delineation of Jefferson's incorrigible racism in another aspect, see David Grimsted, "Anglo-American Racism and Phillis Wheatley's 'Sable Veil,' 'Length'ned Chain,' and 'Knitted Heart,'" in *Women in the Age of the American Revolution,* ed. Ronald Hoffman and Peter Albert (Charlottesville, Va., 1989), 338–444.

65. Jefferson, *Notes,* 215. Jordan observes of this passage that it exhibits a rare depth of feeling, since Jefferson so infrequently used exclamation points or resorted to miracles without skepticism (see Jordan, *White over Black,* 433–34).

66. Tansill, *United States and Santo Domingo,* 10; Miller, *The Wolf by the Ears,* 133; Tansill, *United States and Santo Domingo,* 10. Not even Jefferson's closest political ally, James Madison, shared his obsessive anxiety. Again and again, Madison showed himself far less phobic than Jefferson about the prospect of slave rebellion; sometimes, indeed, he seemed quite coolly unperturbed, and on at least one occasion he said explicitly that Southern whites had more to fear from the enmity of the ex-slaves of St. Domingue than from the insurrectionary example of their independence among the bondspeople of the South (see Irving Brant, *James Madison: Secretary of State 1800–1809* [Indianapolis, 1953],

Yet he had no notion how to achieve such an end that was not predicated on policies of racial purification and that did not premise itself on polarization and purge. He could not conceive of any scheme of emancipation that did not then mandate the deportation of the freed people. The only remotely "practicable plan" he ever projected entailed the exile of an entire generation of black children from their parents. Such separation did not particularly perturb the great *philosophe* in his piedmont fastness. He simply pronounced his satisfaction that the plan would reduce the public charge of abolition and the compensation due to the erstwhile owners. His priority on purse over person was worthy of the iciest Federalist. It was also indicative of his readiness to subordinate every other principle by which he lived to his apprehensiveness about race.[67]

Even the colonization schemes of his contemporaries envisioned multiracial societies that he could not conjure without revulsion. The earliest plans for the removal of freed African-Americans to the West Indies presupposed sanguinity that St. Domingue "could become an exemplar for white-black relations in the New World." And to the time of Jefferson's complicity in the Napoleonic invasion of 1802, such hopes seemed plausible. Correspondents described "a scene of racial bliss as whites and blacks lived and worked in an integrated society run by a black general and white officials." Americans, Frenchmen, and San Domingans of that era all perceived possibilities and actualities on the island in terms other than those of isolation and exclusion.[68]

Nonetheless, Jefferson persisted in his passion for polarization and his adamant obsession with monoracial resolutions of his apocalyptic anxieties. He believed that the Antilles would belong to the blacks as their "permanent home" because he convinced himself that the region "was naturally suited to them." He even avowed optimism that these "purely negro states" in the tropics would allow blacks a stage for their own social development at the same time that their emigration would rid whites of a dangerous incubus.[69]

On just those lines of logic, Jefferson could have assisted St. Domingue to provide emancipated slaves the sanctuary that both his best

---

65, 74, 75, 77, 93, 275). For the one vagrant moment when Jefferson recognized that, rationally, there was nothing to be feared from events in St. Domingue, see Dumas Malone, *Jefferson the President: First Term, 1801–1805* (Boston, 1970), 252.

67. Davis, *Problem of Slavery*, 183.

68. Hunt, *Haiti's Influence*, 164–65.

69. Ibid., 6, 122; Montague, *Haiti and the United States*, 66–67.

beliefs and his worst fears required. He could, indeed, have endorsed its republican revolution as a heaven-sent solution to his ideological dilemma, at once an empirical testing ground of black capacities and a practical arrangement for the separation of the races. But he did not seize, or even see, his opportunity. Over the entire period of his presidency, he pressed instead for the devastation and destruction of the black Jacobins. Even as he maintained his unyielding "aversion . . . to the mixture of color" on the continent, he set himself intransigently against a separate black state in the islands. Even as he "grew increasingly silent and depressed about the future of Africans in America," he moved malevolently against them in the Caribbean. Even as he yearned to be rid of them, he refused to let go of them.[70]

Jefferson simply lost his philosophical bearings when he confronted the question of color, or at any rate when he addressed its African aspect. And his contemporaries understood as much. Friends and foes alike complained of his inactivity in the cause of emancipation in which he purported to believe. Confronted with their complaints, he routinely retreated into a mystical miasma. He counseled his critics to "await with patience the workings of an overruling providence." From a man who had never followed a course of quietude or fatality in public affairs, such counsel was extraordinary. Jefferson had dared the Declaration against his king, organized the opposition against his president, and hardly hesitated to challenge every other entrenched power he deemed inimical to liberty. Only against slavery did he appear paralyzed in policy and immobilized even in imagination.[71]

His recurrent excuse for his refusal ever to speak out against slavery was that such speech would cost him "the confidence and good will of . . . friends" and consequently "lessen [his] powers of doing . . . good." His concomitant assurance to those who reproached him—at least to those friends who reproached him—was that he was always ready to act "should an occasion ever occur in which I can interpose with decisive

70. Jordan, *White over Black,* 470, 467; see also Miller, *The Wolf by the Ears,* 133.
71. Jordan, *White over Black,* 176. In the waning years of his life, in the Missouri crisis of 1820, Jefferson warned that the "anti-slavery conspiracy" might "force the South to secede." It was a way of saying that the maintenance of black bondage was sufficiently urgent—not to say sacred—to justify the dissolution of the national union. Such bald insistence on the sanctity of slavery seems at first a far cry from Jefferson's separatism in the Kentucky Resolutions of 1798; there the affirmation of state rights was inseparable from the affirmation of civil liberties. But in the perspective of 1820, the possibility presents itself that civil liberties and slavery were indissolubly joined in Jefferson's mind (see Jordan, *White over Black,* 174–75).

effect." Then, he promised, he would "certainly . . . do [his] duty with promptitude and zeal."[72]

The rising of the slaves in St. Domingue was just such an occasion. It might have been for Jefferson what it was for a host of Haitian intellectuals from that infant republic's first moments of freedom: a demonstration of black dignity and competence, a refutation of racist theories of African inferiority, and an affirmation of the unity of the divine creation. If Jefferson was as agonized by the discrepancy between Enlightenment ethics and his own quotidian experience as Jordan and others have alleged, the climactic confrontations in Hispaniola in the first years of his presidency offered him an unmatched opportunity to vindicate his abstract ideals. He could have hailed the black republicans, fostered their freedom from colonial tyranny, extolled Toussaint, and treated the improbable achievements of the ex-slaves as indisputable proof of a black genius that had been stifled before by the brutal constraints of their situation.[73]

Yet he did nothing of the sort. So far from celebrating black accomplishments in that more propitious milieu he had always admitted would be essential to a true test of African capacities, he disdained them. So far from cherishing the black republic as a providential incarnation of the very refuge his environmental agnosticism necessitated, he bent his efforts to its enfeeblement. His real revulsion from blacks eclipsed his commitment to equality whenever he descended from pontification to praxis.

He was torn between hatred of slavery and conviction of the incapacity of blacks only to the extent that the theory which animated his philosophy "formed a part of his being." Beyond his "mental enmeshment" in natural rights rhetoric, beyond his infatuation with his own language, his hatred of slavery was always "more abstract than immediate and personal." It was always attenuated enough that he could let it all go, as he did in St. Domingue. If he hated slavery as an actual condition of real men, women, and children, he certainly never so much as said so when the slaves were struggling for liberation. Indeed, he never even hated it enough to withhold his complicity from Napoleon's barbaric effort to reinstate it after those slaves had achieved that liberation. From his early works to his late, over almost half a century, he did not deviate from his racial repugnance. He could not countenance black emancipa-

72. Miller, *The Wolf by the Ears*, 131.
73. Ibid., 429; Nicholls, *Dessalines to Duvalier*, 41–43.

tion in America, and he would not recognize the reality of a multiracial society or a black state in the West Indies. He operated in a cul-de-sac of his own creation, and he was resolute in his refusal of any outlet.[74]

Almost from the moment he assumed the presidency, Jefferson made unmistakable his antipathy to the black Jacobins and his preference for the French. In his first days in office, he announced his intention to recall Edward Stevens from Le Cap in favor of an agent less partial to the San Domingans and more sympathetic to their nominal metropolitan masters. Soon enough, he did in fact depose Stevens. In place of this "brilliant man" to whom Toussaint "often looked for sage counsel," he put Tobias Lear, "a pedestrian person of modest pretensions" who would do as he was told. Lear's previous public service had been performed for George Washington, and it had involved transporting slaves from Philadelphia back to Virginia before they availed themselves of the freedom to which they were entitled by Pennsylvania law after six months' residence in the Quaker state. Lear had done his tawdry task faithfully for the nation's first president, and his experience as a petty fixer in a racist ruse prepared him appropriately to serve another president in another pretense.[75]

Stevens had been consul-general. Lear could claim no comparable commission. He was merely made America's general commercial agent and he accepted uncomplainingly the demotion that attended Jefferson's transformation of substantive San Domingan policy. Jefferson was keen to accommodate France. When the French minister Pichon protested the designation of the American emissary to Toussaint as a consul-general, as if St. Domingue were a sovereign society, Jefferson withdrew at once the courtesy that his Federalist predecessor had always accorded the rebels. His abject concession was only the first of a succession of servile subordinations of his country's immediate interests to his own design of ingratiating America with the French.[76]

74. Jordan, *White over Black*, 431.

75. Tansill, *United States and Santo Domingo*, 78; Logan, *Diplomatic Relations*, 113; Tansill, *United States and Santo Domingo*, 81; Davis, *Problem of Slavery*, 170–71. Washington himself conceded that the work on which he set Lear was but a "pretext" to "deceive both [the slaves] and the public."

76. Tansill, *United States and Santo Domingo*, 81; Logan, *Diplomatic Relations*, 113. Irving Brant claimed that there was "no hint of a change" from Federalist policies when Stevens was succeeded by Lear (*James Madison*, 63). The claim is untenable, even absurd, on Brant's evidence alone: that Lear was a commercial agent, not a consul; that he presented his credentials to a locality, Cap Français, not to Toussaint; that his instructions enjoined him to neutrality, not open partisanship; that his instructors, Madison and Jeffer-

But Jefferson's Francophilia was never so overweening that it impelled his policy. As much as he meant to placate Pichon, and Talleyrand and Napoleon, he meant much more to distance himself from the black republicans of St. Domingue. As Pichon reported to Paris in his very first filing, Jefferson and his secretary of state, James Madison, did not want an independent black government on the island and would not support Toussaint's ambitions of autonomy. As was evident to all by the end of 1801, antipathy ruled American relations with the insurgents. The Department of State permitted "official relations with Santo Domingo to decline to a vanishing point." In November, Lear himself complained to Madison that there had not been "a single line of intercourse" between Washington and his West Indian post in months; and when Lear did finally hear from his superiors, he received only their disapproval of his ceremonial "address of felicitation" to Toussaint. Jefferson and his administration would not exert themselves even to maintain the most trifling cordiality with the rebel government.[77]

Toussaint, with his perennial penetration, divined Jefferson's disdain from the first and divined its deepest springs as well. When Lear was initially presented to him, the general "complained bitterly" that the new American agent carried no personal letter from the president such as he had been accustomed to receive from John Adams. Lear attempted to excuse the slight, explaining that, by the "custom of the Government," his inconsequential consulship did not warrant such notice. But his explanation was "in vain." Toussaint caught the insult and its ultimate origin as well, "saying his color was the cause of his being neglected."[78]

Color countermanded everything for Jefferson. All the fine philosophy, all the generous sentiment, all the brave enlightenment paled before its power. As he told Pichon in the summer of 1801, he "had no reason to be favorable to Toussaint." The fact that the black Jacobin leader fought for freedom, self-determination, and a rather more radical version of the Revolutionary republican virtues Jefferson himself had proclaimed in the Declaration counted for nothing—"no reason"—against the blackness that made the man "a menace to two-thirds of the

---

son, openly preferred French recovery of the colony, opposed a San Domingan declaration of independence, and provided French representatives in Washington $150,000 for use in St. Domingue to promote their preferences (63, 64, 76, 77).

77. Tansill, *United States and Santo Domingo*, 80–81, 76, 85, 88, 77.

78. Adams, *History*, 1:388–90; Tansill, *United States and Santo Domingo*, 82–83.

states." Ideological affinity availed nothing against disparity in skin pigmentation. The similarities in the struggles of the American and San Domingan rebels caused Jefferson not a moment's pause, let alone the deep ambivalence and anguish so often attributed to him by historians. The natural rights philosophy may have constituted "the governing aspect of his theology and his science," but he relinquished its ethical injunctions without an apparant pang of conscience so far as they bore on the blacks of Hispaniola.[79]

Jefferson was not just bent on "reversing the policy" of the Federalists who preceded him. He was actually "entirely willing for France to regain her lost colony" in the Caribbean. The rhetorician who once wanted the tree of liberty refreshed regularly with the blood of tyrants now made common cause with the oppressors themselves. The radical who once swore eternal hostility against every form of tyranny now participated in an impenitent effort to restore slavery itself. The revolutionary who once fought a dire war against imperial exploitation now leagued with Europeans seeking to resurrect a far crueler colonialism. The republican who once resented with unsurpassed eloquence the exactions of executive power now allied himself with a leader of executive energy unparalleled in the history of the modern West. Napoleon was the embodiment of every outlandish Old Whig nightmare about George III. Jefferson had devoted some of the most stirring moments of his public career to denunciations of the dangers of executive aggrandizement. Yet between the Corsican consul and black Toussaint, Jefferson never hesitated.[80]

In an early conference with Pichon, Jefferson promised the French minister that the United States government would act in concert with France to restore her supremacy over St. Domingue. The Virginian acknowledged that such action would undermine the "extremely important" West Indian trade and "seriously compromise" his administration in public opinion. But such dangers did not deter him. His animus against Toussaint overrode all his "scruples about laying plans for his [enemy's] destruction." As Jefferson assured Pichon, "nothing will be easier than to furnish your army and fleet with everything and to reduce Toussaint to starvation."[81]

79. Logan, *Diplomatic Relations*, 120, 80; Jordan, *White over Black*, 431.
80. Tansill, *United States and Santo Domingo*, 79.
81. Carl Lokke, "Jefferson and the Leclerc Expedition," *American Historical Review* 33 (1928): 324; Tansill, *United States and Santo Domingo*, 85, 80–81, 87; Logan, *Diplomatic Relations*, 120. Even Jefferson's most ardent admirer, Dumas Malone, admitted that the

On the president's promise of assistance, Napoleon concluded an uneasy peace with England and hastened to prepare a West Indian invasion of unprecedented scale, savagery, and duplicity. He gathered twenty thousand veteran troops under some of his ablest officers and put the entire campaign under the command of his own brother-in-law, General Charles Victor Emmanuel Leclerc.

"It was the largest expedition that had ever sailed from France," and perhaps the most ill-fated. Within eight weeks, five thousand French soldiers were dead and five thousand more in hospitals, and that was before the yellow fever even began its work. Leclerc wrote desperately for reinforcements, pleading the "mortality of four-fifths of his army and the uselessness of the remainder." In a year, Leclerc was dead and his offensive a failure: Of thirty-four thousand troops who had landed on St. Domingue by that time, twenty-four thousand were already dead, eight thousand were hospitalized, and barely two thousand exhausted men were still in arms. By the time France finally conceded its defeat, a year of unconscionable carnage after Leclerc's death, Napoleon had lost almost all of the sixty thousand soldiers he had shipped from home. The few who remained, at the end of 1803, surrendered to the British sooner than struggle on against the San Domingans and the tropical diseases that decimated them. They would "rot and waste for years in English prisons."[82]

Napoleon had never dreamed it would end that way. He had always intended a "war to the death," but he had plotted a merciless extermination of the blacks. Depending on deception at the outset, he had instructed Leclerc to promise the San Domingans anything until his troops occupied the strategic sites in the colony. Then, when French forces were impregnably fortified, Leclerc was to seek the surrender of all rebels he considered dangerous and to deport or outlaw them if they did not surrender. Finally, when the local leaders had been removed, Leclerc was to dispense with deviousness and proceed to disarm the population, restore French colonial control, and reinstitute slavery it-

---

promise to Pichon went "further than was wise or necessary" (*Jefferson*, 252). Madison intimated no such assistance when Pichon conferred with him prior to his audience with the president, and the British actually refused Napoleon's contemporaneous request for their aid in the campaign, though their own invaluable colony of Jamaica was far more directly imperiled by San Domingan independence than the American South was (Miller, *The Wolf by the Ears*, 136).

82. James, *Black Jacobins*, 274–75, 323, 343, 355, 369. See also Buckley, ed., *Haitian Journal*, xxvii, and Montague, *Haiti and the United States*, 9, for slightly different numbers.

self, by means of mass arrests, banishment of blacks and even of white women who had "prostituted themselves" to blacks, and mass murder if necessary.[83]

Neither Napoleon nor Leclerc had ever had any illusions about what they were doing. They had only attempted to plant illusions among their antagonists and allies. Leclerc wanted to win the blacks over with proclamations that protected their freedom, but he was willing to destroy them if they were not to be won over. Napoleon personally guaranteed "the freedom of the blacks" in a letter delivered directly to Toussaint by the San Domingan's own sons, but even as Napoleon wrote he was plotting the perpetual bondage of the blacks and the execution of Toussaint. Even as the black general read the first consul's unqualified promises, French colonial administrators were giving them the lie by restoring the color line, reopening the slave trade, and reenslaving the black masses in Martinique and Guadeloupe.[84]

Toussaint was not deceived for long, if indeed he was ever deceived at all. Once it was clear that the conflict could not be averted, he minced no words in his orders to his officers: "Leave nothing white behind you." Once his dream of a multiracial society was irrevocably aborted by Napoleon's gratuitous promulgation of race war, Toussaint prepared his people to return racist brutality for racist brutality. He betrayed his humanity only by arranging for his own abduction by the French before the full depth of ferocity had been sounded, as if not to have to witness with his own eyes the destruction of the kingdom in the sun he had come so close to creating.[85]

But Jefferson was deceived—or allowed himself to be deceived—to the bitter end and beyond. He was reluctant to reckon with the implications of the intelligence he received from Robert Livingston, his own minister in Paris, and he was disinclined to seek any other reports on

83. James, *Black Jacobins*, 292–94; Ott, *The Haitian Revolution*, 147. For the full text of Napoleon's directives to Leclerc, see Carl Lokke, "The Leclerc Instructions," *Journal of Negro History* 10 (1925): 88–98.

84. Ott, *The Haitian Revolution*, 151, 147; Davis, *Problem of Slavery*, 150–51; James, *Black Jacobins*, 340–41.

85. James, *Black Jacobins*, 287–88. The analogy of St. Domingue to the multicultural kingdom in the sun of Roger II in Sicily in the twelfth century is from Kennedy, *Orders from France*, 162–63. The interpretation of Toussaint's submission to the transparent ruse by which he was captured and exiled to France to die is my own wistful one, necessitated by the absence of a plausible alternative. Not even C. L. R. James, whose wisdom is wondrous in all else, explains in any convincing way why the brilliant black general fell into French hands on such a simple ploy when he had slipped or foiled so many sophisticated ones.

Napoleon's plans. "At the moment when national interest depended on prompt and exact information," he "withdrew half his ministers from Europe, and paid little attention to the agents he retained." As a result, he "knew almost nothing" of the Corsican's "character and schemes." With an ignorance that was as willful as it was profound, Jefferson simply trusted to his own openness and good feeling to overcome animosities that he attributed to Federalist Francophobia.[86]

When the rumors of the retrocession of Louisiana to France turned to confirmed fact, Jefferson persisted in his cordiality to Napoleon and his minions. When Livingston wrote from Paris that the French expeditionary force was to proceed to Louisiana once it successfully secured St. Domingue, Jefferson renewed his instruction to Lear in Cap Français "to do nothing that might offend the French." When Leclerc expelled Lear from the island for insufficient inoffensiveness, Jefferson accommodated the affront by naming no new agent at all to the post. Even when Leclerc confiscated American cargoes at Le Cap and clapped any American who protested into prison, Jefferson turned a deaf ear to the "widespread indignation" at the general's "high-handed actions." Though Pichon himself rebuked Leclerc for his insolent exercise of authority, the president assured Pichon that the United States government would recognize Leclerc's regulations "in their full vigor." The *philosophe* was prepared to acquiesce in any French outrage rather than impede the effort against Toussaint.[87]

In the heat of the recolonizing campaign, Jefferson lost his purchase on lofty ideals and immediate practicalities alike. Awash in his abhorrence of slaves who had slain their masters, he pursued policies at odds with everything he meant America to mean to the world. The president who had promised "peace, commerce, and honest friendship with all nations, entangling alliances with none," was immoderately eager to forge a triple concert with France and England to forestall the emergence of a black nationalism. The president who had promulgated the

---

86. Adams, *History,* 1:404.
87. Ibid., 1:404, 405–6; Montague, *Haiti and the United States,* 42–43; Logan, *Diplomatic Relations,* 130; Montague, *Haiti and the United States,* 48; Tansill, *United States and Santo Domingo,* 90. Jefferson's apologists insist that he saw at once the significance of the retrocession and reversed at once his St. Domingue policy. See, e.g., Malone, *Jefferson,* 253–60; Miller, *The Wolf by the Ears,* 132–41; Merrill Peterson, *Thomas Jefferson and the New Nation: A Biography* (New York, 1970), 745–50. Their apologies are all alike and alike unconvincing: one part Jefferson's refusal to provide the support he promised Pichon, one part his famous letter to Livingston and its plight of marriage to the British fleet and nation the moment France took possession of New Orleans, and five parts wishful thinking.

rule of recognition of *de facto* governments was adamantly opposed to any such acknowledgment of the Antillean republic.[88]

Jefferson saw the significance of recognition clearly enough. He had articulated it himself, as the nation's first secretary of state, in 1792: "We certainly cannot deny to other nations that principle whereon our own government is founded, that every nation has a right to govern itself internally under what forms it pleases, and to change those forms at its own will." He had enunciated the connection of that precept to his own dearest democratic values: "The only essential thing is, the will of the people." But he did disregard those "principles," "rights," and "essential things" when they collided with his conceptions of racial relations. As Pichon saw plainly, "the fear which a black government inspires" dictated the president's departure from all other norms he prized.[89]

The same fear that debilitated Jefferson's devotion to his own Enlightened ideals also clouded his assessment of affairs. In the interview in which he promised Pichon American assistance in reducing Toussaint to starvation, he also assured the French minister that England "would doubtless participate" in their "concert to suppress this rebellion." Ensnared in his own negrophobia, Jefferson simply assumed that others shared it, a grievously mistaken assumption, as events unfolded. England not only declined to cooperate in the expedition but also ended by fighting with the San Domingans against the French. Less than two years after Jefferson's blithe prognostication to Pichon, the British were supplying Dessalines arms and ammunition; by September 1803 the British fleet was helping to force Rochambeau's retreat from the interior and playing an important part in the capture of several key ports; by November a British blockading squadron was receiving Rochambeau's surrender.[90]

Nothing but color can account for Jefferson's unbudging attachment to a counterrevolutionary enterprise that even the counterrevolutionary British disdained and defeated. Nothing but his own racial revulsion can explain Jefferson's deliberate blindness to the barbarity that the French brought to the Antilles.

Jefferson never did demur at the senseless slaughter, so long as it was

---

88. Logan, *Diplomatic Relations,* 121, 76–77.

89. Ibid., 76–77, 126. Jefferson did admit, in 1801, that the blacks in St. Domingue were "established into a sovereignty *de facto*" and had "organized themselves under regular laws and government" (127).

90. Lokke, "Jefferson," 325; James, *Black Jacobins,* 366; Ott, *The Haitian Revolution,* 180.

directed against the blacks. He never did desist from his endorsement of the endeavor, even as it became a lost cause of mindless savagery.

The president was unperturbed as the war wore on, and Leclerc's men died in droves under the tropic sun, and appeals for supplies from the metropolis went unheeded, and Leclerc resorted to tactics of unblushing terrorism: "Since terror is the sole resource left me, I employ it." The president was unmoved as Leclerc's "war of extermination" worsened, and so many blacks were drowned in the bay of Cap Français that "for many a long day the people of the district would not eat fish." The president was unaffected as 1500 bloodhounds trained to terrorize blacks and tear them apart were imported from Cuba and set loose in an amphitheatre where rich white women in finery watched the dogs disembowel blacks lashed to posts, and the truth became inescapable: the furious killing reflected "not only hatred and fear, but policy."[91]

Indeed, the president persisted in his punitive onslaught past the period when it was doomed to a phase when it was actually pointless. At the end of 1804, a year after the first consul had abandoned his expedition in the Indies, a year after the new nation of Haiti had proclaimed its independence, Jefferson and his party commenced a campaign to cut off all American trade with "the usurped government of that unfortunate island." One after another, Republican representatives in Congress rose to vent their murderous rage. Long after Francophilia or plausible policy could rationalize such rhetoric, they thundered that the only other republic in the hemisphere had to be "destroyed." As one of them put it, he "would venture to pledge the treasury of the United States that the negro government should be destroyed."[92]

Jefferson himself orchestrated the entire endeavor. He professed to do it in order to placate France, and his partisans attempted to follow his lead.[93] But the fact was that France scarcely cared by the time the embargo was instituted in 1806, and neither did the Republicans themselves. Even as Jefferson pushed his party to curtail trade ties with the West Indian rebels, Talleyrand was recommending concessions to entice

91. James, *Black Jacobins*, 344, 349; Ott, *The Haitian Revolution*, 179; Rodman, *Haiti*, 14.

92. Tansill, *United States and Santo Domingo*, 104–5; see also, e.g., Miller, *The Wolf by the Ears*, 133–34.

93. Modern historians have followed his lead too. See, e.g., Hunt, *Haiti's Influence*, 85; Logan, *Diplomatic Relations*, 176–77; Brant, *James Madison*, 270–75; Nicholls, *Dessalines to Duvalier*, 37. Logan does deplore the "unseemly haste" with which the administration acted, and he does report Madison's admission that the measure went "beyond the obligations of the United States under the law of nations" and proceeded not "from any rightful requisition on the part of France" but only from the free concession of America.

Americans into the trade again. Even as Jefferson lobbied, his adherents were thinking other thoughts. As Linda Kerber observed of the debate on the embargo, the Jeffersonian defense of the measure was only ostensibly about trade, profits, and neutral rights; "it kept sliding into the subject of slavery and of whether free Negroes could behave responsibly." Few doubted that the embargo would damage American commerce, perhaps lastingly. But Southern Republicans "seemed unable to stay on the obvious subject." The only issues that authentically engaged them were the "question of American support for a Negro republic" and the possibility of "helping to suffocate Haiti."[94]

Needless to say, it was not in the national interest to let the lucrative trade of the Indies atrophy. As a result of Jefferson's intransigent antagonism, Toussaint and Dessalines turned to the British, whose merchants came to control the commerce of the Caribbean. Jefferson had once been willing to go to war to keep Great Britain from the very power in the French islands that his own policy now delivered to her by default. But that had been when he was secretary of state, before his rage to rebuke the black Jacobins overwhelmed his judgment.[95]

By the time he became president, Jefferson had no purchase on any larger notion of the national interest when the provocation of St. Domingue intruded. He prostrated American policy before Napoleon's will and Pichon's every wish and whimsy. He confided indiscreetly in the French minister, countermanding his own secretary of state as he did. He even made the minister—and his masters in Paris—privy to American diplomatic secrets that should have remained strictly confidential. When Pichon asked to see the Pickering instructions to Stevens and the "Propositions" discussed in Philadelphia between Pickering and Maitland, Jefferson acceded to the Frenchman's extraordinary application and indeed exceeded it. He allowed Pichon to see those "important documents," and he also, "without any hesitation," had the State Department give the papers to Pichon, "who promptly forwarded them to Talleyrand."[96]

94. Tansill, *United States and Santo Domingo*, 103; Kerber, *Federalists in Dissent*, 47–48. The vendetta continued with the extension of the embargo in 1807 and again in 1808. When the ban was finally lifted—upon Madison's ascension to the presidency—American trade did not return. By 1810, United States exports to all the French West Indies amounted to a paltry two percent of the value of goods sold to Toussaint alone, under Federalist auspices, in 1800. By 1822, Haiti ranked twenty-ninth among nations in trade with the United States. See Montague, *Haiti and the United States*, 47; James Padgett, "Diplomats to Haiti and Their Diplomacy," *Journal of Negro History* 25 (1940): 267.
95. Tansill, *United States and Santo Domingo*, 10.
96. Adams, *History*, 1:388–90; Lokke, "Jefferson," 323–24; Tansill, *United States and Santo Domingo*, 88.

It was obtuse to American economic interests to take the side of France in the first place. But even within that willed obtuseness, Jefferson showed startling indifference to his opportunities to advance American interests. The Federalists had collaborated with the British in the quasi-war, but the Federalists had neither disdained to drive hard bargains with their allies nor ignored their own needs for the sake of amiable relations with their putative partners. Over the course of the Adams administration, indeed, the United States had actually moved closer to St. Domingue than it was to England.[97]

Jefferson was so blinded by the racial aspect of the conflict in the Caribbean that he seems never to have asked his allies any compensation for his unflagging friendship and never to have doubted their own equivalent good will toward him. In fact, Bonaparte bore Jefferson no gratitude and contemplated toward him no reciprocity. His secret instructions to Leclerc commanded his brother-in-law to admit American commerce with St. Domingue only during the course of the war with Toussaint. Once the colony was firmly under French control, the Americans were to be excluded as they had been before 1791.[98]

Jefferson could not have known the first consul's mind, of course, but a president less absorbed in his own affections might at least have protected against the possibility that Napoleon was not as ardent for America as Jefferson was for France. A president less blinded by his bigotry might have guessed at Napoleon's malice—as Toussaint and the British did—and taken precautions to safeguard his country's concerns.

Even after the French gave up their grand design of American empire in 1803, Jefferson disdained to make the minimal demands on them that Talleyrand took for granted he would. The Frenchman finally tired, indeed, of waiting for American initiatives and himself prodded Livingston to press for limited trading concessions in Hispaniola. As he reminded the American representative, the French minister of marine and colonies was bound to be receptive to such a request, since the United States could simply recognize the Dessalines regime and claim unlimited legal commerce with it. But Livingston did not dare to pursue the matter. While Talleyrand was offering him better arguments to advance American interests than his own president was, his president

97. Tansill, *United States and Santo Domingo*, 44–45, 55, 58, 64, 73; Logan, *Diplomatic Relations*, 110–11.

98. Tansill, *United States and Santo Domingo*, 87.

was pushing for the prohibition of all American trade with Haiti and thereby conceding the island's commerce wholly to the British.[99]

The truth was that Jefferson did not want to deal with the black republicans and did not want to define American interests in terms of such dealings. When Dessalines wrote directly to him, declaring a desire to renew trade relations with the United States, describing an abundant crop just harvested, and promising protection to American merchants, Jefferson did not even deign to reply. Not even the notorious Dessalines was as antagonistic to whites as Jefferson was to the blacks of Haiti whose overtures he spurned so uncivilly. Months after Rochambeau's men quit their campaign, Madison was still assuring Pichon that Jefferson would "do nothing that might injure the rights and dignity of France." Months after Dessalines had made himself the only effective authority among the Haitians, Madison was still fatuously affirming that France was "the sole sovereign of Saint Domingue."[100]

Inimical as all this studied indifference and animosity was to the national economic interest, though, it was at least explicable. Trade was never at the core of Jefferson's conception of his country, and merchants were never the mainstay of his Republican party. His vision was always westward, away from the Atlantic. His notion of the national interest centered on the creation of a vast yeoman empire, beyond the temptations of Old World commerce and corruption for a thousand generations.

Jefferson's profoundest commitment was to the western country. His preponderant constituency was on the farming frontiers. That commit-

99. Ibid., 101–2. The British did not leap to acknowledge Haitian nationhood any more than the Americans did. But the British were more than willing to accept Dessalines's offer of commercial privileges and protection. Their alacrity in resuming and indeed in monopolizing the business of the island only made the Haitians more eager for an American "counterpoise" to the British, and American merchants also "begged Jefferson to give Dessalines some sign of friendship in order that the British might be forestalled." Jefferson ignored all these invitations and importunities (see Logan, *Diplomatic Relations*, 148; Montague, *Haiti and United States*, 44). John Miller tries to excuse Jefferson, averring that the president's policy "was not actuated by aversion to blacks," only by a fear "that an independent Haiti would fall under the sway of Great Britain" and end in "a British monopoly of the island's commerce." But Miller's attempted exculpation is incoherent. On his own account, British merchants did monopolize the St. Domingue trade, and precisely as "the chief beneficiaries" of the American embargo. If Jefferson had truly put any priority on the prevention of a British monopoly, he could have served such an end best by promoting American participation in the trade, as Haiti implored him to do. But then he would have had to overcome his "aversion to blacks" (see Miller, *The Wolf by the Ears*, 139–41).

100. Logan, *Diplomatic Relations*, 148–49; Brant, *James Madison*, 177.

ment and that constituency alike required control of the navigation of the Mississippi. Without it, there would be no way to avert the inroads of urbanization and industrialization, no way to consolidate a continental union, and quite possibly no way to preserve even the present union that was steadily spreading across the Appalachians.

Jefferson knew more than enough about Napoleon's expedition against St. Domingue to appreciate the ways in which it imperiled his intended empire for agrarian liberty. He had rumors of the retrocession of Louisiana to France as early as his inauguration.[101] He had definite intelligence of Napoleon's plan to invade St. Domingue and reduce Toussaint by July 1801. He could have drawn his own conclusions long before Livingston drew them for him at the end of 1801: Leclerc's forces were "destined in the first instance for Hispaniola," but that was only the commencement of the first consul's colossal design. Leclerc was then "to proceed to Louisiana provided Toussaint makes no opposition."[102]

It was impossible for Jefferson to be "indifferent to the establishment of Napoleonic power at New Orleans." Such puissance would endanger the development of the territories beyond the Appalachians and tempt them to forsake their already shaky American allegiance for a French one. It would make Napoleon master of North America, for he would have in the West Indies the most prolific source of colonial staples in the New World and in Louisiana a limitless granary to supply those tropical plantations. It would therefore preempt American expansion and confine the United States forever within its current boundaries. And in so doing it would fulfill French strategic ideas older than the Consulate itself. In 1795 Fauchet had held that if France controlled Louisiana, she would secure sovereignty over all the Mississippi basin. In 1797 Talleyrand had argued that if France occupied Louisiana and Florida, she would have a "wall of brass forever impenetrable to the combined efforts of England and America." Yet Jefferson ignored all that. He "valued the *rapprochement* with France above any American [strategic] interest in" the one place that stood between Napoleon and his North American ambitions, St. Domingue.[103]

101. Montague, *Haiti and the United States,* 41–42. In fact the retrocession had already been accomplished, in the secret treaty of San Ildefonso of October 1, 1800. See Buckley, ed., *Haitian Journal,* xviii.

102. Montague, *Haiti and the United States,* 41–42; Miller, *The Wolf by the Ears,* 136; Adams, *History,* 1:392. The crucial point about the chronology is, as Miller concedes, that Jefferson "knew of the secret treaty . . . when he offered American cooperation in 'starving' Toussaint" (Miller, *The Wolf by the Ears,* 136).

103. Brant, *James Madison,* 69; Montague, *Haiti and the United States,* 41–42.

By the summer of 1801, rumors of the retrocession were so strong that Jefferson and his secretary of state had to acknowledge them. Nonetheless, their acknowledgment was innocuous to the point of inanition. Madison's instructions to his ministers in Europe were "remarkable for their mildness." The administration offered "no protest" at all "against a scheme so hostile to the interests of the Union." If Toussaint and his successors had not detained, defeated, and finally destroyed Leclerc's legions, "ten thousand French soldiers, trained in the school of Hoche and Moreau, and commanded by a future marshal of France, might have occupied New Orleans and St. Louis before Jefferson could have collected a brigade of militia at Nashville."[104]

Jefferson's insensitivity to the precariousness of his position is simply unfathomable apart from his antipathy to black autonomy. America's most vital interests were under imminent siege, and the president did virtually nothing to defend them. If anything, he very nearly saved Napoleon the trouble of staging the assault. As early as September 1801, he had Madison instruct Livingston to concede the French occupation of New Orleans, if the cession of Louisiana was irrevocable, since prudence dictated doing nothing to irritate an imminent neighbor. Livingston was simply to see if the French might be willing to "make over to the United States" the Floridas, or at least West Florida with its port of Mobile, as a token of good will to "reconcile the United States to a disrelished arrangement." As late as March 1803, Jefferson dispatched James Monroe on a special mission with instructions to "admit the French to Louisiana without condition." Monroe was to seek the sale of New Orleans or the restoration of the American deposit there; but, failing that, he was merely to secure jurisdiction over some other place substantial enough for a trading town or, failing that, to assure Americans

---

104. Adams, *History*, 1:405–6. Even allowing for his highly charged prose, and even assuming his animus against the man who unseated his great-grandfather, Adams remains a more reliable analyst than the legions of Jeffersonian loyalists who have tried to refute him. Take but one example, among many. On John Miller's interpretation, once Jefferson realized that Napoleon was "deadly serious" about Louisiana, he "reversed himself in the matter of . . . the reconquest of St. Domingo." Once it "dawned on the president that St. Domingo and Louisiana were part of a master plan so inimical to the interests of the United States that it must be thwarted at all cost," he did a "singular *volte-face*" and made the prevention of the fulfillment of that plan "the cardinal objective of the United States" (*The Wolf by the Ears*, 136–37). But Miller never explains why it took Jefferson almost a year to see the significance of a plan that so blatantly imperiled the most vital part of his vision of American empire, and he never shows any reversal or "*volte-face*" either. Even on Miller's strainedly sympathetic account, Jefferson simply never moved beyond neutrality in the Indies, a 90- rather than a 180-degree turn. Neutrality is not normally the way presidents pursue "at all cost" their "cardinal objective."

the privilege of holding real estate for commercial purposes in the great port. In other. words, Monroe's orders promoted political capitulation for the sake of a mercantile mess of pottage. Bonaparte "could have satisfied [Jefferson's] every demand by giving the United States, in the terms of the Spanish treaty, a place of deposit anywhere on the banks of the Mississippi, or by merely allowing American vessels to pass up and down the river." [105]

The Spanish intendant closed New Orleans to American merchandise, in violation of the treaty of 1795, and restive American frontiersmen grew militant if not mutinous. Tennessee and Kentucky called for war itself, knowing that Morales's action was merely "a foretaste of what they were to expect from the French," and knowing too that a French army fortified on the lower Mississippi would never be dislodged. But Jefferson did nothing that might even have disconcerted Napoleon, let alone deterred him. [106]

Western legislatures adopted resolutions demanding that the president be more bold on their behalf. "Eighteen months had passed since the seriousness of Napoleon's schemes had become known to him, but as yet he had done nothing that could be construed as an attempt to represent the demands of the western country; all his ingenuity had, in fact, been exerted to evade these demands." As Jefferson told Livingston in October 1802, the French occupation of Louisiana was not, in his estimation, "important enough to risk a breach of peace" with the Bonapartists. [107]

105. Adams, *History,* 1:405–6, 442–43; Brant, *James Madison,* 71; Malone, *Jefferson,* 286.
106. Adams, *History,* 1:421–22.
107. Ibid., 1:431–32, 424–25. A week after Jefferson's confession to Livingston, New Orleans itself was closed to American commerce, and still Jefferson did "nothing to check Napoleon" (ibid., 1:424–25). Jefferson did claim, later, that from the spring of 1802 his administration had recognized the possibility of war and prepared for it. But even his most ardent apologist comes up lame in his qualified endorsement of Jefferson's ludicrous claim. Dumas Malone maintained that Secretary of War Dearborn did as much for the defense of the frontier "as could reasonably have been expected, considering the means at his disposal." But of course it was Jefferson who limited "the means at his disposal," choosing that very juncture to reduce expenditures on the military and naval establishment and leaving the British representative in the United States to marvel at the "perfect infatuation" of the administration in leaving the frontier "almost defenseless." Malone cites the report of the Mississippi territorial governor, William Claiborne, that he had two thousand militia and could conquer New Orleans, "provided there should be only Spanish troops to defend the place." But of course the issue was French troops, not Spanish, and ten thousand of them at that. When the *New York Evening Post* learned, mistakenly, of the departure of the French expedition for Louisiana in February 1803, it took for granted, ruefully, that Napoleon would be in peaceful possession of the province by the time Monroe made his first bow to him in Paris. See Malone, *Jefferson,* 248–49, 272–73, 278.

Since Jefferson declined to defend his own and his nation's deepest, dearest interests, Toussaint and the San Domingans were all that stood between Napoleon and the dismemberment of America. As Henry Adams wrote, a century ago, Toussaint's "fate placed him at a point where Bonaparte needed absolute control. . . . Before Bonaparte could reach Louisiana, he was obliged to crush the power of Toussaint."[108]

Jefferson and his partisans never "grasped the whole truth" of their dependence on the San Domingans; their pride and prejudice would not allow them to do so. They never saw beyond their scorn, nor ever appreciated that what befell the brave black republic would befall their own. They simply left Toussaint to his own devices, "without a friend or a hope except in himself." While "two continents looked on with folded arms," guerilla bands of daring, dauntless blacks fought the most formidable military force Europe had seen in more than a millennium.[109]

Few Americans "felt their own dependence on Toussaint's courage," but he held their future in his hands. "If he and his blacks should succumb easily to their fate, the wave of French empire would roll on to Louisiana and sweep far up the Mississippi; if St. Domingo should resist, and succeed in resistance, the recoil would spend its force on Europe, while America would be left to pursue its democratic destiny in peace."[110]

Toussaint did not live to see it, but the troops he had trained and inspired did resist Napoleon's juggernaut and did deny it the success on which the rest of the French colonial design rested. "The colonial system of France centered on St. Domingo. Without that island the system had hands, feet, and even a head, but no body. Of what use was Louisiana, when France had clearly lost the main colony which Louisiana was meant to feed and fortify?"[111]

Napoleon could read handwriting on the wall as well as any man. When Leclerc could not subjugate the blacks of St. Domingue, Napoleon began to recalculate the costs and benefits of a colony in Louisiana. Louisiana was inseparable from the West Indies in his design. He had

108. Adams, *History*, 1:378.
109. Ibid., 1:390–91.
110. Ibid.
111. Ibid., 2:25. In retrospect, even the racist Napoleon saw the centrality of St. Domingue, listing "among the most costly errors of his career—second only to the invasion of Spain in 1808 and of Russia in 1812—his failure to make Toussaint L'Ouverture an ally and rule St. Domingo through the 'black Bonaparte'" (Miller, *The Wolf by the Ears*, 139). Only the Jeffersonians were unable, ever, to concede the contribution of the blacks.

lost the lushest and most lucrative island in the West Indies, and within a matter of months he decided to dispose of Louisiana.

It was the richest irony of an episode redolent with rich ironies. Jefferson had, by his encouragement of the Caribbean campaign, inadvertently made New Orleans and the Louisiana country more attractive to France than they had ever been before. Driven by his detestation of blacks who sought the same freedoms he did, he had aroused the one man in Europe audacious enough to take over the one part of America that was absolutely indispensable to his own agrarian ambitions. Ruled by his racial antipathies, he had left the very blacks he loathed to do the work of defending the vital interests that he declined to defend himself. It was to those nameless, numberless blacks and their incalculable bravery and sacrifice that he owed his ability to hold his constituents and his country together. It was to Toussaint L'Ouverture—his literal *bête noire*—that he owed the crowning accomplishment of his presidency and the monumental legacy for freedom that he left America, the Louisiana Purchase.

# SEVEN

# The Nursery Tales
# of Horatio Alger

D. H. Lawrence taught us long ago how to approach American literature. "Never trust the artist," he warned. "Trust the tale."[1]

But Lawrence never extended his edict or his analysis to our popular culture, and subsequent students of the subject have often been at such pains to be condescending that they could not be bothered comprehending. Accordingly, we have hardly conceived that the very pressures of propriety that made our major writers such darlings of duplicity must have been even more intense for authors with still broader audiences. We have been inclined to discount all possibility of depth and disingenuousness in our hack writers, seeing them simply at their own stated estimation. And in the case of Horatio Alger, we thereby make a serious mistake.

We have imagined Alger our dreamer of success, our rhapsodist of rags to riches, our avatar of the self-made-man—and it is true that Alger knew that tune and announced it unfailingly. He just never played it. In his tales success was but a subterfuge, and self-made men were nowhere to be found. Yet Alger was profoundly, even prophetically, American, and the deflected drive of his stories is essential to an understanding of the emergence of American industrial society.

Alger wrote more than one hundred novels, but he remained so com-

From *American Quarterly* 24 (1972): 191–209.
1. D. H. Lawrence, *Studies in Classic American Literature* (Garden City, N.Y., 1951), 13.

pletely within the compass of a few recurrent themes that there is no need to engage his entire corpus. Almost any of his story cycles gives access to his sentiments and obsessions. The most interesting of them is perhaps his first and most famous, the Ragged Dick series, whose six novels established the Alger formula.[2]

The tales themselves may be speedily summarized. The first, *Ragged Dick,* is a story of the early adolescence of a New York City bootblack, Dick Hunter; it follows him in alternating episodes of fostering friendship and threatening enmity to a culmination in his dive from a ferry to rescue a drowning boy who proves to be the only child of the wealthy Mr. Rockwell. Its sequel, *Fame and Fortune,* finds the young bootblack ensconced in a privileged position in Rockwell's counting room and assured of the further favors of the rich man, who helps him survive an attempted frame-up by his disappointed rivals. In *Mark, the Match Boy* Dick himself becomes a patron, succoring and sheltering the ineffectual little matchboy when he runs away from his exploitive guardian, Mother Watson, until Mark is suddenly discovered to be the long-lost grandson of a prosperous Milwaukee businessman who is only too delighted to relieve Dick of the young boy's care. *Rough and Ready* introduces another hero, a New York newsboy named Rufus, and traces his flight with his sister Rose from their bibulous stepfather, James Martin; its action is dominated by Rufus's successful struggle with Martin for custody of the little girl and, more briefly, by the newsboy's prevention

2. The Ragged Dick Series, listed as such in the advertising pages of any number of Alger's subsequent stories, was published between 1867 and 1870. For ease of access and common reference, I have used the paperback reprint of the pair that are presently in print; for the other four I have used the editions in the Historical Children's Collection of the Free Library of Philadelphia. Two of these are original editions, the other two are nineteenth-century reprints, and all four are likely to differ somewhat in pagination from other editions other students may find available. The six, in order of initial publication, are: *Ragged Dick* (New York, 1962); *Fame and Fortune* (Boston, 1868); *Mark, the Match Boy* (New York, 1962); *Rough and Ready, or, Life among the New York Newsboys* (Philadelphia, n.d.); *Ben, the Luggage Boy, or, Among the Wharves* (Boston, 1870); *Rufus and Rose, or The Fortunes of Rough and Ready* (Philadelphia, 1898). They will be cited hereafter as *Dick, Fame, Mark, Rough, Ben,* and *Rufus,* respectively.

The representativeness of the Ragged Dick Series may be gauged most conveniently by consulting another modern collection, Horatio Alger, *Struggling Upward and Other Works,* intro. by Russel Crouse (New York, 1945). The four novels reprinted there— *Ragged Dick, Phil the Fiddler* (1872), *Struggling Upward* (1886, 1890), and *Jed the Poorhouse Boy* (1892, 1900)—span Alger's literary career from beginning to end and include both country and city novels; and without exception they exemplify the themes to be developed below. The only stories that do not display all those themes straightforwardly are Alger's tales of the West, e.g, the Pacific series, but even in them his fundamental conceptions and concerns are evident, if somewhat more muffled and convoluted.

of the armed robbery of a stockbroker, Mr. Turner, who rewards him with a job in the brokerage. In *Rufus and Rose* the lad foils another robbery of yet another rich man, Mr. Vanderpool, who adopts him and bequeaths him a small fortune in stocks. *Ben, the Luggage Boy* recounts the runaway of a boy of ten from his stern father and splendid home outside Philadelphia, his six years as a porter in the streets of New York, his chance encounter with a rich cousin (which ignites a new determination to return to the swell life), and his triumphant welcome home.

If such summaries seem overdependent on luck, patronage, and the deus ex machina, it is because Alger was too. And if they do not emphasize free enterprise, it is because Alger did not do so either. Despite his homilies and preachments, he was simply not very interested in business, and he was certainly no exponent of entrepreneurial individualism. His heroes neither possess nor prosper by the virtues of self-seeking, and Alger never espoused them. To call him a social Darwinist, as so many have done, is an inconceivable canard.

Alger did not even think comfortably in capitalistic terms. Some of his characters are "ashamed" to use credit,[3] others do not see in money an impersonal measure of value,[4] and none are enmeshed utterly in the mechanisms of the marketplace. The prices they pay and the wages they receive are as often determined by consideration and decency as by supply and demand. Bargains are struck solely on equity between the boys.[5] Rents are set by people who "don't want to make money," and they are renegotiable "if you find it is too hard on you to pay so much."[6] Alger's heroes are all allowed incomes by their benefactors that are sufficient contradictions in themselves of the primacy of profit in the motives of the benefactors who bestow them.[7] Indeed, Alger in his own voice quite condemned those who charge what the market will bear, insisting instead that "fair prices in the long run are the best for all parties."[8]

His comprehension of capitalistic individuals was no clearer than his conception of capitalist institutions. Figures of frugality pass through his pages with "thin lips and pinched expression," and though they are flourishing merchants they have "an outward appearance of meanness,

3. *Dick*, 78.
4. *Rough*, 233.
5. *Fame*, 12–14; *Mark*, 220–22, 237; *Rough*, 136–37.
6. *Rufus*, 49–50; *Rough*, 63.
7. *Dick*, 214; *Fame*, 134, 161, 216, 272; *Mark*, 371; *Rough*, 297–98; *Rufus*, 139, 141, 249–50.
8. *Mark*, 290.

which, by the way, did not belie [their] real character."[9] Men make great fortunes and find that money alone buys no contentment.[10] People of surpassing villainy "look out for number one" or mind only their own business,[11] and in every volume it is the hero's enemy who is "intent only upon his own selfish gratifications."[12]

Alger's favorites, on the contrary, are strangers to such strategies of self-maximization. For them "the best use of money" is in helping others.[13] Dick never gets "so much satisfaction" as when he depletes his own savings to assist a fellow bootblack who has "supported his sick mother and sister for more'n a year," which Dick takes to be "more good than [he himself] ever did."[14] Rufus puts his money where his morals are, buying a baseball bat from his own earnings to stave off a robbery of a man he does not even know.[15] And all alike lavish charities on the needy, whether worthy or unworthy.[16]

In fact, profligacy prevails over parsimony at every turn. All six stories open on a note of heedless indulgence—for the theater, an apartment, or food—and all six sustain that note thereafter.[17] Boys who are fortunate splurge immediately and to the limit of their luck, sharing their strike with friends if they cannot spend it alone.[18] Others who are down to their last pennies yet yield to "temptation" and buy apples and ice cream.[19] And few of the boys are any more frugal than Ben, who feels "very well satisfied" if he comes out "even at the end of the day."[20] By and large they all place their bellies before their bank accounts and otherwise set gratification above accumulation.[21]

Nor could their self-indulgence have horrified Alger, for he often al-

9. *Ben*, 241; see also 241–45.
10. *Mark*, 235, 371–72; *Rough*, 48–49.
11. *Rufus*, 30; *Rough*, 34. See also *Mark*, 246–47; *Rufus*, 127, 178–79.
12. *Mark*, 340. See also *Dick*, 159; *Fame*, 257; *Mark*, 261, 317, 344.
13. *Mark*, 381.
14. *Dick*, 177; *Fame*, 47. See also *Dick*, 170, 192–93.
15. *Rough*, 246.
16. *Dick*, 133–34, 154–56, 193, 198, 199, 216; *Fame*, 39, 48, 191, 209–10, 279; *Mark*, 304, 381; *Rough*, 15, 65, 225–26. Compare Dick's rival, Roswell Crawford, who gives nothing: *Mark*, 261.
17. Each novel is studded with examples. For some sense of their tone, see *Dick*, 39, 49; *Mark*, 253, 363–64; *Rough*, 138, 173–74, 199, 290; *Ben*, 34, 36–37, 39, 68, 113, 149–51, 165; *Rufus*, 25, 68.
18. *Dick*, 42–43, 45–46, 54, 86–87, 111–13, 121, 133–34; *Mark*, 237, 281, 381; *Rough*, 19–20, 134–35; *Ben*, 12, 135; *Rufus*, 98–99, 250.
19. *Ben*, 39.
20. *Ben*, 164.
21. *Rough*, 37, 56, 58–62, 79; *Ben*, 50–51, 63, 103, 105.

lowed it to lead to decisive transformations in their destinies. Mark gets his grubstake while sleeping on an all-night ferry.[22] Rufus first gains solid ground financially when he finds five dollars in a barroom he enters on an "idle impulse," and he overhears the plans for the robbery he prevents in still another saloon to which he repairs upon "the promptings of appetite."[23] Miss Manning, the kind woman who takes care of Rose after the children flee their stepfather, discovers the perfect lodging for herself and the little girl on "an impulse which she did not attempt to resist" even though the room seemed obviously "beyond her means."[24]

In fact, Alger's favorites are almost always impetuously improvident. Prudent calculation of prospects, so crucial for the capitalist entrepreneur, is simply not their style. Dick springs with such "alacrity" to the relief of the drowning boy that he does not even hear the father's shouted offer of reward. Mark, waking to find a dollar in his pocket, sets out on his own without once looking "forward to the time when this supply would be exhausted." Rufus flies from Martin "without any well-defined plan in his mind" and with no idea where he and Rose "should live in the future." And Ben runs away from his father so precipitately that he arrives in New York "an utter stranger with very indefinite ideas as to how he was to make a living."[25] Indeed, even when Ben finds himself but two cents from starvation, "the time had not yet come to trouble himself" about his prospects; and after six years in New York he still does "not think much about the future" for, "like street boys in general, his horizon [is] limited by the present."[26]

Unconcerned for the future, Alger's vagabonds could hardly pursue goals with the perseverance so celebrated in the success manuals of the nineteenth century. Alger did deliver an occasional descant on diligence, but in the tales themselves his heroes are hares, not tortoises. They work sporadically rather than steadily, and they work when they need money

---

22. *Mark*, 266.

23. *Rough*, 111–12, 240. Ben also gets a good break in a "bad" place (a German beer hall); see *Ben*, 63, 66, 68.

24. *Rufus*, 17, 19. The fates of the villains are sometimes tied to appetite too; see *Rough*, 149–50, 152; *Rufus*, 239. And deeds of generosity were often rewarded by immediately subsequent strokes of good luck; e.g., *Dick*, 133–35, 154–56; *Mark*, 281–87.

25. *Dick*, 208–9; *Mark*, 272, 299; *Rough*, 44; *Ben*, 26. See also *Ben*, 41–42, 61, 83.

26. *Ben*, 55, 154. See also *Dick*, 155; *Rough*, 43, 56; *Ben*, 135, 158–62; *Rufus*, 185. Even when a boy does begin to budget, he invariably makes no provision for contingencies such as sickness or bad weather, so that his accounting is still hand-to-mouth and present-oriented.

rather than for work's own sake.[27] They are more nearly Galahads than Gradgrinds, giving up their own gainful opportunities on a moment's notice to protect the helpless or follow the action.[28] And it is by just that temperamental disposition to knight errantry rather than discipline or steady application that poor boys prosper. Dick is on the ferry to dive for Rockwell's son only because he takes "half holidays" to go on "excursions." Rufus finds economic security only as a consequence of quitting work early one day to wander around Battery Park.[29]

All six stories are studded with kidnaps, captures, and escapes, robberies and false arrests, detection and derring-do. Some of them are strung entirely on such narrative threads. *Mark, the Match Boy* derives its design from the search for Hiram Bates's missing grandson. *Rough and Ready* is an account of abduction and recapture. And the others are laced with chapters such as "Tracking the Thief," "A Parley with the Enemy," and "Suspense." In all, less than one-fourth of the chapters even pretend to show the protagonists at work, while the rest show them established at home or embroiled in adventure.[30]

Only when the boys are thus beset by danger do they disclose concern for what they do.[31] At their employment they evince no emotion at all, betraying not the slightest sign that they like or dislike their assigned tasks. Unlike Weber's Protestant capitalists, for whom the moral worth of work was so central, they find neither purpose nor personal fulfillment in their jobs. They just do what the work requires, gaining no intrinsic satisfaction from it, and they identify the good life with consumption and gratification far more than with production.[32]

Disdaining the ascetic capitalist and the entrepreneurial self-seeker, Alger inevitably anathematized the social Darwinians. Against their assertions of the prerogatives of strength, he held the obligation of the powerful to protect the weak.[33] Against Sumnerian standards of self-

27. E.g., *Ben*, 135. In the very nature of the work, bootblacking and baggage-smashing were unsteady, through the day and through the seasons; see *Ben*, 28–30, 155.
28. *Dick*, 79–83, 102–7, 133, 152, 185; *Mark*, 219–21, 284–86, 296–300; *Rough*, 24, 225–26, 240–51; *Ben*, 100, 211, 246; *Rufus*, 158.
29. *Dick*, 208; *Rough*, 111–12.
30. About six of the twenty-six chapters per novel show anyone *at* work; scarcely any show the actual conditions of work. About five of each twenty-six show the heroes at home.
31. *Rough*, 235, 241–43; *Ben*, 211; *Rufus*, 158.
32. *Rufus*, 101.
33. *Dick*, 125–27, 133; *Rough*, 24, 225–26; *Ben*, 100.

reliance, he suggested an endless round of charitable reciprocation.[34] And against the Spencerian insistence on laissez-faire individualism, he urged that "we ought all to help each other."[35]

Alger admitted quite openly his environmental reformism and his hopes of stirring "a deeper and more widespread sympathy" for the "waifs of the city."[36] He never forgot that they too were "somebody's children, and that cold, and harshness, and want were as hard for them to bear as for those in a higher rank of life."[37] He made endless excuses for them because they "had never had a fair chance" or "a very good bringin' up" on the streets: for him even armed robbers "might have been capable of better things, had circumstances been different."[38] Poverty was not, in his eyes, a measure of personal failings. Many poor boys, he insisted, "have good tendencies and aspirations, and only need to be encouraged and placed under right influences to develop into worthy and respectable men"; more fortunate people might have it in their "power to give some one the chance that may redeem him."[39]

Accordingly, Alger's heroes succeed, to the extent that their own attributes have anything to do with their success, because they are good, not because they have sharper fangs and longer claws than anyone else. Like Rufus, who pinches pennies to buy decent clothes for his sister, their economies and ambitions are as often for another as for themselves.[40] Like Mark, they are frequently "bolder in behalf of [a] friend than [they] would have been for" themselves.[41] Like Dick, they can be even "more pleased at the prospective good fortune of [a] friend than if it had fallen to" their own benefit,[42] and like Rose they can be moved more readily by concern for another than by self-interest.[43] They are all, presumably, destined to develop like the successful stockbroker Alger so admired, who was

34. *Dick,* 193; *Fame,* 238–39, 279; *Mark,* 266, 299, 304, 381; *Rough,* 225–26.
35. *Mark,* 239.
36. *Fame,* viii. See also *Mark,* 291, 304.
37. *Mark,* 299.
38. *Fame,* 238–39, 188; *Rough,* 244. See also *Mark,* 256; *Fame,* 275; *Rough,* 16–18; *Ben,* 22, 30, 178–79; *Rufus,* 12, 47. For unhesitating assumptions that a bad environment could turn a tyke to theft, dirt, dishonesty, and the like, see *Ben,* 22, 30, 31, 85, 152.
39. *Ben,* 11; *Fame,* 275. See also *Rufus,* Preface.
40. *Rough,* 30. See also *Fame,* 47.
41. *Mark,* 316. See also 317.
42. *Mark,* 230.
43. *Rough,* 166. See also *Rough,* 267; *Rufus,* 47.

a large-hearted man, inclined to think well of his fellow-men, and though in his business life he had seen a good deal that was mean and selfish in the conduct of others, he had never lost his confidence in human nature, and never would. It is better to have such a disposition, even if it does expose the possessor to being imposed upon at times, than to regard everybody with distrust and suspicion. At any rate it promotes happiness, and conciliates good will, and these will offset an occasional deception.[44]

Such sentimental reliance on people's kindness made aggressive imposition unnecessary and even undesirable. It is only the Micky Maguires and the James Martins, the young toughs and the manipulators, and the counterfeiters, confidence-men, and others of "few redeeming qualities" who use force and cunning for personal gain.[45] Lads like Dick and Rufus have "a certain chivalrous feeling" that does not "allow" them to exploit anyone weaker,[46] while other boys such as Mark and Dick's friend Fosdick are so "timid" that they require the protection of their sturdier allies.[47] Alger never glorified strength or shrewdness in the struggle for success because he did not believe it was that sort of struggle.

The virtues Alger did exalt, revealingly enough, were the virtues of the employee, not the employer.[48] Since his heroes do not succeed at the expense of others, it is not essential that they build better mousetraps, cut costs, or innovate in any way. They have little enough initiative even in the streets, and less in the shop. Indeed, when they enter upon their white-collar careers, they promise their new bosses primarily to "try to make you as little trouble as possible."[49] Dick will do "anything that is required" in the line of duty,[50] but neither he nor any of the others ever rethink such duties. And no one ever asks them to. Employers themselves assure the boys that they "have only to continue steady and faithful" to be "sure to rise."[51] None but the heroes' rivals—the preening

44. *Ben,* 226–27; see also 87.
45. *Fame,* 136. See also *Dick,* 122–29, 149–53; *Rough,* 34, 83–84, 101–3; *Ben,* 241–45; *Rufus,* 30, 120–21, 127, 151–53, 167–69, 172, 178–79.
46. *Dick,* 133. See also 125–27 for Dick's refusal to fight even under provocation and for the way he finally defeats Micky by defensive prowess. See also *Rough,* 24, 225–26; *Ben,* 100.
47. *Mark,* 271. For Fosdick, see *Dick,* 133; *Fame,* 53. It might be added that even fighting on no provocation but "to check ruffianism" is merely "less censurable" by Alger's lights; see *Rough,* 25.
48. This point was first developed, so far as I know, by John Cawelti, *Apostles of the Self-Made Man* (Chicago, 1965).
49. *Fame,* 36–37.
50. *Fame,* 50. See also *Dick,* 214; *Rufus,* 73–74, 138.
51. *Fame,* 258–59. See also *Fame,* 274; *Mark,* 318, 319; *Rough,* 297; *Rufus,* 141.

pretenders to superiority by birth, such as Roswell Crawford—fail to content themselves with service in subordinate places, and the Roswell Crawfords come to bad ends.[52]

As Alger would have it, then, success follows dependability and a desire to serve others. It attends those who obey orders cheerfully and serve others willingly. And it is available to all, for Alger posited no pinacle of preeminence for which many compete and a few prove fit.[53] The Alger stories were never about the fabulous few who rose from poverty to great riches; they were, at best, tales of a much more accessible ascent from rags to respectability. His nonpareils do not wax wealthy so much as they grow reputable, leaving the promiscuity of the streets for the propriety of a desk job. Dick is barely begun upon a clerical career at the conclusion of *Ragged Dick*, still six months away from promotion to bookkeeper at the end of *Fame and Fortune*, and headed no higher than a junior partnership in a good mercantile house even at the termination of *Mark, the Match Boy*. Rufus can claim only an eight-dollar-a-week clerkship at the climax of *Rough and Ready*, is still on "the lowest rung of the ladder" halfway through *Rufus and Rose*,[54] and is destined only for an undescribed junior partnership when all is done. Mark is restored to his grandfather, a moderately wealthy broker in Milwaukee, and Ben is reclaimed by his father, a coal dealer outside Philadelphia. There is not a robber baron in the bunch, nor even any remarkable fortune. The boys gain only "the fame of an honorable and enterprising man of business," which was all they ever aimed at anyway. "I'd like to be a office boy, and learn business, and grow up 'spectable," Dick confides at his first stirring of ambition; and even as he nears the end of his odyssey he sets his sights no higher. "Take my advice," he urges Mark, "and you'll grow up respectable and respected."[55]

Such commitment to respectability implied also a commitment to others rather than to selfish aspiration. Respectability, in Alger's idea of it, could not come from within but could only be conferred by others. Accordingly, his heroes require the good opinion of the herd for their

52. E.g., *Dick*, 158–60; *Fame*, 118, 126–30, 216; *Mark*, 312–19. Significantly, Roswell's undoing is his attempt to steal from his employer and place the blame upon another; see *Mark*, chaps. 17–23.

53. The essential mobility Alger aimed to inspire was moral mobility, a change in lifestyle more than in life situation, e.g., *Dick*, 108–9, 140–41, 167; *Rough*, 17–18.

54. *Rufus*, 141.

55. *Dick*, 73; *Mark*, 309. For the consistency with which Dick maintains this motif, see *Dick*, 128–29, 132, 167; *Fame*, 22, 25, 159–60, 203; *Mark*, 224, 293. For the other heroes, see, e.g., *Ben*, 11, 278; *Rufus*, Preface.

own sense of success and for their very sense of self.[56] And they seem to believe they can gain it by behaving the way the herd behaves or would want them to behave. Dick, for example, acquires clothes so modish as he moves out into "society" that Fosdick accuses him of dandyism; Dick answers that he wants "to look respectable. . . . When I visit Turkey I want to look as the turkeys do."[57] Rufus shows a comparable concern for respectable appearance and a similar identification of such respectability with doing as others do when he goes to the theater. At expense he can ill afford, he buys a pair of white kid gloves, which he twirls about "in rather an embarrassed way" because he can hardly get them on; "I'd enough sight rather go without any," he admits, "but I suppose, if I'm going to sit in a fashionable seat, I must try to look fashionable." Later, though the gloves still do not "feel comfortable," he looks at his hands "with satisfaction," for "step by step he was getting into the ways of civilized life." (The performance itself he enjoys "almost as well" as the less classy ones he had haunted as a newsboy, which he would have attended even that night had he not suspected that the Old Bowery "was not exactly a fashionable place of amusement," one which he would "hardly have liked to mention" at the boardinghouse table the next day.)[58]

Rufus's integrity counts for no more than his entertainment in matters of reputation, giving him no pause whatever in telling a lie before his sister sooner than lose face with a total stranger. When he finds a fine new house in which to room, he offhandedly informs the landlady that he will send his trunk up later. Rose lets slip that she "didn't know [he] had a trunk," and though he replies smoothly that he does not "carry [his] trunk round all the time like an elephant," he is "a little embarrassed" because "he wanted to keep up appearances in his new character as a boarder at an up-town boarding-house."[59] And appearance is so central for Ben that he bases his entire estimate of his acceptability at home on his outward aspect, building the strategy of his return solely on a plan to "purchase a suit as handsome as that which his cousin

56. *Fame,* 159–60. For the general vapidness of such opinion, see *Rufus,* 96–97, 101–4.

57. *Fame,* 61.

58. *Rufus,* 101–2, 104. See also *Rough,* 254–55.

59. *Rufus,* 60–61. Dick and Fosdick also buy trunks they do not need with savings they do, when they move to new quarters, and they do so quite explicitly for the purpose of respectability; see *Fame,* 17. For other instances of extravagance for the sake of a respectable appearance, often in the face of more immediate necessities, see *Rough,* 37–38, 56; *Rufus,* 51–52, 68.

wore." The thought that he might be as welcome without the suit, simply for himself, never enters his mind.[60]

Even the most elemental virtues of individual character acquire an other-oriented flavor in Alger's hands. Dick may be honest when he informs a fellow boarder that he once shined the man's shoes, but the author admits that Dick "wouldn't have said so" if he thought the man might believe him.[61] Ben may decline to steal, but only because "he still felt that he should not like to have a report reach home"; and on the one occasion he does swipe an apple he feels only a fear for what "his friends at home [would] think of it" if they heard.[62] Rufus may have a superfluity of intrinsic reasons to reject the company of his stepfather, but he spurns him solely from anxiety over what others might think when that "not very respectable-looking object" tries to walk alongside him.[63] And almost all the principal characters pursue education simply because they recognize that there is "something more than money needed to win a respectable position in the world."[64]

The Alger hero's very notion of his own nature depended, ineluctably, upon others. If Alger's world was a Carnegie world, it was surely not Andrew's but Dale's. Alger could not create self-impelled individuals because his stalwarts required a crowd for their sense of self. The quest for respectability imposed a communal derivation of identity and a communal dedication of the self as well. Accordingly, when Alger offered examples outside fiction of the newsboy success story, he cited politicians, journalists, judges, a district attorney, and a clergyman before arriving finally at "still others prosperous and even wealthy businessmen."[65] Businessmen brought up the rear while public figures led because it was primarily the redemption of respectable citizens Alger sought. His aims were social and moral more than they were ever economic.

Alger's inability to conceive convincingly his heroes' inner resources made it quite impossible for him to maintain the traditional connection

60. *Ben,* 193–94; see also 128–29, 275. For other indications of the importance of judgment by appearances, see *Fame,* 256; *Rufus,* 75, 76.

61. *Fame,* 60–61; see also 213–14.

62. *Ben,* 178–79, 85; and see esp. 211.

63. *Rufus,* 108.

64. *Dick,* 130. See also *Dick,* 167; *Fame,* 66; *Mark,* 359; *Ben,* 255–56. Fosdick is, of course, something of an exception. It might be added that Dick also thinks of religious observance as "an important step toward securing that genuine respectability which he was anxious to attain" (see *Dick,* 141).

65. *Rufus,* Preface.

of character and success. He could—and did, occasionally—claim it, but he could not bring it to life. His tales contradicted him at every such turn. The path to wealth was not, as it had been for Franklin, "as plain as the way to market." Instead there intervened always between constitution and conquest the sudden stroke of luck.[66]

The typical Alger story, therefore, was one of casual contingency, not causal necessity. Bootblacks rise by diving for the drowning son of a rich man, newsboys by foiling attempted robbery, matchboys by the belated beneficence of a grandfather a thousand miles away. None ever attain eminence by diligent application; none are ever on a course of notable advancement before their big break. Alger knew the litany of industry and frugality as well as most people, but for him and his characters the failure of firm selfhood and the facts of late nineteenth century life kept getting in the way.[67]

Primarily the problems were that these gamins of Gotham could not get the kind of work Alger wished for them and that, even if they could, they could not afford to take it. In the Algerine cosmos, nothing but a white-collar career would do, finally[68]—protagonists had somehow to quit the street for a store—and in the Ragged Dick series not a single favorite ever secures a clerical position purely on personal initiative. Dick makes "several ineffectual applications" and surrenders for the season. His friend Fosdick solicits fifty appointments and suffers "as many failures." Ben gives up entirely after a few rebuffs; Rufus never even tries.[69] And the reason is always the same: "it was generally desired that the boy wanted should reside with his parents" or "bring good references."[70] Fosdick finds that to confess himself "a boy of the street" is usually "sufficient of itself to insure a refusal,"[71] and the others all share

66. The first developed analysis of the centrality of luck was R. Richard Wohl, "The 'Rags to Riches Story': An Episode of Secular Idealism," in *Class, Status and Power*, ed. Reinhard Bendix and Seymour Martin Lipset (Glencoe, Ill., 1953), 388–95.

67. Alger is such a revealing source precisely because he does not—the temptation is to say cannot—suppress such facts. For some suggestive instances of his literalism and passivity before the flow of his own experience and environment, see *Ben*, vii–viii, 59–60, 172n, 259n; *Rufus*, Preface.

68. It is true that Alger sometimes affirmed the equal honorability of all honest employments, but some were generally more equal than others. See *Dick*, 109, 128, 147; and esp. *Rufus*, 70.

69. *Dick*, 207, 157; *Ben*, 42–45.

70. *Dick*, 157; *Ben*, 88. See also *Fame*, 43; *Mark*, 307; *Ben*, 46–47, 48, 73; *Rufus*, 138.

71. *Dick*, 157. When he does finally obtain employment, it is by the happenstance that Mr. Greyson, a merchant he knows through Dick, enters the very store where Fosdick is applying at the very moment he is being interviewed; even Fosdick admits he is hired

his discouragement in a system that supports no self-made men. They hustle on the streets precisely because they are alone and unaided and consequently can do no better, for they have no access to a counting-house unless they can claim a place in a household. Unsponsored and unspoken for, their success can only be extrasystemic. In the very structure of the situation they can advance by no means but the lucky acquisition of a patron who will provide the protection they require.

In the very structure of the situation too, young men on their own are all but obliged to remain independent rather than seek employment, because the financial price of propriety is too steep. Energetic newsboys and bootblacks in Alger's New York make far more money than beginning clerks do—Dick, for instance, sees at once that on an office salary he would "be nothin' but skin and bones" within a year[72]—and such stalwarts of the street have far fewer expenses besides. They worry little about lodging, less about clothes and cleanliness, and not at all about education. It is all the same to them if they sleep in a box, an illegal hideout between the wharves, or a suitably impressive address.[73] An aspiring bookkeeper, on the other hand, cannot afford to be so cavalier. He has a position to uphold, so he has to incur the costs of a regular room, presentable clothes, and perhaps even a few luxuries for the sake of such respectability.[74] His office job, if he is but beginning, nets him less than the expenses of his own support; and even Dick recognizes this for bad budgeting, asserting as he does his disinclination "to give up a independent and loocrative purfession" for the pittance he would be paid in a store.[75]

Luck, then, does not simply seal the success of those on the proper path. On the contrary, fortune's favor is indispensable to lift poor boys out of the ditch. Ragged Dick is not on his way before he saves Mr. Rockwell's son, for there is no way. Orphans of the city cannot afford

---

"only because Mr. Greyson spoke up for me"; see *Dick,* 161–62. The only other boy to gain an appointment by his own endeavor is Mark, but he does so only at Dick's urging and with Dick's assurance of a reference; see *Mark,* 307–12.

72. *Dick,* 73. Three or four dollars a week was the normal beginning wage in these novels—see *Dick,* 73, 158–59, 177; *Fame,* 44; *Mark,* 312; *Rough,* 297–98—while bootblacks and paperboys could scuffle for a weekly income quite double that—see *Dick,* 166; *Rough,* 111, 297–98; *Ben,* 28–30, 120.

73. *Dick,* 40; *Ben,* 170.

74. E.g., *Dick,* 113–14, 141, 159; *Fame,* 109, 241; *Rough,* 151; *Rufus,* 51–52, 60–61.

75. *Dick,* 159; see also *Rough,* 295–96. For the excess of expenses, see *Dick,* 166, 177; *Rough,* 111, 297–98.

an apprenticeship in respectability, since they have no parental subsidy to tide them over and can hardly survive on status alone. Only by benevolent patronage can they manage their entry upon a white-collar walk of life. Only from parental surrogates who set defiance of the market's determination of wages at "no consequence" can they extract salaries they cannot economically earn.[76] Dick speaks for them all when he admits that he "was lucky" to have "found some good friends who helped [him] along."[77]

So far from telling of a system so bountiful that any earnest lad could succeed if he tried, Alger's tales implied one that held the disprivileged down so securely that only by the unlikely advent of chance and championship could the impoverished even set foot on the social ladder. In the Alger novels of New York a steady undertone of desperation resonated beneath the scattered cries of lucky triumph.

As essential as luck was to the manifest social action of the stories, it was still more imperative at their latent levels of intimate familial relationships and personal fantasies of fulfillment. For if Alger could not in the end cleave a straightforward course from character to success, it was because he could not from the first conceive of any satisfactory character at all. In an era whose leading spokesmen defined character—at least male character—in terms of will,[78] Alger's deepest desire was persistently for a denial of the will.

At first, of course, it does not seem so. His heroes have always to fend for themselves, often in adversity, and generally they enjoy their lot. Dick delights in being his "own boss," trumpeting it as "the difference" between himself and his storeboy sidekick.[79] Mark exults in being "free and independent."[80] Rufus, disdaining another boy's servility, announces that he does not "want anybody to give [him] money."[81] And Ben becomes "so accustomed to the freedom and independence of his street life, with its constant variety, that he would have been unwilling

76. *Rough*, 297–98. See also *Dick*, 214; *Fame*, 134, 216, 272, 277–78; *Rufus*, 139, 141, 249–50.
77. *Mark*, 236. See also *Fame*, 74, 238–39, 255. Alger often added that his hero's luck was deserved; see, e.g., *Fame*, 264; *Mark*, 221; *Rufus*, 253–54.
78. See Donald Meyer, *The Positive Thinkers* (Garden City, N.Y., 1965).
79. *Dick*, 165. See also *Fame*, 121.
80. *Mark*, 287; also 289. The chapter in which Mark secures such freedom is entitled "Mark's Victory."
81. *Rough*, 14–15; also 253–54.

to return, even if the original cause of his leaving home were removed. Life in a Pennsylvania village seemed 'slow' compared with the excitement of his present life." [82]

But such bold sentiments are the artist's asseveration, not the tale's truth, and they are always spoken before opportunity offers. As soon as it does, Dick decides he would rather be Mr. Rockwell's hireling, Mark accepts his grandfather's guidance, Rufus takes Mr. Turner's money and Mr. Vanderpool's too, and Ben goes back home. In every case their independence is only for the interim. In the end they abandon all autonomy, willingly. Ben declares it "a good deal pleasanter resting in the luxurious bedchamber . . . than the chance accommodations to which he had been accustomed." Dick is "rather pleased" that his old rags are stolen, since their loss seems "to cut him off from the old vagabond life which he hoped never to resume." [83]

Not one of Alger's elect is ever self-employed at the end of a novel, nor do any of them ever really wish to be. Mark most obviously needs "somebody to lean on," [84] but even Dick admits that his deepest dreams involve "some rich man" who "would adopt me, and give me plenty to eat and drink and wear, without my havin' to look so sharp after it." It is not with his usual levity that he adds that he would "like to have somebody to care for me," and later, when he wishes explicitly for a mother, there is the same "tinge of sadness in his tone." [85]

Dick's fantasied confusion of men and mothers comes very close to the emotional core of the Alger stories, for though the boys all crave care-taking, they are quite particular about its provenance. Not any parent will do. Each of Alger's prodigies is seeking something very special, and it is no accident that in a nation still two-thirds rural and presumably patriarchal, every story in the series is conditioned on father-absence. Only one of the six tales even admits a flesh-and-blood father, and Ben runs away from him. In the others there are a few self-sacrificing mothers, an indulgent grandfather, a stern stepfather, and a monstrous mother substitute; and only those among them who abdicate their authority succeed in sustaining a relation with their wards. All

---

82. *Ben*, 153–54; also 160–62, 163–64, and *Rufus*, 94. The preference for the city's excitement is echoed by other characters: see *Dick*, 47–48; *Mark*, 310.

83. *Ben*, 285; *Dick*, 215. For Rufus, see *Rufus*, 51–52.

84. *Mark*, 271; also 299.

85. *Dick*, 99, 171. Even this early his fantasy is fulfilled; Frank tells him, "I will care for you."

who play the traditional masculine part—demanding and commanding—discover one day that their fledglings have flown the coop.[86]

Over and over again in these stories, Alger returned to the problem of proper parentage. His fixation was overt in *Mark, the Match Boy* and *Ben, the Luggage Boy,* more muffled in the others—the first two tell quite focally of falls from family and reentry into its bosom, the rest dwell less on literal than on figurative kinships that are reclaimed as the protagonists find their patrons—but it pervaded the entire series.[87] In every novel the hero experiences the unsettling sense that his own parents have failed him, that somewhere else his true parents are waiting to be found by accident and good luck.

Proper parents such as these are invariably defined in terms of nurturance and even indulgence, not discipline and hard knocks. It is because his stepfather "couldn't take care of [him]self, much less of anyone else" that Rufus so often reminds him, "I am not your son."[88] It is because Mother Watson assumed charge of him "rather for her own advantage than his" that Mark finally realizes that she "had no claim on him" and pronounces her "no relation."[89] And it is because his father, though a good provider, is intolerant of impulse and unbending in righteousness that Ben runs away and refuses to return:

knowing his father's sternness, he knew that he would be severely punished. Unfortunately for Ben, his father had a stern, unforgiving disposition, that never made allowances for the impulses of boyhood. He had never condescended to study his own son, and the method of training he had adopted with him was in some respects very pernicious. His system hardened, instead of softening.[90]

Proper parents, then, are permissive. Like Ben's mother, who is "quite different from her husband, being gentle and kind," such parents are sweet but not strong.[91] They give, and they ask little or nothing in return. Every Alger favorite finds a few of them on his way, and the occasions of these encounters are the hinges on which his history turns.

86. Cawelti, *Apostles,* is sensitive to some of these issues, but his analysis is far too Freudian. The heroes' needs are rather more oral than oedipal.

87. The most fascinating development is at the conclusion of *Rufus,* when Miss Manning, Rose's guardian, marries rich Mr. Vanderpool, while Rufus and Rose go to live in his house and Rufus inherits from him.

88. *Rough,* 202; see also, e.g., *Rufus,* 158, 188–89.

89. *Mark,* 271, 286; also 249, 251, 270.

90. *Ben,* 73–74; also 24–25, 59–60, 128–29, 140, 144, 145, 232.

91. *Ben,* 137–38. Significantly, it is "to her that Ben always went for sympathy, in any trouble or difficulty."

Dick's advancement, for example, can be traced quite completely through his successive sponsors, who provide him the incentives and resources for his rehabilitation.[92] Mark's merest survival, to say nothing of his brief flight to freedom, is conditioned on the support, first, of an older street urchin who fends off Mark's former guardian by claiming to have "adopted that boy," and then, of course, by Dick himself, who declares Mark his ward and explains that he will "look after" the little boy "just as if I was your uncle or grandfather."[93] Ben is squired by a series of street people who provide him present comfort and promises of future assistance at any time he is "in need" of them, and later he is assured by a wealthy merchant that "when you need a friend, you will know where to find me."[94] Rufus alone requires scant succor before his decisive break, but only because the focal roles are reversed so that he protects his sister, sheltering her from any obligation "to go out into the street to earn anything" though "many girls, no older than she," do work; and even Rufus dreams of the day Rose "grows up, and can keep house for me."[95]

In truth, almost every character establishes his connection to others on an axis of caring or being cared for, or defaulting on such fostering duties. And the narratives move almost wholly on these matters of maintenance. *Rough and Ready,* for instance, is at its core an adventure of abduction and recovery, of nurture ruptured and restored. Success is so peripheral to the story that Rufus quite literally thwarts the thieves and gains his clerkship in an interlude while waiting to save his sister. His own advancement never does concern him so much as her sustenance, which is why her stepfather steals her in the first place, knowing "that nothing would strike the newsboy a severer blow than to deprive him of his sister."[96] In *Rufus and Rose,* the former newsboy himself escapes from his stepfather and the criminals Martin has fallen in league with; and he is able to do so because one of them unjustly beats the

92. *Dick,* 72–73, 74–75, 87–89, 108–11, 131–33, 143–44, 161–62, 202, 213–14; *Fame,* 91–92.

93. *Mark,* 285, 303; also 265, 273, 298–99, 301, 307. Dick does similar services for Fosdick: see, e.g., *Dick,* 133–36, 155–62; *Fame,* 76; *Mark,* 228, 241.

94. *Ben,* 63, 232; also 66, 69, 89–91, 93–103, 119, 120, 123.

95. *Rough,* 89–90, 174; also 163, 184, 190, 214, 267, 287; *Rufus,* 47, 233–34. Rufus is vitally assisted at one crucial juncture by the young hunchback Humpy; see *Rufus,* chaps. 20–24.

96. *Rough,* 109. Even Martin's ability to manage the kidnap in the first place depends on (Miss Manning's) failure to watch over the girl closely enough; see *Rough,* 152–53. And in the end it is Rufus' nurturant regard for his sister that Alger invokes to justify the lad's luck; see *Rufus,* 253–54.

hunchback guard Humpy, whose "rude sense of honor" had previously held him "faithful to his employer." Humpy determines to betray his masters for that failure—regretting that he "wouldn't have gone ag'inst" them had they been more supportive—and he single-handedly engineers Rufus's rescue.[97] In *Mark, the Match Boy* Hiram Bates triggers the action not merely by setting Dick to search for his grandson but also by having failed, years before, to accept his daughter's love for his clerk. She married the man anyway, Bates "disowned her" and "hardened [his] heart against her," and it is his remorse that drives him to try to make amends when he learns that his daughter and her husband are dead. "I cannot forgive myself," he swears, "when I think of my unfeeling severity."[98] And in *Ragged Dick* and *Ben, the Luggage Boy* alike, the young hero's ascent is fired by first fostering, Dick's when he is encouraged as "nobody ever talked to [him] so before," Ben's when he is assured that his cousin's love for him is unconditional, "no matter how he looked, or how poor he might be."[99]

Ultimately, then, Alger's every novel was a novel of nurturance, a novel whose dearest ideal was to be cared for and indulged, not to be self-sufficient and self-reliant. Each of them begins with a boy alone and on his own, but each of them concludes with that boy safely sheltered in some secure niche where his future is assured because his protector will look after him forevermore. Alger allowed his every hero and half his supporting cast this movement from the streets to Easy Street, and it afforded him the essential drama and the irresistible consummation of all his narratives. Dick gains Mr. Rockwell's undying gratitude, Mark secures "a comfortable and even luxurious home, and a relative whose great object in life is to study his happiness," Rufus has Mr. Turner's pledge that there will be many ways "in which I shall find an opportunity to serve you" while Rose has Rufus's reassurance that she is "safe now, and nobody shall trouble" her, and Ben is welcomed home by all to take over the family firm.[100] In every case the womb is warm; in no case will the hero have to struggle any longer.

97. *Rufus*, 196–97, 223; see, generally, chaps. 20–24. Since Humpy cannot return to his employers after he helps Rufus, the hero promises to take care of him—"I won't forget the service you have done me"—and, through Mr. Turner, Rufus keeps his promise. See *Rufus*, 227–33, for these wheels within wheels of nurturance and patronage.
98. *Mark*, 234–35. Mark's departure from Mother Watson is also due to a deficit of nurturance; see 271.
99. *Dick*, 75; *Ben*, 187–88. For another example of the connection of nurturance and ambition, see *Fame*, 265.
100. *Dick*, 211; *Mark*, 382; *Rough*, 297–98; *Ben*, 280, 281, 285–89.

At this level the public and the private themes of the tales merge and reinforce each other superbly. The quest for a patron that provides much of the explicit action of the stories parallels—and is finally the very same as—the quest for a new and more nurturant parent that provides the covert action. The social and the personal themes are one and the same, and they are both fantasies of fosterage. The hero eludes stern parental authority and secures a more supportive champion who supplies rather than demands. His lot is unconditional love, from a guardian much like the father Ben goes back to, who "seems to have changed greatly" and "is no longer stern and hard, but gentle and forbearing."[101] The thrust of the stories is not the growth of the heroes but the alteration of their environments; Ben can return because his father and his home have changed.

All the stories are, in a similar sense, tales of a return to respectable estate. Their movement is not even from rags to respectability, for their subjects never really start in rags. They pass their formative years in the bosom of a family, and they are quite familiar with its comforts before they run away or are orphaned. In their success, they simply recover a condition that was originally theirs. Like Mark and Ben, they reclaim a literal birthright with a reformed relative; or, like Rufus and Fosdick, they find a fonder patron altogether. In either case their progression is the same: from respectability to rags to respectability, from home to street to a new and more nurturant home.[102]

Indeed, homes are crucial concerns for Alger even before his heroes consummate their quest,[103] for such lodgings symbolize superbly the fusion of public and private aspiration to passive security and indulgence in their desires. The boys move constantly to more expensive and

101. *Ben,* 289.

102. Dick is the only protagonist who does not demonstrably follow this sequence, and his origins are ambiguous.

An interesting index to this retrieval of position is the progression of names Alger allows his heroes. Almost without exception they begin with nothing but their street nicknames, reclaim their given first names as they begin to advance, and assume their full familial names when they are securely settled in a protected place. Thus Ragged Dick becomes Dick becomes Richard Hunter, and Rough and Ready becomes Rufus becomes Rufus Rushton. Ben admits to his father's name only when he is reconciled to returning home, and Mark is discovered as the grandson Hiram Bates was seeking when he reveals his real name to Dick. Even Humpy, the young hunchback who handles Rufus's escape, resumes his original name, William Norton, after Rufus promises to "be [his] friend" and "get [him] something to do" (*Rufus,* 227–29).

103. Symptomatically, Alger devotes at least a part of the first chapter of five of the six novels to a detailed description of the protagonist's place of lodging. In the sixth, *Rough,* such discussion is deferred to the second chapter.

commodious quarters, even though they can scarcely afford to feed themselves and cannot save a penny after they have paid their rent,[104] because they need both to signify the stations of their advancement to social respectability[105] and to simulate the safety of the cradle. As Alger explained, "those young men who out of economy contented themselves with small and cheerless rooms . . . were driven in the evening to the streets, theatres, and hotels, for the comfort which they could not find at home."[106] An ample home is, in Alger, the alternative to the real independence and loneliness of the large city, and none of the boys want such self-reliance if they can avoid it. They pay so excessively for a room because it is so much more important to them than saving. It is a sanctuary, a veritable womb.

So too, in the end, do the dependence on luck and the cultivation of the employee virtues conduce to the same comfort. The reliance on chance issues from a passivity before the environment, an impingement of favorable circumstance upon the individual; the sanction of subordinacy clarifies the heroes' progress by patronage, since the very virtues the boys acquire represent efforts to come to the attention of their superiors and gain such support.[107] And success itself is attained not by fighting to the top in constant, clawing struggle but precisely by moving out of the fray entirely, into another's custody.

If Horatio Alger was the mentor of an emergent industrial society, then the Americans who grew up under his tutelage were surely schooled for service in the corporate bureaucracies that would in time transform the culture. For Alger never encouraged his audience to care so much for work as for the gratifications of income, and he never dared his readers to be as they might be so much as to do as their neighbors did. Beneath his explicit emphasis on striving upward ran a deeper desire for stability and security; beneath his paeans to manly vigor, a lust for effeminate indulgence; beneath his celebration of self-reliance, a craving to be taken care of and a yearning to surrender the terrible burden of independence.

104. *Fame*, 9, 12–14, 152–54; *Rough*, 58–64, 79; *Rufus*, 51–52. At one point Rufus is spending his entire income on rooming costs; see *Rufus*, 51–52.

105. *Dick*, 113–14; *Ben*, 193–94; *Rufus*, 51–52.

106. *Mark*, 222; also *Fame*, 152–54; *Ben*, 201–2.

107. Alger's favorites often snub an immediate superior who is arrogant toward them and could hardly play the patron in any case; but they are unfailingly respectful of the counsel of higher authorities, especially owners, who are kindly and can conceivably help them. See *Fame*, 30–34; *Mark*, 318; *Ben*, 203–7.

# EIGHT

# Faith, Hope, Not Much Charity: The Optimistic Epistemology of Lewis Mumford

The myth of Mumford is that the polymath of power faltered in his last large books. According to this conventional commentary, his prose grew self-indulgent and overheated, his exposition polemical and undersubstantiated. His best arguments were already ingredient in his own earlier work, and now they were tainted by a sour pessimism he had held at bay before: *The City in History* is, on this orthodox account, a darker endeavor than *The Culture of Cities,* and *The Myth of the Machine* a bleaker, more bilious one than *Technics and Civilization.*[1]

Some of the reviews were savage. "There is little here that is really new," said one; *The Pentagon of Power* "does not significantly extend the range of Mumford's social criticism" nor even "advance much beyond" views he propounded in his earliest writing on technology. "Rather than being a fitting capstone for his career," said another, *The Myth of the Machine* "has little that is new or useful to offer us"; it is "not so much a summary as a rehash of bits and pieces of his previous work." Its insights "nearly all reproduc[e] thoughts Mumford had already expressed in 1934," said a third. Its argument is "less well documented than it was" in the work of that year, said a fourth.[2]

From *Lewis Mumford: Public Intellectual,* ed. Thomas Hughes and Agatha Hughes (Oxford: Oxford University Press, 1990), 361–76.

1. Donald Miller, ed., *The Lewis Mumford Reader* (New York, 1986), 102, 160–61, 300.

2. Ronald Weber, "Mumford But Not Vintage," *Review of Politics* 34 (1972): 107; Victor Ferkiss, "The Megamachine Reconstituted," *Commonweal* 93 (1970–71): 499;

Those reviews and others as well marked a "gloomy" progression from *Technics and Civilization,* which they took for "a relatively cheerful and optimistic book," to *The Myth of the Machine,* which they conceived as the culmination of Mumford's "evolution toward disillusionment." One of them went so far as to call *The Pentagon of Power* a "doomsday book." And even Donald Miller, Mumford's literary executor, has posited "a profound change in Mumford's social outlook," a "growing disenchantment with modern life and a gathering pessimism," in the years from Mumford's first major works to his last. Miller proclaims *The Myth of the Machine* "a world removed, in temper and tone, from *Technics and Civilization,*" and he holds Mumford's other writings of the sixties equally the "somber" studies of "a far less sanguine" scholar who had "lost some of his faith in the possibilities of . . . revitalization."[3]

Against all of this conventional wisdom, I mean to argue that neither of the volumes of *The Myth of the Machine*—*Technics and Human Development* and *The Pentagon of Power*—is derivative in its essential thrust from Mumford's earlier masterwork, *Technics and Civilization,* and that neither is inferior to it in originality or importance. I mean to set forth a conception of *The Myth of the Machine* as Mumford's most mature and most audacious work, the ripest and bravest fruition of a lifetime of engagement with the twentieth-century prospect. And I mean to suggest that this last great statement before the concluding autobiographical essays of the seventies is not nearly as dismal or despondent as so many readers have supposed, that it is, on the contrary, the most intriguingly and compellingly optimistic composition of his career.

If that career defies complete comprehension, it can at least be approached in the epistemological terms in which Mumford himself understood it. As he said in his autobiography, any adequate appraisal of his intellectual outlook would have to "take account of [his] lifelong intercourse with both Plato and Aristotle."[4]

Mumford did oscillate, always, between the philosophical perspectives of the two great ancients. But in his early writings the older Athenian yielded priority to his Peripatetic protégé. In his very first book,

---

William McNeill, "A Novel Vision of Mankind's History," *Virginia Quarterly Review* 47 (1971): 299; Robert Multhauf, Review of *The Myth of the Machine: The Pentagon of Power, Technology and Culture* 13 (1972): 299.

3. Multhauf, Review, 295, 296; Hiram Caton, "The Machine Profaned," *National Review* 23 (1971): 41; Miller, ed., *Mumford Reader,* 300, 301, 102, 160–61.

4. Lewis Mumford, *Sketches from Life: The Autobiography of Lewis Mumford: The Early Years* (Boston, 1982), 142–43.

*The Story of Utopias,* Mumford focused less on the psyches of the communards than on their social systems and less on their ideals than on their practices. He still vacillated. Here he insisted on the pragmatic idealism he drew from John Dewey, there on the ecological empiricism he learned from Patrick Geddes. He set himself now to study "attitudes and beliefs," then to do the "regional surveys" demanded by his Scottish master. He affirmed sometimes an intellectual approach—"our most important task at the present moment is to build castles in the air. . . . It will be easy enough to place foundations under them"—and sometimes a sociological one—"the first step out of the present impasse [is to] return to the real world, and face it, and survey it in its complicated totality," because "our castles-in-air must have their foundations in solid ground."[5]

He was still oscillating for decades afterwards. But for all the attenuated idealism of such subsequent early works as *The Golden Day,* he was still, essentially, seeking "foundations in solid ground" to the time of his first great history of technology. In *Technics and Civilization,* he postulated a phasing predicated on technical potentialities and desiderata—eotechnic, paleotechnic, and neotechnic—and he explicated the emergence of each phase from its predecessor in a manner almost Marxian.

After 1945, however, there was a different drift in the direction of his thought and in its epistemological underpinnings, or perhaps simply a turning of the circle. As he addressed the crises he believed beset civilization in the wake of the Second World War, dreading as he did the future that might follow the age of Hitler and Hiroshima—the worst twenty years in human history, as he thought[6]—he came to doubt the empiricism he had taken from his teachers, Geddes and Veblen, and to deepen and clarify his commitment to the primacy of mind in the making of the world. As he found his way to the most daringly original and sweeping syntheses of his entire career, he found his way back to the convictions of his collegiate days, when Plato "took possession" of him for a time. As he surveyed the trajectory of his development, at the completion of *The Myth of the Machine,* he noted that he had begun "as a pragmatist and a positivist" and then moved steadily "closer to . . . platonism."[7]

5. Lewis Mumford, *The Story of Utopias* (New York, 1922), 298, 279–81, 307, 281.
6. Miller, ed., *Mumford Reader,* 301.
7. Mumford, *Sketches,* 142; Lewis Mumford, *The Myth of the Machine: The Pentagon of Power* (New York, 1970), 444 (hereafter cited as TPoP).

He had never, of course, categorically discounted the role of mind, or spirit, or will, or values, in his pragmatic and positivist periods. But he had never thought it all the way through, either. Even as he had affirmed the importance of ideas and designs and the imposition of meaning upon experience, he had still conceded much more to an autonomous empirical reality. He had upheld almost unthinkingly, for example, the conventional disjunctions of means and ends and of science and human values, disjunctions that he would dedicate his later works to denying.[8]

Where *Technics and Civilization* had clung to conceptions of technological succession and sociological stages, *The Myth of the Machine* abandons them for a more contingent appreciation of history and a more Platonistic conviction of the priority of ideas, ideologies, and spiritual forces in the course of human evolution. Impelled by the urgency he apprehends in our contemporary situation, he reaches beyond the ringing Emersonian rhetoric on which he had always relied, ransacking domains as disparate as archeology and physiology, experimental psychology and the history of the ancient Middle East, for the data of a new conception of humanity's destiny.

Where once he had merely gestured, now he specifies. Where earlier he had depended on declamation, now he essays sophisticated elaboration. Where before, at best, he had simply assumed the centrality of mind, now he attempts to account for it.

From the first pages of *Technics and Human Development* to the final pages of *The Pentagon of Power,* his account frames and informs *The Myth of the Machine.* It begins from an arresting assertion of "man's overdeveloped and incessantly active brain" and of the excessive "mental energy" that brain affords, beyond all necessity for "survival at a purely animal level." It insists that that "gift of free neural energy" set the elemental terms of the evolution of human beings, fostering their "exploratory curiosity" and "idle manipulativeness with no thought of ulterior reward" and spurring their creativity for the sheer joy of utilizing their immense resources and expressing their latent potentialities.[9]

Yet the brain, remarkable as it is, remains for Mumford a mere "biological organ." It is sufficient to entail creativity upon men and women as a constitutional function embedded in their neural structure. It is nonetheless amplified immeasurably upon the advent of mind, "the

8. Mumford, *Utopias,* 171–72.
9. Lewis Mumford, *The Myth of the Machine: Technics and Human Development* (New York, 1967), 7, 36, 8 (hereafter cited as T&HD).

most radical step in man's evolution." Mind is a "cultural emergent." It "superimposed upon purely electro-chemical changes a durable mode of symbolic organization." It "created a sharable public world of organized sense impressions and supersensible meanings and eventually a coherent domain of significance."[10]

In positing the emergence of the oversized brain and then of the playful, purposeful mind as the principal drivers of human development, Mumford makes the evolution of *homo sapiens* hinge far more on plenitude than on the scarcity and parsimony that orthodox accounts assume. In affirming the absence of any specialized adaptation and the presence of an extravagant plasticity as human beings' evolutionary advantages, Mumford maintains the power of multipotentiality and epitomizes his insistence that humankind be understood as a species that made meaning before—and much better than—it made tools, or, alternatively, that made signs and symbols, out of the special resources of the mind, as its most formative tools.[11]

In this insistence, he assailed all the exponents of materialist conceptions of man, such as the Marxists and the megamechanicians, and more than a few self-styled psychologists and spiritualists besides. Man, for Mumford, is a "minder" much more than a "maker," a creature of culture and consciousness much more than of artifacts and arms. From their earliest appearance, as Mumford reexamined the evidence, humans had scanned the skies, sacralized ancestral spirits, speculated on death and future existence, and otherwise displayed an awareness that distant, mysterious, and implacable forces might impinge upon their lives.[12]

Where materialists, Maslovian as well as Marxist, predicated hierarchies of human needs in which spiritual and esthetic motives appeared only after more urgent imperatives of survival and amenity had been satisfied, Mumford maintained that an unmistakable consciousness of mystery and concern for artistic effect had marked the human endeavor from the first. As the decisive experiments of Adelbert Ames had demonstrated, cognitive expectancy is indispensable even in the seemingly simplest processes of perception. Men and women always outleap the evidence of their senses, anticipating experience and transcending it. They could no more function now than in the prehistoric past if they did not. And therefore they cannot be comprehended merely as practical problem solvers or as agile adjusters to environmental demands.

10. T&HD, 27, 39, 26, 27.
11. T&HD, 40, 6–7, 43.
12. T&HD, 4, 95, 20–21.

They are, on the contrary, creatures who set themselves gratuitous problems. They press beyond present needs, seeking and hypothesizing patterns of significance.[13]

Their very quest for surplus meaning is what defines them, for Mumford, as a species much more appropriately classified *homo sapiens* than *homo faber*. In the perspective that pervades *The Myth of the Machine*, the mind is not a late-evolving luxury in the course of human development. It is constitutive of the entire enterprise. Those too committed to technological rationalism to acknowledge this "autonomous original nature" only present symptoms of the disease of megamechanical modernity, not analyses of it. Mumford saves some of his sharpest barbs for such "technological men." He assails them savagely as "ghosts clad in iron," catching exactly as he does the deathly denigration of mind and culture and art that only modern humans have dared.[14]

Yet Mumford is too instinctive a dramatist, and his theories themselves too instinct with conflict, to sustain a simple paean to the mind and its priority. The antagonism between the mind and the brain remains. The mental excess that affords humans their evolutionary edge over the animals also exposes them to danger. The "immense psychic overflow from man's cerebral reservoir" is the condition of his creativity, but it is also a source of nonadaptive and indeed irrational impulses.[15]

Such irrationality may be as innocuous as that "most peculiar type of inner activity: the dream," for "the dream itself testifies to a more general organic exuberance that can hardly be accounted for on any purely adaptive principle." From the beginning, "man was a dreaming animal." His dreams, born of psychal superfluity, perhaps precipitated his departure from "the restrictions of a purely animal career" and certainly gave him his first hint of an unseen world "veiled from his senses" yet as starkly real as his food or his hand.[16]

Such irrationality may also be far less innocent or intimative. It encompasses "transcendental aspirations and demonic compulsions" alike. It sanctions and even sanctifies the merest of mischiefs and the most monstrous of "destructions and debasements."[17]

Against such capacity for irrational rage and devastation, Mumford

13. T&HD, 43–44.
14. T&HD, 9, 4, 22.
15. T&HD, 48, 49, 50.
16. T&HD, 48, 50, 49, 54.
17. T&HD, 11, 50–51. See also, e.g., 10, 204.

posits primitive ritual and the vast cultural apparatus in which it eventuated as ancient people's means of controlling, or at least offsetting, their inordinate unconscious. Only their dogged insistence upon the perpetuation of established ways could curb the creativity and the aggression and sadism that steadily imperiled all possibility of social order. Only the tedium of repetition and the interdiction of innovation could contain the teeming fantasies of their overcomplex brains.[18]

Just as the evolution of language—the expression and transmission of meaning—was "incomparably more important to further human development" than the evolution of weapons, so the elaboration of ceremony was immeasurably more vital than the elaboration of tools. Or, more exactly and more audaciously, technics and language alike flow "from the same common source . . . : the primeval repetitive order of ritual" that early man developed "in self-protection, so as to control the tremendous overcharge of psychal energy that his large brain placed at his disposal."[19]

On this striking supposition, Mumford inverts the Maslovian hierarchy. Men and women invented themselves before they ever invented instruments of merely utilitarian efficacy. In human nature and in human history, the making of meaning had precedence—until our own megamechanical age—over the making of tools. Language and ritual were richly developed even in the most technologically backward societies, and toolmaking and tool using were relatively retarded even in the most technically advanced. Communication and ceremony maintained order—literally held the world together—as technics never could have done.[20]

Ranging over the data of early human development with ingenuity and an unsurpassed erudition, Mumford propounds an unprecedented prehistory and a persuasive ancient history to sustain such arguments. He notes that, in excavations of archaic sites, items of bodily decoration—necklaces and the like—are found alongside people's bones even where tools are not. He observes that, in the first firing of sand into glass, the glass was made into beads rather than more manifestly functional objects. In the earliest smelting of ores into metal in the earliest hearths, the iron was made into rings rather than weapons. And he concludes from such evidence of the fundamentality of ornament that "we are never so sure of the presence of a creature . . . like ourselves as when

18. T&HD, 50–51, 57, 63.
19. T&HD, 8, 9.
20. T&HD, 63, 66–67.

we find" these signs of its determination to "establish a human identity."
From the first, men and women found their crowning concern in the
explication of their own purpose and significance. Jewelry was, to them,
more important—indeed, more basic—than mechanical or military im-
plements.[21]

Paleolithic peoples also used clay as a medium of animal sculpture
thousands of years before they employed it as a material of pottery and
in the construction of their housing. They pursued horticulture, with
its focus on fine solitary specimens, long before agriculture, with its
emphasis on economic yields. In far-flung aspects of their lives, they
cultivated artistic refinement more than they prized the apparent prac-
ticality of productivity. And their preference suggests, to Mumford, that
"man began to domesticate himself before he domesticated either plants
or animals."[22]

Spiritual and ceremonial preoccupations similarly took precedence
over quotidian considerations of survival and material interest. Cattle
were harnessed in ritual processions before they were ever yoked for
farm work. Plows were put to the soil in religious rites before they were
turned to regular tilling. The massive walls built around the first towns,
such as Jericho, "performed a magico-religious function before they
were found to furnish a decided military advantage."[23]

Sacred stimuli inspired the earliest wheeled vehicles, which were
hearses for funerary occasions, not farm wagons or army chariots. Cul-
tic requirements may even have set the shape of the earliest organized
killing, since there is better evidence for human sacrifice than for war in
the neolithic community.[24]

And just as Mumford's intrepid rereading of the archaeological record reveals this extraordinary array of instances in which ideation and
the search for significance preceded utility and the desire for material
wealth and power, so his reconception of the historical record suggests
that every epochal transformation of world civilization—the onset of
the neolithic era, the transition to the pyramid cultures, the collapse
of that first megamachine and the reversion to handicraft, and the

21. T&HD, 111, 150, 111. See also, e.g., 151, 252, 253.
22. T&HD, 123, 136, 132, 123. For Mumford's critique of claims that earliest *homo
sapiens* was a hunter, and his alternative affirmation of the primacy from the first of the
body, of the female, and especially of wits rather than weapons, see 99–101. For his argument that, even in mechanization, humans mechanized themselves before they mechanized their tools or other amplifications of their power, see 168.
23. T&HD, 153, 216.
24. T&HD, 153, 150. See also, e.g., 71, 120, 146–47, 218, 254.

rise of modern kingship and nationalism—had its essential sources in altered religious sensibilities rather than in technological revolutions.

A "new cultural pattern" overspread the planet six or seven millennia before Christ, forming "the underlayer on which all higher civilizations until now have been based." A normative and "psycho-social" shift constituted the crux of the "profound change" of the third millennium B.C., submerging the village cultures of the neolithic age in the vast agglomerations of centralized power and coercion that took shape in "the hot valleys of the Jordan, the Euphrates, the Tigris, the Nile, and the Indus rivers." A massive "religious transformation" preceded and exceeded the rather modest technological achievements of those cradles of empire. Men and women of Egypt, Persia, and kindred kingdoms subordinated their ancient "gods of vegetation and animal fertility" to the new "gods of the sky." They established an "abstract impersonal order" of standardization and "strict human control" by withdrawing authority from deities who suffered human debilities and investing it in others more implacable who could not "be swayed from their course." They conceded the imperious central powers that commanded the pyramids and comparable monuments by conceiving of their rulers as godlings "lowered down from heaven." Divine kingship—the identification of the person of the king with the impersonal order of the heavens—was from the first "a religious phenomenon, not just an assertion of physical prowess [or] a mere enlargement of venerable ancestral authority." And even into the modern era, it was the transcendental religions, especially Christianity, that conditioned the rise of the capitalist world system and the nation-state and supplied the twentieth-century megamachine crucial components that widened its province, augmented its efficiency, and enhanced its acceptability to its subjects.[25]

The congruence of these interpretive archaeological and historical accounts with Mumford's epistemological premises is transparent, and the opening they offer for hope for the future, and perhaps even for politics, is almost as evident. Mumford's unremitting onslaught against the American defense establishment and the corporate order that sustains it misled reviewers and subsequent commentators, who supposed *The Myth of the Machine*—and especially its second volume, *The Pentagon of Power*—a bleaker book than its predecessor, *Technics and Civilization*. In fact *The Myth of the Machine* is markedly more optimistic, and its opti-

25. T&HD, 136, 163–64, 167, 173, 175, 263.

mism is ingredient in its enterprise as the optimism of the earlier study never was.

Of course, it should be said at the outset of all consideration of comparative optimisms and pessimisms that neither Mumford's writings nor his sensibility lend themselves to unequivocal conclusions in the matter. In his first works, in the 1920s, when he was treating topics such as utopias and golden days, Mumford still spoke of the "dissipation of Western civilization," the "dismal" outlook for its culture, and the triumph of a machine "servitude" that "paralyzed" the human spirit. In his autobiographical *Sketches from Life*, he describes a "habit of mind" so "mordant" in the 1930s, when he was composing *Technics and Civilization*, that Van Wyck Brooks routinely sought out Mumford's company to compensate Brooks's own lack of blackness in disposition. And conversely, in the mid-1960s, at the very moment he was hurling himself into the strident critique of American culture of *The Pentagon of Power*, he was hailing, unapologetically, "the New World promise of renewal and responsibility." On the human prospect, Mumford can always be quoted against himself. He was unfailingly ambivalent—now hopeful, now despondent, optimistic in the midst of his most virulent denunciations, pessimistic at his giddiest heights—and it is quite impossible to plot any straight line of development in his sentiments or his presentiments.[26]

Indeed, even if clear conclusions were possible, they might not matter very much. Observing that "much has been made of the gap between optimism and pessimism, and whether a particular writer is a 'prophet of hope' or a 'prophet of doom,' " Langdon Winner has dismissed such distinctions as "in the end . . . vacuous." Winner acknowledges that, in contemporary scholarship, "there exists an almost compulsive need for optimism on this topic." But he goes on to observe, trenchantly, that

if one notices that an Ellul or Mumford or some other author is pessimistic in his conclusions, that becomes sufficient ground for dismissing anything he or she might be saying. Pessimism, it is argued, leads to inaction, which merely reinforces the status quo. This is somehow different from optimism, which leads to activity within the existing arrangement of things and reinforces the status quo.[27]

Nonetheless, it makes scant sense to see *The Myth of the Machine* as an expression of Mumford's deepening desolation, if only because it

26. T&HD, 218, 217, 286, 361, 290.
27. Langdon Winner, *Autonomous Technology: Technics-out-of-Control as a Theme in Political Thought* (Cambridge, Mass., 1977), 152–53.

could not have been much more melancholic than *Technics and Civilization* already was. In that relatively youthful study, the hopes that Mumford invested in his notorious neotechnic phase were submerged almost as soon as they were floated, in his somber recognition that neotechnic potentials would probably be denied by the power of the paleotechnicians to pervert or prevent the emergence of the new age. The concluding chapters of *Technics and Civilization* plainly prefigure the impasse at which we have now arrived: the paleotechnic world dead, the neotechnic powerless to be born. Those chapters hold out only the palest, frailest Veblenian hope that the intrinsic impulsion of the technological system might somehow speed the dawning of the neotechnic day. But even in 1934, Mumford knew better. The very quietism of his reliance on ineluctable technosocial process admitted as much.

By 1970, Mumford was much more explicit in his acknowledgment that the renovative implications of modern science and technology would not be realized effortlessly or inexorably. *The Pentagon of Power* announced that deliberate and determined action would be necessary for the fulfillment of those redemptive possibilities. Indeed, it declared that "massive measures" would be imperative merely to avert "destruction and extermination."[28]

In this anxiety over the fate of the earth, Mumford did ply a rhetoric resented by readers who found his late works at once more dire and more dour than his earlier writings. *The Pentagon of Power,* especially, has its boding, brooding passages, and its critics were not entirely wrong in marking its melancholy. Mumford had never before been so unrelievedly acerbic in his attack on the world picture of the modern megamechanics. He had never so scathingly assailed their "under-dimensioned" model of man or their complicity in the ascent of the scientized, centralized, militarized capitalism nascent since the seventeenth century and advanced to its apotheosis in America after the Second World War. He lashed out relentlessly at that megamachine for its hostility to "organic realities and human needs." He denounced again and again its "cult of anti-life" and its readiness to "extirpate" people to make them "conform to the machine." And he traced those characteristics to their theoretical foundations in the earliest envisionings of modern science—in Bacon, Descartes, and Kepler—and their "underlying desire to reduce man to a machine, for the purpose of establishing uniform behavior in the army and the factory, or any other potentially disorderly collection of men." The mechanical mode was from the first "an

28. TPoP, 80.

auxiliary . . . to political absolutism," as Hobbes made manifest in his idolization of automatism and control and his pathological fear of a brutish disorder that did not exist in the primitive societies in which he posited it.[29]

Some of Mumford's most telling thrusts point up precisely such delusive dispositions—such "psychotic irrationality"—in the managers of the modern megamachine. People who style themselves scientists profess to eliminate subjectivity from their operations but end instead by occluding awareness of their "own subjective inflations, distortions, and perversions." Their very ideology of themselves as immaculate aspirants to mastery over nature betrays by that "obsolete military" metaphor their "paranoid fantasy" of "conquest." And the devotion they thereby display to "the existing power system" is made more "pathological" by the "superstitious savagery" of the political and military elites to whom they attach themselves so abjectly.[30]

Over and over again, Mumford poses "the problem towering over all others: how to prevent the human race from being destroyed by its demoralized but reputedly sane leaders." Increasingly, he comes to see another problem "almost as pressing," that those leaders may be little more demoralized than the masses who follow them. Megatechnics touches almost everyone. It offers, "in return for its unquestioning acceptance, the gift of an effortless life," and its "plethora of prefabricated goods" produces, ultimately, an "existential nausea." It provides, without exertion or stress, a repletion that can only be considered evidence of "infantilism or senility," rather like the "organic deterioration" found in laboratory animals under comparable conditions. Just because it sets itself so adamantly against tradition, the megamachine disdains a vast inheritance of ideas and institutions and inflicts an authentic "brain damage" on its subjects. Just because its animus against the past loosens "the binding ties of habit, custom, and moral code," it drives "an increasing portion of the human race . . . out of its mind."[31]

Mumford's deepest indictment of these megamechanical pathologies of presentism and progress brings him back to the epistemological premises with which he began. Man's "overgrown brain," unconstrained by instinct or even by an overriding intelligence for survival, has always been "at the mercy of his unconscious." Man's consequent vulnerability has, historically, been limited only by his culture and its

29. TPoP, 92–93, 91, 94, 84, 100–101.
30. TPoP, 187, 292, 260–61. See also 186, 224, 290, 319–20, 336.
31. TPoP, 253, 338, 340–41, 399, 368. See also 210–12, 298, 358.

repetition compulsions. But the "Power Complex" transfers those "stabilizing repetitive processes" from man to the machine, "leaving man himself more exposed than ever to his disordered subjectivity." Precisely by relieving people of their routine obligations, and of the stressful social participation that enabled them to maintain a semblance of psychological balance, the megamachine allows the demonic impulses their archaic dominion and places immeasurably augmented technological resources at their disposal besides. Precisely by pretending a pure rationality, the megatechnicians enhance the destructive promptings of the unconscious.[32]

Some of Mumford's most haunting exposition (as well as more than a little of his most venomous rage) is given to the pursuit of such ironies. Perhaps the most poignant passages in the book detail the developments by which benevolent men headed, almost unwittingly, the most decisive advances of dehumanization. Francis Bacon sought surcease in scientific collegiality from the fratricidal strife of seventeenth-century politics; he never fully foresaw that his visionary refuge would one day be a positivist prison. Isaac Newton still knew spiritual mysteries and struggled unavailingly with them; he never supposed that his scientific advances—by far the lesser part of his speculative endeavor—would obscure and even obviate such mysteries for those who came after him. Even earlier, others met similar fates. A malign juggernaut began rolling in the Renaissance, and the noblest spirits since have been impotent to impede it. Leonardo da Vinci bent his best efforts to embodying an ampler model of humanity, but the burgeoning colossus ignored his antipathy and incorporated his technological triumphs. Albert Einstein dedicated a lifetime to the promotion of peace but abetted the engines of war incalculably by a single letter to President Roosevelt. Indeed, almost all the early advocates of nuclear power—Fermi, Szilard, and Urey as well as Einstein—were themselves "unusually humane and morally sensitive" people. They were "the last scientists one would accuse of seeking to establish a new priesthood capable of assuming autocratic authority and wielding satanic power." Yet just such authority and power were "the dreadful consequences of their effort."[33]

All this melancholy admitted, however, *The Myth of the Machine* remains a rousing book rather than a resigned one. Its vigor and venom belie its ironic bemusement. Its vibrancy belies its anguished baffle-

32. TPoP, 368–70. See also 378.
33. TPoP, 255.

ment. The very virulence of its impassioned critique and the very energy of its exhortation to renewal and redemption belie the manifest bleakness of its overt message: the engorgement of the megamachine and the closure of the neotechnic opening.

Moreover, Mumford's emphasis on mind, and values, and visions is much fuller and more focal in *The Myth of the Machine* than it ever was in *Technics and Civilization,* and it is in such spheres that Mumford finally finds the sources of solace he can credit. He still implores that the evolutionary studies, such as biology and history, not the timeless ones, such as physics, be taken as exempla of optimal scientific inquiry capable of encompassing wholeness and metamorphosis as well as analytic abstractions of unchanging entities. But he no longer attaches his appeal so substantially to any of the conventional disciplines. He now relies primarily on his own rich elaboration of the growth of the psyche, and he now reserves his most scabrous censure for the ways in which we are complicitous in our own self-diminution and self-denial.

Among many other things, *The Myth of the Machine* is an account of humankind's advancing abdication of its mind—of its subjectivity and inner integrity—before the pretensions and powers of the machine. It is a nervous narrative of a faith that began as the willed, chosen worship of the sun—of light, in McLuhan's hypnotic, anaesthetic sense—and that became over subsequent centuries less freely offered and more harshly demanded. It is a fiery, fearful interpretation of people's increasing propensity to concede increasing portions of their own vitality and autonomy to the megamachine or, more accurately, to their imagination and creation and construction of that megamachine. And it is a searing summons to men and women to cease such self-abasement and recover "for human use the mechanized and electrified wasteland that is now being constructed, at man's expense and to his permanent loss, for the benefit of the megamachine."[34]

As Mumford grew older, he saw more clearly the futility of counting on mechanism to cure the corruptions of mechanism. As he grew more pessimistic about our probable fate, he became more resolute in his refusal of his own rational assessment. As he said, "I still believe in miracles." And as he knew, the realm of miracles was the realm of faith and spirit and mind where he situated *The Myth of the Machine,* not the domain of dialectical, developmental automaticity on which he had depended in *Technics and Civilization.*[35]

34. TPoP, 76. See also 75, 78, 92–93, 98, 191, 210–11, 224–28, 243, 276, 279.
35. Miller, ed., *Mumford Reader,* 302.

The contrast between Mumford and the great French student of contemporary technological consciousness, Jacques Ellul, illuminates Mumford's sensibility and strategies in these regards. In his preface to *The Technological Society*, Ellul ponders the possibility of men and women taking thought about their plight and overcoming the essential determinism of "the technological phenomenon." How is this to be done? Ellul confesses that he does not know, but he proceeds to state that the first step "is to arouse the reader to an awareness of technological necessity and what it means. It is a call to the sleeper to awake." Mumford speaks several times in similar accents, but where Ellul calls for recognition and reasoned consciousness, Mumford hopes for widespread religious renewal. Where Ellul, the realist, insists that "there *are* ways out . . . but nobody wants any part of them," Mumford, the Platonist, discounts people's declarations of their desires because he believes the breakthrough will not be a rational one anyway. Where Ellul demands "a better basis" for rebellion than "blind acts of unreasonable faith," Mumford welcomes such stirrings of religious revolt.[36]

There is irony in Ellul refusing to countenance what he craves and in Mumford entreating what he does not expect. There is irony upon irony in Ellul, a profoundly faithful Christian, austerely renouncing resistance rooted in faith and Mumford, an indifferent believer at best, boldly bidding transformation impelled by religious fervor. But there is also an exquisite aptness in the divergences. In urging any antagonism to *la technique* at all, Ellul violates the assumptions of his own arguments for technological automatism and the technological conditioning of thought. In courting conversions, Mumford follows the flow of his conviction that the source of every profound social shift is spiritual. Having frankly admitted that there is no basis for transformation intrinsic to the megamachine itself—an admission he refused to make in *Technics and Civilization*—Mumford can consistently anticipate alteration from outside the Leviathan.

As if deliberately, Mumford distinguishes himself from Ellul at every opportunity in their essentially concordant analyses, and the distinctions unfailingly disclose Mumford as the more optimistic of the two men. Ellul propounds an irresistibly linear development of modern technique; Mumford establishes a much longer temporal perspective in which history reverses its direction again and again. Ellul argues that technique increasingly obviates individual choice; Mumford insists on

36. Jacques Ellul, *The Technological Society*, trans. John Wilkinson (New York, 1964), xxxii-xxxiii, xvii-xviii.

the imperative of volition. Ellul defines technique in terms of "the one best way"; Mumford celebrates proliferous plenitude. Ellul regrets the impossibility, under modern conditions, of the community he idealizes; Mumford invested vast energies over several decades in the regional project he revered. And Ellul devotes his brilliance, ultimately, to an intensification of the myth of invincible technology; Mumford sets himself to dispel that myth and demystify the megamachine.[37]

Mumford takes up such tasks so ardently because, on his own Platonistic premises, that myth is and always has been the essential support of the megamachine. From its first formulation by Francis Bacon, the modern mechanistic world view was a faith that outran the empirical evidence and remade the world in its own image. To this very day, despite its massive nuclear arsenals, its monstrous bureaucracies, and its multitudinous corporate consorts, the Pentagon depends in the final analysis on the acquiescence and attachment of the people. On just that account, it is far more vulnerable than its adherents imagine.

Mumford's obsessive assaults on the warfare state's vaunted veneer of scientific rationality are more than just raging rhetoric. They are designed to disclose its reliance on "both the human components and the religious ideology" of its bureaucracy and its military-industrial priesthood. They are intended to deny that its pretensions are above the failings of its individual actors and beyond the ravages of time. Above all, they are meant to enable us to see that our awesome apparatus can no more exempt itself from the vortex of change than any other historical formation.[38]

Like the empires of the Pyramid Age—the original megamachines— the two great power complexes that arose after the Second World War are structures of centralized exploitation maintained by military rulers with the sanction and support of religion and science. They therefore require the same priestly monopoly of all "higher knowledge" that their predecessors did; they shroud it in the secrecy of security designations and cloister it as classified information.[39]

The managers of the modern megamachines know, as the managers of the ancient ones did, that not even the "mechanized human parts" of the colossi can be "permanently held together without being sustained by a profound magico-religious faith in the system itself." In the era of

37. Ellul, *Technological Society*, 79–81, 55, 207–08, 215, 263–65, 301–03; T&HD, 224.
38. T&HD, 199.
39. T&HD, 189, 190, 199.

the pharaohs, megamechanical dynasties collapsed when "the grim impositions" of the rulers "became intolerable"—despite their "superb technological achievements"—and when subjects ceased to concede the "religious exaltation" of divine kingship. Even those most aloof and imperious of Leviathans proved to exist "on a basis of human beliefs, which may crumble, of human decisions, which may prove fallible, and human consent, which, when the magic becomes discredited, may be withheld."[40]

Just as "the basic institutional transformations that preceded the construction of the megamachine were magical and religious," so "the most effective reaction against it drew on the same potent sources." The pharaonic power complexes were "as frail and vulnerable as the theologico-magical conceptions that were essential to their performance." And as then, so now. If and when we come to doubt the worthiness of our institutions and withdraw from them our inner allegiance, they too, maintains Mumford, will collapse. Mind remains primary. Mind—more exactly, mind in history—was ingredient in the emergence of the megamachine and will ultimately be equally ingredient in its demise. Platonism comes full circle to politics.[41]

Of course, it is precisely politics that Mumford's critics contend he cannot confront. Several of them doubt that "the gates of the technocratic prison will open automatically, despite their ancient rusty hinges, as soon as we choose to walk out." They suspect instead "that fundamental change may not come about so easily, that whether the technocratic prison is the work of the human will or not[,] it is unlikely that the gates will open automatically but only when we are prepared to make some difficult political and economic decisions, if even then." They lament in that light Mumford's "political naiveté" and his substitution of prophecy for politics. Conceding his contention that we are on the eve of destruction, they merely maintain that "to escape we are going to have to make some difficult decisions, yet Mumford makes them seem easy—simply matters of life over death, good over evil. . . . He tells us what is wrong, but not how to set it right[,] and leaves us feeling both distressed and impotent." And of course there is something to be said for such critics and such criticisms.[42]

But Mumford is not as obtuse to these issues as his detractors sup-

40. T&HD, 229, 230, 190, 230.
41. T&HD, 231, 190.
42. Weber, "Mumford But Not Vintage," 108; Ferkiss, "The Megamachine Reconstituted," 499–500.

pose. He is neither so infatuated with his own prophetic voice as to ignore practical constraints nor so enamored of his historical reconfigurations as to imagine that they can be transposed without trouble to another megamachine in another millennium. He does demand that the popular disillusionment that underlaid the revolts that ignited in "seemingly spontaneous combustion" across India, Persia, Palestine, Greece, and Rome, beginning between the ninth and sixth centuries B.C., be taken with supreme seriousness. He does insist that those risings be seen as evidence of the power of widespread refusal of reverence, in fact as well as in the fancies of that fevered moment at the end of the sixties when *The Myth of the Machine* was taking shape. Yet he is more determined to seek the structure than simply to assert the fact of such successful resistance to the levies of technocracy. He is keen to show that the revolts of that epoch began in the mind every bit as much as the megamachines they helped to overthrow began in the mind. He is much keener to comprehend the conditions and the character of those revolts: the sources of vulnerability of the ancient empires and the sources of strength of the transformations taught by Amos, Hesiod, Lao-Tzu, and other reformers and rebels of that era.[43]

In Mumford's view, the masters of the megamachine have always operated in a state of "anxious tension" even as they promoted the myth of their invincibility. They have always dreaded treason and heresy even as they required "submissive faith and unqualified obedience to the royal will." They have always been obsessed with subversion, and they still are. Their megamachine is "an elephant that fears even the smallest mouse." It tends to a "technological arrogance" that offends even its followers. It is disposed to "misbehaviors of cold intelligence" that provoke reactions of upsurgent vitality and indeed "savage irrationality" among the masses. And simultaneously it is subject to "miscalculations and ignominious breakdowns" that diminish the credibility of its "official caste" and "call into question both their basic assumptions and their ultimate objectives."[44]

These flaws and failings lead to "disintegration and demoralization . . . visible in every culture that the renovated power system has even remotely touched." The beneficiaries of the megamachine themselves show "an increasing unwillingness to keep the system in operation" by their own unstinting efforts. They seek rather to wring from it ever more substantial rewards while "performing ever more reluctantly a

43. T&HD, 258.
44. T&HD, 190; TPoP, 246, 303, 313, 312.

minimal amount of work and accepting an equally minimal degree of responsibility." As they are progressively deprived of old skills and autonomies by automation and new modes of centralized control, they display mounting measures of "psychological absenteeism."[45]

A reservoir of commitment does remain, but it tends steadily to depletion, because it is merely a residuum of an "archaic moral culture" to which the megamachine is inherently inimical. In this attrition of traditional moral and social values, instilled under the auspices of "a more lovable, life-sustaining world," power is "stripped of [its] historic clothes." All that is left of humanity are "two components no longer recognizably human: the automaton and the id." And the system itself is profoundly imperiled, "for it has no values of its own"—no "appealing moral alternative" of rational distribution or social justice—to supplant those it undermines. It has only its megatechnics, empty at its ethical core of every aim beyond the removal of "all limitations on productivity and power." It has only "its own absolute: the support of the power complex."[46]

At this crisis, according to Mumford, there is only one effective way of "conserving the genuine achievements" of megamechanical technology, and that is "to alter the ideological basis of the whole system." The instances of such alteration that he adduces are those wrought by the remarkable moral mentors of the first millennium B.C. Those men confronted a comparable disaffection from power and material wealth abstracted from communal purpose and significance. Those men gave voice to a popular movement that could no longer accept "assumptions that equated human welfare and the will of the gods with centralized power, military dominance, and increasing economic exploitation." Those men, scattered across Europe, the Middle East, and Asia—Isaiah and Buddha, Confucius and Solon, Socrates and Jesus—saw that the elaboration of a new ideological basis of life "is a human, not a technical, problem" and that it "admits only a human solution." They denounced the myth of the megamachine, asserted "the spirit against the shell," and beckoned believers to a new kingdom of righteousness, cooperation, and humility. They challenged those they inspired to become new men and women. They balked at the virtues and achievements of civilization as much as they condemned its evils. Scorning "all the pomps and vanities of worldly success," they persuaded rather than commanded and taught rather than ruled. Spurning all opportunities to

45. TPoP, 344, 347, 348.
46. TPoP, 351, 350, 352, 348, 351, 352.

consolidate their authority, they urged their adherents to "return to their own centers and be guided by their hidden lights." Their new vision diverted energy from the service of civilization "more by withdrawal and abstention than by any overt struggle with the ruling classes."[47]

In Mumford's mind, this Platonic politics of withdrawal and abstention is as pertinent to our present practice as to our ethical ideals. This rejection of the rewards of large-scale organization and this affirmation of the inner identity against the outer suggest, indeed, a more plausible political programme than anything his critics offer at this desperate juncture, and not just because a similar politics of prophecy has prevailed again and again in the past. Mumford means to avoid clashes that cannot be won. He assumes, as the romantic realists do not, that the power complex cannot be conquered by direct confrontation. He knows that such an assault would be a battle fought on the megamachine's terrain by the megamachine's rules, a battle against vastly superior forces. He conjures a rising that does not depend on physical weapons just because such a rising cannot be quelled with physical weapons.

More than that, he entreats avoidance of an overt struggle with the ruling classes because he does not believe such a struggle can be won even if it is won. He is haunted by the emergence of the American megamachine after the Second World War and by the ways he believes the Nazis transmitted their pathologies, irrationalities, and rigidities to their New World conquerors, who rebuilt and perfected the fascist model of the warfaring state. He cannot shake his agonized conviction that any assault on the megamachine would necessarily be conducted in the very image of the megamachine, with the very instruments of centralized oppression it professed to repudiate.[48]

In just such tortured turns, Mumford keeps faith with his understanding of the contingency of history. At the same time, in the multitudinous continuities that run through his writings from first to last, he keeps faith with himself. *The Myth of the Machine* scouts the far frontiers even as it goes over old ground. It is his most searching reconnaissance of contemporary culture and consciousness, yet it returns to his earliest intellectual attachments—to Plato and the primacy of mind, to regionalism and the centrality of the organic environment, to utopianism and its applications in a tangled, troublous world—and also to his first ma-

---

47. TPoP, 352; T&HD, 258, 259, 260, 261.
48. TPoP, 250–51, 360–67, 408.

ture masterwork. It follows *Technics and Civilization* in its determination to demystify the machine, its insistence on history and biology as the most essential of sciences, its awareness of the play of power and money on technology, and its passion for wholeness and its rage against abstraction run amok. It is a worthy and wondrous capstone of his career not least because, in following that brilliant book, it goes so much further. It achieves a more expansive and vivid development of the psychological, epistemological, and spiritual premises of positions latent but still largely inarticulate in *Technics and Civilization*. It wrestles more conscientiously and convincingly with the revolutionary project implicit in that earlier work.

Almost on every page, *The Myth of the Machine* deepens the despair that was already discernible in *Technics and Civilization*. Mumford does not doubt that ours is a culture drifting ever further from human fullness and vitality, ever closer to death. Yet almost always, he refuses to give in. Though he predicates his entire argument on the power of the mind, he disdains the conclusions to which his intellect impels him. Defiantly, he bends his extraordinary erudition to the task of fashioning the only flickering hope he can credit. No one in our time has done better than Mumford in delineating our dilemmas or evoking their urgency. No one has done better at allowing men and women of integrity the faintest faith that we may yet elude our frightening fate.

# NINE

# Dr. Spock: The Confidence Man

In one sense, there is nothing unusual at all in the modern American obsession with child-rearing. Americans have been ill at ease about the younger generation, and preoccupied with it, for centuries.

But in another sense there is something odd indeed about this extravagant anxiety. Few parents anywhere have ever put themselves as hugely and hopefully in the hands of child-care counselors as American parents of the aspiring classes have in the twentieth century. And few parents anywhere have ever had so hard a time raising their children.

These difficulties imply the plausibility of an exploration of the very advice parents attended, but it would be best to be clear at the outset about the logic and the limitations of such an undertaking. For the investigation of advice is, inevitably, a perilous enterprise. We have no clear notion of who heeds such advice, or in what sense. We rarely even know how many parents bought a particular baby-care book, and we virtually never know the social strata from which they came. We do not know whether they ever actually read the book or, if they did, which parts they took to heart. We cannot recover the conditions under which, or the state of mind in which, they sought expert advice, so that, given what we know of selective perception, we cannot be confident of the meaning they made of what they read. And above all we do not know what they really did about what they read.

We do not know, therefore, how to treat the preachments of the past

From *The Family in History,* ed. Charles Rosenberg (Philadelphia: University of Pennsylvania Press, 1975), 179–207.

or even those of the present. In any strong sense of knowing, we prob-ably never will. But our ignorance does not dictate on that account a turning to sources other than those of the prescriptive literature, be-cause the fact of the matter is that such sources afford no easier or more reliable access to parent behavior. We can penetrate the process of so-cialization in the present only for those atypical subjects willing to sub-mit to surveillance in bringing up their children and in the past only for those atypical elites able—or those aberrant minorities obliged—to leave records of their acts and intentions. The relation between these parents and the wider population is at least as problematic as the rela-tion of advice to audience and action.[1] And in any case we can discover almost nothing, either past or present, of the identificational and imita-tive transactions we now take to be most elemental in the enculturation of the young, since such modes are so largely nonverbal.[2]

If we would enter at all, then, into the play of parents and children, we must enter inferentially rather than by direct and definitive observa-tion. And as soon as we recognize that, we have also to see that infer-ences founded on manuals of instruction and idealization are, in prin-ciple, exactly as plausible or implausible as any others. The issue is not the propriety of establishing inferences on the basis of advice but the soundness of the particular inferences built on that basis, and the illu-mination they afford.

Of such inferences, there are three fundamental categories. The first moves backwards from admonition to practice, assuming that parents did, by and large, follow the tuition they were given and that the man-uals do, within vague but determinate limits, present realistically the raising of children. The second moves forward from advice to future outcomes, attempting to predict or explain the sorts of adults to be ex-pected from such regimens of rearing if they were indeed imposed. And the third simply moves sideways or perhaps never moves at all. It con-cedes that the guidebooks are evidence only of values and attempts es-sentially to analyze those values. It focuses, therefore, on parents rather than on children or parent-child interactions.

The first, if it is not entirely tautological, rests on an extremely shaky

1. On the atypicality of contemporary informants, see, for example, Joseph Church, *Three Babies* (New York, 1966), vii. On the atypicality of the most widely studied child-hood of the past, see Elizabeth Marvick, "The Character of Louis XIII: The Role of His Physician," *Journal of Interdisciplinary History* 4 (1973–74): 347–74.

2. See Jay Mechling, "A Role-Learning Model for the Study of Historical Change in Parent Behavior; with a Test of the Model on the Behavior of American Parents in the Great Depression" (Ph.D. diss., University of Pennsylvania, 1971).

empirical bottom. We know from a number of studies that there are significant misfittings between parents' knowledge of proper conduct and their actual behavior.[3] And we know from several other studies that, within given families, mother and father often set distinctly different standards for their offspring, so that it hardly seems safe to infer from a single manual to a single parental mode of rearing.[4]

The second suffers all the debilities of the first, since the prediction of future behavior on the basis of present instruction demands that such instruction be indeed acted upon, and it incurs still others all its own. Empirical evidence, again, suggests that there is no simple and straight-forward transfer from the attitudes inculcated by books to the actual adoption of such habits of mind by children grown to maturity.[5]

The only sort of inference that seems truly tenable, then, and the only one that will be undertaken in earnest here, is to parental and societal values. For it is, after all, adults who write the baby-care books, adults who publish them, and adults who purchase them. We will wonder, briefly, at the end, about the prospect for the future if the adult values delineated in this essay should be successfully transmitted to the generations to come, in child-rearing or otherwise; but it will be worth our wondering only if we comprehend the values themselves compellingly in the first place.

To gain such comprehension, we will have to confront the advice in its entirety. Parents may or may not have read it that way, but there is almost no way to know. We cannot guess the parts they ignored or re-

3. The problematic relation of ideals and actualities is proverbial; conceptualization and demonstration that is apposite in this context include Allen Edwards, *The Social Desirability Variable in Personality Assessment and Research* (New York, 1957), and David Marlowe and Douglas Crowne, "Social Desirability and Response to Perceived Situational Demands," *Journal of Consulting Psychology* 25 (1961): 109–15. For specific applications to parent behavior, see, e.g., Daniel Miller and Guy Swanson, *The Changing American Parent* (New York, 1958), 223; Marian Yarrow, John Campbell, and Roger Burton, *Child Rearing: An Inquiry into Research and Methods* (San Francisco, 1968), 137–40; Grace Brody, "Relationship between Maternal Attitudes and Behavior," *Journal of Personality and Social Psychology* 2 (1965): 317–23; Michael Zunich, "Relationship between Maternal Behavior and Attitudes toward Children," *Journal of Genetic Psychology* 100 (1962): 155–65.

4. See Kenneth Davidson et al., "Differences between Mothers and Fathers of Low Anxious and High Anxious Children," *Child Development* 29 (1958): 155–60; Leonard Eron et al., "Comparison of Data Obtained from Mothers and Fathers on Childrearing Practices and their Relation to Child Aggression," *Child Development* 32 (1961): 457–75; Donald Peterson et al., "Parental Attitudes and Child Adjustment," *Child Development* 30 (1959): 119–30; M. Kent Jennings and Kenneth Langton, "Mothers versus Fathers: The Formation of Political Orientations among Young Americans," *The Journal of Politics* 31 (1969): 329–58.

5. David McClelland, *The Achieving Society* (Princeton, N.J., 1961), 101–2.

jected if they did ignore or reject any, and we could not trust their answers even if we were able to ask them explicitly.[6] So we must eschew all efforts to divine what parents did see in the advice and address ourselves instead to what was there to be seen. We must seek a reconstruction of the pervading assumptions and injunctions of the text. And we must be content with the conviction that, in so doing, we accept a postulate neither more nor less hazardous, in principle, than what must obtain in more traditional domains. For the problems of interpretation and of imputation to an audience are hardly peculiar to the literature of child-rearing. A Puritan sermon too must have meant different things to its diverse auditors and a Roosevelt campaign promise to its readers. We cannot get inside the minds of these audiences either, except by interpretation. We have only the texts. Yet if we are not too chary of interpretation—if we admit its inevitability and ask rather about the adequacy of its specific showings and the insight they invite—the texts may be sufficient.

The text to which this essay essentially attends is Benjamin Spock's *Baby and Child Care.* The best-selling handbook for parents ever published, it is a text that would deserve much closer consideration than it has had even if it were manifestly eccentric. But in fact it is by no means odd or unrepresentative. It appeared at a time when any number of similar counsels were emerging in other quarters, and it appeared in a social context common to them all.[7] The argument to be set forth here could almost as readily have been based on those other advices. We will confine ourselves to Spock primarily to provide, in the integrity of a single text, a concentrated focus for analysis.

But we must begin before Spock if we would understand his impact. We must begin at the beginning of the twentieth century and the advent

6. See Lillian Robbins, "The Accuracy of Parental Recall of Aspects of Child Development and of Child-Rearing Practices," *Journal of Abnormal and Social Psychology* 66 (1963): 261–70; Marian Yarrow, John Campbell, and Roger Burton, "Reliability of Maternal Retrospection: A Preliminary Report," *Family Process* 3 (1964): 207–18.

7. See Celia Stendler, "Sixty Years of Child Training Practices," *The Journal of Pediatrics* 36 (1950): 122–34; Clark Vincent, "Trends in Infant Care Ideas," *Child Development* 22 (1951): 199–209; and Martha Wolfenstein, "Fun Morality: An Analysis of Recent American Child-Training Literature," in *Childhood in Contemporary Cultures,* ed. Margaret Mead and Martha Wolfenstein (Chicago, 1955): 168–78. For some striking convergences with actual practices as well, see Urie Bronfenbrenner, "The Changing American Child—A Speculative Analysis," *Journal of Social Issues* 17 (1961): 6–18; Evelyn Duvall, "Conceptions of Parenthood," *American Journal of Sociology* 52 (1946): 193–203; and Sibylle Escalona, "A Commentary upon Some Recent Changes in Child-Rearing Practices." *Child Development* 20 (1949): 157–62.

of formal psychological prescription for parents.[8] For it was then that American mothers and fathers of the ambitious middle classes faced for the first time a distinctively modern problem: the necessity to cope not merely with the immemorial dilemmas of daily attention to their off-spring but also with the complications induced by the very advice they sought in the discharge of such duties. In the face of that necessity, their behavior began to be fraught with significances they had scarcely sus-pected before. They could no longer even cuddle the baby when he cried, or be impatient with him when he soiled his diapers, without worrying about one scientifically authoritative injunction or another. And more, though they dared not do the wrong things, they could not do the right ones.

They dared not do the wrong things because the experts insisted that a child's character could be so "spoiled by bad handling" that it would be impossible to "say that the damage is ever repaired." They could not do the right things because those experts never did agree on what such things were. Conscientious parents of the first decades of the century confronted, in the collective counsels of traditionalists, progressives, Freudians, and Watsonians, a crazyquilt canon that at once required stern discipline and gentle indulgence, detachment and intimacy, pro-hibition and permissiveness. The more earnest parents were, the more anxious they were bound to be.[9]

Eventually, even the experts could stand back from such work and see that it was not entirely satisfactory. So around the time of the Second World War, a few of them began to add that, in the face of their corrod-ing cares, proper parents ought to relax. The idea was probably about as helpful as a coach telling his team before the big game not to be nervous, but it was where Doctor Spock came in.

Benjamin Spock's first *Baby and Child Care* was published in 1946.[10] Through two subsequent revisions, more than two hundred printings, and sales of over twenty million copies, it has remained as it began: a manual of tension-management for parents, premised on a simple little

8. On the rise of formal psychological guidance over the course of the twentieth cen-tury, at the expense of more strictly medical counsel, see Vincent, "Infant Care Ideas."

9. John Watson, *Psychological Care of Infant and Child* (New York, 1928), 3. On the quandaries of conscientious parents, Helen Merrell Lynd, *On Shame and the Search for Identity* (New York, 1958), 61n.

10. The first edition was published simultaneously in hardcover, *The Common Sense Book of Baby and Child Care* (New York), and paperback, *The Pocket Book of Baby and Child Care* (New York), in 1946. The second edition, *The Common Sense Book of Baby and Child Care* (New York) in hardcover, and *Baby and Child Care* (New York) in paperback, was published in 1957. The third edition, *Baby and Child Care* (New York) in hardcover, and

confidence trick. For even as its author acknowledges at the outset the unease of his readers, he diverts it by directing them from doubts about their functional competence to assurances of their instinctual adequacy. "Trust yourself," he tells them, in the celebrated title of his opening passage. "What good mothers and fathers instinctively feel like doing for their babies is usually best."[11]

The equation of inclination and aptness makes a virtue out of everything spontaneous and a vice out of all that is deliberate or controlled. The mother who "feels like" comforting her crying child should go ahead, without fear of spoiling him. Her very desire to give such solace makes it "natural and right." The father who gets angry with his toddler had "better" avow it openly. His prudential calculation of other responses would be "grim" and "unnatural." For simply "on general principle," it is "safer to do things the natural way." Unrelieved irritations and "suppressed" resentments are "not good for" parents, nor for their children either. Easy indulgence of impulse is what the doctor orders.[12]

Moreover, such celebration of hedonic immediacy depends on Spock's most fundamental notions of human nature. His assumption of the benevolence of the instincts underlies his invitation to trust them. His supposition that what wells up from within will be basically benign sustains his incitements to self-confidence. Babies are, by disposition, "friendly and reasonable." They are "meant" to be "free, warm, life-loving" people.[13]

They are not, therefore, the dangerous little beasts whose terrifying drives haunted the imaginations of older Americans. They move instead in milder climes, where the heats of erotic excitement and the blasts of savage fury rarely reach.[14] Their sexual pleasures are only satisfactions of a "wholesome curiosity," not consummations of an indomitable

---

Baby and Child Care (New York) in paper, was issued in 1968. The alterations are more substantial between the first and second editions than between the second and third, but in both cases the changes serve basically to reduce the original realm of "permissiveness" and enlarge the sphere of parental control. For a discussion of the differences, see Lynn Bloom, Doctor Spock: Biography of a Conservative Radical (Indianapolis, 1972), chap. 6.

So as not to triplicate citations, all references not otherwise noted will be to the third (1968) edition in its more accessible form, the Pocket Books paperback.

11. Baby and Child Care, 3–4. See also 9.

12. Ibid., 320, 20–22, 338, 72, 345, 250. See also 4, 19, 61, 186, 190, 192, 193, 222, 253, 262, 271, 275–77, 327, 329, 339, 345, 439. For a variety of ways in which nature knows best, see 72, 81–82, 123–24, 157, 173, 263; though cf. 170.

13. Ibid, 232, 327. See also 4, 14, 16, 281.

14. For a similar configuration, at almost exactly the same point in time, in the Infant Care bulletins of the Children's Bureau of the U.S. Department of Labor, see Wolfenstein, "Fun Morality."

itch.[15] Their aggressive impulses spring from misunderstanding or parental ineptitude, not native ferocity.[16] So if a child goes upstairs to "play doctor" with the girl next door, or if he smashes his friend's toy or his little brother's finger, his derelictions do not signify the eruption of untoward impulse or prophesy for him a career of urgent craving. They merely represent episodes of exploratory development.[17]

Spock sets the sweet positivity of these inquisitive little innocents in an environment consistent with, and supremely congenial to, their own dispassion. He refuses to concede that "life is a struggle" and affirms on the contrary the elemental harmony of things. In a cosmos that is "peaceful," amid relations that are "quietly friendly," "fond" and "gentle," he discovers all about him a wondrous concordance of human needs and natural supply.[18]

In the feeding of infants, for example, he finds parables on the reliability of the child's instincts and the safety of indulging them. Studies of "self-demand" show that even newborn babies manage well on their own initiative in eating, so a mother may presume that her child already "knows a lot" about his own nutritional needs. She can trust his vagrant fancies. She "doesn't have to worry" if he suddenly spurns string beans. She can give in "without worrying about the consequences" if all at once he has to have ice cream or Queen Anne cherries. He is a satisfactorily self-regulating organism. He will want what he needs and need what he wants, difficult though it is "for us moderns to have this kind of confidence in our children's appetites."[19] And in sleeping, walking, bladder control, and a number of other motor controls and sustenance functions, Spock posits a similar coincidence of appetite and ability and advocates an identical confidence in the provision of nature.[20]

In social behavior, everything works out equally well. Just as the child covets what is good for him, so he seeks willingly what is seemly and convenient for society. He has no propensities that stand in any real

15. *Baby and Child Care,* 372. See also 379.

16. Ibid, 233–34, 319. Spock does occasionally concede that aggression is to be expected in early childhood (see 311, 328), but he acknowledges little or none thereafter.

17. In truth, there is nothing that can count against this assumption; any child who is "preoccupied with sex" or aggression is dismissed as abnormal and shunted off to see "a good children's psychiatrist." See 311, 319, 372, 373.

18. Ibid., 59, 169–70.

19. Ibid., 58, 279–81. See also 61, 68, 69, 125, 303–4, 436, 439. Spock seems to have been profoundly affected by these studies, which were conducted just a few years before the original publication of *Baby and Child Care.* Here and elsewhere, feeding functions paradigmatically for Spock in his conception of the appetites.

20. See, for example, ibid., 81–82, 157, 166–67, 238, 263, 323.

antagonism to civilized convention. He has no need to disengage himself from his fellows to pursue his own identity. He aims merely at an alignment with his world. "Every hour of every day," he tries to emulate his elders and assimilate grown-up modes. With all his heart, he wishes to "fit into the family's way of doing things." He "wants" to accept obligations. He "prefer[s] to be helpful." For the fact is that "three-quarters of the things that we think we must impose on children as unpleasant duties are things that they enjoy learning to do themselves." If anything, it is the absence of imposition that disturbs children, because they know very well when they are "getting away with too much naughtiness" and would actually "like to be stopped" at such times. Their waywardness is no irresistible expression of an imperial id but only a departure from their dearest ideals.[21]

The success of a book based on premises such as these is more than a little puzzling. Ascetic civilizations do not display such acceptance of instinct. Competitive cultures do not so eagerly embrace a conception of human nature so amiable and mild. And yet Benjamin Spock breaks precisely with that dominant tradition in America that has considered children as scaled-down savages, the tradition that modern sociology sustains when it compares the births of successive generations to recurrent barbarian invasions.[22] His nonpareils do not need to be salvaged for society because they are never unfitted for it in the first place. Their socialization is not dependent on the breaking of an obdurate will or the sublimation of a polymorphous penchant. Their growth is not conditional on a gracious escape from depravity. They have only to learn specific roles and routines, because from the moment they draw breath (and as long as they are not undone by adults) they are creative and caring human beings.[23]

The success of the book is also curious because its supposition of the child's perfect endowment is an extraordinarily inconvenient one for the parents of the prodigy. They must bear the fearful burden of preserving his perfection intact through his youth, yet they can claim only the most paltry credit if they manage the task. For theirs is not the Pygmalion part on the Spockian stage. They do not mold the child, nor do they

21. Ibid, 308, 4–5, 326, 324, 247, 330. See also 22–23. Spock imagines the child so perfectly cooperative and companionable that even good manners, the very epitome of artifice, "come naturally" to him; see 327.

22. Roger Brown, *Social Psychology* (New York, 1965), 193. The specific image is from Talcott Parsons.

23. *Baby and Child Care*, 16.

even bring forth his dormant potential.[24] An infant is as inquiring, as expressive, and as good as he will ever be; and his glory is his by birthright. His parents have no portion of it but the blame if he should fall away from it.

Nothing whatever of ill inheres in a child. He does not misbehave unless he is "bossed and disciplined too much." He is not "naturally deceitful,"and he does not tell lies unless "under too much pressure." He is "born to be" inquisitive and enthusiastic, and he does not become lazy unless his initial eagerness for life is "trained out of" him. He is a hearty eater at the outset, and he does not desist unless his mother devotes "knowledge and many months of hard work to make a feeding problem." Indeed, even when Spock is obliged to acknowledge the occasional complicity of the little one in a vicious circle of mutual animosity, he never doubts that "the parent starts it." Children are just not naturally ornery. Any of them who act that way must be products of parental ruination.[25]

And Spock does invoke that spectre of ruination often enough to recall parents after all to the portentousness of their responsibility. For it is they who have the ominous power to shatter the child's primal innocence and set the shape of his discontent "forever." It is their word "uttered in a thoughtless or angry moment" that can "destroy the child's confidence," their nagging that can precipitate troubles that "last for years," and their failure to afford the child love and security that can cause "irreparable harm."[26]

In the face of this forbidding awareness, Spock's appeals for confidence fade. He may know that mothers and fathers cannot come to any assurance of their own adequacy if they have to rely on physicians and psychiatrists in every extremity, but he is nonetheless unwilling to leave parents to their own intuitions at such junctures. Before the mother ever brings the baby home from the hospital, he urges her to leave things wholly "in the doctor's hands." As soon as she gets her charge across the threshold, he tells her she "ought" to have a visiting nurse. And as the days go by, he presses her again and again to "ask the doctor"

---

24. Though cf. the otherwise splendid essay of Philip Slater, *The Pursuit of Loneliness* (Boston, 1970), chap. 3.

25. *Baby and Child Care,* 319, 580, 367, 407, 436, 326. See also 233–34, 263, 279–80, 328–30, 331, 372, 379, and, for further elaboration on the theme of feeding, which serves as a model for other impositions on "natural appetite," 123–24, 439.

26. Ibid., 589, 282–83, 567. See also 200, 408, 418, 517, 521, 522.

rather than decide for herself, in everything from her choice of baby toys to the baby's own bowel movements.[27]

Of course, the mother who could truly trust herself would not be bothered by these aspersions on her competence. She would never have needed a book to be convinced of it in the first place. But with just those mothers who most required confirmation of their abilities, Spock strains to the limit the confidence he commends. He bids such women be natural, and then, dozens of times over, he lets them see how "easy" it is "to be mistaken" in diagnosis and how "absolutely necessary" therefore to have "close medical supervision" of the child.[28] Or he allows them a nominal autonomy and then compromises it by instructions so specific as to stifle their independence anyway. In his advice on bathing the baby, for instance, he encourages the mother to "enjoy it" but orchestrates her action in such detail that he has even to remind her to take off her wrist watch before beginning. In his directions for cleaning soiled diapers he actually tells her to "hold tight" while she rinses the garments in the toilet.[29]

Moreover, Spock has quite as equivocal a faith, ultimately, in Mother Nature as he has in the mothers of children. And in some sense he almost has to. If natural processes and predilections were actually as reliable as he often asserts, there would be no need for child psychiatrists or professors of pediatrics. If babies did infallibly do as their parents preferred, and if vitamin deficiencies and gastrocolic reflex irregularities and a hundred other nuisances of flesh and spirit were unknown in nature, there would be no occasion at all for professional expertise or intervention. *Baby and Child Care* would be a contradiction in terms.

As it is, however, Spock hedges on the sanctity of spontaneous inclinations. He does prefer an image of affairs suffused with moral significance, tending always to the optimal in the best of all possible worlds. He does hold forth fulsomely, when he can follow his preference, on

27. Ibid, 60, 49, 172. For a wider sample of situations in which to consult doctors or psychiatrists, see, e.g., 174, 176–77, 177, 197, 282, 283, 354, 359, 367, 386, 409, 436, 563.

28. Ibid., 205, 199, 190. Spock issues far too many of these injunctions to cite: more than one hundred fifty in all, and eighty-six (well over one every other page) on 395–540 alone.

29. Ibid., 155–56, 176. See also 453–57 for five pages of painfully detailed description of the simple procedure of taking the child's temperature, and 266–67 for a list of thirty-six dos and don'ts hard on the heels of an insistence that parents "cannot prevent all accidents" and will "only make a child timid" if they try.

"how smoothly Nature works things out."[30] But after all his effulgent rhetoric is spent, he knows that there remain a few matters that cannot be contained so felicitously. The breasts, as an example, are susceptible to a number of ills that a can of condensed milk is not. They engorge, they cake, they get infected. The nipples become sore or cracked, or retract. The baby bites so painfully that "nursing has to be stopped."[31] And all these infirmities signify for Spock a very different image of nature and imply for him a very different attitude toward artificial intervention in her vicissitudes.

Where the complementarities of supply and demand unfailingly inspire Spock to exalt the providence of nature, the disparities never do drive him to reflect on her niggardliness or inefficiency. They elicit from him only an austere normative neutrality, couched in a language itself all at once technical rather than teleological, in which aggravations become straightforward somatic problems devoid of moral meaning or emblematic import.[32] And in such circumstances, Spock's advice shifts even as his diction does. He promotes certain parental efforts to "influence" and indeed to "change" the child's natural feeding and sleeping schedules. He recommends some vitamin supplements, for the breast-fed baby as well as for the one brought up on a bottle. He sees circumcision as "a good idea."[33]

If he is nonetheless no apostle of pill and scalpel, it is not because he has no use at all for these tools of this trade. He does write as one trained in the infringement of nature's unimpeded course, and his book owes a part of its authority to its scientific seal. It is, in some measure, a medical manual. Yet to just the degree that it is, its medium inevitably

30. Ibid., 81. See also 14, 61, 123–24, 263, 281. Needless to say, Spock finds a metaphor for this cosmic conceit in the feeding of infants at their mothers' breasts, the harmony between baby's need and mother's milk supply being both a proof that "Nature" does "provide" and a model of the design of creation; see 157. In an even more expansive instance of the doctor's apprehension of nature as morally purposive, Spock supposes that "the reason that the soles of the feet are ticklish and sensitive under the arch is to remind us to keep that part arched up off the ground"; see 239.

31. Ibid., 99.

32. Ibid., 61, 87, 94–100, 127.

33. Ibid, 66, 166–67, 159–60. See also 65, 87, 127, 172, 192, 322, 323–24, 418, 428–29, 462. On a very few occasions Spock does maintain that parents must afford the baby "firm guidance" because the little one "doesn't know what's good for him," but even such uncharacteristic concessions are ordinarily vitiated in definitional assimilation of such directives to nature ("it's [the child's] nature to expect" parental guidance) and to the pleasure principle ("this comforts him"); see 193 and, similarly, 6–7. Spock's one truly contemptuous dismissal of nature as an adequate authority is at 428. There is nothing else of the sort in the entire volume, and nothing like it at all in the original edition of 1946.

violates its message. To just the degree that Spock direct mothers and fathers to medical specialists who then preempt responsibilities he promised they could manage, he obstructs the path he wants to clear for such parents—and their children—to enjoy a ready run of impulse.[34]

Of course, it is no real indictment of Spock's book to cite its internal incoherences. Its unprecedented popularity puts it far beyond quibbles about consistency. *Baby and Child Care* is, to the extent that any single book can be, an embodiment of its culture. And a culture never does resolve its focal tensions. It merely oscillates endlessly about them.

But it is just because American culture has not oscillated about these particular tensions in the past that the very success of the book suggests a shift in the culture itself. And the suggestion brings us back to the questions with which we began. Why should American parents of the mid-twentieth century have been willing, as their ancestors never were, to take up a psychology so farfetched and a program so problematic? Why should they display such overweening concern for self-confidence in the first place? Why should their thoughts turn so ceaselessly on the axis of anxiety?

For despite all his divagations, Spock never really swerves from his transcendent intention to dispel parental anxiety. The easy instinctual release that he counsels is ultimately just a tactic in a grander strategy designed to shore up the psyche by inculcating confidence and averting dread. It is the tactic he celebrates, but it is not the only one he ever advocates. He would far sooner put parents in the care of the technicians than throw them on their own resources if those are inadequate to the occasion, because in the last analysis he is less concerned that mothers and fathers trust in themselves than that they trust and less insistent that they relax in the amplitude of nature than that they just relax.[35]

So if we would understand why so many parents have embraced an instruction premised on such solicitude for emotional repose, we must move beyond persisting misperceptions of Spock as a subversive or, alternatively, as an author of a great charter for childhood.[36] We must remind ourselves that it is, after all, American parents themselves who have bought the doctor's books and propagated his gospel. And parents

34. See, for example, ibid., 59.

35. See, for example, ibid., 58, 175, 201, 210, 295, 347–48, 480, 517, 521, 522.

36. Among the commentators, it has been primarily the politicians who have seen Spock as subversive, the sociologists who have seen him as a liberator of children. See, e.g., Robert Winch, "Rearing by the Book," in *Sourcebook in Marriage and the Family,* ed. Marvin Sussman, 3d ed. (Boston, 1968), 340.

presumably relinquish power no more readily than any other ruling class.

We had best begin, therefore, with the primacy of parents. We had best suppose also, if only as a pragmatic postulate of inquiry, that the permissive mode of child-rearing is as serviceable to the book-buying classes of the present day as older modes were to older audiences. Then, exactly on such a supposition, Spock would be neither savior nor saboteur of the rising generation. He would be merely its universal nanny. His would be the expertise to which mothers and fathers might defer, yet he would hold his dominion solely on their sufferance. His would be the office of nursemaid and mentor to millions, yet he would maintain his position only on the thoroughly conservative condition that, in the immortal round of parents and progeny, his strictures aid the elders and smooth for them their children's inheritance of the ancestral estate.

Indeed, as long as we presume that few parents purposely raise their youngsters to be misfits in society, and that no society encourages them to do so, it is quite unconscionable to condemn—or applaud—*Baby and Child Care* as a spring of revolution before considering it as a source of revelation. At least at the outset, Spock's admonitions and injunctions ought to be taken as functional for parents and for their social order as well. His departure from traditional precepts ought not to be taken to imply an abandonment of obligation to the social system so much as a different definition of it, as appropriate to the emergent order as past sanctions were to preceding configurations.

By 1946, or 1956 or 1966, the contours of such an emergent order seemed obvious. American children would pass their days, as many American parents already passed theirs, under the auspices of the enormous organizations that dominated the economic life of the nation. And in the society that those organizations shaped, certain prerequisites of personality would prevail.

The prerequisites may be seen most conveniently in terms of production and consumption; and of the two, those of consumption were probably the more powerful and certainly the more pervasive. The centralized structure of power that was conceived in the New Deal and born in the wake of the Second World War offered vast numbers of people an unprecedented economic security. It flattened the business cycle, blunted the competitive edge of American commerce, and made credible an existence beyond scarcity. At the same time, and for just those reasons, it accentuated emotional disengagement from work. People who no longer ran their own risks and could no longer identify with the elephantine operations that increasingly controlled their occupational destinies turned instead to realms they could still control. They gave up the satisfactions of getting for the pleasures of spending. They grew impatient of their old habits of deferred gratification and embraced an ethic of indulgence for which it was more than a little comforting to be assured that the provenance of nature was dependable.[37]

As Marcuse among others has seen, this nascent hedonism was absolutely essential in an economy of abundance. Such an economy cannot count on any substantial reserve of demand for its goods and services. It has already appeased most people's necessities. It can all too easily produce more than what most of its members, left to their own unaided imaginations, might consider amenities. It must therefore stimulate appetites relentlessly. And to that end, its customers have to be brought to release old inhibitions and accept the appropriateness of desire. "Controlled desublimation," as Marcuse calls it, was a precondition of the administered demand that became a hallmark of the corporate economy after the Second World War.[38]

Altered circumstances of production did not touch as many men and women as the changed conditions of consumption did, because the mass of Americans could not plausibly aspire to echelons of the great

37. There is an intriguing irony in Spock's celebration of indulgence as "natural" and denigration of restraint as "unnatural," since earlier Americans also defined good and evil by the opposition of "natural" and "artificial" yet aimed exactly at the inhibition of "affectional displays." Those patriarchs saw emotional exhibition as "unnatural" and took moderation and control to be much more nearly "natural." See Bernard Farber, *Guardians of Virtue: Salem Families in 1800* (New York, 1972), 30–31.

38. Herbert Marcuse, *One Dimensional Man* (Boston, 1964), chap. 3. It should be added that the very forces that foster such hedonistic expression also attenuate the resistance to it. For the economy that requires disinhibition to clear its inventories is at the same time an economy that erodes the values that might allow people to stand against the corporate order. It is an economy in which family enterprise plays a steadily shrinking role, so that children grow up steadily less dependent on the family for occupational placement and steadily less subject to the authority of the father. "He has less to offer, and therefore less to prohibit." He becomes "a most unsuitable enemy and a most unsuitable 'ideal,'" because he "no longer shapes the child's economic, emotional, and intellectual future." And the child no longer learns the necessity of repression in protracted conflict with the father. Instead, the ego-ideal is "brought to bear on the ego directly and 'from outside.'" The child is "prematurely socialized by a whole system of extra-familial agents and agencies," and the parents' influence in upbringing is supplanted by that system's "direct management of [the child's] nascent ego" (Herbert Marcuse, *Eros and Civilization* [New York, 1961], 88; Herbert Marcuse, "The Obsolescence of the Freudian Concept of Man," in *Five Lectures* [Boston, 1970], 46–47). For somewhat similar arguments to a similar conclusion, see Fred Weinstein and Gerald Platt, *The Wish to Be Free* (Berkeley and Los Angeles, 1969), 196.

organizations where the alterations were most manifest.[39] But for the strategic cohort that could—and that was in any case likelier to attend earnestly to the child-care counselors—careers in the postwar world of business also implied new terms of conduct and character.[40]

The most suggestive exposition of these terms is still the one put forward by Miller and Swanson.[41] In it, the two social scientists contrast the isolation of the self-made man and the concern for loyalty, morale, and interpersonal adjustment of the organizational staff. They counterpose the emphasis on aggression, ambition, and active manipulation of risk in the entrepreneurial regime and the promise of steadiness and security in what they call the welfare bureaucracy. And, more, they link these attributes of ecological niche in production to practices of child socialization in the family. Maintaining that role requirements of different economic institutions are differentially reflected in the general perspectives of their actors, they attempt to show that these divergent outlooks in turn affect beliefs and behavior in the rearing of children.[42]

At the same time, Miller and Swanson do recognize that there is still substantial pressure to perform in the modern corporation, even if it assumes a somewhat different guise. They shrewdly trace that pressure to the ascendant corporate ethic itself and to the ambiguity inherent in a system that compels the very license it allows. Giant enterprises depend, in daily routine as well as in deeper structure, upon smooth social relations among members. They can scarcely operate without at least a

39. Nonetheless, many Americans could, for it seems to be the case that the bureaucracy of the great corporations facilitates upward mobility. See W. Lloyd Warner and James Abegglen, *Occupational Mobility in American Business and Industry* (Minneapolis, 1955), 150–54, and Seymour M. Lipset and Reinhard Bendix, *Social Mobility in Industrial Society* (Berkeley and Los Angeles, 1962), esp. chap. 4.

40. Orville Brim, *Education for Child Rearing* (New York, 1959).

41. Miller and Swanson, *The Changing American Parent*. See also, among many, William Whyte, *The Organization Man* (New York, 1956), David Riesman, Nathan Glazer, and Reuel Denny, *The Lonely Crowd* (New Haven, Conn., 1950), and Thomas Cochran, *The American Business System* (Cambridge, Mass., 1960).

42. There are not many systematic studies that bear upon this argument, but for a few that bear it out see Paul Breer and Edwin Locke, *Task Experience as a Source of Attitudes* (Homewood, Ill., 1965), Melvin Kohn, *Class and Conformity* (Homewood, Ill., 1969), and Donald McKinley, *Social Class and Family Life* (New York, 1964). It might be added that Miller and Swanson also extend their assumptions to considerations of consumption. They posit that employees in the welfare bureaucracy are more free to enjoy the present than they ever were under entrepreneurial imperatives to self-denial, and more prone to express their feelings than they ever were under mercantile mandates to self-control; and they predict, on just those grounds, that such people are more likely to school their youngsters in similar self-indulgence.

semblance of amiable intercourse in the ranks. And therefore they require, especially of those who would advance into their administration, a degree of freedom from the inhibitions that might impair such outgoing affability. Individuals who are unduly cool, controlled, or independent are, in those respects, ill-suited to act in bureaucracies that would have their agents cooperative and congenial.

In this light, the significance of Spock's obsession with confidence and the management of anxiety becomes explicable. Confidence is essential to the easy camaraderie necessary for success in corporate society, but on just that account the achievement of such assurance is inevitably problematic among the people who need it most. For letting go that is itself constrained is less than liberating. Spontaneity that is part of the job specifications is no simple effusion of self. And vivacity that is compulsory soon bids to become compulsive. The result is that the organization man is caught in such psychological binds that he is very nearly bound to be tense, bound to be worried about his capacity for relaxation and release, bound to be anxious about the adequacy of his impulses.[43]

Spock's insistence on the benevolence of nature and the dependability of instinct serves in this context to counteract, or at least alleviate, such anxiety. It affords about as much solace as may be mustered for parents whose ability to express an easygoing warmth with others is central rather than peripheral to occupational attainment, and it provides about as much comfort as may be contrived for children who have in prospect a society in which similar psychological demands will be similarly the stuff of life. For in the bureaucracies in which parents work and toward which they point their offspring, the chief accomplishments are interpersonal. They are matters of the management of social relations more than of the movement of merchandise. And because they are, parents must be concerned to instill social savvy in their children, for whom they can hardly anticipate a world any less organized or other-oriented than their own.

Spock's sense of human nature and advantageous character interlaces exquisitely with these parental concerns. It was not the only one that might have done so, since it was by no means strictly entailed by the structure of the corporate system, and it may not even have been called forth in the first instance by bureaucratic conditions. Some of its elements were assuredly evident before the war, in areas rather remote

43. Cf. Wolfenstein, "Fun Morality."

from the pressures of big business routine.[44] But if the personality formations promoted in *Baby and Child Care* were not direct responses to the requirements of the corporate colossus, they certainly converged well enough with them. "Without planning by businessmen," as it were, "the new conditioning fitted people for easy and effective participation in an impersonal corporate society where individual eccentricities were suppressed in the interest of harmonious action by the group.[45]

There can be little profit, then, in continuing to conceive Spock as a man gone against the American grain. He is neither an evil genius of degeneracy nor a singular beacon of decency so much as he is a representative man of his epoch, acutely alive to its tendencies and tensions. He may seem more generous in his sympathies than his predecessors in the tutelary trade, but he is as moralistic in his way as they were in theirs. His tutelage is as fully functional for the oligopolistic economy of the mid-twentieth century as theirs ever was for the dicier enterprise of earlier days. Their teachings, in times of chronic scarcity of capital and commodities, emphasized prudent calculation and the containment of immediate appetite; his, in a period of plenty so remarkable that it must unceasingly exacerbate demand, celebrate impulsiveness and inexhaustible desire. Their counsels, in ages when challenges were essentially environmental, stressed independence and an ardent assault on nature; his, in an era when exigencies are primarily interpersonal, commend social facility and accommodative complaisance.

*Baby and Child Care* merely marks an alteration of the national course that it did not cause. It differs from the earlier manuals exactly because it shares with them an adaptedness for preparing children to be the adults they must be in a business civilization and because that civilization itself has changed. The postindustrial order does not need the exaggerated autonomy and aggressiveness that an older mercantile milieu honored. It prefers men and women more mutually supportive, more genial and mild, more benign and bland. And Spock's advice serves its preference superbly.[46]

44. On the emergence of hedonism as a motif in the settlement of southern California, as long ago as the late nineteenth century, see Robert Fogelson, *The Fragmented Metropolis: Los Angeles, 1850–1930* (Cambridge, Mass., 1967), chap. 4. On a more equivocal hedonism, at exactly the same time, much closer to the urban-industrial citadel, see Charles Funnell, "Virgin Strand: Atlantic City, New Jersey, as a Mass Resort and Cultural Symbol," (Ph.D. diss., University of Pennsylvania, 1973).

45. Thomas Cochran, *Business in American Life* (New York, 1972), 273.

46. It might be objected that the popularity of *Baby and Child Care* reflects less its utility to the corporate regime than its accidental priority in the paperback publishing

The most obvious indication of the way *Baby and Child Care* conduces to corporate ends is its unremitting attention to the child's capacity for smooth social exchange. From the first, Spock defines the infant's developmental potential in terms of success in social relations. The baby is "born" for "friendly" fellowship. As long as he has the companionship he needs, he will grow up to be "a person who loves people." And his growth will be no mere incident in a larger maturing of environmental or emotional mastery. It is itself "the most important job in his life." He simply "can't be happy" unless he acquires such social ease. So his parents have to help him "to be sociable and popular." They literally "owe it to the child to make him likable."[47]

They also owe it to the youngster to teach him confidence in his own innate endowment, because he will never be able to use his talents effectively, whatever they may be, unless he does develop such self-trust. Nineteenth-century authorities of the nursery may have demanded the inculcation of a precocious control, but Spock brands their presumption of the dire origins of impulse "unwise." The child who is "appreciated for what he is" will grow up with "confidence in himself" and "a spirit that will make the best of all the capacities that he has." By way of contrast, "the child who has never been quite accepted by his parents" will "grow up lacking confidence" and "never be able to make full use of what brains, what skills, what physical attractiveness he has." A child must be confident to be competent. He "must feel secure" to be outgoing, and he must be outgoing among his peers to advance in their midst, since his gift for cordiality with them sets the shape of his bureaucratic achievement.[48]

The triune tangle of assurance, sociability, and success that is largely theoretical in Miller and Swanson is thus made tangible in Doctor

---

revolution. As the only child-rearing manual on the early list of Pocket Books, the pioneering firm whose Donald Geddes claimed that he "could sell 'em by the hundred thousands, whether or not the book is any good," Spock's guide was for a time the only such book to be widely available to the American public in an inexpensive edition. (Bloom, *Doctor Spock*, 101 and, generally, ch.5.) But it is difficult to believe that the book could have capitalized so remarkably on its initial advantage if it did not serve the needs of parents and the business system alike. And certainly the argument for affinity advanced here is strengthened signally by the convergence of Spock's advices with contemporaneous counsels and conduct in a wide variety of other quarters. See footnote 7, above.

47. *Baby and Child Care*, 4, 383, 20, 391, 328. See also 4–5, 19, 27, 28, 124, 311, 312, 320–21; though cf. the more spacious vision of such other-orientation at 12–13, 16, 317. Spock holds such sociability as essential as physical health itself, asserting that the child needs it "just as much as he needs vitamins and calories"; see 4.

48. Ibid., 430, 5–6, 347. See also 87, 89, 90, 320–21, 563–66, 585, 587.

Spock. His prescriptions rest on an explicit assumption that sanguinity will allow ebullience among fellows and that such ebullience will in turn afford more advantage than any training in the techniques of specific tasks. For in a host of endeavors, it is the child's frame of mind that is more important by far than his actual ability. "The most powerful factor" in a child's performance is "attitude." It is better "to do the supposedly wrong thing with an air of confidence than the supposedly right thing with a hesitant or apologetic manner," because, properly appreciated, almost all things are episodes in interpersonal relations rather than task execution. That is why the father who would have his son an athlete must concentrate less on coaching the boy than on insuring that he feels "approved by his father." Acceptance lets the lad come "around to an interest in sports in good time" where even the most constructive criticism leaves him "uncomfortable inside" and liable to a "feeling of being no good." And in any number of other activities as well, conciliation of the child's confidence profits parents more than any specific schooling they may provide.[49]

Mothers and fathers must therefore foster a basic trust in their offspring, because the alternatives are dismal indeed. The father who puts undue "pressure" on his child only disposes the youngster to be "hard to get along with." The mother who persists in prodding her baby to eat his last few mouthfuls merely manages to "take away his appetite" and build in him "a balky, suspicious attitude." And "once a child becomes balky" and his parents began to fret, "the fat's in the fire."[50] Anxiety is aroused. Further fears and doubts are begotten. Existing difficulties are aggravated, and new ones are animated as well. The child seems unable to sleep at night, or shows a diffuse disinclination to behave. He stutters, or wets his bed, or suffers stomach aches. He develops an asthmatic condition or simply catches a cold. There is no end to the variety of somatic symptoms of such psychic stress.[51]

Though the physician's antibiotics, sedatives, and salves may sometimes "help a little" in these cases, they cannot "do the whole job." No

---

49. Ibid, 353, 426, 320–21. See also 124, 249, 310, 321, 325, 336, 384–85, 465, 491, 508–9, 509, 553, 555, 567, 569, 571, 571–72, 576–77, 580. Given this priority of social relations to specific task orientations, it is scarcely surprising that Spock states plainly in the preface that his book "is not meant to be used for diagnosis or treatment" so much as to give "a general understanding of children"; see xv.

50. Ibid., 357, 124, 282–83. Failure of such early "love and security" inevitably occasions "irreparable harm"; see 408, 567.

51. Ibid., 85, 201, 223, 282, 353, 354, 358, 360, 367, 372–73, 374, 381, 382, 408, 410–11, 445–46, 451, 471, 486–87, 487, 510–11, 512, 513–14, 550, 584, 586.

medicaments can. For treatment turns ultimately on uncovering what is "making the child tense" so as to "take away his worry." Parents ought to do this themselves, but if they cannot thus relax the lad or relieve the pressure upon him, they ought to enlist the aid of a psychiatrist who can.[52]

In fact, they ought to seek professional assistance for less than that. The child who is merely "lonely" or "unsociable" must also be ministered to. His estrangement from his peers is debilitating in its own right, and it often marks as well the diagnostic distinction between ordinary growth and pathology. There may be "no cause for concern" when a child with "plenty of . . . playmates" masturbates, but real reason to "find help from someone" when he is "wrapped up in himself, or unable to enjoy friendships." There may be nothing untoward when a three-year-old who is "outgoing in general and happy with other children" has imaginary friends but grounds for misgiving when he is "living largely in his imagination and not adjusting well with other children."[53]

Spock's sovereign "remedy" for excessive isolation is to provide the sufferer more "companionship with his parents" and more "children his own age to play with." At school the refractory child can be drawn "gradually into the group" and enabled to "find a comfortable place" there. At home the little one who overeats, chews his fingernails, or skips his breakfast can be plied with attention and affection. Like everyone else, he has to be helped to "feel he really *belongs*."[54]

Just because his belief in his belonging is "necessary" and even "vital," the child must be given no cause at all to suppose "that he is different from" his age mates. He must be permitted to "dress like, talk like, [and] play like" them. He must "have the same allowance and privileges as the other average children in the neighborhood," regardless of whether his parents "approve of the way [such children] are brought up." For parents are not to insist upon their own opinions in the face of antithetical conventions among the child's friends. They are not to set the stamp of their own attitudes so indelibly on the child that he is himself made capable of resistance to the judgment of his peers. Moth-

52. Ibid., 353, 515. See also 87, 359, 360, 381, 486–87, 510–11, 513–14, 514. For the remarkable notion of worry as a "psychological emergency" in itself, see 201.

53. Ibid, 445–46, 395, 372–73, 376, 366–67. See also 319, 360, 447–48. For the overt physical infirmities that may attend the child who does not "get along enjoyably with his fellows" or is not "deeply loved," see 445–46, 486–87, 586.

54. Ibid., 367, 408, 411, 405. See also 350, 359, 360, 383, 384–85, 402, 410–11, 447–48. "The main lesson in school is how to get along in the world"; see 400.

ers and fathers have instead to be made to see that their values "won't be of much use" to an heir "unable to get along comfortably with anyone" and to understand that the "other average children" are the arbiters of their own child's conduct.[55]

And such subordination of parental standards to prevailing peer usage prefigures as well the final supercession of parental authority itself. Spock warns parents warmly against inordinate subjection in their offspring, but he does not seriously seek to free the youngsters for whom he begs independence. He simply wishes them removed from the intensities of the immediate family to the mildness of their larger society. The independence he actually affirms is little more than a different dependence, a due submission to the sentiments of the other fledglings on the block and the styles of the other students in school. The child of six or eight who "becomes more independent of his parents" merely grows "more concerned with what the other kids say and do." His "emancipating himself from his family" is mostly a matter of "shifting to his own age for his models of behavior," and the shift is only extended and exaggerated as he grows older. "Independence" in the adolescent is but a "pleasurable sense of belonging" with peers rather than parents and siblings.[56] And Spock sees nothing disconcerting in this Newspeak notion of autonomy, because the adolescent ideal is his own, too. It finds a fitting expression in his valedictory injunction that the child "must belong completely," by which the book brackets itself in neat symbolic symmetry between its opening invitation to assurance and this ultimate invocation of affiliation.[57]

People who espouse affiliation so fondly can hardly hail as well the recompense of conflict, and Spock does not. The children of *Baby and Child Care* do not contend for their identities in bitter struggles against their elders. They do not strain for their souls in furious campaigns against their own concupiscence. They do not even fight for their physical safety against the bully on the block. Their peers are all playmates rather than rivals.

If these children experience sporadic antagonism anyway, they experience it simply as they might suffer an occasional constipation or a spill on the jungle gym. They do not discover the recalcitrance of the cosmos

55. Ibid., 563, 564, 392. See also 242, 422, 565, 566; though cf. 390, 427, 428–29.
56. Ibid., 388, 390, 422. See also 270–71, 385, 388. For monitions against excessive submission to parents, see 170, 186, 193, 270–71, 271, 353.
57. Ibid., 589. See also 585, 587.

in their collisions but just the differences of an instant. And because such differences are merely "facts of life," without wider ramification, parents can presume that the settlement of strife is always possible. Because broils are never embedded in irreconcilable discordances of desire, parents can be sure that the resolution of childish strife requires only their own adroit management.[58]

Among their other offices, then, parents are the personnel directors of the houses that Spock would have them build. They are the ones who can damp the first flaring of friction. They and they alone are the ones who can fan the flames of animosity by mishandling it. They must therefore be every bit as adept as their corporate counterparts in denying extended expression to aggression. They must know that sentiments of obduracy are as impermissible in the intimacy of the family as in the bustle of the bureaucracy, and they must know how to make such sentiments over "into other feelings that are painless and constructive."[59]

The most immediately expedient tactic to alter the child's feeling of being thwarted is simply to let him have what he wishes. And as long as his demands "seem sensible" and the mother does not "become a slave" to them, Spock often urges exactly such submission. Sometimes he suggests that the concessions be made as a matter "of course." Sometimes he advises only that they be made if the child "insists." But again and again, in everything from the toddler's choice of teething objects to his efforts to get out of the playpen, Spock does order that concessions be made.[60]

Nonetheless, the doctor never exhibits any dogmatic attachment to his precepts of permissiveness. The deference to puerile importunity that he encourages is merely a tactic in a grander strategy of conflict management, not an end in itself; and he promotes it only in specific situations, on prudential calculation of its costs and benefits. It is never

58. Ibid., 340. See also 161, 319, 345, 379.
59. Ibid., 340. See also 345.
60. Ibid., 4, 122, 271. See also 59, 233–34, 244, 320. For denials of the danger of spoiling the child, see 61, 189, 191; though cf. 191–92. Again, the justifications for these concessions emerge most paradigmatically in considerations of feeding. The child knows his own appetite. His parents can as easily offer him foods he enjoys as others he cannot abide, within a wide range of nutritional equivalence. And if parents do not capitulate, their intransigence may precipitate strife over eating itself. Thus, Spock presses the menu planner to seek nutritionally similar substitutes for the dishes the child dislikes and to allow some rather unconventional requests "right away, willingly." He argues that as long as parents do not force "a battle," their child will eat "a reasonably balanced diet"; and as long as they instigate no "issue," the child may even eat vegetables. See 304, 283, 299, and also 61, 68, 69, 296, 297, 298, 302, 303–4, 305, 306.

a principle as much as a ploy. It never proceeds from his devotion to the dignity of children as much as from his fears that the fallout from contention could last "for years." And its function is never to provide children maximal protection as much as to afford animosity minimal purchase. When parents are asked to "leave [a child] to his preference," it is primarily because opposition to his inclination would make him "more antagonistic and obstinate" under the circumstances.[61]

Under other circumstances, Spock is perfectly willing to confess that the child and his parents alike would be better off for their interdiction of his demands. A parent can be "a pal at times" without ceasing to be "a parent all the time." It simply "isn't necessary," as Spock explains with some exasperation, "to be a doormat." If grown-ups "can't be comfortable" with a child who is "doing things [they] dislike," they should not "ignore" behavior they were "brought up to be disturbed by." If they are distressed by masturbation or bothered by bad manners, they should attempt the child's reformation. If they are embarrassed by obscenity, they should monitor the books and movies they allow the lad, to be "sure" that such entertainment has "a moral and spiritual tone of which they approve."[62]

The truth is that "strictness or permissiveness is not the real issue" at all. "Good-hearted parents" can "get good results with either moderate strictness or moderate permissiveness." Insecure ones can anticipate comparably "poor results" with either "a permissiveness that is timid or vacillating" or "a strictness that comes from harsh feelings." The "real issue is," accordingly, "the spirit the parent puts into managing the child."[63]

This spirit cannot be caught in explicit definitions any more than it

61. Ibid., 282–83, 233–34. See also 228, 244, 319, 327, 514, 520, 537.

62. Ibid., 332, 443, 375, 396. See also 193, 196, 205, 317–18, 332, 356, 361, 364–65, 365–66, 366, 386, 390, 410, 423, 426. For more ambivalent expressions, see 166–67, 303. Between the first edition and the present one, Spock has grown gradually more appreciative of the place of parental guidance and control in the rearing of children. The alteration is largely a matter of modifications of nuance, and as such its instances are at once too numerous and too trifling to cite in themselves. But for some stunning reversals that indicate, in vastly exaggerated form, the direction of this deeper drift, see the movements from the radically permissive posture of the 1946 edition to the cautiously coercive stance of the 1968 version in regard to right- and left-handedness (1946: 141–43; 1968: 233–34), toilet-training (1946: 184–93; 1968: 258–59), and fictive violence in play and on movies and television (1946: 240–41; 1968: 313–17). For conflicting findings on the wider generality of this trend, see Nathan Maccoby, "The Communication of Child-Rearing Advice to Parents," *Merrill-Palmer Quarterly* 7 (1961): 200, and Michael Gordon, "*Infant Care* Revisited," *Journal of Marriage and the Family* 30 (1968): 578–83.

63. *Baby and Child Care*, 7.

can be epitomized in the crude dichotomy of discipline and indulgence. Model mothers and fathers may display adamantine intransigence in some situations and barely dare lift an eyebrow balefully in others. They may force an assurance they do not feel on some occasions and then go guilelessly on others. And as often as not they may seem merely to make do, decisive one day and evasive the next, improvising as they go.[64] Yet for all that, there are methods in their meanderings. The expedients that vary so greatly from one incident to another can finally be comprised in a few fundamental modes, and those few are all subject to a single standard. Spock's immutable measure of the incessantly shifting disciplinary practices he advises is effectiveness in heading off hostility and preventing pitched battles of the will. The very crux of the parental control on which he insists is its contravention of direct confrontation.

Permissiveness is simply the most straightforward of Spock's elemental modes. It is to be employed in affairs in which something of importance to the youngster is a matter almost of indifference to his elders, and its object is the arrest of needless breaches between parents and children. Mothers and fathers on permissive maneuvers may go no further than to try, "tactfully," to guide the child "if he is willing to be guided." They may not advance beyond such indirection, and, above all, they must not "argue or fight" with the youth.[65]

Evasiveness is another mode in which parents may move, especially when they cannot bend so readily before the child's desires. In this course they try to "distract him" from his intent without exciting his ire, by getting "his mind on something pleasant" in place of the project he cannot consummate. And in this course too, they attempt to prevent asperity even when they cannot so cunningly mask their manipulation. For it is rarely their imposition as such that antagonizes the child, rarely the bare reality of being made to come in for dinner or wash up before bedtime that arouses his wrath. His outbursts are rather the result of insult than of mere injury. So parents must not "scold" their little one lest they spur him "to further balkiness." They must not be "reproachful" lest they "bring out his meanness." They have instead to abandon these moralistic embellishments of their authority for more "matter-of-fact" routines of regulation, in order to escape the corrosive sequels of censoriousness. And they have to carry themselves "cheerfully" in all

64. Spock does declare that "the main source of good discipline" is "a loving family," but he never elaborates the disciplinary manifestations of such mutual affection. See ibid., 336.

65. Ibid., 234. See also 103–7, 282, 410–11.

these operations and maintain a "breezy" bearing and a facade of "friendly encouragement."[66]

Severity is yet another mode in which parents may proceed, setting themselves against the child's demands without any subterfuge whatever. But even in such strident imposition of their own interests, they still oppose their darling primarily to contain more serious cleavage. For when he implores privileges he cannot be permitted—when he pleads not to be sent to school, say, or not to be separated from his mother at night—his parents can be sure that their appeasement would only prolong his resistance to a regimen he must ultimately endure anyway. "If parents are firm, children accept; if parents are hesitant, children argue." So parents must sometimes deal "firmly" with the child's appeals. Their puissance may have to be posed, but the pose must be impenetrable if it is to achieve its end in the preservation of domestic tranquility. They themselves may have to bear with "a little unhappiness" in these brushes with belligerence, but they must harden their hearts for a moment if they would not have "the struggle drag on for weeks."[67]

In permissiveness, evasiveness, and severity alike, then, a persistent ambition controls Spock's teachings. For in all these modes of handling the child's inconvenient conduct, the doctor aims unfailingly at the dissipation of friction. Conflict is not, on his account, a normal social process, nor a natural aspect of the ordering of interpersonal relations, nor even a sometimes seasonable instrument in the settlement of differences. It is simply a source of frustration, because it cannot satisfy the desire it arouses to make an adversary "change his mind" or "see the error of his ways." So if parents would "really" avert trouble, they must try to muffle every clash of wills. They must, indeed, give up the very categories of contrariety, because the polarity of domination and docility itself impels them to one extremity or the other or, worse, to one and then the other, in endless escalation. A mother and father may begin, perhaps, by indulging their child. He discovers that he can "take advantage" of their leniency. They discover that "their patience is exhausted" swiftly in such circumstances, and they "turn on him crossly." But because their displeasure is so much stronger than his misbehavior alone would seem to

66. Ibid., 335, 276, 390, 319, 355–56, 223. See also 275, 277, 319–20, 340, 349, 354, 356, 462.

67. Ibid., 559, 195, 355. See also 196, 205, 276, 317–18, 332, 335, 337, 349, 353, 369, 386, 462.

warrant, they make him "feel guilty." And just because they are aware of that, they suffer sufficient consciousness of their own culpability to begin the cycle all over again.[68]

Spock is sensitive to these crescendos of contrition, since guilt is in the end the veritable bogeyman of *Baby and Child Care*. The doctor's New England ancestors may have hailed heartfelt conviction of sin as a condition of salvation, but he does nothing of the sort. He allows only that it "drives" people to do things that are "not sensible." He admits only that it "can cause" somatic afflictions. He acknowledges only that it may attend masturbation, parental overprotection, and a wide variety of other ills. And he adds that it does most of this damage quite gratuitously. The "sense of guilt" appears, all too often, where "there is no realistic need for it."[69]

Parents must, therefore, resist guilt in their own right and refuse to instill it strenuously in their offspring. They must not fight or in any other way force a concussion of purposes, because they must not do anything to stimulate a stricken conscience. They must never feel "too guilty" themselves—their very "guiltiness" could be "harder" on the child than the "irritation" that touched it off—and they must never make the youngster "feel really guilty" either. A "*heavy* sense of guilt" would impair the confidence he has to have to get on among his friends, and it would quicken his susceptibility to the promptings of the still small voice within.[70]

It is to protect the child from the terrors of interiority and to spare him the cares of self-awareness that Spock promotes the values of peer-group play. For the youth must, at all costs, be kept from himself. He has to be outgoing so as never to be alone long with his inmost ideas

68. Ibid., 276, 275, 331, 369. See also 282–83, 283, 319–20, 439, 512; though cf. 258–59, 562 on the inevitability of conflict. Spock's deep-seated preference for the conciliation of contrariety is revealing in a special sense, since Bloom maintains (*Doctor Spock*, 86–87) that the chief formal sources of Spock's psychological notions were the ideas of Freud and Dewey. Given that Freud always thought conflict inherent in the nature of things, while Dewey devoted his philosophy to the denial of such dualism, it seems clear that Spock's spiritual affinities are far more profoundly with the American pragmatist. For his symptomatically "soft" reading of Freud, see *Baby and Child Care*, 14, 364, 366. (And, in a similar vein, see his domestication of Darwin: 59, 169–70.)

69. Ibid., 573, 520, 353. See also 375–76, 438. Since these occasions of guilt are linked to tension and anxiety, an extensive roster of ill effects also attend guilt through such insecurity: see, among many, 79, 223, 381, 408, 510–14.

70. Ibid., 26, 517–18, 338. See also 25, 190, 193, 345, 366, 374.

and imaginings. He has to be "absorbed in games" so as to find no time for "inner fears." And he has to be extroverted and unceasingly busy in the pursuit of popularity so as never even to dream of descending into regions of his being in which "it's risky and it's wrong" to dwell.[71]

The days of the lad's life are, accordingly, to be spent in the emotional shallows. He is to sound no spiritual bottom of his experience, and fathom no sensual one. He is to shun every current that might carry him beyond the safe mooring of his sociability into a more turbulent inner life. He is to know nothing of "deep" distress, or of "deeply" felt doubt, or indeed of any passion that is not passing. He is to be a vessel of affability and ease, and little more.[72]

Every intense affect that could lead to a deepening of the child's character has consequently to be made to remain "out in the open," where it can dissipate its potential energy. For desires that are "suppressed" do not disappear. They only enter more profoundly into the unconscious, where their denial "doesn't work out well" at all. The lad who tries to "bottle up his feelings" merely makes himself "more tense than ever." His anxieties "accumulate inside." His fears multiply. And his very possession by such demons—his very possession, that is to say, of a distinctive personality—unsuits him for the camaraderie that will be a measure of his manhood. He must be made, on that account, to see a psychiatrist, who can "clear the air" and dispossess him of his particular tendencies. He must be brought "back to the surface again." His eccentricities must be exorcised, his idiosyncrasies "expressed," and his grievances gotten "off his chest."[73]

Americans of an earlier era did not worry so much about the things on a child's chest, because they were more concerned about the things in his heart. They did not strive to scan the child's mind, either, because they were more attentive to the state of his soul. And they certainly did not even contemplate the spiritual search-and-destroy missions that *Baby and Child Care* actually advocates.

Such changes are symptoms of still vaster transformations. Even if only inadvertently, *Baby and Child Care* epitomizes the emergence of a new American ethos, and perhaps the beginning of a new chapter in the history of Western sensibility as well. Though it simply summarizes a traditional American way of life when it invites sociability and a due

71. Ibid., 369.
72. Ibid., 374, 345.
73. Ibid., 345, 190, 52, 22, 346–47. See also 21–22, 370.

deference to the opinions of others, it goes much further when it solicits such ends in the context of a concerted effort to detach the youngster from the moral authority of the immediate family. For that family has been, over the last few centuries, the cauldron of the modern conscience and, as such, the very crucible of identity and individuation in the West.[74]

So when *Baby and Child Care* disdains dependence on parents and urges instead an independence defined as an efficacious reliance on peers, it does not just represent reconceived parental prerogatives. When it subordinates the morality of the family to the mores of the "other average children" in the neighborhood, it does not just betoken the recast claims of the rising generation. And when it aspires to a certain invulnerability to deep-going guilt, it does not just seek to spare the young the anguish of their elders. It is, in addition, a part of a sustained onslaught on the structures of conscience and on the family in which they are formed. And insofar as such siege is successful—insofar as conscience, guilt, and the absorptive family itself are laid waste—it is hard to see how the inner citadels of individuality that have been the mark of modern man can long survive.

74. On the emergence of this familial focus of sensibility, see Philippe Ariès, *Centuries of Childhood* (New York, 1962).

TEN

# Ronald Reagan, Charles Beard, and the Constitution: The Uses of Enchantment

When the lurid headlines that heralded Gary Hart's *liaisons dangereuses* with Donna Rice first appeared, the excitement that they stirred was hard to fathom. When the pictures of the young woman went from furtive telephotos to provocative pinups on the front pages of the tabloids, the significance of that stir was still not easy to see. For several days, debate turned primarily on a simple question: Did he or didn't he? And even if he did, it was difficult to believe that the American public would care in any consequential way.

In a country in which the divorce rate had doubled from the days of John Kennedy to the regime of Ronald Reagan, a country in which sexual exploration of every sort had become a fact of life and literature, an extramarital escapade would surely occasion no more than the most passing of sensations. Even if the Don Juan in doubt was the front-running candidate for his party's presidential nomination, his dalliance would surely provide no more than the briefest of titillations and the barest of lingering embarrassments.

But the media did not treat the affair as sober sociological analysis suggested. As if in defiance of the rampant revolution in American sexual mores, and in the teeth too of their own trepidation at their prurient

This essay was written for a symposium on the seventy-fifth anniversary of the publication of Charles Beard's epochal *Economic Interpretation of the Constitution* and first appeared in *George Washington Law Review* 56 (1987): 81–105. In its details, it is, therefore, a little dated. In its essence, it is as timely—or as mistaken—as it was when it first appeared five years ago.

and unprecedented invasion of a political leader's privacy, journalists worried the story until Hart withdrew from the race.

Those journalists were by no means vindicated by that withdrawal, nor was sociological analysis confounded. Popular response to the revelations was as tepid as the survey data indicated it would be. In one very striking poll, taken after the exposé had gone on for almost a week and the candidate had finally bowed before the mounting mass of innuendo and inference, a certain number of Americans did declare themselves inclined to vote against a presidential aspirant who was unfaithful to his wife even if they agreed with him on most substantive issues. But the proportion who thus claimed to care so strongly about infidelity in a potential president was not only well under a majority of the populace but also well below the proportions who said they would be likely to abandon a candidate with whom they were otherwise in sympathy if he was guilty of drunk driving, lied about his war record, was hospitalized for psychiatric treatment, cheated on his income tax, or used cocaine.

Contrary to the presumptions of the media moguls, the American people cared less about a presidential contender's relations with a young woman who was not his wife than about any other item in the survey spectrum. Where only a minority maintained that it was important for the media to tell of a candidate's infidelity, massive majorities insisted that newspapers and television should reveal a candidate's cheating on his income tax or lying about his military career. Where barely two-fifths of those polled felt it fair for the media to probe private sexual conduct, two-thirds and more felt it imperative for reporters to tell of drunk driving or psychiatric hospitalization.[1]

As if they sensed such popular sentiments and misgivings, the media did not dwell overmuch on matters of morality. Instead, the anointed pundits of the press focused on a pair of other issues: the character of the candidate and the quality of his judgment.

Those who held that the question of the Coloradan's character was the crucial one confronting his candidacy insisted, of course, that the putative trysts were properly subjects of public concern. But on this count as on the others, the polls made plain that Americans did not connect private peccadilloes to public character and presidential qualification as the media analysts alleged that they did. Even after the revelations had run their course, solid majorities still believed Hart more honest than most politicians, and overwhelming majorities still considered

1. Richard Meislin. "Poll Finds Infidelity a Lesser Evil Than Others in Picking Candidates," *New York Times,* May 8, 1987, A1.

him competent to deal with new problems. To the day he withdrew, Hart had suffered only the most minimal erosion of his prior popular support. A third of all Democrats preferred him as their party's nominee, a slippage of only six percent and a following still three times greater than any other contender could command.[2]

Those who proclaimed that the question of judgment was the essential one to emerge from the scandal also, of course, affirmed the appropriateness of the media inquisition. Declining to declare themselves one way or the other on the actuality of events, they nonetheless pronounced themselves appalled by the compromising appearances that the affair presented. Hart, they argued, should have realized that people would be watching, since similar sexual issues had arisen in his earlier campaign for the office in 1984. He was therefore guilty whether he had indeed spent the night with a lover, as the *Miami Herald* reporters who skulked in the bushes on stakeout supposed, or whether he had merely let a casual acquaintance in and out of his Capitol Hill townhouse at odd hours by odd doors, as he himself insisted. Either way, they thundered, he was guilty of "bad judgment" and perhaps even stupidity, and such defects called into question his fitness for the presidency.[3]

On the surface, such assaults seemed absurd. A press and television corps benignly unbothered by an unabating stream of egregious and embarrassing lies by President Reagan himself now professed to be perturbed by a single suspicious story by a mere seeker of the office. Reporters and correspondents essentially indulgent through six years strewn with catastrophic fiscal misjudgments on the deficit, fatal military misjudgments in Beirut, and execrable ethical misjudgments at Bitburg now rose in righteousness to denounce Hart's judgment in romance. Editorialists and analysts unmoved to skepticism by Reagan's moral equation of the mercenary killers who called themselves contras with the Founding Fathers of American nationhood now found Hart too foolish to be president.

Even beneath the surface, most explanations of the media onslaught on the good sense of the Democratic frontrunner seem too jaundiced to develop in detail. But one interpretation does offer itself that may account for the virulence if not the vindictiveness of the commentators.

2. Ibid.
3. See, e.g., "Nightline: Press Hounds Hart," ABC television broadcast, May 4, 1987 (transcript on file at the *George Washington Law Review*).

Perhaps the issue is precisely the one the pundits posed. Perhaps we need only understand what they were saying.

American presidents have always had a fairly free hand in the conduct of the country's foreign policy, or at any rate they have had a far freer hand in international affairs than in the domestic sphere. They were constrained more by the modest place of the United States upon the world stage than by the complex conflicts of multitudinous interests that set the shape of governmental action on the home front. But upon America's emergence from the Second World War as the prepotent nation on earth, that constraint ceased to obtain. In the era of the cold war, the sway of the presidency swelled beyond all previous bounds. Under the aegis of the Truman Doctrine and the anticommunist consensus that sustained it, American presidents arrogated to themselves unprecedented prerogatives of global dominion. Abetted by an ever-proliferating national security apparatus ensconced in the White House and by an ever-increasing reluctance of the Congress to intrude upon executive control of that apparatus, chief executives presumed more and more to order the world by fair means or foul. In an expanding domain defined as essential to national security, this imperial presidency became for all practical purposes a law unto itself, a veritable outlaw and even criminal office. Indeed, neither the public nor the press nor the Congress itself can imagine it any other way any more. In the Iran-Contra hearings, not even the committee members most dubious of the contras or the diversion of funds to them questioned the necessity for cloak-and-dagger operations and illegal activities in the international arena.

In this age of the national security state, the management of the American empire and the adroit oversight of its multifarious concerns has become the principal standard of presidential performance. The chief executive must be able to conduct covert operations and defy the declared laws of the land with sufficient good judgment to escape public responsibility if his illicit policies and pursuits are exposed. In that regard, maintaining discreet appearances in carrying on an extramarital affair is very like maintaining plausible deniability in overthrowing an unfriendly foreign government, murdering a militantly antagonistic foreign head of state (or failing that, his little children), and evading an inconvenient congressional mandate. If a man who would be president cannot even manage an amour without awkwardness, how, the commentators tacitly wondered, could he ever manage the major violations of the Constitution that have attended every presidency since Franklin Delano Roosevelt's?

It was hardly an accident, then, that the newspapers and the networks never did quite decide whether the top story of that fateful weekend was the passion of Gary Hart or the reopening of the Iran-Contra hearings. In a very real sense the two stories were one and the same story of culpability and cover-up.

None of this clandestinity and criminality was provided for in Article II of the Constitution; much of it, indeed, was provided against. The Founding Fathers believed themselves driven to rebellion against the British by King George's abuse of the royal prerogative. They were obsessed with issues of executive excess when they assembled in Philadelphia to draft the Declaration, and they remained mindful of those abuses of executive power when they met again in Philadelphia a decade later to compose the Constitution. For all their fear of the unfettered authority of popularly elected legislatures, they remained republicans. They did not dream of reinstating the executive absolutism against which they had so recently waged an epochal and exceedingly expensive war. The executive they envisioned was only strong enough to offset the legislature, not to overmaster it. The *Federalist Papers* attempted again and again to allay what their authors plainly took to be pervasive popular dread of presidential tyranny. Hamilton himself repeatedly assured readers of his polemics that the chief executive would be restricted by the Congress and would not even be the "sole and absolute representative of the nation in all foreign transactions."[4] As he observed:

The history of human conduct does not warrant that exalted opinion of human virtue which would make it wise in a nation to commit interests of so delicate and momentous a kind as those which concern its intercourse with the rest of the world to the sole disposal of a magistrate, created and circumstanced, as would be a president of the United States.[5]

And Madison was even more explicit. "The constitution supposes," he wrote Jefferson, "that the Ex[ecutive] is the branch of power most interested in war, & most prone to it. It has accordingly with studied care, vested the question of war in the Legisl[ature]."[6]

---

4. [Alexander Hamilton, James Madison, and John Jay], *The Federalist,* ed. Jacob Cooke (Middletown, Conn., 1961), 467.

5. Ibid., 505–6.

6. *The Writings of James Madison,* ed. Gaillard Hunt (New York, 1906), 6:312.

Indeed, much of the distinctive tension that has marked modern American governance surely originates in the determination of the cold war presidents to preempt the powers over "foreign transactions" that the Framers so studiedly vested in the Congress or balanced between the two branches. The most celebrated study of the subject posits a "presidential breakaway" from constitutional limitations after the Second World War, as the White House since the time of Truman "came to see the sharing of power with Congress in foreign policy as a derogation of the Presidency."[7] A more recent survey of the same history similarly sets the decisive divide around 1950.[8] Executive abuses of the war and foreign policy prerogatives of Congress did occur before then, but they were perceived and protested precisely as abuses. Presidential violations in the era of the Korean War and after have occurred far more frequently and under cover of an unprecedented array of legal claims set forth by presidential advisers and apologists that would allow the White House to conduct the country's international affairs and even to launch wars without congressional collaboration and without imputation of illegality.

Before the commencement of the cold war, American presidents could make decisions by themselves about foreign policy, but they could not carry them out without the consent and cooperation of other publicly accountable authorities. Franklin Delano Roosevelt had a brain trust—a handful of valued advisers—but he did not have a Central Intelligence Agency and a National Security Council with their literally innumerable agents in the field and their extensive professional staffs. Only after the creation of those instruments of the executive in 1947, and their severance from all subjection to the State Department, did presidents begin to be able to contemplate an autonomous and imperious role on the world stage. Only then did they possess the bureaucratic capability to transcend traditional constitutional limits and to operate outside traditional institutional channels. Since then, like Kennedy, they have deliberately chosen weak secretaries of state whom they could freely disregard. Like Johnson, they have lied to congressional leaders. Like Nixon, they have willfully humiliated members of their own cabinet officially charged with the conduct of foreign policy.[9]

7. Arthur Schlesinger, Jr., *The Imperial Presidency* (Boston, 1973), 206.
8. Francis Wormuth and Edwin Firmage, with Francis Butler, *To Chain the Dog of War: The War Power of Congress in History and Law* (Dallas, 1986).
9. For a deft summary of these developments, see Theodore Draper, "Reagan's Junta," *New York Review of Books* 34 (Jan. 29, 1987), 5–14.

The progressive insulation of the presidency from conventional procedures and proprieties and from responsibility to the representative
process came to another of its recurrent culminations early in 1986,
when Ronald Reagan signed the notorious intelligence "finding" that
permitted the sale of arms to Iran. Among the many intriguing aspects
of that document was its provision that its contents were to be con-
cealed from the Congress and even from four of the eight members of
the National Security Council. Congress was to be denied knowledge
of the transactions that the finding authorized because of the "extreme
sensitivity" of the information and the "security risks" its disclosure entailed. The four national security councillors—the secretaries of state,
defense, and treasury and the chairman of the Joint Chiefs of Staff—
were to be kept in the dark because they had previously registered insufficient enthusiasm for it. Only a single copy of the order was made, and
it was secreted in the safe of the national security adviser.[10]

The Founding Fathers devised no such structure of stealth. They declared their independence to "a candid world." They took for granted
that sound policy dictated "a decent respect to the opinions of mankind." They created a constitutional system of checks and balances that
required consultation and consent across a considerable range of government operations, and they added to it a bill of rights that insured a
regime of publicity through its protections of opinion and expression.

Their founding vision and its successive institutional embodiments
served the nation until the portentous innovations of the Truman administration provided presidents an alternative. And even then, despite
the obsession with internal security and the communist menace that
haunted the Truman and Eisenhower years, the elaboration of the national security state under the leadership of an outlaw president was not
extensive. Truman was an accidental president, a creature of the political
party leadership who had made his career in Congress. Eisenhower was
our last president sufficiently at ease in himself and in his popular following to be willing to entrust his administration and its foreign policy
primarily to democratic processes.

John Kennedy put no such faith in popular democracy. The principal
novelty of his New Frontier was its unabashed adoration of the best and
the brightest, whom it unfailingly defined in terms of technocratic intelligence. Camelot signaled the supersession of democracy by an unparalleled mandarinism in American politics. Kennedy's national security

10. Ibid., 10.

adviser, McGeorge Bundy, made plain his unconcern for the Congress by treating it as if it didn't exist. And in his disregard for the people and their representatives, he took his cue from the man who appointed him. Kennedy never outgrew the convictions that animated his college honors thesis. His focal fear was that democracy was inherently soft, spineless, and incapable of coping with dictatorship. The weakness of will of plain folk was why England slept. The willingness to defy their constituents was what qualified his selected senators for inclusion in his profiles in courage; those who "fought with the knowledge that they enjoyed the support of the voters back home"[11] were explicitly excluded from his pantheon on that account.

Kennedy was the first of the modern "outsider" presidents. He did not simply stand apart from the government, above politics, as Eisenhower had. He actually set himself and his administration against the Washington establishment. And where he led, others—Nixon, Carter, Reagan—soon followed. His managerial innovations answered needs deep enough to be shared despite abundant divergences of style and substance between him and his successors.

Kennedy dealt not only with Congress but also with his own executive branch as adversaries. He circumvented their sluggish ways whenever he could, issuing executive orders instead of seeking legislation and delegating increasingly broad powers to the tight little band of vigorous men who shared his impatience with conventional democratic routines. Robert McNamara at the Department of Defense and Richard Bissell at the CIA soon found themselves assigned work in areas as disparate, and as distant from their formal responsibilities, as civil rights, space, foreign aid, and foreign policy more generally. As Garry Wills put it, Kennedy "assembled a hit-and-run team to go outside channels."[12] He pitted his "enlightened few" against the many dullards of democracy in what he saw as an effort to save the system from itself and in what Henry Fairlie saw, instead, as an effort to institutionalize "guerrilla government."[13]

An older American liberalism that came down continuously from the American Revolutionaries had feared power and trusted the people. Dwight Eisenhower was an exact embodiment of that republican heri-

11. John F. Kennedy, *Profiles in Courage* (New York, 1956), 243.

12. Garry Wills, *The Kennedy Imprisonment: A Meditation on Power* (Boston, 1981), 169; see also David Halberstam, *The Best and the Brightest* (New York, 1972).

13. See Henry Fairlie, *The Kennedy Promise: The Politics of Expectation* (Garden City, N.Y., 1973), 179–208.

tage. The new doctrines of the Kennedy years were doctrines of crisis and charisma. The young president thrived on crisis and did not tremble to create crisis so as to center the action in the White House, where tough-minded men could ignore the rules and impose their will. Charismatic leadership, as Max Weber defined it, is precisely a product of social crisis, in which traditional and bureaucratic norms no longer suffice and the people turn to a charismatic hero who operates outside the law so as to save them.[14] Great Americans have historically spurned such charisma, as Washington did when he relinquished willingly a presidency he could have kept to his dying day, but Kennedy sought it ardently and his idolaters celebrated it in him.

Since his death, it has become a standard for his successors. Presidential candidates routinely run for the party's nomination against the party regulars. Presidents cultivate the character of the antipolitician if not the outlaw. Even as they inveigh against Congress, Foggy Bottom, the courts, the regulatory agencies, or whatever other duly constituted legal authorities offend them, they draw effective power ever more securely into the White House and their own swelling staffs.

It is possible that the passage of power from responsible representatives to insulated elites was inevitable from the time the nation launched upon a course of empire two centuries ago. Patrick Henry implied as much when he assailed ratification of the Constitution, and the spirit from which it emanated, at the Virginia convention of 1788. "Some way or other," he railed, "we must be a great and mighty empire; we must have an army, and a navy, and a number of things. When the American spirit was in its youth, the language of America was different: liberty, sir, was then the primary object."[15] But the accoutrements of empire—the corruptions and clandestinities of an overbloated executive—did not become an American way of life before the Second World War and indeed before the presidency of John Kennedy.

The covert operations in Southeast Asia that could not be confessed, and the widening war in Vietnam that could never be adequately explained, opened a credibility gap between the presidency, the Congress, and the people, and the gap has done nothing but deepen in succeeding decades. In the 1960s, Americans were still chagrined if not shocked when Arthur Schlesinger, questioned on the discrepancy between his

14. See generally *Max Weber on Charisma and Institution Building: Selected Papers,* ed. S. N. Eisenstadt (Chicago, 1968).

15. Pauline Maier, *The Old Revolutionaries: Political Lives in the Age of Samuel Adams* (New York, 1980), 288–89.

account of the Bay of Pigs invasion to the press at the time of the attack and his very different version in his subsequent study of Kennedy's thousand days, "simply remarked that he had lied;"[16] or when Arthur Sylvester, assistant secretary of defense for public affairs, exploded in exasperation to the press corps in Saigon in 1965, "Look, if you think any American official is going to tell you the truth, then you're stupid. Did you hear that?—Stupid."[17] By the 1970s, official untruth had become customary and, indeed, compatible with honor. Richard Helms could admit that, as director of the CIA, he had lied in sworn testimony before Congress and, in the wake of that admission, win recognition from the Justice Department for "outstanding public service." By the 1980s, government disinformation campaigns directed at the American people were acknowledged public policy and objects of White House pride, high-ranking government officials had to be "authorized" to tell Congress the truth rather than fabricate fictions under oath, and Oliver North perjured himself, falsified testimony for others, shredded and stole essential evidence, and emerged as a national hero.[18]

A congressman sitting on the Iran-Contra committee summarized the first phase of the hearings as "a depressing story . . . of not telling the truth to the Congress and to the American people."[19] But he was only depressed, not surprised. After Vietnam and Watergate and the Pike and Church committee investigations of the intelligence agencies, he was prepared for revelations of the readiness of government figures to deceive and defy the public and its representatives. The Iran-Contra conspirators may have been more brazen than the Watergate burglars and the men who gave them their orders. To this day, none of the current crew have evinced even the crocodile contrition of John Dean, and North and Poindexter still think their schemes "a neat idea" and a necessary one. The Iran-Contra conspirators may have been more audaciously undaunted by the expressed will of the American people than the CREEP crowd. Fawn Hall caught the spirit of her superiors when she confided to the joint congressional committee, "Sometimes you just have to go above the written law."[20] But her slip simply made palpable

16. See Noam Chomsky, *American Power and the New Mandarins* (New York, 1969), 325.

17. Edward Herman and D. Gareth Porter, "The Myth of the Hue Massacre," *Ramparts* 13 (May/June, 1975), 8.

18. See *New York Times,* July 13, 1987, A8.

19. *New York Times,* June 10, 1987, A14.

20. Ibid., A15.

the practices and principles of systematic deception that have long been policy at the intelligence agencies.

In truth, the testimony of her boss, Oliver North, betrayed the bias of the national security state even more fully than Fawn Hall's *faux pas*. North conceded a long litany of dishonest chronologies, altered data, shredded and stolen documents, and fraudulent testimonies to the Congress. He claimed as justification his determination "to spare American hostages and secret Iranian intermediaries from harm" and his desire "to prevent domestic repercussions." [21] But his defenses did not exculpate as much as they exposed, for in the end they both warranted lying all the time.

Over and over again, North insisted that he had had to choose between "lives and lies." [22] Yet in covert operations lives are always at stake; a covert operator always confronts North's dilemma and, to judge by his testimony, always feels free to resolve it in favor of deceit. Throughout, North presumed that he had to protect the president from any outcry against pursuit of his objectives. Yet in covert operations the president's darker designs are always in peril; a covert operator always faces a prospect of protest if his enterprise is uncovered and, apparently, always aims to deflect discovery by duplicity. In every case, a higher priority takes precedence over obligations to honesty, even in deposition before the elected representatives of the American people. In every case, mendacity is the means to keep out of ordinary governmental channels any endeavor to which the White House or its national security surrogates fear democratic opposition.

North's disdain for the democratic process extended to the creation of an unofficial government acting outside all constitutional constraints and to a plan to supersede the Constitution altogether. According to a memorandum written by Arthur Liman, chief counsel to the Senate panel investigating the Iran-Contra affair, North and the National Security Council ran a powerful parallel government from 1983 to 1986: a "whole secret government within a government, operated from the [Executive Office Building] by a Lieutenant Colonel, with its own army, air force, diplomatic agents, intelligence operatives, and appropriations capacity." [23] Over the same span, North also drafted a secret contingency plan that would have suspended the Constitution, turned

21. *Philadelphia Daily News*, July 7, 1987, P.M. edition, 4.
22. *Philadelphia Inquirer*, July 9, 1987, 1A.
23. Alfonso Chardy, "Reagan Aides and the 'Secret Government,'" *Miami Herald*, July 5, 1987, 1A, 14A, 15A.

state and local governments over to military commanders to rule by martial law, and conferred control over the United States itself upon the Federal Emergency Management Agency in the event of a national crisis. Among the circumstances that constituted a national crisis in North's plan was any outbreak of domestic opposition to an American military invasion overseas.[24]

It is not yet clear how far approval of this contingency plan ran. Attorney General Smith apparently minuted his opposition to its provision for an "emergency czar," but he addressed his protest to Robert McFarlane, a partisan of the scheme, and it went no further.[25] President Reagan may or may not have penned an executive order authorizing preparations for the course of action envisioned in the plan.

But is it now very clear indeed that Oliver North was no "loose cannon." Even if he did not invariably have explicit approval, as he maintained in the Iran-Contra hearings, he did act generally at the direct behest of the topmost officials of the American garrison state, the national security adviser and the director of the CIA. He did work on the assumption, uncontradicted in several years of service, "that the President was aware of what I was doing and had, through my superiors, approved it."[26]

North was not abashed when the president denied such knowledge and approval because he had always taken for granted that he was promoting presidential policies that could not be acknowledged openly. The recourse to covert operations was necessary, as he said repeatedly before the joint congressional committee, to provide the president "plausible deniability" of involvement in illegal undertakings."[27] The national security adviser similarly told the committee of insulating rather than informing the president to enable him to dissociate himself from illegal actions if they were exposed.[28]

In a revealing exchange during the hearings, Louis Stokes admonished North that "we did away with" the concept of plausible deniability after the congressional intelligence investigations of the 1970s. "There is no plausible denial as far as the president is concerned . . . there is no plausible denial to Congress. What we seek to do in covert operations is to mask the role of the United States from other countries,

24. Ibid.
25. Christopher Hitchens, "Minority Report," *The Nation* 80 (1987): 245.
26. *New York Times*, July 8, 1987, A8.
27. *New York Times*, July 13, 1987, A1, A8.
28. *New York Times*, July 16, 1987, A11.

not from our own government."[29] Unmoved by the representative's rebuke, the lieutenant colonel retorted, "Congressman Stokes, I would beg to differ."[30] And in this case the lieutenant colonel was right and the representative wrong. The very crux of plausible deniability in the 1980s is concealment of covert operations from Congress. The law to which Stokes alluded, a product of the Pike and Church panels and their intelligence inquests, was indeed designed to curtail covert operations and preclude plausible deniability. It mandated a presidential "finding," or authorization, for all covert operations, and it required that Congress be notified of all such findings. On just that account, as a former deputy director of the CIA explained, the very "process of getting a Presidential finding automatically removed plausible deniability."[31] Rather than comply with the conditions of the law and relinquish plausible deniability, the deputy director went on, the CIA had simply shifted its activities to more furtive fronts such as the one over which Oliver North presided and about which the lieutenant colonel had not scrupled to deceive the Congress.

Deception and duplicity have simply become standard operating procedure in the national security state. Concealment from the public and from its elected legislators is now routine in realms from the most tawdry to the most terrifying. Norms of disingenuity are now taken for granted by flunkies as well as by their bosses. Evasion of the will of Congress is as conventional in quotidian concerns of military procurement as in top-secret projects of highest priority.

The tokens of the new mendacity are all about us. Some of them are individual and perhaps idiosyncratic. Assistant Secretary of State Elliot Abrams deliberately misleads congressional questioners about solicitation of contra money and, when the fraud is found out, excuses himself on the ground that he was "not authorized" to be forthcoming, which prompts the chief counsel of the Senate committee to wonder why Abrams "needed the permission of the Secretary of State to tell the truth."[32] Or again, Abrams is chastised by Representative Jack Brooks for his unresponsiveness to the committee and, when asked whether he can "survive as Assistant Secretary of State"[33] if he persists in such recalcitrance, answers that, "fortunately," he does not work for Brooks

29. *Philadelphia Inquirer,* July 15, 1987, 8A.
30. Ibid.
31. Ibid.
32. *Philadelphia Daily News,* June 10, 1987, P.M. edition, 6.
33. *Welcomat* (Philadelphia), June 10, 1987, 4.

and that George Shultz "seems to be pretty satisfied with the job I've done for him,"[34] which might prompt an ordinary citizen to wonder why Abrams supposes himself answerable solely to Shultz and not to the American people.

But some other tokens of the times are more structurally settled. The army awards a $39 million contract to General Dynamics to develop an antiaircraft gun on which General Dynamics spends $57 million. The Justice Department unwittingly indicts General Dynamics and four of its officers for conspiring to overcharge the government to recover on the discrepancy, but the department is forced to drop its indictment when it finds that the army knew full well that the weapon could not be developed for the contracted cost. There is no conspiracy to defraud because the Department of Defense colluded in the scam in order to frustrate efforts by Congress to control the cost of the program. As an army contract specialist tells the Justice Department, the army underfunded the project to stay within congressionally legislated limits, with the understanding that the company would recoup its costs from other government accounts. And this case is so far from being singular that the contract specialist says the Pentagon customarily "closes its eyes" when contractors use "other money" in such circumstances. As a matter of course, the Department of Defense colludes with contractors to defy the spending ceilings set by law and to shield that defiance from the lawmakers. Congressional investigators of this system of "contracts signed with a wink and a nod" estimate that Pentagon acquiescence in and instigation of illegal overruns cost the country "hundreds of millions of dollars annually."[35]

Even such staggering sums—"the most serious white-collar crime"[36] confronting the nation, according to John Conyers—are still paltry set against the immense bulk of the "black budget," the Pentagon's term for a vast cache of secret accounts for projects it prefers to shelter from all scrutiny. The black budget exists beyond the oversight of Congress, the General Accounting Office, and the Pentagon's own accounting agencies, and it is growing faster than any other major component of government spending. Appropriations to its inscrutable categories tripled in the Reagan years to the point that they now dwarf all federal outlays on the environment, exceed by billions all federal expenditures on education, agriculture, and transportation, and rival federal spending on

34.  Ibid.
35.  *Philadelphia Inquirer*, July 30, 1987, 1A, 10A.
36.  *Philadelphia Inquirer*, July 31, 1987, 3A.

health care. And precisely as these uncounted and unaccountable programs proliferate, Congress grows more indulgent of them.[37]

If, as the gospels of Matthew and Marx alike assure, men's hearts are likely to abide where their treasure is, then the cold war climate of the last quarter-century reveals a clear inclination of American hearts to the engorgement of executive prerogative and an unmistakable disposition to abandon the nation's democratic heritage.

The men of the American Revolution understood the fragility of republican institutions. The Framers of the Constitution hoped to stay the ravages of history when they enshrined in their new charter the rule of law. For they understood, by bitter experience with arbitrary imperial power, the consequences of allowing governors to operate outside the law, exempt from responsibility to and reliance upon the people they governed. They would have known in a moment what to make of William Casey's wish for a secret fund to underwrite an "off-the-shelf, self-sustaining, stand-alone entity, that could perform certain activities on behalf of the United States" without ever informing the Congress of its conduct.[38] They would have seen in an instant the significance of consigning crucial aspects of the country's foreign policy to types like Albert Hakim and Richard Secord on the faith that such men could "do things better than the government [could], because they [could] do them without the restraints that are placed on government."[39] And they would have known in their bones the fate of a people who do not know what to make of such wishes and do not see the significance of such consignments.

We seem, today, to have forsaken the devotion to civic virtue on which the Founding Fathers predicated the preservation of their republican experiment, and it is incumbent upon us to wonder why. We have grown obsessed, as Edmund Muskie said for the Tower Commission, with a secrecy that is the antithesis of the openness and candor that the men who made the Constitution admired.[40] We have conceded unprecedented claims to executive privilege and, at the same time, allowed unprecedented pretensions to executive irresponsibility for the most dire of political debaucheries. We have made our peace with a government

37. See generally Tim Weiner, "The Pentagon's Secret Cache," *Philadelphia Inquirer*, Feb. 8, 9, 10, 1987 (three-part series).

38. *New York Times*, July 13, 1987, A1 (statement of Oliver North).

39. *Philadelphia Daily News*, June 10, 1987, P.M. edition, 6 (statement of Arthur Liman).

40. *Forum: The Newsletter of the People for the American Way Action Fund* (Summer 1987): 7.

that disinforms us and delights in doing so. We have come to terms with a contagion of state criminality, not always as grotesque as that of the notorious CIA agent who considered his career in the Company "fun, fun, fun"—"Where else could a red-blooded American boy lie, kill, cheat, steal, rape, and pillage with the sanction and blessing of the All-Highest?"[41]—but amply appalling nonetheless. As Jonathan Kwitny recently warned, "the license to commit crimes in the name of national security has been granted too often and too lightly."[42]

We confront, then, a crisis if not an essential collapse of the classical conception of citizenship. We confront a citizenry that cannot inform itself because its government operates so substantially by stealth and deliberate deception, and we confront a citizenry that does not care— or dare—to inform itself because it is preoccupied with private fulfillment. In the days of the Framers, civic participation was an assumptive attribute of the man of virtue, just as virtue was almost inconceivable apart from political engagement. In our own day, as Robert Bellah has observed, sustained involvement in public affairs is so exceptional that we scarcely have a term for it. We call men and women "good citizens" if they merely cast a ballot every year or two, since most Americans no longer do even that much.[43] The eagerness of the electorate to give up its civic entitlements and obligations is mirrored in the keenness of the Congress to avert its attention from executive usurpations, and that keenness in turn heartens the executive to attempt further usurpations.

The crucial questions concern the sources of such shifts. Why do recent presidents reach so recklessly for prerogatives of which their predecessors never dreamed? Why does Congress let them get away with it? Why do ordinary citizens abandon the exercise of rights and privileges for which their ancestors fought and died?

These questions seem to be political questions. But since the processes to which they pertain proceed apace in both Democratic and Republican regimes, under both self-styled liberals and self-styled conservatives, when a single party controls Capitol Hill and the White House and when partisan stalemate prevails, these questions seem unlikely to yield political answers. Deeper forces must be at work, setting the contexts of political activity and conditioning the entire political system.

41. Martin Lee and Bruce Shlain, *Acid Dreams, The CIA, LSD, and the Sixties Rebellion* (New York, 1985), 35.
42. Jonathan Kwitny, "Crimes of Patriots," *Mother Jones* 23 (1987): 12.
43. Robert Bellah et al., *Habits of the Heart: Individualism and Commitment in American Life* (Berkeley, 1985), 181.

For all their vaunted and visionary radicalism, the Founding Fathers were fundamentally realists. They were realists not only in their beliefs but also in their behavior, not only in their bleak estimate of human nature but also in their experience of their social milieu. They moved in a world in which rhetoric bore some reasonable relation to reality, a world especially in which political language bore some substantial resemblance to political life.[44]

For all our professions of hardheaded pragmatism, we are much more nearly ideologues and even fantasists. We move in a world in which rhetoric comes unmoored from reality, a world especially in which political forms drift ever further from political practice. The evidence is on every hand. The Constitution assigns Congress sole power to proclaim war, Congress has not done so since 1941, yet a succession of presidents have fought a succession of wars without such authorization. The Constitution appoints the Senate to advise and consent with the president in the promulgation of foreign policy, yet senators quail to tangle with presidents on any issues that activate the anticommunist consensus or the bipartisanship orthodoxy. The Constitution accords the House the power of the purse, yet budgetary initiative has passed almost wholly to the president, the Pentagon, and a vast concourse of military and nominally civilian defense contractors whose handiwork is subject to little more than the most cursory review by a few complaisant if not complicitous congressmen. The Constitution establishes an elaborate system of checks and balances to avert arbitrary and overbearing government, yet a proliferating array of agencies of the garrison state get past those checks and balances with impunity.

Such disjunctions of form and function dominate our days, and not just in the purlieus of politics. Comparable uncouplings of old ideals and new necessities color our economic and social experience.[45] And the less the old values inform or even illuminate present practice, the more compulsively they are invoked in wistful ritual. Their very sclerosis seems, paradoxically, to promote their pathetic ceremonial survival.

Some of the most penetrating accounts of contemporary society converge to a common explanation of these developments. Jacques Ellul puts it most unsparingly when he maintains that "technique"—by which he means not only machine technology but also, and far more

44. The classic account of the Founding Fathers as realists is Richard Hofstadter, *The American Political Tradition and the Men Who Made It* (New York, 1948), 3–17.

45. See generally Thomas Cochran, *Challenges to American Values: Society, Business, and Religion* (New York, 1985).

fundamentally, the encompassing modern commitment to standardiza-tion and rationalization in the organization of economic life and indeed of existence itself—"cannot be otherwise than totalitarian."[46] Robert Merton concurs when he warns that "only the naïve can really believe that the world-wide movement toward centralism results from the machinations of evil statesmen."[47] And in more muted tones, a host of other analysts add their assent. The scale of the modern economy and the pace and priorities of modern technology demand a political consol-idation to match, and the demand imperils, if it does not preclude, pres-ervation of our representative democratic tradition in any vigorous, vital way.

The modern industrial system, as its interpreters from Weber through Mumford and Galbraith to the most current of contemporary analysts have seen, is a structure of extraordinary control.[48] Its sophisti-cated hierarchical organization entails imperatives to specialization, centralization, standardization, and planning that are all inimical to the republican spirit of '76 and even to the chastened constitutional faith of 1787.

The sheer span of time that giant corporate enterprise requires be-tween the commencement of an endeavor and its completion, and the sheer magnitude of the commitment of capital, call forth a precision of planning and presuppose a situation of social stability beyond anything the eighteenth century could have contemplated in earnest. Planning replaces the market in modern managerial calculation, and planning therefore propels modern managers toward collaboration with the state, sometimes in corrupt and sinister schemes, much more often in innoc-uous efforts to minimize uncertainty and attain the predictability that planning predicates.

The immense technological systems of what Mumford calls the megamachine presuppose stable economies and sustained economic growth. They require trained labor, regulation of aggregate demand, and a considerable constancy in prices and wages. And they cannot se-cure any of these essentials on their own. In the United States as else-where around the world, they therefore turn to the state as the one

46. Jacques Ellul, *The Technological Society* (New York, 1964), 125.
47. Robert Merton, "Foreword," in Ellul, *Technological Society*, vii.
48. See generally John Kenneth Galbraith, *The New Industrial State* (Boston, 1968); Lewis Mumford, *The Myth of the Machine: The Pentagon of Power* (New York, 1970); Lewis Mumford, *Technics and Civilization* (New York, 1934); Max Weber, *The Protestant Ethic and the Spirit of Capitalism* (New York, 1930); Langdon Winner, *Autonomous Tech-nology: Technics-Out-of-Control as a Theme in Political Thought* (Cambridge, Mass., 1977).

power that can supply their needs. As they do, "the boundary between private industry and government [becomes] increasingly indistinct, in some cases virtually non-existent."[49] Political and economic power fuse, not necessarily in collectivism or totalitarianism, but at least in indissoluble relationship.[50]

When Ellul speaks of the inherent totalitarianism of technique, then, he speaks metaphorically of its aggregating, integrating drive to homogenize and control its environment. He speaks elegiacally as well of the way that drive renders "cherished democratic institutions" mere "empty forms which have no visible connection" with the actual conduct of nominally democratic nations.[51] The centralizing imperatives of planning and predictability that underpin the twentieth-century technostructure cannot be made compatible with the unwieldy if ingenious federalism of the Constitution. They war with its astonishing tolerance for multiple sovereignties and its intricate separation of powers even within the central component of those sovereignties. It is no accident, then, that the outlaw impulsion of the postwar presidency is precisely to surmount such multiplicity and to stifle the perennial conflicts of state and central authority and of executive, legislative, and judicial claims within the central sphere. It is no accident that the cold war White House sets itself to overawe the states and to bypass the other branches of the national government. The mature corporate megastructure demands an order and a consolidation commensurate with its own.

Amid the vast combines of contemporary technological society, the personal independence that was prerequisite to civic virtue for the Founding Fathers becomes precarious if not impossible. In the simplest of senses, economic autonomy ceases to be a plausible prospect in an organizational order in which more than ninety percent of the labor force works for others.[52] In more subtle ways, the slippage of self-reliance is even more serious. Modern corporate enterprises are "massive aggregations of human and nonhuman parts, rationally ordered, working in precisely coordinated actions and transactions,"[53] Such juggernauts shape their employees to their own ends far more than they respond to their employees' needs or to the wants of the people they

49. Winner, *Autonomous Technology*, 152; see also Galbraith, *New Industrial State*, 316.
50. Ellul, *Technological Society*, 157.
51. John Wilkinson, "Jacques Ellul as the Philosopher of the Technological Society," in Ellul, *Technological Society*, xix-xx.
52. See U.S. Bureau of the Census, *Statistical Abstract of the United States: 1985* (Washington, D.C., 1984), 395.
53. Winner, *Autonomous Technology*, 202.

supposedly serve. Their technologies themselves impose harsh discipline, for the machines must be used according to their ordained functions and by their in-built rules or not used at all. "In modern civilization, great amounts of time, energy, and resources are expended in making certain that procedures are followed and that the conditions are met."[54]

A century and a half ago, surveying the far more primitive industrial equipage of his day, Ralph Waldo Emerson could already see that the tools of the new technology would be reagents, affecting their operators even as they were used by them. In the incomparably more complex and encompassing mechanical, electronic, and organizational technologies of our time, men and women at work are often reduced to rationalized fragments of themselves that travesty the human integrity at the heart of the Madisonian assumptions.

More than that, such men and women are almost invariably reduced—as the Founding Fathers would have understood; raised, as they themselves generally suppose—to specialists. Technological axioms and corporate ideologies alike take for granted that, in a sophisticated division of labor, every actor has a role to play and will play it better by unremitting refinement of it. At the same time, as a veritable corollary of those axioms and ideologies, the modern economic system also demands that every actor accept unquestioningly the expertise of all trained specialists outside his own area of competence so long as they are in theirs. As Langdon Winner argues, citizenship in the technological order "consists in serving one's own function well and not meddling with the mechanism."[55]

Such citizenship and such reverence for the mechanism are, of course, essentially antithetical to the classical conception of self-government and of citizenship itself. Such deference to the determinations of the designated authorities in every realm beyond one's own tiny patch forfeits all possibility of personal independence, of autonomous judgment, and even of participation as an authentic agent in one's polity. It confesses an incompetence for the fullness of public experience that would have repelled Americans of the eighteenth century, who supposed a citizen a whole man.

The new technicians avidly claim all that a decadent citizenry abandons. As Ellul says, twentieth-century specialists seek "the joy of consti-

54. Ibid., 198.
55. Ibid., 207.

tuting a closed group in which the layman has no part at all." The quest may be unconscious, but it is no less potent for that. The sophistication in which the experts clothe themselves "takes the form of a secret vocabulary which is incomprehensible to the outsider."[56] Under the aegis of technique, the practitioners of each isolated mystery create "a kind of secret society," in the end "excluding the public from the technical life," in a development "decisive for the future of the democracies."[57]

James Madison was as much an adept in the eighteenth-century science of government as any inventive scientist in his discipline or high-powered manager in his delegated department today. The *Federalist Papers* arose out of his extraordinary erudition and out of the deep and purposeful reading he and his collaborators had pursued in political theory and history. But even if the authors of those classic papers had an exceptional fund of information at their disposal and some very real qualms about casting their conceptions before the populace, they did ultimately address their ideas to the citizenry. The *Federalist Papers* were written precisely out of passion and necessity to take that acquired expertise to the people and share it with them rather than to shut them out of it.

The modern ideology of specialization and expertise separates each man from his neighbors, into whose work he no longer even seeks to enter imaginatively or sympathetically, and it renders each man remote from the lives and sufferings of the others around him. It precludes, therefore, the informed and active citizenry whose part in the political process the Framers presupposed.[58]

Almost the only modifications of the classical conception that pretend to preserve a broader sense of civic adequacy are a range of arguments that define participation in modern public life in terms of consumption rather than of production. These cheerless rationalizations acknowledge, by their very emphasis on spending, the impossibility of meaningful mass determination in making. They struggle solely to re-

56. Ellul, *Technological Society,* 162.
57. Ibid.
58. These are not merely speculative deductions. See, for example, W. Russell Neuman, *The Paradox of Mass Politics: Knowledge and Opinion in the American Electorate* (Cambridge, Mass., 1986), 171, for survey data indicating that only one in twenty American adults can be counted as active and attentive citizens and that fully a fifth are wholly unresponsive to civic issues. Or consider the essential unconcern of the country when unemployment reached double digits a few years ago and the verbal legerdemain by which the deprivations of the substantial numbers still unemployed today are dismissed as "structural" by contemporary economists and administration apologists.

deem a residue of modern existence that is not so directly dominated by the demands of employment and occupation. And as they do, they reveal themselves as pale trivializations of the robust producers' ideologies that conditioned republican understanding of participation in the eighteenth century and connected political life to economic livelihood in responsible engagement rather than in purest parasitism.

Even contemporary consumer activists, even in their most expansive ambitions, aim at little more than inducing or obliging giant corporate producers to act more responsibly. They ask the manufacturers to attend more conscientiously to the quality of the commodities that Americans purchase, but they do not ultimately ask for anything more than their money's worth. They do not seek to inform themselves of the technical processes of production. They aspire simply to bind producers to a probity that might eliminate all need for a critical comprehension of technics. By their very indifference to the inner workings of the technologies that set the shape of their days and ways, consumerists concede, tacitly, "that systems are too large, too complex, and too distant to permit all but experts an inside view."[59]

Thus, the Enlightenment vision of a virtuous, self-determining people intelligently enacting the public business daily dissipates. Thus, the sophisticated technoeconomic system of the second half of the twentieth century increasingly achieves in its stead the old Baconian ambition to turn government over to a technical elite. The advocates of the Baconian ambition insist—and for the first time in modern Western history they possess the power to make effective their insistence—that the good society is the society founded on scientific progress and that the proper governors of such a society are the technically trained specialists. This technocracy allows only the most paltry place in governance to popular participation, because the scientific solutions and technical truths on which it predicates advancement are beyond the competence and even the comprehension of the masses. Its priorities are priorities of planning, and since it cannot reconcile planning with any real role in ruling for the electorate and will not brook popular or political interference with its plans, it dispenses with such a role and obviates such interference. Its predilections are predilections of elitist expertise, and since it cannot accommodate the prerogatives of expertise to the traditions of responsive representative government, it lets such government go.[60]

59. Winner, *Autonomous Technology*, 288.
60. Some theories of democracy and planning do struggle to square these incompatible claims, but Ellul's anathema upon them is apt: "To reason like this is surely to move

In the sixties, the Diggers declared American culture "extinct" and pronounced American politics "as dead as the culture they supported."[61] In the years of the bicentennial of the Constitution, most of the news confirms their bleak view. Day after day, the Iran-Contra revelations mark the distance we have traveled over two centuries from the audacious experiment of the Framers to the demise of their dream in our own time.

Where they sought only to establish islands of order in a vast sea of uncertainty—a stable executive and judiciary to steady the tumultuous legislature, a degree of safety amid the general inconstancy of currency and contracts—we demand a pervasive order and are prepared to establish a police surveillance state to secure it.[62] Where they dreaded power and devised a multitude of means to fracture its force, we cultivate consolidation and conglomeration and the concentration of unprecedented power, despite our daily experience of its rampant abuse. Where they were wary of the military and unalterably opposed to standing armies, we build our economy and our polity alike on the foundation of national defense, despite our dismal knowledge that modern war dooms democracy.

Nonetheless, the dark has not entirely descended yet. The Congress rouses itself now and then to ask a few questions about secret government. The courts occasionally balk the administration's most intemperate plans. The constitutional machinery does not run of itself, does not really even run, but it rumbles and heaves. Men and women of good will still look to it as a palladium of possibility if not necessarily of liberty.

Intriguingly, those who look most fondly and protectively upon the Constitution are those who could be called liberals. Those most prone to look past it, those who seek to overset it, those who clamor most ardently for a constitutional convention to draw up a new charter for

---

in a world of dreams. The good faith of these intellectuals compels one to think seriously of pathology" (*Technological Society*, 178, n1).

61. Lee and Shlain, *Acid Dreams*, 172.

62. Even as I was writing this piece, in my own city of Philadelphia, the National Park Service was denying permits to protesters at the ceremonial session of Congress commemorating the bicentennial of the Constitution (*Philadelphia Inquirer*, July 2, 1987, 1B); the Philadelphia police force was infiltrating and otherwise holding under surveillance an extensive variety of civic and political groups (ibid., June 28, 1987, 1A; June 30, 1987, 1A; July 8, 1987, 1A); and the federal court was partially upholding the Park Service and entirely upholding the police (ibid., July 11, 1987, 1A; July 15, 1987, 1B).

the nation as it approaches the twenty-first century, are those who call themselves conservatives.

This represents a remarkable rearrangement of the contending ideological camps that have dominated American political thought for the better part of the past century. Before the Reagan revolution, liberals thought of themselves as Emerson's party of hope and considered conservatives the nineteenth-century sage's party of memory. Liberals promoted programs of progressive reform, while conservatives clung to the constraints on change that they believed were embodied in the Constitution. Liberals, to come at last to the subject of this symposium, embraced Charles Beard's epochal interpretation of the movement for a new frame of government and the motives of the men who convened in Philadelphia to create it in the steamy summer of 1787, while conservatives execrated that iconoclastic account.

*An Economic Interpretation of the Constitution of the United States* was a prominent part of the progressive project that Morton White has called the revolt against formalism. In many ways, indeed, it epitomized that project. Twenty-five years after its first publication, when they were asked about "Books That Changed Our Minds," American intellectuals cited it more often than any other book but *The Theory of the Leisure Class*[63] and invoked Beard himself more often than Dewey, Freud, or any other thinker of the age but Veblen.[64] The revolt against formalism was a revolt against an overruling moralism and a rejection of abstract logic and deduction as the essential methods of social research. Its adherents insisted that the life of society was not logic but experience. Instead of reasoning from first principles and doctrinal desiderata, they set themselves to historical and cultural inquiries capable of "containing the rich, moving, living current of social life."[65] They determined to desacralize the shibboleths of their Victorian heritage and to demystify the congealed pieties and proprieties that still occluded critical analysis in the early twentieth century.

Charles Beard understood his early work as a part of that enterprise. Against the prevailing veneration of the Constitution as a work of demigods, he insisted upon its "human origin" in impulses anything

63. Thorstein Veblen, *The Theory of the Leisure Class* (New York, 1899).
64. See Richard Hofstadter, *The Progressive Historians: Turner, Beard, Parrington* (New York, 1968), 220.
65. Morton White, *Social Thought in America: The Revolt against Formalism* (Boston, 1957), 11.

but "independent of all earthy considerations."[66] Against the dominant view of the document as the product of an undivided people "acting under divine guidance," he asserted a series of sharp social cleavages and conflicts originating in a medley of mundane economic interests.[67]

Beard's dismissal of the conventional conception of the Constitution as the miraculous emanation of "the whole people,"[68] and his disdain for the conventional interpretation of the fabled frame of government by "vague abstractions"[69] and "devotion to deductions from 'principles,'"[70] provided progressives such crucial comfort that they no more troubled to test his hypothesis than conservatives bothered to read it. In an era when conservative judges consistently invoked the Constitution to invalidate liberal economic legislation and thwart popular economic initiatives, Beard's bold study provided an invaluable alternative to the histories that justified such judicial decisions. *An Economic Interpretation* disenchanted the Constitution, stripping away its deific aura and revealing its foundation in very human interests. To those inclined to read it in such a way, its import seemed inescapable. What human interests had made, human interests could unmake and remake.

Nonetheless, neither Beard nor his liberal admirers leaped to associate themselves with the Americans who, during the debates over ratification itself, had seen and said many of the things Beard was saying. Liberals relished a clever debunking as well as anyone, but through the first three-quarters of the twentieth century they remained cosmopolitan as well as confident. They identified with the Framers, not the anti-federalists, because they could not imagine themselves as localists or losers. Indeed, increasingly over the years, they learned to laugh derisively at the misguided provincialism of the anti-federalists.

Now, for the first time, liberals ought to be able to sympathize with the plight of those they so long scorned. Now that a constitutional convention looms, two states shy of approval, in a nation in which the new conservatism stands at a peak of political power, liberals ought to be able to appreciate the Constitution as anti-federalists valued the Articles of Confederation, as a fortress of the accustomed freedoms of a past becoming increasingly problematic as the country's ruling elements

66. Charles Beard, *An Economic Interpretation of the Constitution of the United States* (New York, 1935), xiv, x.
67. Ibid., 1.
68. Ibid., viii.
69. Ibid., 8.
70. Ibid., 9.

grow harder and more heedless of the common people. Now, as two hundred years ago, a preponderant majority of the population is more liberal than those in positions of power and influence. Just as survey research shows that most Americans remained liberal in their social and political sympathies even though they elected Ronald Reagan to the highest office in the land, so historical research reveals that most Americans who cast ballots in 1787 and 1788 voted against ratification even though their representatives eventually approved the Constitution.[71]

In their anxiety over the prospect of a constitutional convention, liberals today recognize as anti-federalists two centuries ago were forced to recognize the persuasiveness of power and money. Just as opulent Federalists turned massive anti-federalist majorities among the elected delegates into narrow Federalist majorities in the final voting in the New York, Virginia, and Massachusetts ratifying conventions, so liberals fear the effects of similar advantages at a constitutional convention for the Far Right.

Beard may have been mistaken in his obsession with the part played by depreciated government securities in the deliberations of the delegates in 1787, but he was not wrong in his more basic belief that the work of that sultry summer was a Thermidorian moment. The Constitution was, as he insisted, the enterprise of an economic elite who stood to benefit from it, by the broad stimulus it afforded their cosmopolitan commercial interests more than by any windfall profits they accrued from the "personalty" they held. It was the endeavor of a cadre of "national-minded" men who sought to centralize authority to an extent unprecedented in a country where the preponderance of the population was still recovering from its protracted Revolutionary struggle to preserve local liberties. It was the effort of influential magnates to tame the turbulence of the lower orders, alarmingly evident in popular uprisings such as the Shays Rebellion, by buffering the government from the direct power of the people.

By a delicious irony in which Beard and his fellow rebels against formalism would have reveled, however, the conservatism of 1787 has become something very different in recent years. The Constitution that served the purposes of an emergent cosmopolitan elite so superbly then

71. See generally Thomas Ferguson and Joel Rogers, *Right Turn: The Decline of the Democrats and the Future of American Politics* (New York, 1986); Daniel Yankelovich, *New Rules: Searching for Self-Fulfillment in a World Turned Upside Down* (New York, 1981); Charles Roll, "We, Some of the People: Apportionment in the Thirteen State Conventions Ratifying the Constitution," *Journal of American History* 21 (1969): 56.

seems more the residuum of a far more radical impulse than any we can muster now. Its undeniably centralizing and antipopulist design appears decentralizing and democratic today, in the age of the mature corporate state. Indeed, its limited order and hierarchy now prove insufficient to serve the incomparably more voracious appetites for control of the corporate colossi and the national security apparatus.

Just three generations after Beard intimated that undue reverence for the Constitution might be an impediment to progressive fulfillment of American ideals, that Constitution seems to his liberal successors a bastion—one of the few remaining—against the maneuvers and machinations of the Mafia, the multinationals, and the garrison state. Just three generations after the Constitution stood as an impregnable bulwark against liberal legislation, its very perpetuity comes into question as certain dominant elements in American society begin, for the first time, to doubt its utility to them.

In this twilight of the twentieth century, the Constitution suddenly emerges as one of the only sources of effectual resistance to the forces it originally expressed, forces Beard began to lay bare in 1913, forces far more dangerous and malign today. Its position becomes precarious yet, for that very reason, precious. And one of the few factors that favor its survival is the immense and intense affection that the American people have come to feel for it. They may not know much about its particular provisions or its intricate evolution, but they treasure it anyway.[72] An aura of the sacred attaches to it after more than two hundred years, an aura the Articles of Confederation never had time to acquire.

In the campaign to avert a constitutional convention and preserve the Constitution, such sanctity may be the one essential asset that liberals have at their disposal against the money, power, and momentum of the Far Right. And that peculiar configuration compounds the irony of recent developments. For the irony is not simply that the Constitution has grown dearer to liberals as it has come to be perceived as an impediment by conservatives. It is also that liberals now scurry to assert the sanctity of the document as conservatives gingerly intimate its shortcomings. The transformations suggest something of the recent trajectory of the republic from the not-so-distant day when Beard and his adherents believed that they had to disenchant the Constitution in order to advance the sacred cause of liberty.

72. See generally Michael Kammen, *A Machine That Would Go of Itself: The Constitution in American Culture* (New York, 1986).

Liberals today are not so sublimely certain as liberals were before the First World War that that cause of liberty is advancing. They are not so innocent as to imagine that the imperial outlook and the armamentarium of the national security state will wither away if they stave off a constitutional convention. But they are not naïve, either, if they exult that the very anachronism of the Constitution preserves an essential tension and thereby enables the perennial conflict of liberty and order to continue.

| | |
|---|---|
| Compositor: | Graphic Composition, Inc. |
| Text: | 10/13 Galliard |
| Display: | Galliard |
| Printer: | Thomson-Shore, Inc. |
| Binder: | Thomson-Shore, Inc. |